CHATEAUBRIAND

Other Books by
André Maurois

ARIEL

BYRON

CAPTAINS AND KINGS

DISRAELI

MAPE

LYAUTEY

THE SILENCE OF COLONEL BRAMBLE

GENERAL BRAMBLE

DICKENS

PROPHETS AND POETS

THE THOUGHT-READING MACHINE

CHATEAUBRIAND IN 182
by Hilaire LeDr

Chateaubriand

Poet
Statesman
Lover

by

ANDRÉ MAUROIS

Translated from the French by
VERA FRASER

Blue Ribbon Books · New York

1940
BLUE RIBBON BOOKS
14 WEST 49TH STREET, NEW YORK, N. Y.

CHATEAUBRIAND
Copyright, 1938, by André Maurois
Printed in the United States of America
All rights in this book are reserved.

REPRINT EDITION PUBLISHED BY
ARRANGEMENT WITH HARPER & BROTHERS

CL
PRINTED IN THE UNITED STATES OF AMERICA

CONTENTS

	Introduction	ix
I.	Childhood and Youth	1
II.	Soldier and Voyager	35
III.	Exile in England	57
IV.	Le Génie du Christianisme	87
V.	Journey from Paris to Andalusia	128
VI.	The Valley of Wolves	156
VII.	The Partisan	193
VIII.	The Upward Climb. The Dizzy Heights. The Fall	233
IX.	The Monarchist against the Monarchy	269
X.	Towards the Grave	305

Introduction

SEVERAL reasons have led me to apply myself to the study of Chateaubriand's life. The first was a great admiration for the writer, one of those who have exercised the most lasting and profound influence on French literature; the second the desire to compare a French romantic with the English romantics I had studied, and especially to find in Chateaubriand the original of which Byron was so often a copy; the third a keen interest in that strange existence which found itself bound up with the whole history of France throughout the most dramatic period of that history. The Old Order, the Revolution, the Empire, the Restoration, the July monarchy, Chateaubriand knew them all; he was banished by the Republic, a rival of the Emperor, a minister and afterwards an opponent of the King; he lived in England and in America. In his time he was traveller, soldier, novelist, ambassador, religious writer and political publicist; he was loved by the most beautiful and sphinx-like woman of her age. In all this there is so much material for a biography that it is surprising to find that Chateaubriand's has, all things considered, been rarely written. There exist numbers of special studies; fine scholars have pieced together, minute by minute, the use of his time; literary critics have dealt with his style; psychiatrists and psychologists have analysed his character. Comprehensive studies, however, are scarce and the most recent, that of M. Henry Bérenger, was written before the latest discoveries—discoveries which are infinitely precious.

It would seem that the reasons for this abstention are on the one hand the fact that Chateaubriand himself, in the *Mémoires d'Outre-Tombe*, wrote his own life, on the other the vast labour of research essential to the study of so long and complex an existence. These two objections have not withheld me—for these

Introduction

reasons: (1) The *Mémoires d'Outre-Tombe* are far from being wholly trustworthy—moreover, Chateaubriand put into them only a fractional part of all that went to make his real life. (2) The labour of research has been lightened for me in that, for the last few years, there has existed in Paris a Société Chateaubriand which has brought together all the scholars engaged in the study of that writer, classified fresh documents and, finally, issued a bulletin to spread the knowledge of those documents. To the president of that society, Dr. Le Savoureux, and to his archivist, Mlle. Darenberg, I owe my warmest thanks for their careful checking of my work, the proofs of which they have been good enough to read. Without their help, I should never have dared undertake it.

The Société Chateaubriand has begun the publication of a complete bibliography. It is vast and I shall make no attempt to summarise it here. I would only point out all that this book owes to the excellent work of M. Collas and M. Aubrée on Chateaubriand's youth, of M. Bédier and M. Chinard on the American journey, of MM. Le Braz, Baldensperger and Marcel Duchemin on the London exile, of M. Yves Le Febvre on *Le Génie du Christianisme*, of M. André Beaunier on Mme. de Beaumont and Joubert, of M. Agénor Bardoux on Mme. de Custine and the Duchesse de Duras, of MM. Villemain, Cassagne, Beau de Loménie and Hubert Gillot on the political life of Chateaubriand, of the Abbé Pailhes and Mme. Marie-Louise Pailleron on the Vicomtesse de Chateaubriand, of M. Maurice Levaillant on the *Mémoires d'Outre-Tombe* and on Mme. Récamier, and finally of Mme. Marie-Jeanne Durry on the Roman embassy and Chateaubriand's last years. These books, together with the Correspondance Générale edited for Champion by M. Louis Thomas, Edmond Biré's annotated edition of the *Mémories d'Outre-Tombe* and, needless to say, Sainte-Beuve's *Chateaubriand et son groupe littéraire* are essential to all those who, after reading this book, are desirous of pursuing further their study of the man and his work. I have also to thank Mme. la Comtesse de Durfort, née Chateaubriand, for her kindness in permitting me to visit the castle and the archives of Combourg.

A. M.

CHATEAUBRIAND

CHAPTER I

Childhood and Youth

> I was burdened with a superabundance of life.
> —CHATEAUBRIAND

1. LORDS OF THE MANOR, FARMERS AND CORSAIRS

IN THE open fields near the Breton village of Guitté, there may still be seen an old and strongly-built stone house which is now no more than a farm, but which the lawyers of two hundred years ago named, with respect, in their deeds the Manor or Château des Touches. In it there lived, at the opening of the eighteenth century, Messire François de Chateaubriand, "High and puissant Seigneur of a dove-cot, a toadery and a rabbit-warren." One of his ancestors, Brian I, had fought at the Battle of Hastings. Later Geoffroy de Chateaubriands had accompanied St. Louis on the Crusades. The Chateaubriands had twice allied themselves with the royal house of England, once with that of Spain and three times with the house of Bertrand du Guesclin. They had presided over the *États bretons* and had stood surety for the Kings of France. Even in the younger branches of the family, there was no member but could lay claim to an amazing number of quarterings, though all that many among them possessed beneath the sun was a field too barren to supply their bread.

Such was the lot of François de Chateaubriand, Seigneur de Villeneuve et des Touches. When he died in 1729, two-thirds of his meagre goods passed, in accordance with Breton custom, to his eldest son, a Rabelaisian curé turned country-priest. Three other sons shared an income of 1,166 livres. In such straits, the younger sons of a noble house in Brittany had only two paths open to them. Some went back to the plough and "in the course of a few generations were swallowed up in the labouring classes"; others took to the sea. The eldest of the three younger Chateaubriands, René-Auguste, chose the sea. He would have liked to serve as an officer in the Royal Navy, but the family was not rich enough to keep him at Brest for the period of training and it lacked patrons in the Admiralty to speed up his commission. Every Breton household, however, had friends or relations among the Merchant Adventurers of the Armorican coast, and it was to St. Malo that René-Auguste went in search of fortune.

About 1740, St. Malo—that rich stone city crouching on its island behind noble ramparts—was at the height of its vigour and prosperity. Trade seemed closely bound up with warfare. The corsairs, legalised pirates who were granted their letters-of-marque by the State, kept a sharp look-out for enemy ships (almost invariably English), attacked them when they were not too well armed and sold the booty for the benefit of the privateer. Though to all appearance a peaceful cod-fisher, the Newfoundlander also had often a bone to pick with the English, who were jealous of his rights on the Bank. Finally there was the less dangerous slave-trade, which consisted in carrying off negroes from the coasts of Guinea and selling them to planters in the French American islands.

René de Chateaubriand plied all three trades. "Whether as cabin-boy, apprentice or lieutenant, one may imagine his silent rage as he, whose ancestors had captained their vassals at Bouvines and seen service as Commanders-in-chief of the Breton squadrons, paced the quarter deck with clenched fists, seeing himself condemned to drag out his existence in the lower ranks, at the beck and call of merchants."[1] At twenty-eight he became a captain and drew his share in the profits, but kept the right, shared by the whole crew, to ship a private cargo. On one cruise to the coast of Guinea, Captain de Chateaubriand signed on his brother Pierre (afterwards M. de Chateaubriand du Plessis) as first mate. Though it was a slaving-expedition, there was nothing surprising in such traffic on the part of younger sons of good family. Not only was the slave trade held to be non-derogatory and as legitimate as any other, but it was encouraged by the authorities equally with other

[1] Collas.

Childhood and Youth

sea-ventures and the King readily ennobled the bankers who exercised it. On this occasion, the *Apollo*, commanded by René de Chateaubriand, carried 414 blacks, of whom only 16 died on the voyage. This was a remarkable success, for the average losses varied from 5 to 30 per cent.

In 1753 the captain married. A few leagues from the manor of des Touches, where he was born, there lived near the village of Plancoët a charming and cultured family of the ancient lineage of the Bédée, Seigneurs de la Bouëtardais. Messire René de Chateaubriand, Chevalier, took to wife the noble demoiselle Apolline de Bédée. She was a girl of twenty-seven, "lively, vivacious and gifted with a pretty wit." A great reader of Fénelon, Racine and Mme. de Sévigné, "her manners were elegant, but her person was small, brown-skinned and homely." After his marriage, René de Chateaubriand made but few voyages and, by 1757, had established himself as a ship-owner at St. Malo. His success was rapid. Privateering and slave-trading were by no means easy avocations. They meant the buying of cargoes, the choosing of cotton-stuffs and glass beads, the supervision of shipbuilders and a good eye for a craft. An experienced man of business, shrewd, silent and unyielding, M. de Chateaubriand brought to the conduct of his affairs something akin to genius and, in thirty-three years, amassed a fortune of nearly 600,000 livres. In the eyes of the gentleman-corsair, however, money was merely a means to an end. Humiliated by the poverty in which he had seen his people sunk, he longed to restore his house to the rank and honour befitting it. From the moment he became rich, his one dream was the purchase of a castle and an estate. That of Chateaubriand was not to be had, for it had merged into the house of Condé, but the beautiful feudal fortress of Combourg was on the market, since the Maréchal de Duras, to whom it had come by marriage, wished to be rid of it. In 1761, the ship-owner bought Combourg for the vast sum of 340,000 livres. Doubtless the possession of its four towers, the assumption of the title of Comte de Combourg, Seigneur de Granges and other places, and the certainty of his eldest son's inheriting the estate and titles were the most deeply-rooted joys of that proud, violent and gloomy nature.

Ten children were born to René de Chateaubriand and Apolline de Bédée. Four died in infancy, of meningitis. Six survived—a son,

Jean-Baptiste, the heir to the title and the castle; four daughters—Marie-Anne, Bénigne, Julie and Lucile, and lastly, François-René, the youngest, who was born half-dead on September 4th, 1768, a day when the old houses on the Ramparts echoed with the howling of a storm.

Any attempt to bring up so sickly a child in St. Malo would have been foolhardy. His mother put him out to nurse in the country, on the Bédée estates near Plancoët. The milk of his first foster-mother dried up. The second, seeing that the child was wasting away, put him under the protection of the Virgin, roughly carved in granite, whom the village-folk called Our Lady of Nazareth. She promised that, in honour of the Virgin, the boy should wear only blue and white until the age of seven. He lived, and spent the first three years of his life in that enchanting village which remained, till the end of his days, "the abode of happiness." A pretty stream, the Arguenon, flowed through it, between two wooded hills. Mme. de Bédée, a kindly old lady who had been given the sound education of all girls brought up at St. Cyr, shared with her sister Mlle. de Boistelleul an unpretentious house with terraced gardens where her grandchild loved to play. Not far away, in the Château de Monchoix on the Lamballe road, his uncle Bédée, Seigneur de Plancoët, was cheerfully squandering both his capital and income. The Seigneur, nicknamed the "Artichoke" by reason of his corpulence, had three daughters and a son, the Count de la Bouëtardais, "all of whom shared his sunny disposition." Monchoix forever echoed with music, dance and song and there was no lull in the gaiety. To leave its even tenor for the gloom of the paternal roof was a change indeed.

When, at the age of three, François-René was taken home, his father was gradually dissociating himself from ship-building and had already taken up residence in the Château de Combourg. Meanwhile his mother who (even if somewhat scatter-brained) was a woman of some learning, devout, and much given to politics and society, stayed on at St. Malo, in the vast town-house on the Place St. Vincent, where the ground-floor was given up to the offices of the firm of Chateaubriand. Her preference for her elder son, Jean-Baptiste, was so marked that the younger, "Franchin" (or the Chevalier, as they came to nickname him) suffered from

Childhood and Youth

a sense of injustice. From the very day of her marriage, Apolline de Bédée had surrendered to her husband's turn of mind. "The restraint it put upon her changed her light-hearted gaiety to sadness." Driven to silence when she would fain have spoken, she made amends in her master's absence. All day long she gadded about the narrow streets and the drawing-rooms of the little town where the privateers' families lived on the most intimate terms. She came home only to scold, and there could be no more natural butt than her son, the Chevalier.

Gifted with a daring and violent nature, that imp of mischief would make his escape to play with the urchins of St. Malo on the causeway of Le Sillon. He would come home at night with torn clothes and a grubby face to the distress of his mother who sighed:—"How ugly he is!" She was too absent-minded to notice how he suffered from being shabbily dressed and from having no money to buy toys and cakes like other children. Trivial sorrows, maybe, but are any sorrows trivial to the seven-year-old? When the Comte de Combourg succeeded in tearing himself from his estates and came to St. Malo for a few hours, he had to listen to endless complaints about his younger son and replied unsympathetically that all the Chevaliers de Chateaubriand had been drunkards and brawlers. François' elder brother was at boarding-school; his sisters blushed for such a ragged and dirty scamp. The only persons who shewed the least kindness to the baby of the family were an old servant, La Villeneuve, who stuffed him with sweets and his youngest sister, Lucile, who was as neglected as he.

"Picture a thin and gawky little girl, too tall for her age, shy, reticent and unteachable. Dress her in a cut-down frock. Lace her narrow chest in a boned bodice that bruises her sides; hold her head high by means of an iron collar covered with brown velvet; scrape her hair back on top of her head under a black cap; and you will have some idea of the poor wretch who greeted my eyes when I returned to my father's roof."

Lucile had tasted far deeper humiliations and was far more sinned against than her brother, so, although four years her junior, he took her under his protection. When they were sent for their first reading lessons to a pair of bent and hump-backed sisters who scolded Lucile, the young barbarian flung himself on them tooth and nail. Thus, from their earliest years, the two youngest of the family shared their woes which—however trifling—had power to sting.

At seven years old, François-René was taken with due ceremony to Our Lady of Nazareth to be dispensed of his vow. Mass was celebrated at the Abbey of Plancoët and the ceremony of which he was the hero left a deep impression in his mind. In his sermon, the Prior recalled Geoffroy de Chateaubriand's departure for the Crusades with St. Louis and added that François de Chateaubriand, like his ancestor, might one day find the road to Palestine and visit the Virgin to whom he owed his life. At Plancoët the child had another glimpse of his delightful grandmother, with her gathered frocks and lace caps tied under her chin. She told him scores of tales about the court of Louis XIV while her sister, Mlle. de Boisteilleul, sang him songs of her own composition. One of them began: "There was a hawk which loved a lark," a situation which struck her great-nephew as odd. At Monchoix, Uncle Bédée was still going the primrose-path to ruin and "his gaiety was inexhaustible." After the scoldings of the Place St. Vincent, "the junketings and festivity" of Monchoix seemed Paradise indeed.

A few days later François de Chateaubriand returned to St. Malo. There was an odd pleasure in the streets smelling of tar and brine, in the shops, their doors ajar, with their rolls of cotton and chests of glass beads, in his fearless companions and the daring games on the causeway of Le Sillon. The children of St. Malo laughed at spindrift, bestrode the piles amid the surf and welcomed tempests with delight. Chateaubriand was to love the sea with his last breath:— "that sea which had been his first foster-mother, which had seen his first stumbling steps, awakened his first passions and stilled his earliest storms." Throughout his life, too, he was to remember Christmas Day in the Cathedral of St. Malo, when the old salts knelt down and the young women read their Book of Hours by the light of a farthing-dip, while tempests shook the stained-glass windows and the arches of the nave quivered.

As he sat on the shore, he delighted in "gaping at the blue horizons" or in watching the wind-swept mists which furled about the squat black rocks of the Grand Bé. The dreams of a pugnacious young man are all too short-lived. There would come a schoolfriend such as Gesril, who lived on the floor above the Chateaubriands in the Place St. Vincent and who amused himself by emptying water-cans down the necks of François' elder sisters as they stood on the balcony, or perhaps Captain Pierre de Chateaubriand's son, Armand, and the band would be off on some mischief which terrified the servants. In the evening they would come back to the Place St. Vincent, to the drawing-room with its yellow-damasked armchairs and buttercup-yellow hangings. Mme. de Chateaubriand, who was always mutinous and inclined to the party of La Chalotais, would tell her visitors sadly that the fish-wives of St. Malo obstinately refused to sell their sole and turbot to the partisans of the Duc d'Aiguillon. La Villeneuve would go bedwards to her attic and stretch herself on a rickety cot under an inadequate feather-mattress while the child fell asleep to the rise and fall of the waves which beat on the shore in perfect and monotonous rhythm.

2. BRETON SCHOOLS

In May 1777, M. de Chateaubriand, who was living in retirement at his castle, sent for his wife and children. His swarthy little spouse had to resign herself to leaving St. Malo, though sorely against the grain. A heavily-gilt coach, harnessed with eight horses as gaily caparisoned as Spanish mules, bore the noble family, which drove up the hornbeam-avenue of Combourg with a pomp befitting the Marquis de Carabas. From an outer gateway the carriage, with all its bells a-jingling, turned into a vast grass-grown courtyard. At its far end the "austere and gloomy" pile of a feudal castle rose amid a grove of trees, touched with splendour by the setting sun. Four towers, "arranged like chariot wheels" were linked by machicolated curtain walls, while the pointed roofs seemed poised above the battlements "like a cap on a Gothic crown." The fortress was lit by few windows, lost in the huge walls, and even those were latticed like Moorish grilles. Never had François de Chateaubriand beheld anything more terrible and fair. Compared with Combourg, Monchoix and La Bouëtardais were mere hovels, and—proud of being a son of such a house— he "snatched a fearful joy."

The drawbridge had been replaced by an ugly flight of steps which led to the guard-room. At its top, the Comte de Combourg awaited his family. "M. de Chateaubriand was tall and gaunt, with an aquiline nose and thin, pale lips. His deep-set greenish eyes were small, but, when he was angry, their shining pupils seemed to start out and come at you like bullets." That day, however, "the arrival of his family in a place of his own choosing softened his mood." The exploration of the castle and the park, the cork-screw staircases, the secret passages, the Moor's tower, the lake which mirrored the great trees and the birds and flowers of spring made the ensuing fortnight one of witchery for the children. Combourg seemed to them a dread and wonderful place. Had they not been told that it was haunted, especially by the ghost of an old nobleman with a wooden leg, whose cat followed everywhere at his heels? From then on, however, François was to be given regular schooling, since his father intended him for a commission in the Royal Navy. Though he shed a few tears he was confided to the headmaster of the nearest school, the Collège de Dol.

It was a very small school, staffed by a few priests. There were two buildings at right angles, a courtyard, a meadow and trees—no more. Hitherto the Chevalier de Combourg's studies had been somewhat desultory, but the masters at Dol found him a gifted pupil. Both in Latin and mathematics he shewed quick intelligence and a phenomenal memory. So naturally did his phrase slip into Latin pentameter that the Abbé Egault, who taught the subject, nicknamed him the "Elegiast." Later, he would doubtless have called him the "Rhetorician." In the company of his schoolfellows he suffered at first, as he had at St. Malo, through having no pocket-money and being the shabbiest of them all. Later, they came to respect his courage and admire a temperament so violent that it flared into open rebellion if a master threatened even to lay a finger on him. Besides his gifts as a Classic, he loved games and, as he was "neither bully nor slave," his natural charm soon made him a centre of attraction.

He passed four well-spent years in the Collège de Dol and acquired a sound classical background. Towards the end of that time he was troubled by an early adolescence. It is the period when a growing boy becomes aware of new and unfamiliar de-

Childhood and Youth

sires within himself, when—because he does not understand them—he searches every book he reads for some enlightenment on the mysteries which disturb and bewitch him. Cut off from women, he calls out to them, not knowing that he calls. It is they whom he seeks in poems, in novels, in the Scriptures even, and he quivers at meeting a voluptuous word among the pages. In Chateaubriand such impulses were very strong.

"There chanced to fall into my hands two very different books, an unbowdlerised Horace and an *Histoire des Confessions mal faites*. No one would believe the upheaval that those two books occasioned in my mind. An unfamiliar world grew up about me. On the one hand, I suspected the existence of secrets which, at that age, I could not understand, an existence other than my own, pleasures that outrivalled my sports, charms undreamed of in a sex which I knew only in the persons of my mother and sisters. On the other hand, ghosts—breathing fire and dragging their chains—warned me of the eternal torments reserved for those who left one mortal sin unconfessed. . . . I was construing the Fourth Book of the *Æneid* and reading *Télémaque*. In Dido and in Eucharis I suddenly discovered a beauty which swept me off my feet. I awoke to the mighty harmonies of those great verses and of that old-world prose. One day, my unseen translation of the *Æneadum genetrix hominum divumque voluptas* of Lucretius was so spirited that M. Egault snatched the poem from me and bustled me on to Greek roots. I purloined a Tibullus; when I came to *Quam juvat immites ventos audire cubantem*, the sad sensuousness of the verse was a revelation of my own nature. From that time the volumes of Massillon that contained the sermons on the Magdalen and on the Prodigal Son went everywhere with me. I was allowed to browse, for no one guessed what I found in them. I stole candle-ends from the chapel so that, during the night, I might read those bewitching descriptions of the disorders of the soul. I would fall asleep murmuring incoherent phrases in which I strove to capture the melody, the rhythm and the grace of the writer who came nearer than any other to transmuting into prose the music of Racine. If, in after life, I have succeeded to some degree in giving a true picture of the promptings of errant hearts and the Christian subjugation of the passions by right reason, I am persuaded that I owe it to the chance which led me, at one and the same time, to the knowledge of two hostile and warring empires."

At the age of thirteen, he discovered in the work of the Christian orators those harsh discords in which the ideas of sin and of pleasure are mingled even as, in the Latin elegiacs, pleasure went always hand in hand with the regret that joy should be so fugitive. Before making his first communion at Dol, he hesitated till the last to confess his imaginings, but—at the very moment when he was about to receive absolution—he owned up bravely, dreading the torments attendant on bad confessions. The Superior was alarmed by the sensuous and fiery temperament thus unexpectedly revealed to him. He foresaw the stormy passions to come, and feared for his pupil. Next day, however, the boy made his Communion with the utmost reverence. "In the course of the ceremony, I might have met with my accustomed humiliations, pinpricks though they were. My clothes and my bouquet were not as fine as my companions', but that day was wholly God's and wholly for God. I verily understood the meaning of Faith. The Real Presence of the Victim in the sacrifice of the altar was, for me, as sensible as that of my mother at my side. When the Host was laid on my lips, it seemed that all my being grew full of inward light."

During the holidays, it was a delight to see the little world of Combourg again. M. de Chateaubriand, as he grew old, was proving an exacting and cantankerous overlord to his tenants. To make amends for his long deprivation of feudal rights, he formally revived even those almost forgotten, however quaint their nature. There was, for instance, the pair of white gloves which the parishioners of Mont-Dol owed the Seigneur de Combourg, or the crisp loaf which the parishioners of Québriac had to offer on Whit Sunday, together with five sols in coin.[1] On certain fairdays, he compelled his vassals to take up arms and so give a semblance of force to the levying of a toll due to the Counts of Combourg on every head of cattle. In good years the levy had been known to bring in as much as from sixty to eighty thousand livres. When his son petitioned for a horse to go riding in the

[1] M. L. Pailleron—*La Vicomtesse de Chateaubriand*.

woods, he was told that a naval officer should only ride the waves. His two eldest daughters, Marie-Anne and Bénigne, he married on the same day, to two men of rank in Fougères, M. de Marigny and M. de Québriac. A little later (in 1782) the gentlest and loveliest of the four girls, Julie, married another gentleman living in Fougères, the Comte de Farcy, a captain in Condé's regiment. The three sisters, who were of considerable social standing in the little world of Fougères, soon set about introducing their odd young brother and sister.

When the boy left the Collège de Dol, François' father decided that he should go to the Jesuits at Rennes to work for his naval examinations, as the mathematical teaching was better. The Jesuits had thousands of pupils and the Chevalier de Chateaubriand met some of his old friends from St. Malo, Gesril among others. In the bustle and turmoil of such surroundings his faith was swamped. He had no time for meditation, no place where he could find solitude. His progress in mathematics was rapid enough. François de Chateaubriand had a clear head and a concise mind; there seemed every likelihood that he would make a good naval officer or engineer. Yet he still remained the *enfant terrible* of St. Malo and of Dol. He was mixed up in all the school rags, but ready to own up cheerfully when the moment of retribution came.

He stayed two years in Rennes. After Julie's wedding—when for the first time he had the unforgettable experience of seeing at close quarters a beautiful woman not related to him (Thérèse de Moëlien de Trojolif, "a slender, lively Amazon")—he set off for Brest, where he hoped to get his midshipman's certificate. Paris delayed, the certificate never came and the Chevalier remained what was called in Brest a "soupirant" exempted from regular studies. M. de Ravenel de Boistelleul, a sea-captain who was a first cousin once removed of the Chateaubriands, introduced him to a good eating-house and found him masters for fencing, drawing and mathematics. In Brest he found solitude at last and the "blue distances of far horizons." He would watch the bustle of the port, with its seamen, customs officers and convicts, and the sloops that came and went in the harbour. Round about him he would hear old salts telling the tale of their voyages and campaigns. Lapérouse was there supervising the equipment of his frigates before putting out to sea. "I drank it all in, watching everything that happened without ever uttering a word, but there was no sleep for me the next night. I spent it in waging imaginary battles or in discovering unknown lands."

One day, as he was watching the return of a victorious squadron, an officer flung his arms round his neck. It was Gesril, who had been wounded, and was going home to his family. The chance meeting awoke in Chateaubriand an intense longing to see his own people. Was he really anxious to become a naval officer? He no longer thought so. Though the sea and far voyages tempted him, he was inwardly conscious that he could not obey that compulsion; moreover, as his certificate had not been sent off in time, he was very near the age-limit. Without a word to his uncle, without writing to his parents or asking anyone's leave, he set off one morning for Combourg where he appeared "like a bolt from the blue."

"Between her scoldings my Mother kissed me whole-heartedly and Lucile rapturously." The indifference of his father, who contented himself with silent head-shakings, is explained by the lack of importance which he attached to a younger son. What was to be expected of the boy? He said now that his true vocation was religion. So be it! He should be sent to the Collège de Dinan to complete his education in the Humanities.

At Dinan, Chateaubriand played prisoners' base in the meadows bordering the Rance, and had a narrow escape from drowning while swimming in the river, in the intervals of writing Latin and even Hebrew prose at the dictation of the Abbé Duhamel. Holidays at Plancoët alternated with holidays at Combourg. It was all pleasant enough, but in his heart he no more wanted to be a priest than to be a sailor. Little by little, he protracted his stay at Combourg until he came to remain there altogether, since his father found that it was a saving of expense.

3. Lucile's Year

By 1784 Combourg, which was always gloomy enough, had become nothing short of funereal. The Comte de Chateaubriand was sixty-six and already threatened by paralysis. A persistent tremor in one arm deprived him of its use and, as he watched himself slowly dying, he was filled with self-reproach for a life in which he said he had not done enough for either his family or his name. He would spend whole days at his work-table, ill-lit by a loophole in the thickness of the wall, studying the family genealogical tree which hung above the chimney-piece or in fighting neighbours and vassals alike in defence of his rights. A true miser, "he kept his sugar-loaf and his candle locked in a cupboard in his room, side by side with rich and splendid clothes and a silver service worthy of the *Arabian Nights*."[1] Mme. de Chateaubriand, too, was growing old and all her thoughts turned to religion or to the six weeks which her stern husband allowed her to spend in St. Malo once a year. The three eldest daughters were living at Fougères; Bénigne had lost her first husband, M. de Québriac, and was about to become Mme. de Chateaubourg. Only Lucile remained with her parents.

At twenty, she had developed a strange, but very real, beauty, although her rather large features were irregular and there was something slightly theatrical about her pale face, her long dark hair and the "fiery sadness" of her glance. Like her sisters, she might doubtless have found favour in the eyes of some gentleman of Fougères, but "scared of men and of life" and overwhelmed by griefs which were for the most part imaginary, she pleaded a longing for the convent. Through the instrumentality of her parents, she was admitted as a Canoness of the noble Chapter of Argentière and so enjoyed a prebend and the title of Countess. Thenceforth the ceremonious society of Combourg always referred to her as "Mme. the Canoness" or "Countess Lucile," while the prodigal son was "M. le Vicomte."

Every evening, in the vast fortress built for a company of men-at-arms, the four members of the family and the handful of servants scattered to their quarters. The old Count, who was a maniac on the question of solitude, had relegated his son to the top of a tower and his valet to a vault. To reach his room, the young Chevalier had to climb a spiral staircase and circle the battlements, from which there were glimpses of sheeted waters and the treetops of the forest. When the wind whistled in the towers and the castle echoed with the answering tu-whit-tu-whoo of the

[1] M. L. Pailleron.

owls, this nightly journey must have been eerie enough, but François de Chateaubriand was no coward. It was enough that his father should say: "Can it be that M. le Chevalier is afraid?" and all the ghosts were laid.

In his mind, "honour had already made its lonely dwelling, like a seignorial manor on a Breton heath."[1] Spread out at the foot of the castle, below the battlements of Combourg, were the wretched hovels of the villagers. Their bitter poverty, the dirt of the hamlets and the abominable state of the roads were such as to shock the English traveller, Arthur Young, in the course of his journey through France. Between those serfs, with their long curls and sheep-skin tunics, and the "fierce and gloomy negro-slaver" who surveyed them from the height of his towers, there was probably no bond of common feeling save that of mutual hatred. Always in François de Chateaubriand, there was to remain something of that ignorant and uncompromising pride.

It may be that if they had ventured to open communications, the two youngest children and the old man might have drawn closer together, for the three were akin in their quality of extremes. On rare occasions, when M. de Chateaubriand came out of his shell of silence and told his children the tale of his youthful poverty and all the rubs of his later life, his son would listen eagerly. Years later, long after the old nobleman's death, he was to write:— "I have treated our most praiseworthy of fathers as he deserves. I have depicted him as he was, a man of courage and genius." When he heard so stern a man lament his fate in brief and bitter terms and, the tale ended, saw him rise abruptly and begin once more his ceaseless walking to and fro, his eyes would fill with tears, but the Comte de Combourg encouraged neither gush nor confidences.

The daily routine was unalterable. Winter and summer alike, the father rose at four. His son had no fixed time and, though he was supposed to study till mid-day, he spent most of his time doing nothing. After breakfast, the Count hunted or fished, his wife shut herself up in her oratory, Lucile in her room, and the Vicomte wandered about the country. Dinner was at eight o'clock. On summer evenings they sat on the terrace and the father, armed

---

[1] Maurice Barrès.

with his gun, took pot-shots at the owls which flew out of the battlements, while the three others sat silent, gazing at the woods, the sky and the first stars. In winter, the family remained in the great hall when the meal was over. Lucile and her brother ensconced themselves by the fire, Mme. de Chateaubriand stretched herself on a day-bed, while the old Count began the regular prowl which ended only with his going to bed. "He wore a gown, or rather a kind of cloak of white ratteen, such as I have never seen on anyone else. His head, already half-bald, was covered by a big cap which stood up of its own accord. When, as he paced the room, he drew away from the fire, the vast hall was so poorly lit by a single candle that he was lost to sight. Only his step could be heard in the darkness. Then he would come slowly back towards the light and emerge ghost-like from the shadows, with his white robe, his white cap and his long pale face. When he was at the other end of the room, Lucile and I would exchange a few words in an undertone, but we fell silent at his approach. As he passed he would ask: 'What were you talking about?' Terror fell upon us and, when we made no reply, he went on walking. For the rest of the evening we would hear no sound but the rhythmic fall of his steps, my Mother's sighs and the murmur of the wind.

"Ten struck on the castle clock. My Father stopped. The same spring as had raised the hammer of the clock seemed to arrest his steps. He drew out his watch, wound it, took his great silver candlestick with its tall candle, went to the little West tower for a moment, then came back with his candlestick in his hand and advanced towards his bedroom, which opened out of the little tower on the East. Lucile and I stationed ourselves on his path, kissed him and wished him good-night. He would bend a dry and withered cheek towards us and, without answering, go on his way to the depths of his tower, where we heard the doors shut to behind him."

No sooner was the old man gone than his wife and children relaxed in a torrent of words. Some time later, when he had escorted his mother and sister to their rooms to protect them from ghosts, the son gained his room in the tower. At four o'clock he was awakened by his father's voice. Nothing broke the monotony longings of adolescence. Like most young men of his age he was in love, but knew not what he loved. "I was a mystery to myself. I could not look at a woman without being stirred, yet I blushed if ever she spoke to me." He drew upon Virgil, Tibullus and Massillon for a clearer image of the object of his yearning, but the only women about him were his mother and sister and he banished, as shameful, thoughts which might offend their purity. One day, however, a Combourg neighbour called at the castle with his extremely pretty wife and, as the young man was stepping hurriedly to a window, he found himself hedged between the lady and the wall. "Even now," he wrote later, "I do not know what went on about me, but—from that moment—I glimpsed the supreme happiness of loving and being loved in a way I had never known."

A boy who reaches puberty amid surroundings of easy virtue can never know the essential strength of passion, for his desires meet with an object of flesh and blood and so fail to stir the imagination. He has found the primrose-path of pleasure and lost that of genius. On the other hand a shy creature such as Rousseau or a youth such as Chateaubriand, cut off from the woman whom he might have loved by physical or moral barriers, must create his heroines or his mistresses of his own flesh. "Hence I formed a woman of all the women I had ever seen. She had the figure, the hair and the smile of the unknown lady who once held me against her heart. I lent her the eyes of one village girl and the freshness of another. The portraits of the great ladies of the time of Francis I, Henry IV and Louis XIV, which hung in the drawing-room gave me other features and I even went the length of stealing beauty from the Madonnas in the churches.

"This delirium lasted two whole years, in the course of which the faculties of my soul reached the last height of exaltation. I spoke little or not at all, I went on studying only to throw my books aside. My taste for solitude redoubled. I had every symptom of strong passion. My eyes grew hollow and my body lean. I could not sleep. I was absent-minded, sad, fiery and unapproachable. My days flowed on tameless, weird, crazy yet all compact of bliss." With this woman, moulded to the heart's desire, his imagination created the fairest of romances. He had only to read the description of a far country for it to become the setting against which his dream-mistress and he lived out their love. Thus grew up the perilous lover who was to go seeking the Sylph in all women, and to become, at last, the writer who depicted, as none has ever done before or since, the moidered passions of youth.

It was at Combourg that he became free of woods and fields, of reeds and heather. From its tree-tops the bird sang to him, as it sang to Siegfried, of love and fame. If, throughout his life, he was to love trees and plant them with his own hands, to speak of the throstle and the nightingale as a man who had often listened to their song, to describe the moon and "the great sad secret she loves to whisper to the immemorial oaks and to the age-old shores," it was to the long loneliness of Combourg that he owed it, to those months when Nature herself seemed only the image of his secret heart and his rapture was so keen that he bounded through the woods like a young faun until he dropped exhausted.

Close on the heels of such midsummer madness there followed a discouragement as intense. He would come to himself suddenly and pass severe sentence. What was he? The younger son of an old man, a Breton nonentity in a pigmy body, an uncertificated sailor, a cleric with no vocation, a lover without a mistress. What future could there be for him? To what end was he born? Deeper even than sadness, he knew "the burden and the weary weight of all this unintelligible world." It is a feeling well-known to fiery souls who have no outlet for their ardour. He was "overwhelmed," less by real anguish than by "superabundant life."

"There were times when I seemed to myself of no account, a creature incapable of rising above the common herd. At others, I was aware of qualities which none could ever appreciate. Everything tended to foster my bitterness. Lucile was unhappy, there was no comfort in my Mother, and my Father was for ever on the watch to nag me." So intense did that bitterness become that he one day attempted to shoot himself with a fowling-piece, but the gun misfired. Eventually he fell sick and the doctor said that he must be removed from the fens of Combourg as soon as possible. He begged to be allowed to go to India or Canada. In 1785 the question of his sailing for those distant lands with a Captain Morand was mooted, but he doubtless preferred going as an army officer, for in June 1786, Jean-Baptiste got into touch with M. d'Andrezel, a major in the Navarre regiment, with intent to secure a commission for his younger brother. During these negotiations the young Chevalier spent most of his time at St. Malo, grieving that he could no longer find the familiar surroundings of his childhood. He was only seventeen, yet his friends were already scattered and the house where he was born had been converted into an inn. What, then, was this world in which nothing endures? "Here below we are mere spectators at a play. If we turn our heads but for an instant, the whistle blows, the enchanted palaces dissolve, and, when our eyes again seek the stage, they see only a wilderness where the actors are strangers." He maintains that he was on the point of hurling himself into the Rance from some rocky height, when a message from Combourg called him home.

"M. le Chevalier," said his father, "it is time to put an end to your follies. Your brother has got you a commission as Second-Lieutenant in the Navarre regiment. You are to start for Rennes and thence for Cambrai. Here are a hundred louis; husband them well. I am old and ailing and have not long to live. Let your conduct be such as befits a man of quality and never tarnish your name." A trembling and emaciated arm, steadied with difficulty by another, only slightly more serviceable, held out to the young man an ancient sword. A few days later, the Chateaubriands' gig took the road past the lake with its skimming swallows, that same road as had brought them, long since, to the castle.

4. The Subaltern

To join his regiment at Cambrai, Chateaubriand had to go by way of Rennes, where the Public Prosecutor, M. Duparquet-Louyer, an old family friend, put him into a carriage with the wife of a silk-mercer of the town, Mme. Rose—a charming milliner who consented to share travelling expenses. Looking at the boy's handsome face, she may have hoped for a brief adventure or a few sweet nothings, at least. She was grievously disappointed. For a lad who had spent three years dreaming of imaginary women, it is no small ordeal to be shut up in a carriage for three days with a woman of flesh and blood, jolted against her with every bump in the road. Yet reverence and shyness triumphed over desire. He squeezed himself into a corner to avoid touching a woman's frock and, on their arrival in Paris, Mme. Rose dropped her silent companion a slight ironic curtsey. "Your servant, Sir." He never saw her again.

She set him down at the Hôtel de l'Europe, in the Rue du Mail, a very second-rate hostelry. There he was visited by his brother, Jean-Baptiste, who, having bought the office of Master of Requests was living in Paris. Together they went to the convent where their sister Julie, Mme. de Farcy, was staying. She had come up from Fougères, "to consult specialists" as she said, but doubtless to breathe the air of fashion also, for Julie was a great success in Paris. With her caressing blue eyes, "coloured like the sea," and loosely-waved brown hair, she was infinitely lovelier than Lucile. Her arms and shoulders were models of grace and whiteness. Brilliant, animated and cultured as were all the Chateaubriand children, a translator of the *Jerusalem Delivered*, it was she who said: "What account of my life shall I render to God? I know nothing but versing?" When she kissed her young brother and, clasped in her arms, he felt her ribbons, her laces and her posies, he took heart. Already he was of that company of men "for whom nothing can take the place of a woman's affection, delicacy and devotion," yet they terrified him. When his cousin Moreau (for naturally he found a cousin in Paris) saw fit to initiate him into the ways of the world and so took him to call on Mme. de Chastenay, a somewhat ripe beauty who, on his second visit, received him lying down and stretched out a bare arm to young Chateaubriand, he promptly took to flight.

On his first visit to Paris, he had no liking for it. His father had been right in saying that there Brittany seemed farther off than ever it did in China. Round about him, conversation turned on another world. There was talk of the Court, of financial schemes, of meetings of the Academy, of the women and the scandals of the day, of the latest play and triumphs of the stage. Fine topics these, for the familiar of nightingales and of the moon that etched the clouds above Combourg. He rejoiced when the time came to leave for Cambrai and his regiment. There he was a marked success. A man among men, he was no longer troubled by the dangerous cross-currents of reverence and desire. Gay-tempered and the best of company, he was a good listener, always ready for a game of dominoes in some café. Before long, his fellow-officers got into the way of dropping in to see him, the older among them to narrate their campaigns, the younger their love-affairs.

In September 1786, a letter recalled him to Brittany. His father was dead and he mourned him sincerely. Death brings forgetfulness both of the harshness and weaknesses of those who have gone, leaving us only regret for our silences. Those self-same mannerisms and tricks of speech which once seemed tiresome or ridiculous take on a touching sadness when we know that we shall never see them more. In his dreams, François de Chateaubriand still seemed to hear his father's steps drawing near the great fire-place or fading away again. The old man had loved him in his heart.

Mourning and the division of the inheritance reunited the family at Combourg. It was natural that the castle and almost all his father's fortune should go to the elder son, Jean-Baptiste. François-René fell heir to the modest sum of 62,740 livres. The dowager countess took up her abode in St. Malo, in the narrow Rue des Grands Degrés. Now that he was rich, Jean-Baptiste set off once more for Paris, where he was to marry Mlle. de Rosambo, the daughter of the Président de Rosambo and grand-daughter of the Minister Malesherbes. For a time at least, the two youngest went to live at Fougères, near their married sisters. The second-lieutenant had been granted long leave. He loved the country, and the countryside about Marigny was beautiful. In that little circle of provincial society, he himself was far from being a failure.

"I knew him," wrote a young girl in Fougères, "at the time when his taste for literature was becoming manifest. He was the gayest and most likeable of people. He gave an original twist to everything he uttered and could make the merest trifles amusing. Hence, if anyone wanted to repeat what he had said, the charm was lost, since it lay rather in his impressions than in his thoughts. For the rest, he was very good-hearted and the gentlest of companions. He loved children and, with his usual kindliness, was always ready to take an interest in them.

"That is how he struck me when I first knew him. . . . I have often heard my father say that he was very fond of him, that such an imagination could not fail to make a stir, and that M. de Chateaubriand would end by writing."

Childhood and Youth

A life so free from struggle might perhaps have bred in him a not unwilling sloth, but in the following year (1787) a letter from his brother summoned him to Paris. Jean-Baptiste was anxious to present his younger brother at court; it appeared that M. de Malesherbes thought it unbefitting that a Count de Chateaubriand, the husband of his grand-daughter, should remain a Master of Requests, since the post made him a gentleman of the robe and so forbade access to the King's coaches. He therefore advised entering the army and suggested that, as a reminder of their claims and noble lineage, the Maréchal de Duras, a kinsman of the Chateaubriands, should present François at court, since, as an officer, he could aspire to that honour. His brother's letter went on to say that, once he had been presented, the Chevalier could hardly fail to be offered a company of horse and even, if he would take the tonsure, the benefice of a knight of Malta.

The young barbarian's first impulse was to refuse. His elder brother had both the title and the inheritance, so the honour of the family name was his affair. "If the king had need of a soldier in his army, he had no need of a poor gentleman at court." When they read it, this noble and theatrical reply moved his sisters to mirth and since, if there was one thing he disliked more than another, it was family discussions, he answered "Have it your own way" and went to Versailles. The etiquette of the Court was still impressive in the extreme and the monarchy had never seemed more firmly established. As the Maréchal piloted the cadet from Brittany to the King's presence, the courtiers lining the way asked of each other: "Who is he?" When M. de Duras named his protégé: "Sire, the Chevalier de Chateaubriand," Louis XVI looked at the young man, hesitated and passed on without a word. The Queen dropped him a noble curtsey; she seemed enchanted with life. Next day, the "débutant" in his grey coat, red waistcoat and red trousers was to join the King's stag-hunt. For a shy person the ordeal was cruel. An untried horse bolted with him. As a result he did the one thing against which he had been warned and was in at the kill before the King himself. Louis, however, did not lose his temper, but said, with a hearty laugh: "He didn't stick it long." Such unwonted graciousness led everyone to believe that the Chevalier would be seen again at Versailles, but his one thought was to escape to his own province. The few weeks which he had spent in a hotel in the Rue du Mail, while awaiting his presentation, left him only a sense of sadness. He was weary of brushing against unknown and beautiful women, as he nightly took his dreaming walks through Paris, and incapable of enjoying the unromantic pleasures of the Palais-Royal. As soon as he could, he set off for Brittany.

On this occasion he found life at Fougères a little tedious and, though he was paying respectful court to "a pleasing, if homely, girl," it seemed that beauty must forever be beyond his reach. All things considered, he would have preferred the loneliness of Combourg, which at least had some character. "When I stayed with my sisters, the County had taken itself to the fields. We went from neighbour's house to neighbour's house, dancing or getting up plays, in which I sometimes acted very badly. Winter in Fougères meant putting up with the society of a little town and all its balls, assemblies and dinners, yet I could not pass unnoticed, as in Paris." He was glad to cut short the boredom of his stay for a period of service with a battalion of his regiment, garrisoned at Dieppe. Once more he saw his mistress, the sea, and as he drilled on the beach to the shouts of the corporal:— "Form fours! Charge! Shoulder arms!" he gazed with longing and delight at the waves breaking on the shore. On his return to Fougères, he found that Julie and Lucile were bent on leaving Brittany. Julie had enjoyed her Parisian triumphs and as her husband, Count Annibal de Farcy, an infantry captain, rarely lived in Fougères, that charming lady decided that her ill-health gave her an excellent pretext for the change. Moreover, now that he was the grandson-in-law of a Minister, her brother, Jean-Baptiste, could open all doors to her, "Driven by the instincts of genius and beauty to a vaster theatre," Lucile took it upon herself to overcome her brother's unwillingness and "the tender band of the three youngest nestlings" took the road for Paris. Needless to say, the journey was severely criticised by Bénigne and Marie-Anne, sensible and managing people both, who never now referred to their youngers save as "The Canoness and her scapegrace brother." Between the stay-at-home Breton clan and the clan agog for adventure, the family was splitting up.

5. MANKIND ON HOLIDAY

The three young fledglings went to nest in the shadow of the powerful Jean-Baptiste, who was living with his father-in-law, the Président de Rosambo, in the Rue de Bondy. Their chief ambition was to be made free of that world of Letters in which each of them hoped to find fame. Julie's beauty and the clannishness of the Bretons in Paris were introduction enough. During her earlier stay, Mme. de Farcy had tamed a minor philosopher, Deslisle de Sales, a worthy man, even if "heartily commonplace." He it was who inscribed on the pedestal of his bust: "God, Man and Nature, he has all explained." Deslisle introduced them to Carbon de Flins des Oliviers, a man "more rich in names than in laurels." Flins, in his turn, fell in love with Julie, and introduced Fontanes, the translator of Pope, a serious-minded poet, upright in life and a gay companion, square-cut as a boar. Chateaubriand, however, preferred the elegies and erotic poems of the Chevalier de Parny. He compassed a meeting with the illustrious Creole, and there sprang up a friendship between him and the "amant d' Eléonore." To their little group, the Breton Guingené, a former pupil of the Collège de Rennes brought the bilious and witty Chamfort, who lived in the same house as he, and the poet Le Brun, who thought himself a second Pindar, though Chateaubriand, if ever he risked a morning visit, grew used to finding him surrounded by unwashed dishes and a charwoman, while he declaimed the verses composed during the night to the refrain of the hairdresser's: "Would you be good enough to turn your head, Sir!"

Save for Chamfort and Fontanes, it was but a second-rate literary set. Even so, its reputation dazzled the three young provincials from Fougères. When Fontanes invited him to dinner in the company of his mistress, Guingené, Flins and Parny, Chateaubriand saw himself as a made man, with a dash of the rake. In the society of those free-thinkers, his faith foundered. He realised that, in the eyes of his new friends, the Christian creed was incompatible with intelligence, and found all the artists, all the wits and, indeed, all men of parts leagued against religion. His reading at Combourg had already shaken his beliefs. In Paris, he was the more easily carried away by "Philosophy" in that he found his brother's household sharing the same ideas. It was a period when "minds and manners were alike at sixes and sevens. . . . Magistrates blushed to wear the robe. . . . The priest avoided uttering the name of Jesus Christ from the pulpit, and referred to him only as the Christian Lawgiver."

Président de Rosambo had three charming daughters, Mmes. de Chateaubriand, d'Aunay and de Tocqueville, who welcomed the newcomers kindly. M. de Malesherbes, who had now retired from public life, willingly sought the society of his children and grandchildren. Though perhaps a little common, "he was always natural, thoroughly good-natured, with a fund of simplicity and commonsense, and so outspoken as sometimes to border on rudeness. When one saw him first," said Boissy d' Anglas, "in his brown coat with deep pockets and gold buttons, his muslin cuffs and snuff-stained jabot, an unkempt wig askew on his head, and heard him talk with no effort at affectation or refinement, it was difficult to remember that one was actually in the presence of such a man." "But," added Chateaubriand, "the first words he uttered betrayed the bearer of an ancient name and a prince of magistrates." His great knowledge caught fire on his lips and Chateaubriand compared his conversation to the "ceaseless bubbling of a brew simmering in the pot."

The old man delighted in expounding the world to a youth filled with the passionate curiosity which he himself had never lost. "The amazing thing about him was his vigour of expression in advanced old age. Could you have seen him sitting silent, with his eyes a little sunken below shaggy greying brows and that kind look of his, you would have taken him for one of those august beings whom Le Sueur delighted to paint. Yet, touch but the right chord, and he was up in a flash. His eyes opened wide; his burning flow of words and animated expression brought to mind a young man in the heyday of his powers, while that hoary head and the indistinct speech that comes of being sans teeth betrayed the septuagenarian. The contrast redoubled the charm of his talk, as a blazing fire in winter is a foil for its ice and snows."

It was not revolutionary ideas which M. de Malesherbes instilled into Chateaubriand, but those principles of reform to which so many right-thinking people in France pinned their hopes. His heart's desire was not to destroy, but "to uphold and regenerate. .... He was of the race of Vauban and of Fénelon rather than that of Mirabeau and Condorcet." He had been the friend and patron of Rousseau, and Chateaubriand, thanks to the atmosphere of Combourg, was already sympathetic to the Genevan's landscape: he was soon steeped in *Emile* and the *Contrat Social*. It was not unusual for the talk of the ex-minister and the young man to turn on botany and geography. Malesherbes encouraged Chateaubriand to learn the names of flowers. He made him read Linnaeus and sent him to the Jardin des plantes. As they bent over their maps, the Minister and the second-lieutenant planned voyages which Malesherbes could only plot, but which Chateaubriand might one day make, and it was this which fired the youth with the idea of journeying to America to discover the North West passage.

M. de Malesherbes' patronage of the three provincials was not idle. He promised the Countess Lucile that he would help her to exchange the Chapter of Argentière for that of Remiremont, which was not only more aristocratic, but more remunerative. Meanwhile, Jean-Baptiste, who had entered the army, insisted on his brother's becoming a Knight of Malta, an honour to which no layman might aspire unless he took the tonsure. This the ecclesiastical authorities were by no means ready to grant, but the Bishop of St. Malo felt himself under an obligation to Mme. de Chateaubriand, who was one of the saints of his diocese. François went to stay with his Mother, who was living alone in her narrow street and spending her days between knitting and prayer. Absent-minded as ever, she would start out for High Mass with a bedroom-slipper tucked under her arm instead of her missal. To her son she recited poems of her own composition, doleful ballads, which had more style than sense. Thanks to her, he was granted his tonsure at once, and now that she was delivered from a plaguy husband, he thought his Mother charming.

All this happened in 1788. In December the États bretons met at Rennes. There was talk of taxes, of the Affair of the Necklace, of the *Mariage de Figaro*, of Cagliostro and of Mesmer. Discontented as ever, the aristocracy of Brittany was plotting against the Court. Even burly Uncle Bédée, nicknamed the Artichoke, was given to speechifying from chairs which collapsed under his weight.

Chateaubriand clamoured with the rest, fought with the university students and held his own against the servants of the king, but always in cold blood and always as an onlooker at the game. For most of the young noblemen involved, such activities were merely a renewal of schoolboy rags. It never occurred to them that by fighting the Court they would end by being engulfed in the same abyss.

From Rennes, Chateaubriand made a bee-line for Fougères, where he lodged with Madame de Marigny and he found his four sisters once more united in their little town. The letters written in 1789, the year when he came of age, to a friend and contemporary, the Chevalier de Châtenet, have come down to us. They are concerned with Lucile, with women and with love, a theme on which he delighted to play the rake *à la Valmont*. Paris and the regiment had spoiled him. "I have kept my pledge in the matter of my sister. Your addresses have been duly paid and she resolutely awaits your coming to continue the romance. My courting may not have been as spirited as yours, but I drew a picture of your person, and that should be enough. I hereby invite you to make her acquaintance as soon as you please. I am not quite sure when I may be leaving, so write to me here. I have often thought of you since we were separated and the barracks idea grows on me more and more. With two or three beings such as you and a mistress (for she would prove a necessary evil) in some country retreat a few leagues from Paris, or even in Brittany, we could while away delightful and quiet days. I promise that as soon as I reach Paris or Brittany, as the case may be, I will set about putting that tempting plan into execution. To spend my whole life in the company of charming friends, such as I might esteem, would be pleasure indeed. Tell Eugénie of our scheme. I am sure she would rejoice to make one of the party, but I can picture her explaining to you, in all good faith, that she is heartbroken to have to decline it. Give her a thousand greetings from me, as tender and as well-turned as you can make them. That should not call for much effort on your part. I swear to transmit faithfully to the Countess Lucile all that you would have me say. My portrait of you has made her greatly wish to meet the original. Deal gently with her, if you must seduce her, my dear Châtenet! remember that she is a maid." If one side of the character he was acting for the benefit of his friend resembled the heroes of Laclos, the other was reminiscent of St. Preux. "Your leaning towards melancholy is habitual with me also. . . . Your keen sensibility has encouraged mine. . . . My greatest need is to unburden myself upon your heart." Such was the way of writing in 1789, and how can a lad of twenty break free from the style and phraseology of his age?

The visit to Brittany was protracted by sick-leave, which allowed the subaltern not to rejoin his regiment. Hence it was only in June that "the three" returned to the Paris they longed to conquer. The journey was marked by unrest. Peasants held up the carriage and demanded passports. In Paris, the whole town seemed at fever-heat. Shopkeepers were on their doorsteps, while nervous and expectant crowds pressed round tub-thumping agitators. The Oath of the Tennis Court had already been taken. The Third Estate had refused to vote to order. "Yet the sense of security was still pushed to extremes. What could be more absurd, said Necker (June 29th, 1789) than the fears to which the organisation of the States General has given rise?"

The taking of the Bastille itself brought no enlightenment. For some days the event seemed to make the nation of one mind. Amid the ruins of the fortress, ambassadors and dancing-girls mingled gaily with the half-naked workmen who were battering down its stones. Young Chateaubriand, who had been present at the assault, was more far-sighted. Already he foresaw its consequences and the probability of mob-rule. Though far from hostile to the ideas which had inspired the attackers, their deeds were abhorrent to him. He had seen one of the conquerors of the Bastille wearing on the lapel of his coat a fragment of the wretched Flesselles' heart. His intellect could have desired to see great changes, his instincts swept him into the threatened camp. He was neither a man of the people, as was Rousseau, nor a bourgeois unjustly thrashed, such as Voltaire. It was from the turrets of Combourg that his young eyes had first taken stock of the world. Had the Revolution but shewn clean hands, it would doubtless have carried him away. A ghastly spectacle sufficed to alienate him. From the windows of his hotel he saw two maimed and dishevelled heads carried by on pikes. They were those of Foulon and Bertier. An eye, prized from its socket, dangled against the darkened face of one of the dead men, while the pike pierced the black cavern of his mouth. "Ruffians," cried he, "is this what you mean by liberty?" Had he had a gun, "he would have shot the villains down like wolves." His sisters and the bystanders rebuked him sharply for that rash cry, which came near to bringing about the massacre of them all, but it was his deepest self which had spoken. He was appalled by what must come and, from that moment, longed to leave France.

Nevertheless he hesitated for some time. A trifling love affair held him back; moreover, his natural melancholy was "the sister of inaction." The majority of the Court were emigrating, while army-officers, disheartened by the unruliness of their troops, were resigning from the service. Among his former friends, the men of letters, he noticed surprising changes. From being a passionate aristocrat, Parny—the lazy—had become a Terrorist. The Breton Guingené, a former pupil of the Jesuits, exclaimed on the day of the Feast of the Federation: "That is something like a feast! For its better illumination they should burn four aristocrats at the four corners of the altar." Others had no thought but for their love affairs. Mankind, freed from the restraints of a crumbling society, thought itself on holiday. It had not yet discovered "the new tyrants begotten of licence."

Amid such disorders, Chateaubriand remained strangely level-headed. He was a man divided against himself. Within him, intellectual sympathy for the doctrines of his age was at strife with passionate loathing of its crimes; hence he refused to take sides. M. de Malesherbes and his daughter, Mme. de Rosambo, clung obstinately to their liberalism; the President and his son-in-law, Jean-Baptiste, were fiercely anti-revolutionary. "As for me," said Chateaubriand, "I attached to the questions then raised only such importance as sprang from general ideas of liberty and the dignity of man. Personal politics bored me. My true life was in higher regions." The bitterness of passion in a man such as Chamfort amazed him. "It has always astonished me that a man with his knowledge of humanity should espouse any cause soever with such warmth. Did he not know that all governments are alike?"

About him, illusions were as tenacious as ever. The Royalists still believed ingenuously "that it would all end one morning with a parliamentary decree." The Revolutionaries "equally unthinking in their hopefulness" foretold "the reign of peace, of happiness and of liberty." Sceptical and perspicacious even then, Chateaubriand wished to have nothing to do with either camp. He remarked in the presence of the Chevalier de Panat: "I am in search of something new. Nothing is left to do here. The King is doomed and there will be no counter-revolution. I am going to imitate those Puritans who, in the seventeenth century, emigrated to Virginia. I'm for the forests. That is better than going to Coblenz." When he spoke of exploring, his friends thought him a little touched, but there was more wisdom in his folly than in their inertia. He was right in considering that the France of the day was no place for a man such as he, and could justify his choice of America by arguments cogent enough. He saw in it a refuge for those who loved true liberty. If only he could discover the North West Passage, he hoped to win there that renown which the nightingale of Combourg had promised him. Above all, he had conceived the idea of depicting the manners and customs of uncivilised peoples and of writing the epic of Man and Nature. The artist in him felt the need of accuracy and he lacked the true colours.

It must be admitted also that his old friend and master, M. de Malesherbes, worked him up to a pitch of excitement about the voyage. "I used to go and see him in the morning. With our noses glued to maps, we would compare the various outlines of the Arctic circle. We calculated the distance from the Behring Straits to the depths of Hudson Bay; we pored over the divers narratives of voyagers and navigators, English, Dutch, French, Russian, Swedish and Danish. We sought information concerning the land-routes to be followed in attacking the shores of the Polar Seas. We yarned of the difficulties to be overcome, the precautions to be taken against the rigour of the climate, the onslaughts of wild animals and the lack of provisions. And that famous old man would say to me: 'If I were younger, I would set off with you. I would spare myself the sight of all the crime, the cowardice and dastardly folly which greets me here. But, at my age, one must die where one is.'"

In January 1791, Chateaubriand came to a final decision. Disturbances were on the increase. Moderation and impartiality were no longer safeguards, but crimes. To render him suspect it was enough that a man should bear a noble name. One morning, in his brother's house, Chateaubriand took farewell of M. de Malesherbes, who said to him: "You are young, you will see many things; as for myself I have but a little time to live." Thereupon the explorer left for Brittany, to make preparations for his voyage.

As for money, he proposed to use what was left of his small inheritance. He had also earned a little, in the most unlikely way, by dealing in cotton stockings. One day, when a debt of honour was weighing on his mind, M. de La Morandais, the son of a former bailiff of good family at Combourg, had put Chateaubriand in touch with a stocking-manufacturer at Angers and the Chevalier had turned merchant with surprising orderliness and attention to detail. He bought several hundred gross of white stockings and even more of mottled "which sold better." Though their spelling left much to be desired, his letters to the manufacturer were in the best commercial jargon: "Sir, I am thoroughly satisfied with your prompt delivery. I hope that I may find considerable market for your goods among my acquaintances. Kindly reply by return of post, enclosing your account and the delivery note for the last two bales I ordered of you, for it is my intention to await your letter here and you would not have me hindered in urgent affairs requiring my presence in Brittany by any delay on your part." Before turning Lord of the Manor of Combourg, the Count de Chateaubriand, his father, had proved himself a shrewd business man. The son inherited from the old corsair and slave-trader not only his thirst for adventure, but a taste for form and order in his actions.

At that time, the crossing to the United States was by no means an easy matter. Chateaubriand went to St. Malo, where he found the *St. Pierre*, a brigantine of only a hundred and sixty tons, captained by Dujardin-Pintedevin, ready to sail for Baltimore with a group of Sulpician priests and a few ecclesiastical students destined for the seminary in that town. The fare for the passage was very reasonable. A Breton who had once seen service in the United States, the Marquis de la Rouërie, known, during the War of Independence, as Colonel Armand, gave the traveller a letter of introduction to Washington. Chateaubriand went to Combourg for a last visit. The courtyards were desolate, the windows barred, and the terrace on which he had last seen his father, deserted. An un-

Childhood and Youth

known caretaker opened the door to him. Only the faintest gleam of light filtered through the closed shutters. He rushed from the castle and left without daring to turn his head. Back in St. Malo, he took a long and tender farewell of his mother, whom he left in tears, and went on board. For some time the vessel was becalmed "in the roadstead." Afar off he saw "the domes and steeples of the churches where he had prayed for Lucile, the walls, the ramparts, the forts and towers of the city, the shores where he had spent his childhood with Gèsril." Then the night drew down. Lights twinkled from the town and the beam of the lighthouse cut the dark. Though no breeze sprang up, the ebb tide swept the *St. Pierre* out to the open sea. When Chateaubriand, who had gone down to doze in his hammock, came back on deck, "the land of France was out of sight."

What manner of person was this lad from St. Malo who, at twenty-three years old, on board a sorry ship, with only a handful of priests for company, set sail for an unknown world? What did he owe to his blood, to his province, to his relations, to his age? To the Celtic spirit he might owe his melancholy, his independence, his obstinacy, his cross between sensuousness and reserve, his taste for heroic poetry and for those sad joys wherein love and death are mingled. To his father, the daring and saturnine old slave-trader, he owed the violence, the delight in risks, the pride of name, the constitutional melancholy and world weariness of great men of action. To his mother he owed that taste for literature which she inherited from hers and bequeathed to all her children, a consuming imagination, a Christian upbringing and the irresistible gaiety and kindliness of the Lords of the Manor of Plancoët. To his schoolmasters at Dol and Dinan and to the Jesuits of Rennes, he owed a sound classical background and a reverence for great works of art. To the battlemented towers, the still pools, the woods and moonlight nights of Combourg he owed the sense of his own dignity, the love of solitude, the strength of his desires and his knowledge of Nature. To his age, to M. de Malesherbes and his Parisian friends, he owed his scorn of despotism and his strange veneer of sceptical philosophy over a Catholic soul.

Because he was a Chateaubriand, he was a Royalist. Because he was a disciple of Rousseau he could not hate unreservedly the ideas of the Revolution. Because he was the son of the Lord of the Manor of Combourg, he was a feudalist; because he was the impecunious cadet of an all too wealthy elder brother, he neither was, nor ever would be, a true Conservative. Because the most sensuous of poets had awakened in him a precocious development, he desired all women; because he was a rustic, brought up by a pious mother in a lonely park, he dreaded and fled them. From all that torturing world of contradictions and longings he could find no escape save in creation, in mystery and in frivolity. Yet, as he set foot on the deck of the *St. Pierre*, the grace of youth was, of itself, enough to shed an atmosphere of gaiety and tenderness over such a turmoil of passions. He was short of stature, too short for the head which seemed sunk on his shoulders, but he had a fine brow and his hair curled delightfully. His gently-mocking eyes were thoughtful, his chin long and stubborn, while his neck was as delicately modelled as his sister Julie's. "Youth," he was to write one day, "is a charming thing. At the outset of life, she goes garlanded with flowers to spread her conquests further, as the Athenian fleet set out for the subjugation of Sicily and the fair fields of Enna." Chateaubriand's own youth bore more resemblance to the frail bark that carried him. Before hoisting him on their foamy crests, the giant waves of wars and revolutions were to plunge him into the black depths of poverty and exile, but the bark was stout and would weather the storms.

CHAPTER II

Soldier and Voyager

> The reader replied that he threw his whole soul into everything.
> —Father de Mondésir

1. The Crossing

THE hull of a sailing-ship of a hundred and sixty tons is a frail wall between life and death. As he hung for three months "above the grave face of the abyss," Chateaubriand learned to know what few French writers had noted before him: "the awful majesty of ocean horizons." Born in St. Malo of a corsair father, he was rather delighted by the beauty of the high seas than moved by their perils. During the crossing he proved himself a good sailor and listened enthralled to the Breton boatswain's descriptions of negroes and American Indians. Wrapped in his cloak, he would sleep on deck beneath a sky heavy with stars and, in the morning, climb nimbly to the top of the main-mast amid the applause of the crew. There may have been a touch of the theatrical in his daring. "One day," writes a fellow-voyager, Father de Mondésir, "we ran into a gale. M. de Chateaubriand, always a great imitator of the Homeric heroes, had himself bound to the main-mast after the example of Ulysses. There he was drenched by the waves and well battered by the wind, but—braving air and water—he cheered himself with the cry: 'Oh storm, thou art not yet as fair as Homer made thee!' "

His attitude to the ecclesiastical passengers was an odd mixture of vainglory and awkwardness. The will to please clashed with the desire to shock. Sometimes it was the Knight of Malta who strove to impress them by his learning, or who, on Good Friday, clasped a great crucifix in his hands and preached a sermon full of "telling and burning phrases" to the crew assembled on deck. Sometimes, on the contrary, he irritated Sulpicians and seminarists alike by sneers worthy of an ill-bred rake. When the vessel touched at the Azores, he came back bubbling over with tales of the impiety of the Spanish monks, but his gibes were those of a subaltern proud of being a free-thinker and loosed at last from the constraint of France. The truth of the matter was that he was brimming with youth and strength and simply did not know how to kill time on board.

"For lack of better occupation and to while away the days," says Père de Mondésir, "he would willingly be present at our spiritual exercises, not, of course, prayer or the rosary, but at the devotional reading which was held in common. We were studying *l'Âme élévée à Dieu* and Père Rodriguez: *De la Perfection chrétienne*. Now Chateaubriand, the impetuous, preferred reading aloud to listening in silence. It was often his turn. One day, M. Nagot, the leader of the Sulpician mission, pointed out to him that a work of ascetic theology should not be declaimed after the manner of a tragedy. The reader replied that he threw his whole soul into everything." The upshot of the master's reminder was that the rôle of reader no longer suited the viscount. Moreover, it caused Chateaubriand to take a strong dislike to M. Nagot, whom he characterised as having "the wily mind of an old priest."

With the French seminarists there sailed for Baltimore a young Englishman of good family, Francis Tulloch, a former artillery officer and ex-Anglican whom M. Nagot had converted to Catholicism. This youth, whom Nature had gifted with a well set-up person and a charming face, was highly cultured and spoke several languages. Chateaubriand, the philosopher, took it upon himself to point out to Tulloch that to renounce his wealth and his career, not to mention breaking his mother's heart, in order to roam the world in the train of a seminary of foreign priests was the most egregious folly. When the ship put in at the Île St. Pierre, these two romantic lads ranged the mist-shrouded mountains, reciting Ossian and making plans for the future. Chateaubriand, who had "thrown his whole soul" into his philosophical disquisitions as into everything else, believed that he had succeeded in un-converting Tulloch, but M. Nagot—far more skilled as a fisher of souls—won the neophyte back in a trice. It was not long before he was chanting in processions and turning the cold shoulder on Chateaubriand.

The latter's attitude was not so simple as his Voltairian outbursts suggested. More than any other passenger, he was responsive to the divine beauty about him. At sunset, when the crew took off their tarry hats and sang some simple hymn to Our Lady of Good Succour, tears welled into the young Breton's eyes. When he recalled the voyage in after years, it was in all sincerity that he wrote:— "The vessel tossed at the mercy of a slow and thudding swell, while fiery sparks flickered along the foam that creamed about its sides. Myriads of stars twinkled against the dark azure of the vaulted sky, a shoreless sea, infinity in heaven and on the deep! Never has God so disquieted me by his greatness as in those nights when I had immensity above my head and immensity beneath my feet." At the actual moment of the voyage, however, it was not of God that he meditated upon the waves. It was the unknown woman, created of his dreams, that he saw there and he would have "bartered eternity for but a single kiss." That is a somewhat lofty way of saying that he was twenty years old, that his desires were keen and that it was enough that a bare-legged fisher-girl should pass near him on the rocks of Saint-Pierre to turn the barren island to "an abode of bliss."

His companions thought him too hot-headed, but was not his the natural state of a body glowing with youth, cribbed, cabined and confined within a narrow space? Spurred by pride and boredom, young Chateaubriand could never envisage a feat of daring, however difficult, dangerous or vain but he must carry it through with a stubbornness at once Breton and quixotic. For instance, he took it into his head to bathe in mid-ocean. In vain the sailors urged the perils of cross-currents and of sharks. Stripped of his clothes, the Chevalier insisted on being lowered into the sea on a pulley and it was not till some little time later, when he was hauled up again, half-smothered by the waves, that he thought his honour saved.

Such escapades did not prevent others from discerning his future promise. After recalling Chateaubriand's prowess. Père de

Mondésir notes that "the young man had already observed and read a great deal." One episode of the voyage gave him a chance opportunity of shewing unexpected eloquence and maturity of judgment. The ship lost an anchor and the captain claimed that those who had chartered the vessel were liable for its replacement. When they touched at Saint-Pierre, the case came into court and Chateaubriand was entrusted by his companions with the defence. He was brilliantly successful. "There is no gainsaying," wrote the Reverend Father, "that he was a man of parts, whether in word or deed."

Even so, his fellow-voyagers were unaware of the most serious side of his life, for it was the most hidden. From his earliest youth there had been developing in Chateaubriand a writer, in love with the perfect phrase, at first only dimly apprehended but sought with as keen a yearning as the unknown woman of his dreams. When he beheld some great natural spectacle, the sun going down into the sea or the giant billows of mid-ocean, it was not of their beauty only that he thought, but of the compelling, half-realised duty of giving that beauty expression. His own mind gave back Lucile's phrase at Combourg: "You ought to paint that." When he climbed to the mast-head and clung there, dominating the waves, it was not only to dumbfound the crew and the seminarists, but that he might wrench from Ocean herself the words which should arrest her ever-changing aspects, "her colour, like that of liquid glass" and her waves which "breaking in a fleece of foam, looked like white flocks scattered over some dark moorland."

It was thus that one morning, after three months' crossing, he sketched in a few concise and accurate lines the arrival in America:— "Only the crests of a few maples rising above the water gave any hint of a coast." In the evening, Chateaubriand disembarked from the launch in Chesapeake Bay. No sooner had he set foot on land than he was struck by a charming picture. In the neighbourhood of a farm, negroes were sawing planks and white men hoeing tobacco plants. "A negro girl of thirteen or fourteen years old, almost naked and of singular beauty, opened the farmyard gate to us like some young figure of Night. We bought maize-cakes, chickens, eggs and milk and went aboard again with our demi-johns and our baskets. I gave my silk handkerchief to the little African girl. It was a slave who welcomed me to the land of Liberty." He was still too enthusiastic to reflect that therein lay perhaps a symbol.

2. Sojourn in America

America surprised and, at first, disappointed him. He had come out to seek a world twice new, in its impressions and in its customs. Yet, on the road by which he journeyed from Baltimore to Philadelphia, swallows skimmed the pools as they did the lake at Combourg. Brimming with enthusiasm for republics after the pattern of the Ancients, and nourished, like many a young Frenchman of his time, on legends of America, he expected to meet with a Cincinnatus, a Cato or a Franklin at every crossroad. The disparity of wealth, the unscrupulousness of banking and gaming-houses, the rowdyism of ballrooms and theatres shocked him. These free citizens were more like the subjects of tyrants. It was amusing but pitiable.

He arrived in Philadelphia, full of the tales of the Abbé Raynal beloved of his father, and asked to be shewn one of those famous Quakers, "the godly and sober descendants of William Penn. What was my surprise on being told that if I were curious to discover the lengths to which self-interest and business immorality could be carried, they would shew me two Quakers trying to buy something of each other and to get the better of the deal. With every succeeding day my illusions faded further and—it hurt."

Washington even ... After his victory, should not that legendary general have shewn his respect for Roman tradition by goading on his oxen and driving the plough? Chateaubriand saw him go by in a spanking four-in-hand with spirited horses. Cincinnatus in a four-in-hand upset the traveller's preconceived ideas. However, when he went to proffer to the President of the United States his letter of introduction from the Marquis de la Rouërie, he discovered the ancient simplicity at last. The house was small, there were no sentries and no men-servants. "Walk in, Sir," said a young maid. Washington made his appearance at once. "Colonel Armand!" he exclaimed when he saw the Marquis's signature and he listened without overmuch impatience to his young visitor's exposition of the journey he was planning. The plan was startling enough. Chateaubriand would have liked to go right across the continent from East to West in a wagon drawn by four yoke of oxen, touch the coast North of the Gulf of California, thence go due North in quest of his Passage on the open seas and finally return to the United States by way of Hudson Bay, Labrador and Canada. When Malesherbes heard those plans, his eyes had sparkled; Washington's opened wide. He invited the young madman to dinner, but gave him no encouragement.

Another interview with a fur-dealer in Albany to whom he had a letter of introduction, brought it home to Chateaubriand that for the present, at least, the scheme which was to cover him with renown could not be realised. He could, however, "enrich his palette with colours and his mind with feeling." The explorer gave way to the poet, though the poet did not give up his preparations for exploring. Telling Mr. Swift that he would content himself with going first to Niagara and then Pittsburgh, he bought two horses, engaged a sturdy Dutchman as guide and set out. Without waste of time he let his beard grow and his hair float about his neck, bought a complete outfit from the Indians, a sheepskin toga for his guide, a horn to call the dogs, a trapper's cartridge-belt, and thus costumed as a romantic hero, went off to hunt the carcajou. It is only an inoffensive little beast not unlike a squirrel, but *carcajou*. ... The word was satisfying and Chateaubriand worshipped words.

He found great happiness in that forest-journey. True, the savages, like the Quakers and Washington, proved rather disappointing. Chateaubriand had believed in the unspoiled child of Nature, in the primitive liberty which preceded the "social contract," in the "noble savage" whom only the conventions of our societies have corrupted. "Soft living" in a polished and artificial world had made the men of the Eighteenth Century forget how thin, in each and all of us, is the rind of convention that covers the formidable brute within. Before long, the traveller had to admit to himself that the Iroquois had their vices, much like Bretons or Parisians, that their passions were dangerous, their vengeance cruel and their tortures appalling. Yet so enduring and tenacious are prejudices that when, in after years, he pictured savages, it was as heroes, philosophers and poets that he drew them, with delightful lack of verisimilitude. In the diary he kept during the journey it is to Nature rather than men that his enthusiasm goes out.

When, for the first time, he penetrated into woods that had never known the axe, the sense of untamed liberty went to his head. "Right and left I went, from tree to tree, saying to myself: 'There are no more roads here, no more towns, no more monarchy, no more republic, no more presidents, no more kings, no more men.' To see whether I was re-established in my birthright, I would indulge in wilful action which infuriated my guide, who—in his heart of hearts—thought me mad."

Rightly to understand his ecstasy, one must evoke yet again the curbed impetuosity of his youth, the proud yet shy younger brother, the youngster from the provinces presented at a ceremonious and indifferent Court. Let loose in the forest, which he believed to be yet virgin, he at last enjoyed "the royal happiness of Adam, sovereign and splendid in Eden." His diary has come down to us: "Primeval Liberty, I have found thee at last. I take my way as that bird flying before me follows his trackless path, with no care save to choose among the leafy shades. Such as the Almighty created me I am, lord of all nature, borne triumphant over the waters. The river-creatures bear me company as I go, the birds of the air sing hymns to me, the beasts of the earth greet me, the trees of the forest bow their tops as I pass by. . . . Run, shut yourselves up in your cities! Go, submit to your petty laws, earn your bread in the sweat of your brow or devour the bread of the poor. Butcher each other for a word or for a master's whim. Doubt the existence of God, or worship him in idolatry! I, for my part, shall roam my solitudes. Not one of my heartbeats shall be checked, not one of my thoughts enchained. I shall be free, as Nature is free!"

This sense of liberation was not the only joy which he found in the exuberant nature of America. Its beauty held him spellbound. The actual extent of Chateaubriand's journey matters little. It seems that he saw the Niagara Falls, the Great Lakes, and the fort of Pittsburgh, and that he roamed the regions round about the Ohio and the Upper Mississippi for some weeks. Did he really ever set eyes on the latter river? It may be doubted. The sparkling beauty that he lent it was such as the real *Meschacébé* never knew. Whatever the case, he used his powers of observation to bear back to France colour and imagery such as no writer before his time had ever caught. In camp, by the glow of wood-fires or the "faint blue haze about the moon that, at her going down between the boles of the trees, laid sheaves of level light within the deepest heart of the glades," he took countless notes. None has ever believed more strongly than he in the necessity of painting (or, at least, of sketching) from life. Brought up among woods and by the sea, the familiar of trees and waves, he was always to be severe in his judgments on painters and writers who trusted to their imagination alone.

"Let us beware of thinking that our imagination is richer and more fertile than Nature. . . . As a rule, landscape painters have no love whatever of Nature and very little knowledge. . . . It is in the heart of the country that they should take their first lesson . . . Sometimes the landscape painter, like the poet, for lack of having studied it, will do violence to the character of a spot: he will set pines on the bank of a stream and poplars on the mountains. . . . Night, even, has her colours. To make the moon beautiful, it is not enough to make her pale. . . . If a landscape is to be a likeness, it should be drawn, so to speak, from the nude, and every line, muscle and bone accented. Studio sketches and copies of copies can never take the place of drawing from life."

These precepts Chateaubriand applied in his own writings and invariably drew the forms and shapes of nature "from the nude." Yet he had no hesitation in changing the grouping of those forms as best suited him or in fusing them with imagery borrowed from other writers for the composition of his pictures. Rivers changed their courses, mountains were moved, fauna and flora transformed, nor did he ever scruple to introduce into a landscape the whirlpool, star or crescent moon which might make it yet more fair. "As a pedestrian musician might transcribe the notes dictated to him by some great master of harmonies," throughout this journey Chateaubriand made exact and careful jottings of the elements of some fine landscapes which he was afterwards to use repeatedly and with subtle skill. Thenceforward his *Nuit chez les sauvages de l'Amérique* and his *Coucher de Soleil sur l'océan* were the indispensable properties of his stage-settings. He was often to draw them from their portfolios, to touch up their colours, simplify them, abridge them or infuse them with sunshine or despair as the circumstances of the moment might dictate.

One side of his work was to derive wholly from the diary of his youth. It was there he found colour: "The foliage was lavish of every imaginable hue—fleeting scarlet on red, deep yellow on gleaming gold, glowing chestnut on russet brown, green, white, misty blue—a myriad shades, that flushed from a faint tinge to burning splendour." He was to find sound there: "Sound has called unto sound and the forest is all one mighty harmony. Is it deep organ music that strikes upon my ear, while fainter strains drift lingering among the arches of the trees? Brief silence falls. The aery music wakens anew and all about me there is a soft plaining, murmurings within murmurings; every leaf has its own tongue; every blade of grass gives back its individual note." There again he found little pictures of Indian life, but above all he recaptured the memory of what he had felt:— "Enchanted meditations! Secret and ineffable charm of a soul joying in itself! It was in the heart of the vast deserts of America that I drank deep draughts of such delight."

If, with him, this exaltation turned more readily to sadness than to joy, if he sought in the ancient burial grounds of the Indians the twofold solitude of nature and of death, it was mainly that in those forests as old as the world itself, he still walked companioned by the sorrows of his childhood, the gloom of Lucile's thoughts and the dreary evenings at Combourg. It was, too, that his exaltation remained as objectless as the unused powers roused in him by youth and desire. "Ah! Could I but have shared my experience of ecstasy with another! O God! hadst thou but given me a woman moulded after my desire; if, as to our first father, thou hadst led me by the hand an Eve fashioned from my side. . . . Heavenly Beauty, I should have fallen prostrate in worship before thee. . . ." But, in those woods, he met with no woman's welcome save from two wretched Floridans, one proud, one sad. He hardly saw them, yet later, when dowered with European souls, they were to serve as lay-figures, one for Atala and the other for Celuta.

Quickness of sight and of understanding is the prerogative of genius. Chateaubriand spent only five months in America, but what does a great writer need? An incense-breathing night, an Indian encampment, a few teeming and motley visions, the clang and splendour of an exotic vocabulary. Of these he can create a world. From his memories and from his reading he can orchestrate a mighty symphony, while from a few half-forgotten impressions he can fashion the wonderful opening of *Atala*. Yet, at the time of his leaving America, nothing had taken shape. If there existed a first draft of *Atala* it was a narrative very different from that which he eventually published. As for the *Natchez*, they were then but the vague forecast of an epic of heroic simplicity, due partly to the reading of Homer and partly to the spectacle of the life of a primitive people. Who were to be the characters? Himself, Lucile, his Floridans, an old sachem (whose recollections of the court of Louis XIV were to be based on those of Mme. de Bédée), a young Indian, Chactas, into whom he was to pour much of Chateaubriand, lovely Indian girls in whom the Sylph was to take flesh and, shed over all, the dazzling colour of the virgin forest and the fragrance of its nights. If he did not begin his book, it was already foreshadowed in his mind, he was playing with it, accumulating material for it. "I had gleaned no light on the chief end of my journey, but I was companied by a world of poetry."

Why did he suddenly decide to return home? Because, for him, everything was quick to lose its savour, because he was already growing bored and because he longed to taste literary fame. He knew, with never a doubt, that in the notes he was taking back with him there was a new and unfamiliar beauty which would ravish the men of his time. Whatever might befall him in after years, he was never to be parted from those manuscripts. He was now far more eager to figure in European eyes as the man who had visited the solitudes of America than to explore the solitudes themselves. Throughout his life he was to glory in his self-styled nickname of the Savage, but he used the prestige of the barbarian to subjugate the most civilised of ancient societies.

He left, too, because honour demanded it. One day, on entering an American farmhouse and taking his seat in the ingle-nook of the living-room he found an English newspaper which had slipped to the floor at his feet. He began idly to read it, stooping over it in the firelight. There he saw in big print: *Flight of the King*. It was an account of Louis XVI's escape. The paper described the progress of emigration and the mustering of army officers under the flag of the French princes. Though Chateaubriand had scant belief in monarchy, his belief in fidelity was unshakeable. He felt that he must go home and join his fellows. Though he had no money left to pay his passage, he found a captain willing to give him credit and embarked on December 10th, 1791.

3. THE RETURN

He landed at Le Havre on January 2nd, 1792, after a crossing so stormy that the ship lost her mast. Chateaubriand narrowly escaped death, yet he made notes on the tempest which was to figure later in the *Les Martyrs* and the Mémoires. The captain asked for his passage money, so the passenger, who had not a shilling in the world, wrote to his brother Jean-Baptiste. Generosity seems to have been one of the last failings of the head of the family. He forwarded the note to their old mother and it was she who, from St. Malo, sent her younger son the necessary sum. In the same letter she told him that his Uncle Bédée and his sister Lucile had taken refuge with her. François-René determined to join them and seek their council.

The journey from Le Havre to St. Malo proved to him all too clearly the necessity for emigration. Menace brooded over the countryside. Everywhere the deserted castles had been looted. Their owners had taken refuge in the towns, but it was doubtful how long they could remain there in safety. The tiniest village had its club, affiliated with the Cordeliers of Paris. To the "unarmed and outworn" despotism of the old monarchy there was succeeding the worst of tyrannies, that of the mob: and every hamlet trembled beneath some local Tiberius. A Frenchman should never desert France. So thought Chateaubriand, but it was easy for a man who held such a point of view to talk: "No-one persecutes

45

him, he may go where he will without fear of insult or even of assassination; his house is not burnt down over him, he is not hunted like some wild beast and all because he is named Jacques rather than Pierre and because his grandfather, dead these forty years, had the right to a special pew in church and two or three liveried Harlequins to walk behind him."

On his return to St. Malo, Uncle Bédée and even Lucile concurred in his decision. Glad as they were to see him, they regretted his homecoming when the times were out of joint. They told him that his brother, deeply compromised by the vehemence of his opinions, was making ready to leave. Family opinion was unanimous in thinking that he should himself join the Princes' Army as soon as might be; honour and prudence alike dictated such a course. Yet, if he was to go, he had to have money. He had devoured his inheritance and who could thenceforward come to his aid? At that point his sisters took a hand. They had thought of everything and had a rich fiancée in the background. Her name was Céleste Buisson de la Vigne. She was seventeen, an orphan, and lived with her grandfather, an old seadog, at St. Malo. Noble? The patent was very recent, but she came of excellent family. Rich? By his sisters' account she had five or six hundred thousand livres, for her father had been a director of the India Company. Pretty? It was possible to find fault with her short stature, her longish nose and receding chin, but she was slim and well-made with delicate limbs and a white skin. "Her beautiful fair hair curled naturally and she allowed it to hang loose as a child's." Intelligent? She had a good head on her shoulders and was decidedly witty. Having been well brought up at the Benedictine convent in St. Malo, she spoke Latin and would end her letters with a *vale et me ama*. When she wrote French her style was vivid and racy. Besides, it was inconceivable that an ill-educated girl should have conceived an affection for Lucile. Would she consent? Lucile, whom little Céleste idolised, had turned catechist and sung such praises of her brother that the girl was in love with him before even they met. What would ensue once she knew him?

Chateaubriand felt himself ill adapted to marriage. How should he, who was possessed of all women in his dreams, be content with one? How could he submit to ties when he felt his energies, always fierce, redoubled by his lonely journeyings and when he must have liberty, if he was to write? He knew that it would be madness to agree, but he had a horror of family scenes and knew himself capable "of agreeing to a century of bondage to avoid an hour's fuss." He gave them his favourite answer: "As you will." Lucile pointed Mlle. de La Vigne out to him as they walked on the Sillon and he got into the habit of recognising her by her pink pelisse, her white frock and fair, wind-blown curls.

Romantic as it was, the marriage was difficult of attainment. In the Buisson de La Vigne family there were partisans of the new ideas who hated the thought that a young girl related to them by blood should marry an aristocrat and a ruined one at that. Devout as ever, Mme. de Chateaubriand, insisted that her son's marriage should be solemnized by a priest who had not taken the oath. It took place on February 29th, 1792, in her drawing-room in the Rue des Grands-Degrés, among the yellow damask armchairs to which the old lady had remained faithful. Buard, the officiating priest, was given twenty sous for his pains. Though the certificate bears the signatures of Mme. de Marigny and of Lucile de Chateaubriand, those of the bride's family are conspicuous by their absence. One of her uncles, M. Bossinot de Vauvert, a Jacobin, protested and egged her grandfather on to bring an action against the offender. Reft from her husband by authority of the court, the newly-wed Mme. de Chateaubriand was lodged in a convent till a decision should be reached. Proceedings had already been instituted when, to spare two reputable families the scandal bound to follow, a compromise was effected: Duhamel, the conforming parish priest, agreed to solemnize the marriage afresh. A legal contract was concluded with M. Buisson de La Vigne and on this occasion was signed by Bossinot himself. The contract shews that Céleste was not nearly so rich as her fiancé's sisters believed. In point of fact she had only thirty-four thousand five hundred livres invested in confiscated ecclesiastical property, which at that time yielded no income. Moreover, the capital could not be realised till the young woman came of age, not to mention that it was held jointly with a married sister, thus making a loan impossible. When, on March 19th, that accursed marriage was performed (for the second time), Chateaubriand knew that, without love, he had thrown away his liberty in vain.

He had yet to make the acquaintance of his wife. From the first he realised that he would never love her. It was not that she had no outstanding qualities. She was virtuous, devout and subtle, a shrewd observer with a happy knack of expression. Yet, though a better person than he, she was less easy of intercourse. Wit she had and to spare, but none of that poetry without which he could not breathe. Like most men who live on their imagination, he was willing to give way on everything (matters of honour always excepted) if only he were left to dream in peace. Now the wife he had taken unto himself proved stubborn, jealous, and mocking. Worst of all, she must needs take it into her head to love him. Lucile had made a dangerous mistake.

Meanwhile preparation for the Chevalier's emigration was pressing. The Legislative Assembly had just declared war on Austria: the effect was to hurry the last of the nobility out of France. "Royalists could no longer remain in their own homes without being dubbed cowards." After a short stay at Falaise, the young couple set off for Paris, duly accompanied by Julie and Lucile. Amidst the three youngest of the brood, the bride must have felt a cuckoo in the nest. The family had rented a flat for them in the Cul-de-sac Férou, off the Boulevard St. Germain. Chateaubriand found the town very different from the Paris he had left in 1790. To the days of Mirabeau, when there was still some hope of compromise, had succeeded those of Danton. The guillotine, in its single strength, upheld "a rule of blood and steel." In the streets, the curiosity and enthusiasm of the early days had given place to faces stamped with cruelty and fear.

Chateaubriand was anxious to meet his old acquaintances. Guingéné and Chamfort, who were converts to violence, disquieted and offended him. It was to M. de Malesherbes, who had strongly urged his departure for America, that he went to narrate his adventures and expound his plans for a second expedition which was to last nine years. "I would dash to the Princes' Army and dash back again to smite the Revolution hip and thigh: it would all be over in two or three months, I would hoist my sail and away to the New World again, with one revolution the less and one marriage the more." On the actual principle of emigration he consulted

Soldier and Voyager

M. de Malesherbes. Did honour really demand that François de Chateaubriand should take up arms against his country for a system of government in which he did not believe? He was amazed to find M. de Malesherbes passionately hostile to the Revolution. The fierce anarchy of which he had been an eye-witness had filled the old man with such horror that even so great a Frenchman as he, who had suffered under Louis XVI for his liberalism and tolerance, had come to long for a foreign invasion and the triumph of despotism. Thus does violence beget violence. M. de Malesherbes cited instances: Had the English in America hesitated to call on the French armies and the French fleets for aid against England? "Every government," said M. de Malesherbes, "which, instead of guaranteeing the fundamental laws of society, itself transgresses the laws of equity and the rules of justice, ceases to exist and throws mankind back to the state of nature. When that happens it is permissible to defend oneself as best one can and to have recourse to whatever means seem most fitted to overthrow tyranny and to restore the rights of each and all."

Young Chateaubriand was not convinced by his reasoning. A natural pragmatist, he was not blind to the fact that we will commend deeds done in support of our own views which we should reprobate if they benefited the opposing party. He knew that there was no course open to him but to emigrate, yet he regarded emigration as a piece of "stupidity and folly." It was characteristic of him that, before leaving, he should make a pilgrimage to Montmorency in memory of the man who more than any other was responsible for all that he was thenceforward to combat, and that he spent two successive days in the forests which had sheltered Jean-Jacques Rousseau's Hermitage. It was an odd way of reconciling his dead hopes with his living wrath.

The question of money had yet to be solved. As Céleste could not touch her property, since it was held jointly with an émigrée, it was manifestly impossible for her to help her husband. Lucile, who had still some small credit on her inheritance, volunteered her signature and a solicitor agreed to advance 10,000 francs. Chateaubriand was taking them home, in assignats, to the Cul-de-sac Férou when, in the Rue de Richelieu, he fell in with a fellow-officer of the old days in the regiment of Navarre, who haled him off to a gaming-house. There he lost all but 1,500 francs and those he left behind him in his cab. By a stroke of luck he discovered the next man to hire it, a worthy friar, who returned his 1,500 francs. Had he not found the friar, he would have been unable to leave: and what might his after-history have been? It was a question he often asked himself: but we who realise that character is fixed know that it would have been the same in its main outlines, if not in detail, even had it started in the other camp.

M. de Malesherbes was insistent that Jean-Baptiste should leave with François. The brothers secured false passports for Lille and disguised themselves as wine-merchants, members of the National Guard of Paris, on their way to Lille to tender for army contracts. Their departure had been fixed for the 15th; they spent the 14th in the gardens of Trivoli, which belonged to a kinsman of Malesherbes. With its grottos, its ornamental lakes, its statues and its tiny artificial stream, "the very image of a river," it was a place which the taste of the time found delightful. The Rosambo family was there, so were Mme. de Farcy, Lucile, Céleste and, of course, the two Chateaubriand brothers, all in the best of spirits, for at that time emigration seemed an adventure straight out of opera. Next morning the travellers pulled on the greatcoats of the National Guard, girt themselves with the tricolor and, at six o'clock, boarded the stage-coach for Lille.

4. The Princes' Army

By little lost paths through the wheat-fields and sunken roads the two brothers crossed the no-man's land separating the armies and scoured by both French and Austrian patrols under cover of darkness. Eventually, in the clearing of a wood, a company of Uhlans bore down upon them. "Officers on their way to join the Princes," cried they. Their tricolor sashes were insulted. When he recounted the episode in after days it was some satisfaction to Chateaubriand to think that these colours, enemy colours to him then, were soon to be imposed by a victorious France on a vassal Europe.

Every campaign brings its shirkers and its heroes. In Brussels Chateaubriand found the émigrés "foppish and worldly." The cadet despised them. "Vanity Fair was in full swing even beneath the cannon of Dumouriez." Pretty women had their salons there as in the days of soft living and managed to keep their relations and especially their lovers about them in some vague post such as aide-de-camp. "Never," said Roederer, "did more religious care go to preserving in Rheims the holy oils for the sacring of a King of France than the émigrés devoted to preserving the vices necessary to the maintenance of a throne." Chateaubriand had no patience with the brand-new uniforms of those glittering chevaliers who reversed the traditions of the Chansons de Geste by making love the path to glory. His own meagre luggage had been safely smuggled into Brussels. It consisted only of a little linen, his old uniform of the regiment of Navarre and the manuscript of the *Natchez*. Those "precious papers" were the only things from which he could not bear to part since he felt for them as a father and creator. The resplendent aides-de-camp of Brussels had nothing but scorn for the shabby young gentleman from the provinces who, in his threadbare coat, was actually making for the fighting-line. François de Chateaubriand, poor and lonely as he was, abominated this kingless court, but Jean-Baptiste, who had money and influence, was not slow in deciding to stay in Brussels as aide-de-camp to the Baron de Montboissier, his wife's uncle. It is as hard for a man comfortably married to live heroically as for a poor devil, tramping with a knapsack on his back, not to be something of a Jacobin.

The younger brother set out for the army by way of Liège, Cologne and Coblentz. On his arrival at Trèves he found the heroic émigrés far more worthy of respect than the fops of Brussels, but even less oncoming. In the eyes of the gentlemen who formed the Princes' Army, the late-comer was an opportunist who had waited to see how things would turn out before making up his mind: "This young Breton arrived when victory was assured. There was no further need of him." They were convinced that, at their first encounter, the Republican armies would fly before them. "There was not one of these knights of La Mancha, ailing, footsore, their nightcaps tucked beneath their three-cornered beaver hats, but firmly believed that in his single strength he could put to flight fifty sturdy young patriots." Luckily Armand de Chateaubriand, Uncle Pierre's (M. de Chateaubriand du Plessis') son was there in the Breton company and took his cousin under his wing. Thanks to him, Chateaubriand was able to explain himself: he was but lately arrived from America, where he had been living among the savages, hence his delay in emigrating; besides, had he not joined up before the first shot was fired? The Savage had charm, so all was well. He entered the Breton company, for the army had been organised by provinces. Noblemen served as privates and the aristocracy thus strangely reverted "to the status of their first beginnings."

It was a stouthearted army, touching in its mingling of generations and the sincerity of its feelings, but none was ever worse equipped. The arms served out to the men were German throw-outs. Chateaubriand went through the whole campaign with a musket whose hammer refused to function. Yet he loved life in camp. His travels had trained him for it—it was among the Iroquois, he said, that he learnt to kindle a fire in the open air; he was a very good hand at making soup as they do it in Brittany; he loved trees and birds. Whenever he had a free moment he would read Homer, contemplate nature or spread his manuscripts on the grass of some meadow by the Rhine and emend his American notes. That done, he would put them back in his haversack with his greatcoat and his pocket Homer. The burden weighed so heavily on his unaccustomed shoulders that he thanked God when a thief lightened it for him by stealing his shirts.

When he crossed the French frontier under arms, he felt "a chill at his heart." The strange thing was that only revolutionary precedents and the abstract conception of a social contract subject to repeal could in any way justify the Princes' enterprise. To a disciple of Rousseau, and to him only, the fatherland might seem not a plot of earth but an entity of laws and guarantees. Once the contract was broken, duty expired. Experience was to teach Chateaubriand that a man's true country—that land of memory, of the same culture, the same tongue and the same dead may not be transplanted by an argument. It was grievous for him to hear the same shout: "Look out, sentry!" arise from either camp and in the same tongue, whether its accent were Breton, Provençal or Picard. When the attack was sounded, insults flew back and forth: "Aristocrats! Sedition-mongers!" yelled the defenders of Thionville. "Scoundrels! Traitors!" came the answering shout of the assailants. Yet always the words were French.

With no artillery, ill-equipped and lacking in a strong command, the émigrés never had the slightest chance of victory. Their only hope lay in the success of the Prussian army. Chateaubriand himself was far too clear-sighted to imagine for a single moment that a handful of valorous gentlemen could vanquish a nation in arms. To one of his fellow-soldiers he maintained that the chief victim of emigration would be the king. It was not long before the Breton d'Aboville, who was in command of the French artillery, wiped out the German batteries. The Prussians abandoned the struggle and the Princes' army had to be disbanded. Chateaubriand could not follow his friends; he had been hit in the thigh by a splinter of shell and the wound was extremely nasty. Moreover he was badly pulled down by fever and within twenty-four hours developed small-pox. More than half dead, covered with scabs, his beard unkempt, his bleeding thigh bound up with a swab of hay and his uniform in rags, he dragged himself through the Low Countries and Luxemburg towards Brussels, whence he hoped to reach the island of Jersey, to which the Bédée family had emigrated.

At this dreadful time, when he was driven to live on the charity of women and fainted by the wayside from exhaustion, he was often revisited by thoughts of religion. At last, thanks to the compassion of peasants who gave him a lift in their carts, he succeeded in reaching Brussels. He presented himself at his brother's town-house, where he saw the Comte de Chateaubriand stepping out of his carriage with the Baron de Montboissier. Jean-Baptiste was terrified at the apparition. He had medical care given to his young brother, told him of the massacres of September and lent him twenty-five louis to get to Jersey. On M. de Malesherbes' advice, he himself was making preparations to return to France to avoid the confiscation of Combourg. With the aid of false certificates of citizenship and of residence he had thus far escaped being entered on the list of émigrés, but district supervision was becoming daily more severe. As for the younger brother, though his leg had turned gangrenous he was in haste to quit Brussels, which was again packed with "armchair heroes."

At Ostend he took passage on a barque. Heavy seas completed his exhaustion and when they touched at Guernsey he believed himself to be dying. When the sailing-ship could at last dock at Jersey, he was delirious. Message was sent to his Uncle Bédée, who came to fetch him. For four months Chateaubriand lay in the room looking out to sea which his uncle had taken for him, lovingly tended and cosseted by the kindly family. There, despite all unhappy circumstance, the Bédée succeeded in being as gay as before the Revolution, and the three young girls forgot their present sorrows in reminding their cousin of the jests shared at Monchoix.

Smuggling boats, plying between St. Malo and Jersey, carried letters between Mme. de Chateaubriand and her brother's landlord. Couched in mysterious terms lest they should betray the émigrés' refuge, one of them referred to "782 livres in assignats for the child suffering from small-pox, together with twelve golden apples." These "yellow pippins" were evidently louis and the poor lady urged that great care should be taken of them "for everybody's resources are exhausted and it will be a long time before you can expect more. . . . Céleste has been asked for a winter coat and whatever else her kindness may suggest. . . . My heart is like lead for the weight that lies heavy on it." Céleste was with Julie and Lucile at Mme. de Farcy's house in Fougères. Though not without difficulty, they had managed to get away from Paris after the September massacres, but Fougères, where Chouans and Jacobins clashed, was far from being a sure harbour of refuge. Jean-Baptiste was about to return "and his relations did not know where to put him." The Terror was at its height. Towards the end of January, 1793, Chateaubriand saw his uncle come into his room in Jersey dressed all in black. He trembled to learn of a death in the family, but it was Louis XVI who was dead. "It did not surprise me," said he, "I had foreseen it."

Though his lungs were still affected, he was gradually gaining strength to get up. He saw poor Uncle Bédée drawing to the end of his resources and reproached himself for being a burden to him. Already M. de Bédée had been constrained to send his son La Bouëtardais to London to "live on hope." What was to be done? Return to Brittany? The news from there was anything but good. The Marquis de la Rouërie, who had founded a Breton Association, was dead; his friends had been arrested and guillotined. Could a young man in Chateaubriand's weak state endure the life of caves and forests to which the Chouans were reduced? The Prince de Bouillon, who was looking after the émigrés in Jersey, thought not. Should he join his cousin, La Bouëtardais, in London? How was he to earn a living? Yet, there was no other solution. Thirty golden louis sent by Mme. de Chateaubriand made the journey possible. The farewells were sad. Would they ever meet again? In taking leave of the Bédée family he said goodnight and goodbye to the only happy memories he had known.

The packet which took him to Southampton was laden with émigrés. During the voyage he talked very agreeably with M. Hingant, a Councillor to the Parliament of Rennes, and reencountered Gésril, his old friend of St. Malo and Brest. Not one of all could foresee his future, but could it be any stranger than the past? In that month of May, 1793, Chateaubriand was twenty-four. He had been in turn a cadet of a great family, officer, explorer, fugitive, private and dying man. He had crossed oceans and frontiers; he had seen active service and had married. Now he was alone on deck with neither family, nor wife, nor money—his only riches the thirty louis that Mme. Apolline had sent and the manuscripts from which he would never be parted. Of what may he have thought while his first foster-mother, the sea, rocked him once more? Of the poor old woman, fluttered and absent-minded, who doubtless prayed for him every morning in her lovely wind-swept city of stone? Of the three women in Fougères who were perhaps talking of him at that moment as they strolled round the garden at Farcy? Of the approach of his own death, which he believed to be near? In all likelihood it was rather of the children of his dreams—Chactas, Atala or Celuta. After two full years, with all their hardships, was he very different from the young man who had pored over maps of America with M. de Malesherbes? Opinions, being begotten of feeling and passion rather than of events, are only slowly modified by them. Thereafter his tolerance of doctrines would be mingled with a dread of their effects. From his voyages he returned with a new conceit of himself. In his own eyes he was to be thenceforward the man of oceans and of desert lands, the man of storm and tempest, the man who had not feared to make his abode with the savages of America. If he is to endure his individuality, every human being must needs set before him the person whom he at first is fain to be, then believes himself to be and sometimes ends by becoming. With the adventures of his youth behind him, Chateaubriand's personality was beginning to take shape in his mind.

The passengers who met him in 1793 on an overloaded packet off the shores of England saw only a youthful emigrant, pale, thin, badly-dressed and racked by coughing. They could not guess that the unhappy boy was companied by a world of poetry. Chateaubriand himself knew it and already there stirred in him a vague hope that, if others could be moved as he had been moved, those images of enchantment that he had carried home, seas and forests, incense-breathing nights, sheaves of level moonlight, skies heavy with ocean-stars, might one day lead him "to win love by way of glory."

When he disembarked at Southampton on May 18th, 1793, the Mayor gave him a travelling warrant, on which he was thus described:—"François de Chateaubriand, French officer in the emigrant army. Height—five foot four inches—Slight—Brown hair and moustache." The mayor should perhaps have added: "Special peculiarities: Indifference, pride and genius."

CHAPTER III

Exile in England

> I was filled with religion and I thought as a mocker; my heart loved God and my mind knew him not.... But does man always fathom his own desires or know, of a surety, what he believes?
> —CHATEAUBRIAND—*René*

1. LONDON AND POVERTY

SINCE the outbreak of the Terror many French émigrés had made their abode in London. "Some took to dealing in fuel, some, with the help of their wives, wove straw hats, while others taught the French they did not know themselves. They were all in the best of spirits." ... "Women of the highest society worked ten hours a day to buy their children bread. In the evening they dressed in all their finery and gathered for singing and dancing." Exile had brought no reconciliation between the parties. The traditional monarchist would have nothing to do with the constitutional "monarchy dog." The old nobility—those who had ridden in kings' coaches—looked down on the gentry and the men of the robe. In all this broil of brothers the one meeting-ground was an astounding optimism. "Anyone who rented quarters for more than a month was held in ill repute. It was better to take them by the week since there could be no possible, probable shadow of doubt of their being on the eve of a counter-revolution which would call them home." Whoever was sceptical of the imminence of the Restoration was suspect. Chateaubriand heard two old bishops talking as they walked in St. James's Park. "Monseigneur," said one, "do you think that we shall be in France by June?" "Well, Monseigneur," replied the other after a period of ripe reflection, "I fail to see why not." The odd thing was that many of these royalists were still steeped in the ideas of the Eighteenth Century. The great Burke, who had his eyes on them, remarked: "They care only for the monarchy, or rather for the persons of the late king and queen. In every other respect it is as Jacobins that they speak." Some time was yet to elapse before Bonald and Maistre came to imbue that aristocracy with ideas better in accord with their interests.

His family alliances might have made the Chevalier de Chateaubriand free of the highest society, but his shyness, his poverty and the ties of friendship bound him to the Breton émigrés. La Bouëtardais, his portly cousin, found him lodgings of a sort in a Holborn attic and marched him off to doctors for he was pale and thin and had begun spitting blood. A Doctor Godwin told him with brutal frankness that he might last a few months, perhaps even a year or so, provided that he avoided all fatigue. "Do not count on a long career" was the gist of the consultation. The sense of approaching death called up the ghosts of Combourg, with Lucile as the genius of the tomb. The sick man developed a taste for churchyard meditations and, as he wandered in Westminster Abbey among the graves of poets and heroes, he thought how soon his own was to open. Emigration, by leading young Frenchmen to read English and German writers, had completed the work of Rousseau. Sensibility, already tinged with romanticism, was gradually taking the place of the clear dry light of the century which was drawing to its close. In Kensington Gardens Lucile's brother would indulge in the agreeable luxury of melancholy as he contrasted his lonely wretchedness with the careless gaiety of the crowds. From afar he gazed on the young Englishwomen with "bashful longing," but who among them would ever have spared a glance for an ailing foreigner sitting quietly under the trees? They were sometimes very lovely, those women who passed like the phantoms of a dream and "death, drawing ever nearer as he thought, lent mystery to the vision of a world from which he was all but parted."

Yet, even at death's door, a man must live and the thirty louis sent from St. Malo could not be expected to outlast him. Only two means of livelihood ever entered his head—the sword and the pen. The sword had been reft from him. The pen? The notes brought back from America and the scheme of a great epic on the savages were hardly likely to appeal to a publisher. It was a time when French readers put political preoccupations before all else. The revolution, now as dreaded as it was once desired, remained an enigma. Why should Chateaubriand not undertake a comparative study of revolutions, dealing with those of Greece, of Rome and of France? It was a project worthy of Montesquieu. Meanwhile, who would be ready to print it and to maintain the author till its success was assured?

By good fortune Jean-Gabriel Peltier, a journalist and royalist pamphleteer, chose that moment to offer his services to Chateaubriand as a fellow-Breton. "Tall, thin, devil-may-care, with powdered hair, for ever shouting and cracking jokes," this Peltier, who managed to combine the service of his lawful king with employment as ambassador of the negro King Christopher of Haiti to the court of George III, was a scapegrace and a rake, but a man of parts and very obliging. Chateaubriand told him of his plans for the book. "It's a grand idea," cried Peltier, and there and then suggested taking a room in the house of a printer named Baylis, who would set the book up in type as it was written. By a miracle Baylis agreed and even went so far as to provide the books needed by the improvised historian, who plunged into them straightway.

Throughout his life, Chateaubriand loved "eager compilation" and those vast works of learning in which a divided mind finds a heaven-sent way of escape and the most secret form of protective trifling. He enjoyed tackling vast subjects, reading abstruse and unknown authors, and embroidering his countless extracts from French, English, Latin, Greek and even Hebrew authors with ideas of his own, with his musings and with recollections of his travels. In this political essay there was soon as much of Montaigne as of Montesquieu. Chateaubriand worked on it through half the night. By day he made translations from Latin and English to earn his living. They were very ill-paid. He shared his poverty with Hingant, the Councillor to the Parliament of Rennes whom he had met on the Jersey packet. Hingant, too, was trying to write in a garret, but it was a novel on which he was at work. Every evening the two Bretons met to dine at a shilling ordinary and then went for a stroll in the fields.

Despite their growing poverty, they tasted some moments of happiness. "In a land where we were of no account we still had our festivities. Above all, we had our youth. Lads who had entered on life through adversity brought the fruits of their weekly toil to make merry at dances like those of home. Friendships sprang up. We used to pray in chapels that seem no whit changed now that I have just seen them once again. On January 21st we wept openly, since the funeral oration pronounced by an émigré priest from our village stirred us to the depth of our hearts. We wandered along the banks of the Thames to watch the ships, laden with all the riches of the world, come into port and to feast our eyes on the country houses at Richmond while we were so poor, so far from the roofs of home. . . . Those joys were very real."

Still, they had to eat. There came a time when the joint resources of Hingant and Chateaubriand were only sixty francs. They cut down rations "as men do in a beleaguered city." They halved the amount of bread with their morning tea and abolished butter. Worn out by fasting, Hingant went slightly crazy. He developed a persecution mania and laughed and wept without a cause. When they were down to their last shilling, they agreed to buy a penny roll, to let the landlady bring up their hot water as usual rather than admit that they had no more tea, and to drink the water with a few grains of sugar. Five such days went by.

"Ravening hunger gnawed me. I was burning hot. Sleep had fled me. I dipped scraps of linen in water and sucked them. I chewed grass and paper. It was torture to pass a baker's shop. On one bitter winter evening I spent hours rooted to the ground outside a shop where they sold preserved fruits and cooked meats, while my eyes drank them all in. I could have devoured not the food only, but the boxes and baskets as well."

On the fifth day of the fast Chateaubriand dragged himself to see Hingant and found him smothered in blood. In an attempt to make an end, the poor wretch had given himself a two-inch wound with a penknife. The maid rushed to fetch a surgeon, who said that the wound was dangerous. Chateaubriand wrote to M. de Barentin, a former Keeper of the Seals, who was related to Hingant and was himself an émigré. He came to fetch the wounded man and carried him off to the country. Just when Chateaubriand himself reached the point of despair, his kindhearted Uncle Bédée sent him forty crowns. He felt as though he were gazing on "all the gold of Peru." To eke out his fortune he gave up his room and took a garret which looked out on a graveyard. La Bouëtardais, who was also at the end of his resources, came to share the wretched hole and the soup that none could make better than Chateaubriand. Since the only garment remaining to that Councillor to the Parliament of Brittany was his magistrate's red robe, he shivered beneath the purple yet lost none of his old wit of the days of Plancoët. In the evening he would sit naked on his pallet, put his square cap on his head and warble sentimental ballads to the accompaniment of a three-stringed guitar. One night, as he was singing thus, he was caught by what Chateaubriand called a "dangerous draught." Actually it was a fit of apoplexy, for his mouth twisted and he was left paralysed.

What was to be done with the invalid? The forty crowns were melting rapidly and nothing more could be expected from the family, which was at bay in a Brittany rapidly going over to the Revolution. It was Peltier, "the resourceful," who once more came to Chateaubriand's rescue. A boarding school in Beccles, a small town in Suffolk, was looking for a French master. Peltier heard of it and offered the post to his friend. The young viscount's pride was up in arms at once. Had not one of his ancestors once replied to a suggestion of the kind: "A Chateaubriand has his own tutors; he does not teach other people"? Peltier, "shouting and joking as usual," pressed the point: "So you want to starve?" By main force he haled Chateaubriand and La Bouëtardais with "his twisted mug" off to dine in a tavern, where he stuffed them to bursting-point with roast-beef, underdone, and plum pudding. After that they turned a more kindly ear on his persuasions and, three days later, Chateaubriand, whom the generous Peltier had fitted out at his tailor's, set off for Beccles.

2. The First Love

Rural England, with its charm and its sadness, pleased him for it called to mind a richer Brittany. "Wherever I went there was the little, lonely country church with its tower, Gray's country churchyard, narrow, sandy lanes, valleys teeming with cows, moorlands dotted with sheep, parks, castles, manors, not many woods of any size, not many birds, but the wind and the sea." He took the name of the Chevalier de Combourg for Chateaubriand was hard to pronounce and his pupils found it all too easy to turn into *Shatter-brain*. Schoolmastering was by no means to his taste and he bewailed "the dulness of spending his days, at the age of reason and of thought, in making his neighbours' stupid children repeat words parrot-like." Nevertheless, he got on fairly well and was offered a good deal of private coaching in the neighbouring manor-houses. Young girls were very ready to learn French, or even Italian, from the young emigrant with his handsome face. It was not long before no party was complete without him; letters were submitted for his inspection, that he might analyse the character of the writer from the handwriting; Anglican parsons were glad to welcome him for his learning and eager thirst for knowledge; the squire of Beccles, Robert Sparrow, who was a gentleman and a humanist, made him free of the rich library at the manor.

Yet he was not happy. His touchy and almost morbid pride could ill endure that he should be an underling. Even the kindliness of others was painful to him. "The sight of poverty," he wrote, "arouses different feelings in different men. The great, that is to say the rich, cannot look on it without loathing. Nothing can be expected of them save insolent pity, gifts and civilities a thousand times more galling than insults." He notes in the margin of his manuscript that in England the best of men is condemned to the life of a recluse if he has no money. No-one asks: "Has that man brains?" but "Has he any guineas?" All the English folk in Suffolk were good horsemen. By his father's fault, Chateaubriand rode badly and his pride suffered. During those years of poverty he developed a dread of society which he never afterwards shook off. The diffidence of the poor émigré so strengthened that of the rustic and the younger son that he could not overcome it. Like Stendhal, Chateaubriand was then of opinion that rich women had no common sense, that they were "empty-headed and ill-bred." He had taken the measure of gentlemen farmers, with their virtues and their limitations. "Is a man what is called a gentleman farmer? Then he sells his wheat, goes in for agricultural experiments, hunts the fox or shoots partridge in Autumn, eats a fat goose at Christmas, sings *The Roast Beef of Old England*, grumbles about the pass to which things are coming, brags of the good old days, which were no better, and is for ever cursing Pitt and the war which has sent-up the price of port. Then he stumbles drunk to bed to begin the self-same life on the morrow."

For himself, he preferred to shut the door of his little room, get down to the *Essai sur les Révolutions*, extract the marrow of the Greek and Latin texts borrowed from Robert Sparrow's library, draft, from the narratives of Carver, Bertram and Charlevoix, a first version of the *Natchez* which, though the author had no money to buy paper, grew into a manuscript of 2,383 pages, or again to draw up rules of conduct for the hapless, a subject which touched him, alas, all too nearly. He stressed three in especial. "The first is to weep in secret. Who is likely to have the least interest in our tale of woe? Some listen with one ear while it goes out at the other, some are bored, but one and all hold it in despite. The second, which follows from the first, is to seek complete isolation. In times of suffering society must be shunned, since it is the natural enemy of the unfortunate. Third rule: Intractable pride. Pride is the virtue of the evil-starred." What remedies does he suggest? Those which he had himself proved: the love of nature and of reading. To wander lonely through the countryside, studying flowers and trees, to carry back to one's little room the spoils of the fields and to classify the booty; at close of evening to open some good book and share, in imagination, the sorrows of Héloïse and of Clarissa; finally, at three o'clock in the morning, with the wind and the rain battering at the windows, to commit to paper all that one had learned of man—such was Chateaubriand's advice to the unhappy and such was then his life.

For he was indeed a hapless wight. It was the time when, in France, the Revolution, which had thrown down a kingly head as a challenge to Europe, was turning its rage against itself; when the Cordeliers, who had ordered the massacre of the Girondins, were, in their turn, delivered up to Fouquier-Tinville; when Robespierre sent Danton's head to follow Hébert's on the scaffold; when—through the length and breadth of the country—popular commissions became purveyors to the guillotine. One evening while young M. de Combourg was at his cheerless dinner, an Englishman, who was reading aloud the headlines from the newspaper, quoted with complete indifference the names of some of the Frenchmen whose heads had fallen on the block a few days before. Among them were M. de Malesherbes, his daughter, the Présidente de Rosambo and his grandchildren, the Count and Countess de Chateaubriand, all of whom had died on the same scaffold at the selfsame hour.

Chateaubriand had the courage not to cry out, but he left the table and the emotion he could not conceal led him to disclose to those who knew him only as the Chevalier de Combourg his real name and his kinship with M. de Malesherbes. As a result, the young schoolmaster's prestige went up considerably in the county. The end of the bad news was not yet, however. Through Uncle Bédée he learned that his mother had been arrested and taken to Paris. The discovery of the Marquis de la Rouërie's conspiracy had unleashed persecution in Brittany. The fair Thérèse de Moëlien, the first woman whom Chateaubriand had ever admired in the days of Combourg, had been guillotined. Julie and her sister-in-law Céleste had been arrested and taken to the castle of Fougères, whence they were moved to Rennes. Lucile, who had pledged herself to watch over her brother's wife, asked to follow them. The same cart had borne "Julie Chateaubriand, married-name Farcy, ex-noble, aged twenty-seven; Lucile Chateaubriand, ex-noble, aged twenty-five and Céleste Buisson, married-name Chateaubriand, ex-noble, aged eighteen." The reason given for their arrest was: "Kinship with an émigré." Thus the exile's dread of losing them was coupled with grief that he should himself be the cause of their peril.

He was finding it ever more difficult to reconcile his impenitent Rousseauism with his loathing of the crimes plotted by Robespierre "in the hollow cavern of his heart." He remembered a remark of Malesherbes at the time of his leaving France: "There was a time when Condorcet was my friend, but at present I should not have the least scruple in assassinating him." True, that same Malesherbes had said on another occasion: "We shall never grow used to Court." Neither to the Court, nor to the Revolution. What then? Chateaubriand was beginning to seek the pattern of political life in the English among whom he lived. Though the individual

Exile in England

Englishman often irritated him, he admired the discipline of the nation. "Therein may be seen the miracle of a free government. The explanation is that the name of the law is all-powerful in this country. Once it has spoken, there is none who resists."

It was through his study of the laws of England that he first conceived the potentiality of "an illustrious alliance between honour and liberty" and envisaged the possibility of restoring a monarchy to which he believed he owed his fealty while yet guaranteeing the control of French affairs by a free assembly and a free press. It was in England he discovered that between despotism and anarchy, between tyranny and revolution, there is an intermediate state—reverence for the law. All these discoveries were to be of great importance in Chateaubriand's later life, but in 1793 he was very young and, for a time, love was to distract him from politics. Four leagues from Beccles, in the little town of Bungay, there lived an Anglican parson, the Reverend John Ives. As vicar of the neighbouring hamlet of St. Margaret's, this minister had few parishioners, few duties and a pretty good income. There was a legend that the Duke of Bedford had given him the living following a duel of the bottle in which the parson saw the Duke under the table. Yet the Reverend John Ives was not merely a hard-drinker—he was a great Hellenist, a great mathematician and a great traveller and, when the women left the table with the coming of the port, he enjoyed talking to the young officer, who was teaching his daughter Charlotte French and Italian, about America, about Newton, or about Homer. In 1795, when Mr. Brightley, the owner of the boarding-school at Beccles, retired, Chateaubriand took a room in the Ives' old house at Bungay, where he was perfectly happy.

He, too, was a success. When he happened to be at his ease, altogether at his ease, "he voiced his meditations with such verve and fancy" that women were enthralled. The vicar's wife had "a charming face and delightful manners." As for his daughter Charlotte, Chateaubriand has described her raven hair and her arms as white as a lily-chain under the name of Celuta. "Her figure was tall, delicate and supple. A hint of dreaminess and of suffering mingled with a grace that still had much of the child. The Indians, when they would paint the sadness of Celuta, said that she had night in her eyes and dawn in her smile. She was not yet unhappy, but was a woman destined to be acquainted with grief." Charlotte Ives and her Mother questioned Chateaubriand about his family and his early days with gentle compassion. At tea-time Charlotte usually sang, the vicar dropped off to sleep, and the young folk discussed the *Divine Comedy* or the *Jerusalem Delivered*. For the first time in his life, Chateaubriand experienced "the shy delight of a spiritual affection."

"Charlotte Ives and I were of an age. . . . It is rare to know all that makes for happiness in love, youth, beauty, the time and place together, the concord of heart, of tastes, of character, of grace and of years. . . . Having been thrown from my horse while riding, I spent some time in Mr. Ives's house. It was winter; my dream-life began to pale before the reality. Miss Ives grew more reserved; she no longer brought me flowers and would sing no more."

The parson and his wife were not blind either to the young folks' constraint or to their love, but they were far from being displeased by the signs. Granted, the Frenchman was a penniless foreigner, but he was related to Malesherbes, he came of good stock and the Revolution could not last for ever. Besides, were they not rich enough to keep the pair as long as need be? The only difficulty was that the man would not come to the point. His attitude was a mystery. Finally, on the evening before he was to leave them, Chateaubriand was greatly surprised to see Mr. Ives carry off his daughter at the close of a cheerless dinner. Mrs. Ives seemed profoundly embarrassed: "Sir," said she in English, "you must have noticed my confusion. I do not know whether you care for Charlotte, but a mother's eyes cannot be deceived, my daughter has certainly grown attached to you. Mr. Ives and I have put our heads together, we like all that we have seen of you and think that you would make our daughter happy. You no longer have a country, your kin are lately dead and your possessions sold. What is there to take you back to France? Till you inherit our all, you will live with us."

"Of all the griefs I had endured," writes Chateaubriand, "that was the keenest and touched me most nearly. I flung myself at Mrs. Ives's knees, covering her hands with kisses and tears. She thought I was weeping for joy and began to sob with happiness.

Exile in England

She stretched out a hand for the bell-cord and called her husband and daughter. 'Stop!' cried I, 'I am married.' She fell in a dead faint. I went and, without even going to my room, set off on foot."

On his return to London his loneliness and despair were such that his old friends thought him mad. He was haunted by Charlotte's image and cursed the absurd marriage which cut him off from happiness. He persuaded himself that he was a fateful being, "so scorching and ravaging hearts that love could nevermore grow where he had passed." Unquestionably, he had brought unhappiness on Charlotte. How? By his stubborn silence, by that "spirit of reserve and interior loneliness" which forbade his speaking to anyone soever of the things that caused him the most acute suffering. In after life he was often to be accused of insincerity, of a constant urge to play a part. It matters that these failings should be traced to their original cause and to the period when they meant no more in him than difficulty of expression and a painful consciousness of the falseness of his position.

Literary genius may spring of such a union of suffering and silence. The passions, too tightly pent within the compass of a human heart, fuse as imaginary characters. René was doubtless born in London, after that return from Suffolk, of the dumb griefs of a Chateaubriand whom no man knew. René was to be a hero very different from those beloved of French readers before his time, for Chateaubriand himself had travelled far from the *Valmont* tone of his letters of 1789. The woes of exile "so rich in sad and tender feeling" and the reading of English poets and novelists had given the émigrés a taste for a wholly new sensibility, more sentimental than that of the sons of Voltaire, less oratorical than that of the sons of Rousseau. Until then the French lover had been a conqueror; the émigré, inexpert in the use of a foreign tongue and bereft of the arrogant self-assurance that comes of rank and wit, had to rely on the pity and compassion aroused by his ills rather than on the magic of his gallant speeches. The new hero no longer made the first move. Despite herself, it was the woman who came to him. Thus Chateaubriand, the Breton, rediscovered the Celtic idea, expressed once and for all in *Tristram*, of the fatal suddenness of love. "You wear your heart on your sleeve," a fair Irishwoman was to tell him later. It was that his heart was at once his only adornment and his most dangerous weapon. Moreover, only a proud melancholy was to save him from despair.

Never was he more sincere and René's sadness was his own. It was the state he has described as "the wave of passions," a state very natural to young men who had all the desires and ambitions of their age but whom exile debarred from all hope of finding an outlet for their idle powers. Finding no scope for activity in the external world, those powers ate into their inward beings. Reading took the place of action and the study of history disillusioned minds which as yet had no experience. "We are undeceived before we have enjoyed; our desires remain but our illusions are gone.... With full hearts we dwell in an empty world and before we have tasted any gladness, we are utterly disabused." Eaten up by boredom, which is the sense of the monotony and vanity of human existence, we come to play with the idea of death, which alone can bring us to those unknown regions for which our hearts cry. "Be swift in your rising, oh longed-for storms which are to bear René to the space and amplitude of another life." René does not imitate Werther—he but finds in the very range of his misfortunes a strange matter for pride, "a two-fold sense of pleasure and melancholy" which seems a revelation of his own nature.

Idleness and poverty were even more painful to Chateaubriand than to his friends, for his temperament was more fiery and his illhap more complete. Not only was he an exile, but his mother and sisters were prisoners, his brother and his protector dead on the scaffold; though married, he could neither live with his wife nor begin life again with another. "A dreary present, an unsettled future, the upheaval of his country, the prospect of poverty and ruin if ever he should return thither, love that was pain, the unrest of a man whom his fellow-countrymen held at a distance, cut off from their public life, concerned from afar—more or less consciously—for the nation's fate and suffering from having no part in it"... these were enough to make the background of despair against which the character of René develops. If the hero was to be understood by the reader, there remained to give him affliction which would rouse feelings akin to those of his creator at the time of the Charlotte episode. Chateaubriand could not make René a married man—the resemblance to his own life would be too marked.

Exile in England

Hence he had to endue him with the memory of a guilty passion which René had aroused in the heart of his sister Amélie. At this point the remembrance of Combourg and of Lucile were to serve the poet in good stead. He used everything, even the rough drafts of his letters to Charlotte, mere jottings never sent, found their place in the *Natchez*. Every novelist knows, however, that there was no need for Amélie actually to have been Lucile that Lucile might beget her, nor for Lucile really to have been in love with her brother: For the artist living beings are shapeless material. He moulds, groups and disposes them as his heart and the requirements of his work best dictate.

In 1796, back once more in the house of Baylis the printer, and very lonely, Chateaubriand toiled the harder at his *Essai sur les Révolutions*. Into it went his reading, his memories and his dreams. While doing a certain amount of private coaching to earn his living, he worked—now in public libraries, "where he undertook a hasty erudition," now in some village tavern to the accompaniment of beef and beer. In France events were following so rapidly on each other's heels that he was hard put to it to keep pace with his material. "At night I had often to scrap the picture I had drawn by day. Events moved faster than my pen." The 9th Thermidor (July 1794) justified the hopes to which the émigrés clung. Among other consequences it set Chateaubriand's mother and sisters free from their prisons in Rennes or Paris. Though there were rude shocks yet to come it was no longer rash to foresee an end of the Revolution. How would it come about? Perhaps by a military despotism which would precede the king's return by a few months.

Only once does Chateaubriand mention the little Corsican general who had recently taken over the command of the army of Italy, but, for the rôle of Monk, he often thinks of Moreau and still more of Pichegru. He compares the splendid victories of the French republicans with those of the republic of Athens and dreads that the fate of both nations may be the same. Thus, reading, compiling and composing all day long he finished the great historical work which he hoped might draw him from obscurity. In the evening, sitting under the trees in Kensington Gardens or on Hampstead Health, he pencilled down René's sighs or transformed a passage of the *Natchez*, begun as a straightforward narrative, into the style of the Homeric epic. If France were to settle down to calm, it might be that by this novel on the savages, which he knew to be original, he might find renown, might astonish Parny, Guingené and Fontanes and win the love of some new incarnation of the Sylph. "If peace comes I can easily get my name taken off the list of émigrés. Then I'm for Paris, where I shall take up my lodging near the Jardin des Plantes. I shall publish my *Sauvages*. I shall see all my friends once more." The tone might well be that of Stendhal.

3. THE FIRST BOOK

The first, and only, volume of the *Eassai sur les Révolutions* was published in March 1797. It was a teeming and ambitious work, shot through with flashes of style and brilliance. On re-reading it after thirty years, the author himself defined it as "A chaos wherein are met Jacobins and Spartans, the *Marseillaise* and the songs of Tyrtæus, a voyage to the Azores and the *Periplus* of Hanno, the praise of Jesus Christ and criticism of the monks, the golden verses of Pythagoras and the fables of M. de Nivernais, Louis XIV, Charles I, lonely walks, views on nature, human ills, melancholy, suicide and politics, the opening snatch of *Atala*, Robespierre, the Convention and discussions on Zeno, Epicurus and Aristotle—all in a turgid and bombastic style, full of solecisms, of foreign idiom and defects of language."

The description is accurate, but severe and incomplete. On beginning the work, the young author had followed a well-thought-out plan which he explained in the prospectus. To those who, like himself, had been whirled by the French Revolution into a "chaos" of schemes, of suffering and of doubt, he claimed to offer a means of forecasting the political future and of regulating their conduct accordingly. Having, indeed, observed that the cycle of revolutions was no new phenomenon and that Greeks and Romans had, in turn, experienced a succession of events very similar to those which had lately gone to the head of France, only to steep her in blood, he thought that the consideration of the great revolutions of the past should prove a means of foretelling the issue of the present discontents. The author therefore proposed to answer the following questions: "I. What revolutions have occurred in the govern-

Exile in England

ments of men? II. Are any among these comparable to the present Revolution in France? III. What causes originally brought about the latter revolution? IV. What is the present nature of the government in France? Is it based on sound principles and can it endure? V. If it does endure, what will be its effect on the nations and on the other governments of Europe? VI. Should it be overthrown, what will be the consequences for the age and for posterity?" To sum up, it was a question of using the study of the past to throw light on the present.

The plan was a fine one and vast and even if its fulfilment left something to be desired, the wonder was that so young a man could have conceived it. There is another characteristic which must strike readers of the *Essai*. In a period of violent political passions, this émigré—their victim—soars proudly above all faction. "I am no partypolemist and I can well believe that there may be very worthy people whose notions of things differ from mine." Gifted with a sense of relative values very rare in his age, he parades neither hatred nor worship of the Revolution. "Every age is a river which, when we let ourselves go, sweeps us away as our several destinies dictate. Yet it seems to me that we are one and all outside its course. Some (the Republicans) have crossed it impetuously and hurled themselves upon the further bank. Others have preferred not to embark and remained on the hither shore. Both parties bawl abuse, according as they are on one side or the other. Thus the former carry us out of ourselves into imaginary perfections, by making us outstrip our age; the latter hold us back, refuse to see new light and, in this year of grace 1797, are bent on remaining men of the fourteenth century."

Why vex oneself for movements as inexorably determined as the course of the stars? "Man, whose powers and whose genius are weak, can only repeat himself endlessly. He goes round and round in a circle from which he tries in vain to escape. Events, which do not depend on him, but seem rather the sport of chance, are forever reproducing themselves in their essentials." Of old, Thrasybulus led the Athenian exiles home. Who is to become the Thrasybulus of the French Revolution? None knows as yet, but the lessons of history justify the prophecy that he will be found.

From this fatality it follows that "a man truly persuaded that there is nothing new in history loses the taste for innovations, that taste which I regard as one of the greatest scourges which afflict Europe at this present. Enthusiasm comes of ignorance. Remedy the latter and it will die a natural death; the knowledge of things is an opiate which, only too well, drugs all exaltation to sleep." This knowledge of things shews that, as far as the human race is concerned, the ratio of vice to virtue is more or less constant. They were mistaken who believed that the abolition of privileges was, of itself, enough to make all men virtuous. Whether under a monarchy or under a republic, there will always be knaves and men of life upright, despots and slaves.

"O famous philosophers who believe that there is such a thing as liberty in civic life, who prefer the number five to unity and who believe that greater happiness is to be found under the rabble of the Faubourg Saint-Antoine than under the bureaucracy of Versailles, what ought we to have done? I cannot tell. All I know is that, when the lust for destruction came upon you, you should at least have rebuilt a dwelling-place fit for Frenchmen and, furthermore, have been wary of enthusiasm for the institutions of other lands. Imitation is the gravest of dangers. What is good for one nation is rarely good for another. I, too, would fain spend my days under a democracy such as I have often dreamed as being, in theory, the most sublime of governments. I, too, have lived, a citizen of Italy and of Greece. It may be that my present opinions are but the triumph of my reason over inclination."

His present opinions? What are they, then? The one sure effect of revolutions is to make those whom they at first beguiled homesick for order and reverent of the past. Chateaubriand who, in 1789, had been a disciple of Rousseau and of Raynal, had come, by 1797, to regret the monarchy. When his heart dominated his intellect, he always came back to that visionary conception of absolute liberty which he had followed beyond the bounds of ocean, for—in the depths of his being—he was ever an anarchist. "It is in vain that we torment ourselves, make epigrams or fine speeches, the greatest misfortune of mankind is to have laws and a government. . . . All government is an evil, all government is a yoke." Yet wisdom and prudence get the mastery at once: "We should not therefore conclude that it must be overthrown. Since it is our lot to be slaves, let us drag our chains uncomplaining. Let us learn to beat them into rings for the fingers of kings or tribunes as the age or custom may dictate. And, publish what they may, let us be sure that it is better to yield obedience to a rich and enlightened fellow-countryman than to an ignorant mob which will crush us beneath the burden of all ills."

While thus recognising democracy as the ideal state, but admitting that the corruption of morals has made it impossible, republican by inclination but royalist by reason, professing equal loathing of the man-eaters of sans-culottism and of the slaves of despotism, this sceptical and inspired adolescent ends surprisingly enough by inviting his readers to seek for some conception of natural liberty among the Canadian savages and to follow the author, but for one night, through the forests of America. It makes a pretext for introducing one of his favourite purple-patches, a silent moon floating above the crests of the forest, diaphanous and changing clouds and, afar off, the solemn roar of the Niagara falls. The passage so delighted him that not long after he had borrowed it from the *Natchez* to put in the *Essai*, he borrowed it from the *Essai* to put in another book which was to make more stir. Moon, clouds and falls, however, were a strange ending to a great political essay. The historian suddenly effaced himself before the poet, for doubtless the poet in Chateaubriand was more living than the historian. His dazzling mind would now and then light up dark jungles of fact, but he was too lacking in patience and submission to reality to be capable of ensuing and laying hold on the truths which he saw through a glass dimly.

One of the last chapters of the book bore this title: "What will be the religion to take the place of Christianity?" for—as at the time of his emigration—he still believed that Christianity must pass. Though, in the *Essai*, he often spoke of the Divinity, all established religions seemed to him caricatures of the natural: "Religions are born of our fears and of our weaknesses; they spread through fanaticism and die through indifference. The priests of Persia and of Egypt differed no whit from our own. Their minds likewise were all compact of fanaticism and of intolerance." In one copy of the *Essai* (over against reflections on God's cruelty in creating beings destined only to grief), he has added, in his own hand, the marginal note: "There is no answer to this objection which overthrows the Christian system from top to bottom. Besides, no-one believes in it any more."

Opposite the words: "God, Matter and Fate are one," he writes in the margin: "That is my system, that is what I believe. Yes, all is chance, hap, fatality in this world—reputation, honour, riches—virtue even. How can we believe that a divine Intelligence shapes our ends? Look at the knaves in office, see how the wicked flourish while the man of upright life is robbed, butchered and scorned. There may be a God, but he is the God of Epicurus. He is too great, too well-content, to concern himself with our affairs and we men are left upon the face of the earth to devour one another."

On the other hand, there are many passages of the *Essai* in which he speaks feelingly of the Gospels as "of real service to the comfortless since therein are found pity, tolerance, loving-kindness, hope that is sweeter yet, all that goes to make the balm of hurt minds. . . . Their divine Author is not content with idle preaching to those who mourn. He does more—he blesses their tears and drinks their cup to the dregs." For country-priests he has naught but praise: "I have known some among them who seemed less men than kindly spirits, come down to earth to bind up the wounds of humanity." Here and there, he breaks into song with the Psalmist: "There is a God . . . the grasses of the valleys and the cedars of Lebanon bless him, the insect bruits his praise and the elephant trumpets him at the rising of the sun. Birds hymn his being among the leaves, the wind whispers him in the forest, the thunderbolt crashes his power and the Ocean declares his immensity. Man alone has said in his heart: 'There is no God.' In the midst of his afflictions, has he never raised up his eyes unto heaven? Has his gaze never wandered to those vast spaces of the stars, where worlds are sown like grains of sand?"

By turn Christian, deist and atheist in the course of that imperfect and powerful book which is rather the diary of a soul in torment, the record of the feelings of the unhappy than the learned treatise of a scholar, Chateaubriand passes many a time and oft through such contradictory states. Sometimes his pain fills him with horror and scorn for a world grown too cruel, sometimes the divine beauty of the universe brings him forgetfulness of its injustice. Sometimes, in his scepticism, he goes so far as to question every moral rule, then the social conservatism taught him by family misfortune vanquishes his natural anarchism. "Truth is not good for evil men. She should remain buried in the breast of the Sage, as Hope lay buried in the bottom of Pandora's box. Had I lived in the time of Jean-Jacques, I should have wished to become his disciple, but I should have urged my master to secrecy." It might be said that, in Chateaubriand's mind, the *Essai sur les Révolutions* marked the end of the enthusiasms and the visionary dreams of youth were it not that, despairing of choosing between the parties, he clung to the hope, alas! too ingenuous, of reconciling them. Once he had lost that last illusion, he was to become—so far as action was concerned—a party man, but—till the day of his death—he remained at heart the sceptic of his earliest work.

4. The First Friend

A book dedicated "to all parties" cannot fail to dissatisfy them, one and all. The *Essai* displeased the very few Republicans who took the trouble to skim it through. ("What a charlatan," said Sieyès. "Could you get to the end of it?") It shocked the monarchists in London; it grieved and even stunned Chateaubriand's own family. His mother, his wife and his sisters had suffered far too greatly at the hands of the Revolution to descant on it under the aspect of eternity. In Fougères, where Julie de Farcy was living a life of holiness, as in Saint Servan, where—sunk in the apathy consequent upon her many bereavements—Mme. de Chateaubriand was drawing, in poverty, to the close of her death-in-life, the *Essai* seemed scandalous and heretical. Even the worthy Uncle Bédée, though he continued to sign his letters from Jersey: "Your old gaffer of an uncle," and to end them: "With my dearest love," spoke regretfully to the Prince de Bouillon of this "modern, high-browed nephew." "There are all too many of the type," replied the prince.

Nevertheless, the book had made the author some friends among the intellectuals of the émigré colony in London, who—with the exception of Peltier's absolutist group—were, for the most part, "Monarchy dogs" and moderates. After the publication of the

Essai, Chateaubriand drifted apart from the Breton set in London and took up with the West End, where lived "the bishops, the court circle and the Martinique planters." There he met Malouet, Montlosier, Mallet du Pan, the Chevalier de Panat, Dom Dulau (a Benedictine turned bookseller), and—in the drawing-room of the beautiful Mrs. Lindsay—Auguste and Christian de Lamoignon. It must be admitted that the philosophisings of the *Essai* were none too much to the taste of such moderates, but when Chateaubriand talked of his *Sauvages* and read them some of the good things from the famous manuscript of 2,383 folio pages, good critics said: "There is undoubted talent in all that."

Through the conversation of his new friends, Chateaubriand came back into contact with French minds, after three years of intellectual solitude. He was surprised to find that such gifted men had travelled far from the ideas of the *Encyclopédie*. Honour had bound them to religion because it was persecuted, as it had bound them to the monarchy because it was banished. The virtues of the exiled clergy, which the Anglicans themselves extolled and which may have had some share in paving the way for the Oxford Movement, conjoined with the quality of pathos which the poverty of the Church and the memory of a martyred king lent to its worship, favoured the renaissance of an emotional Catholicism. Even those who persisted in their unbelief regarded the Christian tradition of the French as the greatest of counter-revolutionary forces. In a gay brush with the Chevalier de Panat in Mrs. Lindsay's drawing-room, Chateaubriand at first battled for the ideas of Rousseau. He began to go back on his position when, in September 1797, the Royalist and Catholic party in London was reinforced by yet another exile, Louis de Fontanes, who—in the old days—had been one of the first friends of the three young Chateaubriands.

Fontanes was a classical poet who came of a Protestant family on his father's side and a Jansenist on his mother's. Like all the men of his age, he had been a Voltairian at twenty and in 1789 "a friend to enlightenment" like Malesherbes and Chateaubriand himself. As early as 1790 he decided that the Revolution was going too far, published a newspaper under the conciliatory title of *Le Modérateau* and finally—by an opportune disappearance—

succeeded in surviving the Terror and even in being enrolled,
while still very young, among the new members of the Institute.
His originality lay in remaining, in an age of upheaval, a writer
and thinker of the Seventeenth Century. Fontanes had a horror
of all obscure and assertive ideologies. His respect for the Ancients
and for the Grand Siècle was sincere and he maintained that any
legislation not founded upon morality was necessarily decadent.

Upright, prudent, ambitious within reason, a born administrator who believed that Paris was worth a mass or absention from
attending it, as the whirligig of time might come round, he had
waited for the reaction of Thermidor to flaunt his traditionalism.
Fructidor, which brought a swing to the Left on the part of the
Directory, had recently shewn him that a man may speak out
too soon and he decided that, till the wind veered once more, the
air of London would be healthier than that of Paris. Thus there
drifted into England "various layers of exiles" thrown up on
her shores by the tempests blowing from the coast of France.
In 1797, Fontanes was forty. He was a burly man "squareset as a
Limousin," with the teeth of a boar and a gargantuan appetite.
Chateaubriand was dazed by the way in which his ideas had
changed. "The Crimes of the Convention had given him a horror
of liberty. He loathed newspapers and philosophisings. . . ."
Chateaubriand had to admit that Fontanes had more knowledge
of the new France than he and so accepted his guidance.

Now, what Fontanes affirmed, as the two men loitered under
the tall elms in the English meadows, dined in a quiet Chelsea
tavern or came back to London by night "under the waning light
of the mist-bound stars," was that France was returning to
Christianity or rather that she had never left it. In the Eighteenth
Century two groups of intellectuals, the rationalist Deists headed
by Voltaire and the sentimental Deists headed by Rousseau, had
waged war against Catholicism among the upper classes, but the
bulk of the country clung to its beliefs. There was proof enough
in the fact that from 1796, when the doors of the churches were
once more set ajar, devotion had shewn itself even more alive
than before the Revolution. Though, in the society of his closest
friends, Fontanes remained a Voltairian, he was convinced that
the ancient faith was better than the new. "The human imagina-

tion," said he, "must have healthy diet if it is not to feed on poisons."

The ideas of a hard-headed man like Fontanes struck Chateaubriand the more in that a firm friendship had sprung up between the two in London. Fontanes had kept a lively memory of Chateaubriand whom he found "grown by a cubit." A man of taste and a good judge of literature, he saw that in the *Essai*, in the *Natchez* and in the rough draft of *Atala*, more especially in the style, there was a strength and originality which could not fail to please. Though he was himself a neo-classical writer, his advice to Chateaubriand seems to have been fairly sound. "It is to him," said the latter, "that I owe whatever rightness my style may have. He taught me to respect my ear." In this embryo genius Fontanes put up with audacities that he himself would never have dared. Here and there he polished some rugged epithet, criticised English turns of phrase, protested against Chateaubriand's over-fondness for new coinages, but—on the whole—praised and encouraged him. "Let him be, gentlemen," said he to the scoffers among the émigrés, "let him be, he will outshine us all."

It was again Fontanes who took his friend to see the Princes' agent, M. Dutheil. Despite their poverty, the Comte de Provence, pretender to the throne of France, and his brother the Comte d'Artois maintained in London and various other towns representatives whose duty it was to band their friends together and rekindle their zeal by small subsidies. Fontanes advised M. Dutheil to make a friend of young Chateaubriand, who had undoubtedly a great future before him, and to help him publish his books. That Dutheil took the hint, we know from a letter of Chateaubriand's: "How to express my gratitude to M. Dutheil I really do not know. His services are so kindly done as to leave me poor in thanks. I beg him to believe that I am deeply sensible for his goodness and can give him no greater proof than by urging our great affair on his attention as soon as he has a moment to himself. The Natchez are naughty children, real savages, lazy, ill-bred and ravenous. They count entirely on M. Dutheil, for their father cannot provide for them single-handed." The Natchez likewise devoured a few louis sent by poor M. de Chateaubriand through the good offices of Caroline de Bédée, who was a milliner in London, and a few guineas which the English Literary Fund subscribed for the help of the French writer. Thus, though straitened, life was not hopeless.

When, in July 1798, Fontanes thought that he could return to France without undue risk, he went by way of Hamburg, which the émigrés regarded "as a kind of Purgatory." From there he wrote Chateaubriand the most tender of letters: "If you have some regrets for my leaving London, I swear that mine have been no less real. You are the second person (the first was Joubert) in all my life in whom I have found a kindred heart and imagination. Never shall I forget what a son of consolation you were to me in exile and in a foreign land. My dearest and most constant thought since leaving you is for the *Natchez*. The passages you read me, especially in our last days together, were admirable and will ever remain in my memory. Work, my dear friend, work. Grow famous. It is in your power. The future is yours." Chateaubriand replied on August 15th: "If I am the second person with whom you have found some spiritual kinship, you are the first in whom I have found all that I sought in man: character, brains— you are all as I would have you and I feel that henceforward I shall be bound to you for life. . . ."

5. Le Génie du Christianisme

At the time of Fontanes' departure, that is to say towards the middle of the year 1798, Chateaubriand was still engaged in altering the *Natchez*, of which *Atala* and *René* then formed part. It was this American epic which he had submitted to Fontanes, it was it that he read to his émigré friends when he invited them to drink a glass of punch in his new lodgings, it was on it that he counted to escape from poverty. Yet Fontanes had advised him to undertake further works. The *Essai* proved that Chateaubriand had in him the stuff of a historian and a polemist. Why should he not use his powers to defend the political and religious ideas for which a convalescent France was thirsting? The conclusions of the *Essai* shew that at that time, Chateaubriand himself had come to desire a reaction, though rather by reason than inclination. An impulse from the heart was soon to quicken the trend of his mind.

On May 31st, 1798, the dowager Mme. de Chateaubriand died at Saint-Servan, aged seventy-nine. The news reached the émigré in a letter from Julie de Farcy. Restored by sickness and suffering to the religion which, in the wild hey-day of youth, she had not forsaken but neglected, Julie de Farcy, whose nature was as fiery as that of all the Chateaubriands, had come to practice extreme austerity. This bewitching and witty young woman, once so proud of her lovely shoulders and of her poems, had made a bonfire of ribbons and manuscripts alike. She wore a hair-shirt, slept on bare boards and lived only on bread and water. During her thirteen months in prison she had been a pattern of patience, or resignation and heroic self-forgetfulness. The long and painful detention had gravely affected her health. Knowing that she was dying, she strove to win her brother back to ideas nearer hers:—

"My Dear, we have but now lost the best of mothers. I grieve to have to give you such a news. When you cease to be the object of our care, we shall have ceased to live. Could you but know how many tears our beloved mother shed for your errors, how lamentable they appear to all thinking people who profess not devotion merely, but right reason; could you but know, I think that your eyes might be opened and that you would give up writing. And if heaven, touched by my prayers, should again unite us, you would find in our midst all the happiness that may be known on earth. The happiness would be of your giving, for we can know none with you away, the more that we have cause to be anxious for your fate."

The death of his mother was a keen sorrow for Chateaubriand. In the old days he had thought her "charming," with her mixture of absent-mindedness, poetry and devotion. The Revolution had brought out her more sterling qualities. At the time of their common poverty, she had stripped herself to help him. With the courage of a saint she had endured first prison, then privation. The thought that he might have embittered her old age broke her son's heart. Even a short time before, he had written in the margin of his copy of the *Essai*: "There are moments when I am tempted to believe in the immortality of the soul, but then comes reason and will not let me admit it. Let us then not desire to outlive our ashes; let us die utterly lest we should suffer elsewhere. Life here should cure us of any passion for being." To deny the immortality of the soul is easy in the abstract; the problem is very different when it touches a being one has loved. The memory of his mother called up that of the religion in which she had bred him, of the cathedral in Saint-Malo and of his first communion at Dol.

"I have not yielded, I well grant, to great supernatural lights. My conviction springs from the heart—I wept and I believed." He was sincere, but the inward strife between faith and doubt went on. "When the seeds of religion first bourgeoned in my soul, I blossomed like an untilled field which, cleared of thorns and briars, bears its first harvest. Then came a frost, a killing frost and parched the soil. Heaven was pitiful. It sent its warm dews, but then there came again the chill and wintry blast. For long this alternation of doubt and faith made my life a cross between despair and joy unspeakable." Filial affection, the faith of his childhood, the Breton tradition of loyalty, the exhortations of his friends and the spirit of the age finally counselled reverence for what the spirit of another age had led him to mock. Fear of ridicule, the probable sneers of a Guingené or a Chamfort, the resistance of his own argumentative reason dragged him back in the direction of the sceptical philosophy of the *Essai*. Indirectly, however, Fontanes' arguments had predisposed his reason itself to wish that his heart might get the victory.

While he stood thus at the cross-roads there arose an opportunity for the defence of Christianity, and that from an unassailable standpoint. At the beginning of 1799 one of his former friends, Parny, published an erotic poem, *La Guerre des Dieux*, in which he depicted in flat and abstract terms the arrival of the Christian gods on Olympus, the wrath of the pagan deities, the struggles of Odin and Jupiter against the Father, Son and Holy Ghost, the loves of the Christians and the Bacchantes and other engaging episodes of the sort. The book aroused a storm of indignation among the émigrés in London. The bookseller Deboffe, who had been sent some advance copies, hurled them on the fire. Chateaubriand was struck by the strength of hostility stirred up by a book which, ten years earlier, would hardly have shocked a soul.

Fontanes was right then and many Frenchmen were ready for

a revival of Christianity. Might not Chateaubriand himself be its poet and philosopher? Following the emotions awakened by his mother's death, the idea fell on good ground. During the spring and summer of 1799, he thought a good deal about a little work to be entitled: *Sur la Religion chrétienne par rapport à la morale et à la poésie*, for at that time he thought he was capable of writing only an aesthetic defence of Christianity. There still exist some of his letters to a certain Baudus, an émigré settled in Hamburg, who was running, at the expense of the princes, a paper called the *Spectateur du Nord*. In these letters, dated April and May 1799, Chateaubriand offered Baudus a short manuscript. "The book is highly Christian and wholly in accordance with the present trend. . . . It is an occasional work, begun at the instance of Fontanes, and is a kind of reply to the poem of poor Parny, our one time friend, who has just brought dishonour on himself wholly gratuitously. I do not believe that the little tract on religion can fail to sell, by reason of the numbers of people, both without France and within, whom it will reach." In October, Chateaubriand informs Baudus that the book will be called: *"Des Beautés poétiques et morales de la religion chrétienne et de sa superiorité sur les autres cultes de la terre,"* and that it is printing in London, at Dulau and Co.'s.

Doubtless his first idea was to write only a pamphlet, but—as soon as he got to work—he felt that he had got hold, not only of a great subject, but of the one best fitted to his powers.

"It seemed that a huge emptiness in my breast was filled. All the time I was writing it, I was devoured by a kind of fever." Unskilled in writing a doctrinal work, in which deductions must be linked on the most rigorous of plans, he was completely at ease when he had only to bring together "fragments" drawn some from his recollections, some from his reading and bind them together in the framework of an original style. In such a work he could make the concord of nature and religion an excuse for the finest descriptions of his American travels, the treatment of religious feeling would lead to recollections of a youth spent among priests and to the stories of René and Atala, slightly christianised in order to serve as examples, while the subject of dogma would allow of introducing all that he had learnt from the Fathers of the

Church, whom he read at the time of writing the *Essai* only that he might refute them. "The memory of Charlotte interpenetrated and kindled it all, while, to clinch matters, the longing for glory first set my fervid imagination afire."

Was not this feverish enthusiasm deceiving him on the quality of his work? He tried reading some of the rough sketches to his émigré friends. The warmth of praise with which they were greeted left him no more doubt. The Chevalier de Panat, who had joined battle with him at the time of the *Essai*, wrote:— "Faith I owe some interesting reading this morning to your extreme kindness! Among its defenders our religion had numbered great geniuses and illustrious Fathers of the Church. Those athletes were vigorous in wielding every weapon of argument; unbelief was vanquished, but it was not enough. There still remained to shew all the charm of this wondrous religion, its consonance with human hearts and the incomparable pictures it offers the imagination. It is no longer the theologian of the schools, but the great painter and the man of feeling who is opening new horizons."

He would greatly have liked Fontanes' advice on the matter, but an exchange of letters was becoming increasingly difficult. The Minister of Police was plunging the émigrés into alternations of hope and terror. Fontanes, who was suspect of royalism (and not without cause) was driven into hiding and lamented his woes. It was to "Citoyenne Fontanes" that Chateaubriand, in August 1799, confided the plan of the book. "There is not a word of politics in the work which could hinder its sale. It is purely literary and we know how kindly you are disposed towards the author. We believe you will like what you see. It is perhaps the best work he has yet done; moreover the *Natchez* are introduced to give the public a foretaste of that epic of uncivilized man."

A few days later he learned that his sister Julie was dead and the untimely end of one so young and fair reawakened, in all its strength, his feeling for his mother's death. On this occasion it was to Fontanes himself that he wrote. The tone of the letter was new to him, for it was the first time that he turned moralist in private life:— "I have lately lost a dearly-loved sister, dead of grief in the place of privation where He who oft-times smites his servants that He may prove them and bring them to their reward in another life had bestowed her. A mind such as yours, whose friendship must be as enduring as it is lofty, will not easily be persuaded that all things come back to a little brief cherishing in a world whose creatures are so swiftly sped and there is naught to do but buy so dear a tomb. Yet God, who saw my heart, that it walked neither in the ways of proud iniquity nor followed after the abominations of gold, knew where to strike, for was he not Himself the potter of this clay and shall He not know its strength and its weakness? He knew that I loved my kinsfolk and that therein was my vanity. He has bereft me of them that I might lift up mine eyes unto Him. Henceforward all my thoughts are for Him—and you." There was perhaps some clumsiness of thought and language in putting God and Fontanes on the same level, but the sincerity of his feeling for Julie's death cannot be in question.

Meanwhile the young renown of Bonaparte was giving heart to the banished. A month after his return from Egypt the general had overthrown the Directory on the 18th of Brumaire (November 9th, 1799) and announced his determination, not to disavow the Revolution, but to bring it to an end in a fusion of the parties. "From the time of Clovis to that of the Public Safety, I regard myself as responsible for all." That was as much as to say that "the field would be open to brains," whatever the political past of their possessors. Whether in the hope that Bonaparte would constitute himself the champion of Louis XVIII or whether they accepted the idea of entering his service, many monarchist émigrés were returning to France and scraping together the remnants of their possessions. Chateaubriand watched the departure of his friend, Mrs. Lindsay, who—in her turn—summoned the Lamoignons. Already they were preparing to leave. Was he to be left alone in London?

Fontanes' sudden stroke of luck helped to make up his mind. It was a kind of miracle. Persecuted by Fouché, Fontanes had addressed to Bonaparte one of the excellent letters for which that modest, affectionate and peaceable man had such a gift when writing to the warriors whom he needed. "It is commonly reported that you do not care for praise. At this juncture mine would seem too interested to be worthy either of you or of myself. Besides, when I was free—before the 18th of Fructidor—it was open to all to see that, in the paper to which I contributed, I referred to you constantly as the glory of your soldiers. I will say no more. History has shewn you well enough that great captains have always defended against oppression and adversity the lovers of the arts, especially poets, who have grateful hearts and thankful voices."

A few weeks later Bonaparte resolved that an encomium on Washington, who was lately dead, should form part of the ceremony of the flags of Egypt. The praise of a republican hero was to be a means of reassuring the ex-members of the Convention, whom Bonaparte had made anxious. It was vital, however, that so dangerous a panegyric should be delivered by the most tactful of orators. Garat, Talleyrand and Chénier were suggested to Bonaparte. He refused them all and chose Fontanes. Why? In all probability he had read an article of Fontanes on Washington in the *Mémorial* and doubtless remembered the letter which had reached him, the "thankful voice" and the man who had skill in praising. However, there remained only thirty-six hours before the ceremony and Fontanes, who was somewhat indolent by nature, came near refusing. It was his friend Joubert who forced him to comply and thus made his fortune, for it sprang entirely from that speech, which made a great stir. Fontanes, who, the night before, had been a hunted man, found himself on the morrow "sought-after, fêted and made much of. From then on he was known as the new Bossuet."

Chateaubriand lost no time in adjuring his "best and dearest of friends" not to forget him. He was about to return to France. Would Fontanes find him a publisher, would he prevail on the Consul to have his name removed from the list of émigrés, above all— would he pave the way for the book's success by laudatory articles: "It is my only hope. If I succeed, I shall be out of the wood for a considerable time. If I fail, I'm sunk beyond plunge of plummet." In March 1800 Chateaubriand obtained from the Prussian Minister a passport made out in the name of La Sagne, resident in Neufchâtel. He stopped the printing of *Le Génie du Christianisme* at Dulau's, packed the pages already in type with the rough-drafts of Atala and René, to go with him, locked the rest of his manuscripts in a trunk which he left in charge of his London hosts, and set off for Calais, where "he landed in France with the century."

He had lived seven years in England. It was a long stay and, made at the age when mind and character are still plastic, it was to leave a deep impress on Chateaubriand. To the English poets, Milton, Gray and Young, he was to owe some of his finest themes; to English law his respect for liberty and his belief in a constitutional monarchy; to English manners, which helped to strengthen his Breton reserve, the "buttoned-up" reticence which was to mask the violence of his passions. In the course of that trying exile, poverty and humiliation had developed in him the impenitent rebel born of his position as a cadet, while the crimes of the Revolution and family adversities had taught him the bounds of rebellion. Though the "good sort" of Plancoët and of Monchoix was thoroughly alive in him and emerged from torpor in the warmth of friendly surroundings, he had discovered that there was a prestige in the beauty of adversity. He had learnt to make of melancholy a shield and buckler against suffering and to seek the storm-wind that it might disperse the vapours of tedium. At the time of his return he was, more than ever, an odd mixture of arrogance and simplicity, of standoffishness and shyness, of passion and good sense. Yet the doctrines he defended were no longer the same. In 1791, when he left for America, he endeavoured during the crossing to "un-convert" an Englishman. In 1800, he returned from England bearing a book which was to convert the French. The fact was that, in those ten years of bloodshed, France and he had suffered much.

CHAPTER IV

Le Génie du Christianisme

> From the time of the Gospels to the *Contrat Social*, it is books
> that have made revolutions.
> —BONALD

1. FIRST CONTACTS WITH FRANCE

THE passport was made out in the name of Jean-David de La Sagne, native of Boveresse, near Neufchâtel in Switzerland; the man who presented it to the Calais police was François-René de Chateaubriand, native of St. Malo, but after so long an absence, his manners, his tastes and his opinions were those of a foreigner. He was surprised by the distress of the population, by the peasants' clogs, by the sight of women in the fields, by the dung-heaps and the noise. Such reactions were typically English, but there were others which might have betrayed the Frenchman and the émigré.

In the musings of the exiled royalists revolutionary France had assumed a fabulous and even monstrous aspect. As Mrs. Lindsay's carriage bore Chateaubriand from his inn in Calais to the gates of Paris, he looked with eager interest at the ruinous castles, the belfries empty of bells, the graveyards with never a cross and the headless statues of saints. When Fontanes came to fetch him at Mrs. Lindsay's, intending to get him into Paris by the Étoile turnpike, he thought he was about to go down into Hell. Fontanes had to explain that it was merely a question of going down the Champs-Elysées. Chateaubriand was amazed to hear the merry din of violins, clarinets and drums and to see men and women footing it in dancing-halls. The Place Louis XV, where the guillotine had stood and where he still felt that his feet were slipping in blood, lay silent and bare. Even the police seemed well-disposed. He had been greatly afraid of compromising Fontanes and of finding them on his own track. When he went to get his passport visa-ed, there was no difficulty about granting a permis de séjour to the Swiss, La Sagne. What he did not realise was that the prefect of police had him watched, but decided that he was harmless. "He frequents none but scholars and booksellers," said the reports. His opinions? "He says little." There is some advantage in English manners.

Fontanes, to whom he had written from Calais: "I have just arrived, my dear and best of friends. . . . I beg you to find me somewhere to live quite near you," at first carried him off to his own house in the Rue Saint-Honoré and afterwards found him an entresol in the Rue de Lille. Somewhat reassured, Chateaubriand plucked up his courage and began to look about him. The sight was well worth seeing. A Paris, which had long been scattered, was coming back to life. "The émigré was returning and talking peaceably with the murderers of his nearest and dearest. . . . Those revolutionaries who had made their pile were beginning to move into the great town-houses of the Faubourg Saint-Germain. Busy becoming barons and counts, the Jacobins spoke only of the horrors of '93, and of the necessity of punishing the proletarians and quelling the excesses of the populace." Chateaubriand had hardly arrived in France when, on June 14th, 1800, Bonaparte consolidated his authority by winning the victory of Marengo.

What use would the Consul make of that authority? Some among the monarchists still hoped, rather naïvely, that Bonaparte would be willing to become Louis XVIII's High Constable. The ex-Conventionals, on the other hand, wished to believe that the Revolution was marching on. From Fouché to Grégoire, from Carnot to Benedetti, there were many such among the associates of the Consul and the Jacobin spirit was as flourishing in the army as at the Institut. On visiting Guingené at his house, Chateaubriand saw inscribed over the porter's lodge:— "Here the title of citizen is regarded as an honour and thee and thou are the customary forms of address." The republicanism of Citizen Guingené seemed unaltered, but Talleyrand, Bourrienne, Roederer and a hundred others were egging Bonaparte, who turned a willing ear, in the direction of personal power. "Day by day there progressed the metamorphosis

Le Génie du Christianisme

of republicans into imperialists and of the tyranny of the many into the despotism of the one."

In the past, Fontanes had been a monarchist from love of order and hatred of extremes. It was from the Consul that he now hoped for the reaction needed. Following his acceptance of the princes' subsidies there had come the famous panegyric and, from that time, he had become an official of the new régime, hitching his wagon to the star of Lucien Bonaparte. That "gawky, black-haired creature," short-sighted, daring and absent-minded, had played a leading part in the 18th of Brumaire. After the success of the coup d'Etat, his brother Napoleon had him appointed Minister of the Interior and Lucien, who prided himself as a writer, surrounded himself with men of letters. To Fontanes, "so devoted to the consular government," he had given the post of Reviser Extraordinary of Literature and the Drama. It was a well-paid sinecure. Fontanes had achieved a closer link with the Consul's family by becoming the lover of Elisa Bacciochi, the sister of Napoleon and Lucien, an energetic person—as lean and swarthy as were all the Bonapartes —who did the honours of Lucien's house. It was on "this wonderful woman," his friend's friend, that Chateaubriand counted to have his name removed from the list of émigrés and to regain his civil status.

Obliging and persistent, Fontanes had long been seeking a publisher for *Le Génie du Christianisme* and found the bookseller Migneret, who promised to make the author an advance and keep him going till the book could prove a success. Meanwhile, Chateaubriand was recasting it, on the advice of Fontanes, for "only in his own country can a man write temperately." In spite of these advances, life was not easy. *Chateaubriand to Fontanes:* "Will you do me two services? First, give me a note to a doctor, next—try to lend me twenty-five louis. I have had bad news of my family and do not know how to last out till I get another instalment from Migneret. It is hard to have to take thought for my life while I am doing the Lord's work. Oh, fine and just Revolution! They have sold all. Here am I as I came from my mother's womb, for even my shirts are not French. They are the alms of another nation. Get me out of this hole if you can, there's a good fellow! Twenty-five louis would keep me going till the publication of the book which is to decide my fate. It will pay for all if such be the good pleasure of God, who has not shewn me over-much favour as yet." For a religious writer the tone was strangely cavalier.

There was nothing to hope from the family. Though somewhat mistrustful of her "scapegrace brother," Mme. de Marigny, his elder sister, had sought out and traced the Swiss, La Sagne, difficult as was the task. She told him that all the Chateaubriands were ruined—that Lucile, who had married the old Chevalier de Caud, Governor of the Fort of Fougères, had left him, had subsequently become a widow and was now more or less penniless, while poor Céleste, once the Buisson de la Vigne inheritance was settled, had only a capital of twenty thousand livres on which she was living at Fougères until such time as her mythical and invisible husband should send for her to join him. Through all this period it was Fontanes alone who came to the rescue of his friend. He was an affectionate soul, always ready to help, and *Le Génie du Christianisme* served one of his dearest plans, that of restoring the Roman Church and attaching to the service of the Consul—and of internal peace—a clergy whose prestige in France, despite the Revolution, was enormous.

There were many indications that Bonaparte might be favourable to such a design. No doubt like most men of his age, he had been a Deist of the school of Rousseau in his time, he had made a civil marriage and had played the Mussulman in Egypt. Yet he had been brought up as a Christian, he had not forgotten and, more especially, he regarded Catholicism as a fundamental principle of order. Persuaded that the metaphysical speculations of the ideologues were dangerous, he granted that only immutable dogma could put an end to them. "Religion," said he, "is the vaccine of the imagination." Moreover, he thought that Catholic ritual beautified and sweetened the life of a nation. He would have understood, though not subscribed, to this letter of Fontanes to Lucien: "Where there is no worship, there is no government. After a victorious army, I know of no better ally than those who direct consciences in the name of God. I see that shrewd conquerors have never quarrelled with the priesthood. It is possible to content them and yet make use of them at the same time. Whatever people say, that is

Le Génie du Christianisme

sound philosophy. One may smile at augurs, but it is as well to eat the sacred chickens with them. So, at least, Cicero, Pompey and Caesar, who had himself made Pontifex Maximus, believed. All those men were of your stock, which has inherited their great qualities and should imitate them in all things."

Cynicism is always bad politics. Bonaparte was far too shrewd and serious for such utterances and realist enough to see that France was still Christian and Catholic at heart. As early as June 5th, 1800, when with the army of Italy, he received the parish-priests of Milan and said to them: "No society can exist without morals and there is no sound morality without religion. It is religion alone which gives the State a firm and lasting prop. A society without religion is like a ship without a compass. Grown wise through adversity, France has at last re-opened her eyes. She has realised that the Catholic religion was the only anchor which could hold her steady when tossed by all her storms." After Marengo, he wrote to his Consuls on June 18th: "Today, let our Paris atheists say what they will, I am going in great state to attend the *Te Deum* which is to be sung at the cathedral of Milan." Finally, to the Royalist emissaries: "I intend to re-establish religion, not for your sakes, but for mine."

Fontanes and Chateaubriand were, therefore, justified in counting on the goodwill of the master, but they had every cause to fear the enmity of the still-powerful Jacobins, who were not men to go to the wall without a struggle. It was to keep them in check that Lucien revived the former *Mercure de France* and made Fontanes its editor. The new *Mercure* aimed at "destroying, both in contemporary thought and style, the traces of barbarism which the influence of the 18th of Brumaire was gradually obliterating from the revolutionary laws." Friendship apart, the editor had therefore doctrinal reasons for bestowing advance praise on *Le Génie du Christianisme*. In the very first number, Fontanes added a postscript to the article in which he attacked Mme. de Staël and spoke of a book on the beauties of religion, "which had chanced to come into his hands." In another article in November, he named *Le Génie du Christianisme*, "a work which may end the literary quarrel between the philosophers and the partisans of religion."

Towards the end of 1800 the party of political and religious reactionaries lost its practical sense and tried to go too fast. Lucien, who was anxious for the future of the Bonaparte clan, was so unwise as to foretell not only the restoration of the old religion, but the establishment of a new dynasty. Sure of finding an echo in the army and in one section, at least, of public opinion, the Jacobins protested. There was a great outburst against Lucien, and Bonaparte, annoyed by such lack of tact, banished his brother to Spain. Fontanes had to lie low. While the storm raged, Chateaubriand offered to take up the cudgels for his friend and patron and it was he who, in the December number of the *Mercure*, undertook to reply to Mme. de Staël's protests against Fontanes' criticisms. His contemporaries reproached Chateaubriand with the ill-nature of the article. Today it rather sets our teeth on edge by its mingling of apologetics with personal publicity. "You are not unaware that my maggot is to see Jesus Christ everywhere, as Mme. de Staël does perfectibility. . . . What I propose to say to you in this letter will be drawn partly from my forthcoming book on the beauties of the Christian religion." The book, however, was not nearly finished. In order that it might strike the right note and that a pamphlet against Parny should become the epic of French Catholicism, there needed the intervention of a group which could steep the young man in the atmosphere of serious, of moral loftiness and of culture necessary to the unfolding of his work.

2. The Little Society—Atala

Before his meeting with Chateaubriand, Fontanes' best friend had been Joubert. As soon as might be, he brought the two men together. Joseph Joubert, at the close of 1800, was forty-six. He was a man of letters of exquisite taste, but he never published, "for he had fashioned himself an idea of perfection which prevented his finishing anything." He was too subtle to avoid the snare of preciousness whenever he wrote, and too delicate of perception not to be aware of it. Of his own thoughts, he said that they were the dreams of a shade. Since he was rich enough to live as he chose, he spent the greater part of the year in the country, at Villeneuve-sur-Yonne, reading and re-reading his favourite books, which ranged from Plato to Mme. de Sévigné and from Virgil to Bernardin de Saint-Pierre. He had arranged them by kindred

Le Génie du Christianisme

spirits, tearing out the pages which displeased him, covering those he liked with cryptic symbols and, when he grew weary of reading, giving a gentle polish to their leather bindings. His modesty and his vast learning gave him that rightness of judgment to which only those writers who subordinate their own work to an eager interest in others' ever attain. He was the most delicate confidant and sensitive critic of his age, but his qualities were hardly known outside a small, enchanted circle.

A woman once said of him that "he looked like a soul which had met a body by chance and tried to make the best of it." The remark pleased him, but there needed perhaps to add that the soul, surprised by the encounter, may have attached too much importance to the ills of the body. Joubert spent his life in believing that he was ill. "He was for ever changing his diet and his treatment, living on milk one day and mince the next." Since his heart was as susceptible as his stomach was frugal, he preferred the gentle warmth of sentimental friendships to the keen wind of love. "I am," said he, "like those Æolian harps which give out a few harmonious notes, but never play a tune." His wit and learning won the admiration of his friends, his crotchets and his originality their affection. Even men of letters were ready to forgive the infallibility of his taste, since his trifling absurdities tempered the brilliancy of his mind.

Joubert and Chateaubriand took to each other at once. "M. Joubert," writes Chateaubriand, "had a strange hold on people's hearts and, once it took possession of you, his image was graven there as a kind of fact or a thought that would not be dispelled. . . . He prided himself on his calm, yet none was more disquieted than he. He kept a watch on himself to check his spiritual emotions, for he thought them injurious to his health. . . . He was an egoist whose thoughts were all for others." As for Joubert, no sooner were Chateaubriand's first pages submitted to him than he recognised a great writer: "Your savage is a charm," said he. "We must wash the Rousseau, the Ossian, the Thames mists and all the revolutions, ancient and modern, off him and leave him the cross, the missions, the sunsets in mid-ocean and the American savannahs. Then you will see what manner of poet we shall have to cleanse us from the traces of the Directory, as of old, Epimenides purified Athens from the plague with his lustral rites and his verses.

The fine bonds of friendship became intertwined. In Joubert, Fontanes had given Chateaubriand all that he prized. Joubert, in his turn, introduced the wonderful Savage to the being, whom on earth, he held most dear—Mme. de Beaumont. Pauline de Beaumont, the daughter of Louis XVI's minister, M. de Montmorin, had given her father that boundless admiration which sometimes makes the daughters of gifted men rebel against marriage. Nevertheless, she had been married at eighteen to a Count de Beaumont, who was wholly unworthy of her. The couple separated almost at once and Pauline began again to act as her father's secretary. Then came the Revolution to break up that life as it had so many others. M. de Montmorin, who had been imprisoned in La Force, perished in the massacres of September. Mme. de Montmorin and her children had meanwhile taken refuge with their cousins, the Sérillys, in the Château de Passy.

Thither in 1794 came three scoundrels to hale them to the guillotine. It is said that they refused to take Pauline de Beaumont, since she was spitting blood, but men of their type were not afraid of blood—it was merely that she was not on their list. Now that she was utterly alone, she left the castle and took up her abode in a hut lent her by a peasant. It was then that Joubert, who lived near and had heard of the young woman's tragedy, went to see her, was amazed by her intelligence and became her friend, the mentor of her reading and her confidant. There can be no doubt that Joubert loved Mme. de Beaumont in his fashion, but the spirit, which had strayed within a body, was content with the shadow of love as with the shadow of fame. He asked no more intimate favour than to be allowed to choose the books that Pauline de Beaumont kept at her bed's head. That grace was granted.

Others had had of her more carnal gifts. At the time of the Directory she had shared the natural abandon common to many young women who had unexpectedly escaped the Terror. "Mme. de Beaumont is a true Frenchwoman, all or nothing according to the time and the person," wrote the Swiss, Charles de Constant. Consumptive and always slightly feverish, she had all the despairing sensuality of creatures who know that their life itself is threatened.

Le Génie du Christianisme

In men she cared more for worth than looks. André Chénier and François de Pange had been, not her lovers, but her friends. "She herself," wrote Joubert, "seemed more like a Muse than a Grace and even more like those figures in Herculaneum which flow silently upon the air, scarcely housed within a body." "She looked," said another of her friends, Chênedollé, "as though she were fashioned of elements forever tending to break free and forever fleeting. Fragile as she was, her courage, her strength of mind and her good sense were amazing. One of her friends had given her this device: 'The least thing stirs me, the greatest cannot make me quake.'"

Towards the end of 1800, Mme. de Beaumont had reinstalled herself in Paris, where her friend Etienne Pasquier gave up his apartment in the Rue Neuve-du-Luxembourg for her use. It was not far from Joubert, who lived in the Rue Saint-Honoré. Immediately there grew up about her a small and vastly agreeable circle. "The happiness of being together again, after so many years of restraint, made everything run smoothly. Shades and divergences of opinion which would never have been tolerated before 1791 were all forgiven each other." They were monarchists at heart, but their longing for peace and quiet forbade hatred and rancour. They admired Bonaparte, who gave Mme. de Beaumont "raptures." Joubert said: "He is a wonderful inter-King. . . . Without him there could be no more enthusiasm for aught that is living and powerful. Thanks to him, wonder has returned to gladden the sorrowful earth."

It was into this fastidious drawing-room, where all talk was in undertones and the conversation of Joubert and Mme. de Beaumont, a colloquy of shadows, set the tone, where fine shades of fine shades were at once perceived and Pauline's old friend, Mme. de Staël, appeared like a whirlwind, that Joubert was rash enough to let loose his Savage. When he came in, Mme. de Beaumont saw "a Breton, short of stature and ill-proportioned, with high shoulders on which the strong head sat awkwardly, since—though it was very fine—it was obviously made for another body, starchy manners and an engaging smile." The moment he opened his lips "the swift originality of his thought," the beauty of his voice and the charm of sorrowful legend which he knew how to cast about him won the heart of a woman so "susceptible to quality." When he read fragments of *Atala* and *Le Génie du Christianisme* at her apartment, she was among the first to define the sensuous and pleasurable quality of his style: "M. de Chateaubriand's style thrills through me like a quiver of love. He plays upon my every fibre as on a harpsichord." She would willingly have said of him what Joubert did of Rousseau: "None has ever conveyed so well as he the sense of flesh that touches spirit and the bliss of their union."

Chateaubriand, like many others, thought that Mme. de Beaumont bore more resemblance to a Muse than to a Grace. He admits that her face was rather plain than otherwise, but his fine portrait of her explains her charm: "Her face was pale and thin. The fire of her almond-shaped eyes might have been too brilliant had it not been softened by the languishing sweetness of her glance, as a ray of light is subdued on its passage through the crystal of clear water. There was a kind of inflexibility and impatience about her character which came of the strength of her feeling and the consuming sickness from which she suffered. Dowered with a lofty soul and high courage, she was born for the world from which her spirit had withdrawn from choice and from misfortune. Yet, when a friendly voice called that lonely mind outwards, she came with heavenly balm upon her lips. Mme. de Beaumont's extreme weakness made her utterance slow and there was something touching in that slowness."

"There was a hawk that loved a lark." Aunt de Boistelleul's song comes to mind unbidden. What havoc would a bird of prey not wreak in that blue drawing-room of the Rue Neuve-du-Luxembourg, softly lighted by a single lamp? How must the sensitive soul of Joubert have shivered when the keen wind of passion arose suddenly to blow through the muted and tender feeling which he had cultivated in Pauline de Beaumont? He refrained from envying Chateaubriand, a little because it would have been dangerous to his health, but chiefly because he was of too fine a fibre to be unjust. Yet he suffered and took in the situation with regret. There came a sad day when he entered in his note-book: "On Mme. de Beaumont. Senses uppermost. No inward seclusion. Too naked." The hawk bore off a willing prey.

One friendship attracted another and the little society grew.

Le Génie du Christianisme

Chateaubriand brought Chênedollé, a poet who—like himself—had returned from exile and one with whom he enjoyed discussing great literary projects at a café in the Champs-Elysées where nightingales sang in a cage. This Chênedollé was so sad that he never drew near a window but his friends dreaded that he might throw himself out. By reason of his settled gloom and his black humours, the little society nicknamed him "The Crow of Vire" (for that was his native town). Chateaubriand was the illustrious Crow of the Cordilleras (sometimes, too, the Cat), young Guéneau de Mussy was the Little Crow, Mme. de Beaumont, the Swallow, Fontanes, the Boar, and Joubert, the Stag, because of his life in the woods. The women who frequented the salon, Mme. de Vintimille, Mme. Hocquart and Mme. de Saussure shewed themselves worthy of the converse of such men as Bonald, Pasquier, Joubert and Molé. "In the little society good company and celebrity were met together. It was perhaps the only gathering in Paris which, without even thinking about it, was unremittingly busy in giving praise where praise was due."

It was thus that the launching of the Enchanter soon became the main preoccupation of the group. Since his readings had proved a triumph, Chateaubriand, who thirsted for fame, was pawing the ground. Yet, to publish *Le Génie du Christianisme* at the beginning of 1801, when the counter-attack of the philosophers was at its height, would have been madness. The wisest of his friends advised him to extract the episode of *Atala* which, being politically inoffensive and emotionally moving, could not arouse the same outburst and would whet the appetite of its readers.

It was "the little trial balloon which is sent up before the larger to test the state of the atmosphere." Besides, there was launched only a refurbished *Atala*, purged of its Rousseauism and christianised as befitted the work of a future religious restorer. Fontanes himself watched over the emendation and made Chateaubriand rewrite Père Aubry's speech at Atala's death-bed. "It's bad. Recast it?" Chateaubriand, as engagingly biddable as he had been with his sisters, obeyed. A discreet and misleading preface explained why this little work came out before the main one promised. The pretext given was the loss of a set of proofs and the groundless fear of plagiarism. The real reason was far simpler—it was nothing but the author's impatience. On the eve of the book's publication, he said to a friend with whom he was dining at a café in the Champs-Elysées: "Tomorrow decides my fate. Either I'm sunk or up I go like a sky-rocket."

Mme. de Beaumont was on tenterhooks. Joubert cheered her with the authority of his infallible taste: "I do not share your fears in the least, for whatever is beautiful cannot fail to please and there is in this work a Venus whom some will see as heavenly, others as earthly, but who will stir them all.... There is a spell, a talisman in the craftsman's fingers. He will have cast it over all the book, for it is the work of his hands, and where that gramarye, that imprint and that character are, there also will be a soul-satisfying pleasure. I would I had time to enlarge on all this and make you understand, if only to drive away your fears, but I have only a moment to give you today and want to tell you at once how unreasonable you are in your misgivings. The book is done and the critical moment is therefore past. It will succeed because it is the work of the wizard."

Joubert was right and its success surpassed all their hopes. "It is from the publication of *Atala*," said the author, "that the stir I have made in the world dates. I ceased to live of myself and my public career began. After so many military successes, a literary success seemed a miracle. It was for that they hungered." Within a few days *Atala* or *Les Amours de deux sauvages dans le désert* had conquered the Faubourg Saint-Germain, the Tuileries, France and finally all Europe. Before long every Waggoner's Rest was adorned with red, green and blue prints representing Chactas, Père Aubry and the daughter of Simaghan. In the booths, on the Quais, Chateaubriand found wax models of his characters while, on the boards of one of the theatres in town, he saw his heroine tricked out in a head-dress of cock's feathers. Skits and caricatures—it was fame.

Why so much ado about a little book? Its success had been wonderfully prepared by the articles of Fontanes and Peltier and by the public readings in London and Paris. Public opinion craved for an original literature which should correspond to the glory of the new France and what could be fresher than the music of this prose—a music such as had never been heard in France: "It was a halcyon night. The genius of the air shook his blue locks, fragrant with the scent of pines, while there breathed a faint aroma of amber from the crocodiles basking at length beneath the tamarinds of the rivers." Or the description of the *Meschacébé* with which the book opens, picked out with yellow water lilies, green serpents, blue herons, rose-red flamingoes and golden sails.

In an epoch of great events and great souls, literature was at last returning to the portrayal of great emotions. Chateaubriand had read deeply in Homer and the Bible. That might have its dangers if he sought to imitate their methods of composition (a danger which was to appear later), but in *Atala*, he had striven only for the noble simplicity of their lines. He might, perhaps, have been accused of overdoing his taste for striking pictures and of needing to plant some arresting and majestic statue on the promontory of every paragraph. Yet these somewhat studied "effects" would have jarred the more if Chateaubriand, with an infinite skill which touched Joubert, had not known how to steep too dazzling imagery in the luminous mist of vague words. ". . . When a breath of wind comes to animate all these solitudes, to set these wavering forms aquiver, to merge all these masses of white, of blue, of green and rose-red, to mingle all colours and gather up every whisper of sound, then—from the heart of the forest—there come such harmonies, such things pass before the sight, as I should strive in vain to describe to those who have never trodden these unravished fields of nature." Can you feel the vague splendour that the humdrum word "things" lends to all the foregoing picture?

With matchless art the magician knew how to mingle the holy enchantment of the Christian virtues and the fiery, sensuous poetry of the Bible with memories of ancient spells and pagan cantrips such as have not lost their power upon the Western mind. The Abbé Morellet wondered why the moon, in Chateaubriand, loves to tell her great sad secret to the ancient oaks. It was that the moon was woman and goddess both and that she came from Virgil as the "genius of the air" came from the poets of the East.

The book was fiercely attacked and as passionately defended. The Jacobins of the old school, the "sons of Voltaire," scoffed at its highly-coloured imagery, at its devout savages and at Père

Aubry's sermons. Marie-Joseph Chénier, in his satire on the New Saints, had a bitter jibe for the Massillon of the desert:

> O terrible Atala! *tous deux avec ivresse*
> *Courons goûter encor les plaisirs de la messe* . . .

But "France was laughing no longer." After her many sufferings she welcomed a gravity of tone which accorded with such sober memories and the hostility of the critics only fanned the enthusiasm of the admirers. "All this hullaballoo served to increase the stir of my appearance. . . . I was in love with fame as with a woman, with my first love. Yet, coward as I was, my affright rivalled my passion . . . My natural shyness kept me humble amid all my triumphs. I fled from my renown. I kept in the background, seeking to dim the aureole about my head. When My Superiority dined for thirty sous in the Latin quarter, he swallowed awry, embarrassed by the interest which he felt he was arousing. I contemplated myself. To myself I said: 'Amazing creature, it is nevertheless you who are eating like the next man. . . .' There came thronging about me, besides the young women who weep salt tears over novels, the crowd of Christian women and those other noble enthusiasts whose soul sets up a throbbing in the blood. Sexless children of thirteen and fourteen years old were the most perilous for, knowing neither what they want nor what they want of you, they mingle your seductive image with a world of ribbons and flowers. . . . I was smothered beneath a heap of perfumed notes. If those notes were not today the letters of grandmothers, I should be hard put to it to recall with befitting modesty the rivalry there was for the least word I wrote and the way in which they would pick up an envelope I had addressed and hide it blushingly, with bent heads, under the falling veil of their long hair."

Even Mme. de Staël became his friend, though she trembled for the danger to her ideas of human perfectibility represented by this young champion of the past, who had so perfidiously attacked her in the *Mercure*. She could not resist such celebrity and pushed her taste for lion-hunting to the point of letting herself be devoured. Besides, Chateaubriand and she found a bond of union in their Anglomania. He was soon her *Dear Francis*, while he ended

Le Génie du Christianisme

his letters with a *God bless you.* True, she was the friend of Fouché and might be useful in getting his name removed from the list of émigrés, for it was more than ever necessary now that he had published a book in his own name.

It was at Mme. de Staël's house that he one day saw the loveliest woman of her age—Mme. Récamier. Christian de Lamoignon had already taken him to see her, but as he was "still a savage coming out of his woods," he had not dared to raise his eyes to a woman surrounded by worshippers. One morning, after the publication of *Atala,* when Mme. de Staël had admitted Chateaubriand while her maid put the finishing touches to her dress, there entered suddenly Mme. Récamier, wearing a white silk frock. "I hardly answered, for my eyes were glued to Mme. Récamier. I wondered whether it was a portrait of candour that I saw or of voluptuousness. My imagination had never conceived her like and I was more than ever discouraged. My loving wonder turned to spleen against my person. I believe I prayed the heavens to lend years to that angel, to strip her of some little of her divinity that there might be less distance between us. When I dreamed of my Sylph, I clothed myself with all perfections to find favour in her sight; when I thought of Mme. Récamier I bereft her of her charms to bring her nearer me. Clearly I loved the reality more than the dream." Mme. de Staël's talk flowed steadily on. Mme. Récamier rose without having said a word. Twelve years were to pass before Chateaubriand saw her again. How surprised he would have been if, in 1802, some Cagliostro could have foretold that this virginal beauty, grown old and blind, would one day watch, almost alone, by his death-bed.

3. TE DEUM LAUDAMUS

The little balloon of *Atala* had shewn that the currents were favourable. Chateaubriand was now eager to launch his larger work, but the odds had yet to be weighted on his side, for it was an enterprise in which his whole fortune was at stake. In this spring of 1801, his literary and political advisers, Joubert and Fontanes, still counselled discretion. Of Bonaparte's intentions there could be no doubt. "My policy," he reiterated in a thousand forms, "is to govern men as the greater number wish to be governed." That, in France, this majority desired the revival of its old religion the Consul was sure, but the opposition promised to be fierce. The philosophers of the Institut raged to see their colleague Bonaparte "leading the Republic to confession." In the army, the anti-clerical generals were doing their best to stir up the grenadiers. Mme. de Staël was anxious and put her friends on their guard: "There is hardly a moment left to you. Tomorrow the tyrant will have forty thousand priests in his service." When to the difficulties of this campaign are added the delays of negotiations with Rome and the resistance of Talleyrand and Fouché, Napoleon's brusque changes of mood are easily understandable. Fontanes had to endure their repercussions and, through him, Chateaubriand. Writing from London, Peltier opined that the success of *Atala*, by alarming the philosophers, had let loose a reaction. "We greatly fear that, in all this, the worthy M. de Chateaubriand has been the dupe and will shortly be the victim of a proud and shuffling cabal." "Shuffling" is superb. Chateaubriand must have envied Peltier the word.

Men are so ingenuously pleased with their laurels that they readily imagine that happiness to be universally shared. Jealousy, criticism and opposition even, strike them as an injustice. Following the triumph of *Atala*, Chateaubriand was wounded and indignant at the inevitable backwash of opinion and immediately spoke of "going to die on a foreign soil." Then he took the wiser decision of surviving in France and putting the finishing touches to *Le Génie du Christianisme* while waiting for the wind to turn. Under the sobering influence of Joubert and Mme. de Beaumont he could now envisage more clearly the mighty scope of his plan, which was to link up a France which had outlived the Revolution with her long Christian tradition. Mme. de Beaumont, who had just taken a house at Savigny-sur-Orge for the summer of 1801 offered him house-room while he worked. He accepted. It meant placarding their relationship, but Pauline de Beaumont was free, she had never lacked courage and, dimly aware of the gravity of her condition, she was loath to die until she had known a little joy. Besides, she thought it wiser to snatch from the women-admirers of *Atala* a Savage all too easily tamed. "A fig for life!"

Le Génie du Christianisme

Margaret of Scotland had once exclaimed. Mme. de Beaumont was greatly taken with the remark, which she thought capital.

For Chateaubriand this loving retreat was not without its dangers. Himself a husband, he was about to publish a book in which the sanctity of marriage was exalted as the "pivot of social economy," yet he was finishing that book in the house of a mistress. The adventure might well lay him open to the witticisms of the philosophers, but its delights were worth the risk. Never had Mme. de Beaumont known her friend "so calm, so gay, so childlike and so tractable." No sooner had seclusion sloughed off his vanity than he became the tenderest and best of good fellows, and the most easy to live with. A happy couple can find mirth in everything—even their dealings with the landlord made them giggle with delight. The house nestling against its vine-grown slope, the dog and the cat drowsing beside the lake, the long walks in the woods all enchanted the Enchanter. From morning till night he ransacked, with more zeal than method, histories of the Church, the *Lettres édifiantes* and the *Livre des Missions* to find facts and quotations with which to buttress his fair building. Mme. de Beaumont found a rapturous delight in helping. It is often the secret grief of a woman in love to feel that the beloved's thought is remote from her; the sharing of toil crowns the union of the flesh with that of the spirit. When darkness fell, she taught Chateaubriand the names of the stars and told him that he would one day remember that it was through her he had learned to know them.

Poor Joubert, the confidant at once of the romantic escapade and of the pious researches, was not without his misgivings. He was resigned to seeing his friend carried off by a younger man, whose genius he admired. "Forty-seven years," he noted with a sigh . . . *"Fiat voluntas tua!"* and accompanied by Mme. Joubert and his son, he went to visit the lovers of Savigny. It was not long since the Directory, and manners were still lax. Yet he dreaded for a young woman of such sensibility the inconstancy which he divined in their friend, and for the book, over whose unfolding he was watching, the floods of erudition in which the two labourers were threatening to drown it. To Mme. de Beaumont's ceaseless demands on his rich library, Joubert replied with unfailing good-nature. He lent *Le Père Charlevoix* and *Le Cardinal*

Fleury and, if need arose, even went the length of buying books not in his possession, but he besought them to be sparing in their use of such a medley: "Tell him, moreover, that there are too many of them; that the public will care not a straw for his quotations but a great deal for his ideas; that it is in his genius rather than in his learning that they are interested; that it is beauty—not truth—which will be sought in his work; that it is his mind and not his teaching which may make its fortune; finally that they rely on Chateaubriand to make Christianity popular and not on Christianity to make Chateaubriand. . . . A rule which is too often neglected, though one which, by virtue of their charge, scholars themselves should observe up to a point, is this:— *Hide your learning.* I do not suggest that one should be a charlatan or practise the tricks of the trade, but that there must be no sacrifice of art. *The true art is to conceal art.* In former days the audience at the Opéra used to be irritated by the noise of the bâton beating time. What would have been the effect of interrupting the music to read an apologia for every tune? Though he writes in prose M. de Chateaubriand bears no resemblance to other prose-writers; by the power of his thought and his sense of words his prose turns to music and verses. Let him mind his business. Let him bewitch us."

Apart from the Jouberts, few visitors came to disturb the work at Savigny. Lucile had been introduced to Mme. de Beaumont by her brother and the two young women had found a meeting ground in their common admiration of Chateaubriand. Lucile, ever prompt to believe herself persecuted, no longer got on either with her sisters or her sister-in-law, Céleste: "Quick-tempered, imperious and unreasonable, she thought herself a prey to secret enemies." She gave false addresses, scrutinised suspiciously the seal of every letter that reached her, conceived passionate affections for people and as quickly grew to hate them. She came to Savigny, where she probably heard the best passages of the *Génie* read aloud. One wonders, a little fearfully, what that odd and feverish creature must have felt as she listened to the tale of Amélie and it is noteworthy that, in the letters written after her visit, she is quick to remind her brother of their childhood's purity.

There was some talk, too, of Chateaubriand's going to Brittany. Mme. de Beaumont was bound to dread it lest it brought him and his wife together, but Lucile who, after taking Céleste under her wing with jealous and dictatorial eagerness, had more or less quarrelled with her, felt constrained to dissuade him from a meeting. Besides, Mme. de Chateaubriand had in the past shewn as much detestation of her husband's writings as Mme. de Farcy. Brittany and a wife were put out of mind. The only break in the lovers' work was a visit to Mme. de la Briche, at the Marais, where Mme. de Beaumont shewed herself "gay, lively, witty, athirst for pleasure and lenient to a fault." Her hair cropped short and wearing a cotton frock, she would go for twilight walks round the lovely, sheeted lake of the Marais and when her friends, trembling for her delicate lungs, said: "You're doing your best to kill yourself," she merely answered: "What does it matter?"

In autumn Chateaubriand, whose enthusiasms were as brief as they were keen, at last decided that the book was finished. Such was not the opinion of Mme. de Beaumont, who doubtless wanted the researches to continue that she might be left alone with the researcher. "What startles me," said she, "is the lighthearted way in which he puts forth opinions which must be presented with the utmost delicacy and skill if they are not to rouse alarm." She thought that the apology lacked a well-defined doctrine but that "there was no help for it," since, if anyone said a word to the author on those lines, he fell into the Slough of Despond and straightway threatened "to go and die on a foreign soil." Mme. de Staël, into whose hands there chanced a few pages about that time, lighted on the chapter *De la Virginité* and said to Adrien de Montmorency: "Oh la, la! My poor Chateaubriand, how flat it's going to fall!"

Mme. de Beaumont's misgivings were as ill-founded as Mme. de Staël's rejoicings. Such as it was, the book was to please and carry conviction, for it brought to a still wavering epoch what it desired—aesthetic and sentimental arguments for returning to a religion after which the age yet hankered. In considering *Le Génie du Christianisme*, its first and real title: *Beautés de la religion chrétienne* should never be forgotten. The essential aim of the author was to shew that Christianity is capable of inspiring an art and a poetry, of beautifying the life of the individual and adorning that of the country with noble ceremonies.

To his long consideration of the poetry of Christianity, of its worship and its ceremonies, he had added a whole book on dogma and doctrine. It was that section which the critics, whether clerical or lay, thought the weakest. Chateaubriand was neither a theologian nor a metaphysician. His mind was rather poetic and concrete—he knew how to paint the passions he experienced and the nature that he loved. His intellect, which—both in its tastes and its way of functioning—was closely akin to Montesquieu or Fontanes, was like a fish out of water when dealing with the symbolism and the deep intuitions of Christianity. If truth be told, his faith was all but a stranger to dogma, paradoxical as the fact may seem. "Apart from the Gospels," his wife was to say later, "M. de Chateaubriand denies everything." He had no real understanding either of the mysteries, which he confused with the mysterious, or of the sense of sin, or of Christian humility. "If anyone smites you," said he, "return the blow fourfold. Never mind about the cheek!" All his life he went from mistress to mistress and never shewed the least sign of repentance. The furthest he would go was to say that Christianity, by binding up earthly passions with distant hopes of heaven, gave rein to inexhaustible dreams.

His adversaries, particularly Guingené in a notable article in the *Décade*, had therefore no difficulty in pointing out the weaknesses in the dogmatic side of his work. Yet no sooner does he touch on the springs of religious feeling, in the French especially, than Chateaubriand moves because he is himself moved. "He was," said Sainte-Beuve, "an Epicurean gifted with a Catholic imagination." He should have said "tradition" rather than "imagination." From the beauty of Catholic ceremonial, from the works of art inspired by Christianity, from the changed life it demands and, finally, from the harmonies of nature he deduces the truth of religion. Is the method so exceptionable and is not beauty the coinage of truth? The Angel of Rheims, the Cathedral of Chartres, the thorns of the monstrance and night with its thousand stars are there in proof. One thing is indisputable—the poet's reasonings

Le Génie du Christianisme

touched countless souls whom the arguments of the theologians failed to reach.

His opponents, the philosophers of the Institut, were to have a thankless task in jibing at this emotional religion, at this tenderness for crocodiles and serpents as works of God, at the eulogy of virginity which ends with a startling sentence: "God is himself the great Solitary of the Universe, the eternal Celibate of all the Worlds." Fontanes, a man of taste, dreaded their attacks. Chateaubriand reassured him: "The great moment draws near; take heart! It seems to me that you are downcast. 'Sdeath! up with you—shew your teeth. They are a cowardly race, it is easy to make short work of them do you but look them in the face." Nevertheless, with intent to bolster up his spiritual defence with powerful earthly forces, he linked the fate of his book to that of the First Consul by means of a preface: "Every man who may hope for a few readers does service to society by endeavouring to rally its members to the cause of religion and, even at the cost of losing his reputation as a writer, he must, in conscience, unite his powers—puny though they be—with those of the strong man who has snatched us from the abyss."

From this "strong man" and all "the family" besides he now awaited the indispensable favour of having his name removed from the list of émigrés. He counted especially on the "adorable" Elisa Baciocchi, Fontanes' friend. "Fontanes may have told you, Madam, what I feel. The Consul's sister is all-powerful and I have grounds for hope since she is graciously willing to shew some interest in me." In exchange for her protection he did not stint compliments. "Because of you, I never stop talking from morning till night. There are myriads of questions to answer. 'You are lucky,' people say, 'to know the Consul's sister! What is she like? There is always so much good said of her and one hears so many stories of her kindness!' Then I take rein and lose myself in long descriptions: 'Picture a woman who is at once unpretentious and witty, noble, gentle, generous and compassionate; it is amazing how many hearts she wins for the Consul.—Where is she? She is at Barèges. Is there anything the matter with her? She has serious gastric trouble—Oh dear, oh dear! she shall be remembered in our prayers.' The upshot is that I have the happiness of writing to Madame

Baciocchi and I vow that whoever does not love the lady is a scurvy knave and a traitor. It is the challenge of the knights of old, we are back in the age of heroes."

"The family" did not hold out long against such blandishments. In July 1801 Chateaubriand heard that his name was no longer on the black-list. Shortly afterwards Fontanes introduced him to Lucien Bonaparte, who had returned from his Spanish exile, and prevailed on the Consul's brother to read the proofs of the *Génie*. The author thought his marginal commentary "commonplace." In 1802 events moved fast—on March 26th the Peace of Amiens which, it was thought, meant the end of the wars of the Revolution, was signed with England; on April 8th the Tribunate and the Legislative Body promulgated the Concordat; April 14th saw the publication of *Le Génie du Christianisme* and four days later, on Easter Sunday, April 18th, a solemn *Te Deum* was sung at Notre Dame in thanksgiving for the restoration of peace and of religion.

Within the cathedral, where all the bells were ringing a full-throated peal, a papal legate, the Archbishop of Paris and thirty bishops awaited the First Consul. When he came, in his red coat, he was led to a seat beneath a canopy. Some of the general officers about him disapproved of all this mummery. In the evening, when General Delmas was asked for his impressions, he replied: "There wanted only the hundred thousand men who gave their lives to put an end to all that." Yet, in the streets, the people were singing: "Sunday, let us keep the feast, Alleluia!" That same day a proclamation of Bonaparte's in the *Moniteur* was followed by Fontanes' review of *Le Génie du Christianisme*, which thus appeared to be both a godly and an official book.

"I wanted a great bruit," said Chateaubriand, "so that it might rise up to the place where my mother dwells." It may seem surprising that communications between sinners and the elect were better assured by noise than by humility, but Chateaubriand undoubtedly experienced the greatest stir that ever surrounded the birth of a work of the mind. It might have been supposed that the bells were ringing, the troops lining the streets and the bishops officiating only to do honour to the new-found fame of the poet-restorer of religion. It was "a triumph of the stage and the altar," a conquering day that Chateaubriand was never to forget and that worked a change in his idea of himself. From that time forwards he conceived an almost boundless political ambition and regarded himself as one of the leading figures of Christendom. He had found himself linked with the vast designs of Bonaparte—thenceforth he thought in terms of "he and I" and as Europe had once joined the Pope and Emperor in a common awe and reverence, desired that men should speak of the Poet and the Consul.

Years later, on writing his *Mémoires*, he recorded with pride the prodigious effect of his book: "Literature grew dyed with the colours of my religious pictures . . . Atheism and materialism were no longer the bases of belief or unbelief in the mind of youth. . . . No longer were men rooted to the spot by anti-religious prejudice. The impact of *Le Génie du Christianisme* on the intellect dragged the Eighteenth Century out of the rut." That is all perfectly true, but it was a remarkable fact that *Le Génie du Christianisme*, which had power over so many minds, was powerless to change the life or morals of its author.

From 1802 onwards there was a great gulf set between the real and the imaginary Chateaubriand, between the personage and the person. Seriousness, which is a complete identity of thought and expression, was never again within his reach. Emphasis and rhetoric wrapped their studied folds about a thought which could no longer endure the naked truth. A mind disquieted and divided against itself seeks to flee the searchlight of lonely meditation. It takes refuge in frivolity, which is a rejection, and in learning, which is an escape. Such, until the time of the fine *Mémoires*, was to be the progress of Chateaubriand. Only at moments (happily fairly frequent) of self-forgetfulness, of tenderness or of pity, did friends and mistresses find once again the lovable youth who, in the days of his obscure poverty, had won the hearts of the "little society" in the Rue Neuve-du-Luxembourg.

4. "You Can Get Me Sent to Rome"

To Fontanes: "I cannot come and see you this morning, my dear fellow, for there is so much to be done that I do not know where to turn. I only want to tell you that the omens seem favourable.

Only yesterday Migneret sold a thousand crowns' worth of copies. That same day I saw the powers that be, who appear well-disposed. Put in a good word for me with all boldness, there's a good soul. Remember that you can get me sent to Rome."

To Rome? From the time of the publication of the *Génie* such was indeed Chateaubriand's distant ambition. Though he was essentially a man of letters, he thought and wished himself to be a man of action. Literary success, as he saw it, was merely the road to success in politics. The controversy that raged about his book annoyed and saddened him. Attacked on the left by Guingené, who criticised the weakness of its thought, the ingenuousness of certain chapters, such as that on virginity, and the injustice of its treatment of the philosophic sect, to which (as he pointed out) Chateaubriand had himself belonged in his youth, he found that he was being attacked on the right by the royalists in London, who were indignant at his collaboration with the Usurper. He wanted to get out of such a kettle of fish, to escape from men of letters, to forget his resentments as an émigré and devote himself wholeheartedly to the new master who alone could open to him the way of action. Who could be better fitted than the author-restorer of Christianity to represent France at the Vatican? Naturally he did not aspire to go there, in the first instance, as ambassador, but since there was some question of the Consul's sending his own uncle, Canon Fesch, to Rome, why should he not give him the author of *Le Génie du Christianisme* as a secretary. The decision depended on Bonaparte alone—it was the business of Fontanes and Elisa to predispose him in Chateaubriand's favour, as he made no bones about reminding them.

It was immediately after the publication of his book that, at a party given by Lucien, he met Napoleon Bonaparte for the first time. When *Atala* came out, Elisa, in order to please Fontanes, had attempted to press the slim volume on the Consul. Its reception was not of the best:— "More romances in A'! I have so much time to read your trash, haven't I?" *Le Génie du Christianisme* was another matter—the book came opportunely and the author might be of some service. In Lucien's drawing-room, Bonaparte bore down on Chateaubriand with his usual abruptness and, without preamble, talked first of Egypt and the Arabs and then of Christianity with

Le Génie du Christianisme

a strong and unexpected sense of poetry. The young writer, who had no gift for swift repartee, found nothing to say, but the great are sometimes flattered by respectful silence and Fontanes told him that he had passed muster. He, on his side, had been taken with Bonaparte's eyes and the lingering kindliness of his smile. There was nothing theatrical or affected about the Consul. From that moment Chateaubriand was hopeful, the more so that Fesch's rapid rise seemed to pave the way to the embassy. Archbishop of Lyons, then Cardinal, it was a high destiny for an ex-seminarist who, during the Revolution, had been store-keeper to the army of the Alps, had made his fortune by selling the booty looted from Italy, and shone rather by the strength of his ambition than the austerity of his morals. Doubtless the Vatican considered that the return of France to the bosom of the Church was worth a biretta. Like all men of lively imagination, Chateaubriand was a person of eager longings and as swift discouragement. When the expected nomination delayed, he began speaking of retiring to the country or to the banks of the Mississippi.

To Chênedollé: "If my request is not granted within a month, I shall throw up the sponge and God knows what will befall me unless I can make a success of vegetating." *To Mme. de Staël:* "There is nothing here but jobbery, cabal, party-spirit and faction. The only honourable things left are quiet and obscurity. I am hesitating between complete seclusion in the depths of the country and re-emigration."

Whatever his longing for quiet and obscurity, he did his best to escape them. One among the steps he took was sending his book to the Pope: "If Your Holiness will deign to glance at the fourth volume, he will see how I have striven to avenge the Church's altars and her ministers on an injurious and false philosophy. He will see my reverence for the Holy See and for the spirit of the Pontiffs who have sat in the chair of Peter." Yet no definite pledges came either from Paris or Rome and Mme. de Beaumont grieved: "Our friend is in a state of uncertainty. His future is more problematic than ever and everything is sadly in the air."

To beguile the time he gadded from country-house to country-house. The old French nobility lionised the author of *Le Génie du Christianisme* and, since the Consul tarried in giving him what he wanted, his monarchism took a fresh fillip. Among the women whom he often met at that time, the most eager to please him was Mme. de Custine. Née Delphine de Sabran, she had been christened by her mother's lover, the famous Chevalier de Boufflers, "The Queen of Roses," by reason of the fair delicacy of her complexion. Married at sixteen to the Comte de Custine, she had led, throughout the period of the Revolution, the most romantic of existences. In the presence of the Revolutionary Tribunal she had made a heroic defence of her father-in-law, Général de Custine. Her husband had gone to the guillotine, after writing her this fine phrase: "Why should I fear? To die is as necessary and as easy as to be born." Widowed at twenty-three, she had vainly endeavoured to leave France, but had been imprisoned in the Carmes, in the same cell as Joséphine de Beauharnais. There, "to Joséphine's certain knowledge," she had become the mistress of Alexandre de Beauharnais. Later, she had loved Boissy d'Anglas, Antoine de Lévis, M. de Grouchy, General Miranda and M. Berstoecher, the Swiss tutor of her son Adolphe, for she was a tender-hearted and generous person. The Queen of Roses complexion which, despite her joys and sorrows, was still unfaded at thirty-three, her long, silky hair, a sensuality which always made her the slave of the beloved and an odd shyness which made her dread society more than the scaffold made her singularly attractive to men. "She disliked society," said her son, "it intimidated, bored and irked her." Even Fouché, to whom Joséphine de Beauharnais had introduced her, had been captivated and, after Thermidor, it was he who had helped the lady to recover part of her possessions. She called him "Chéché" and the dreaded Minister of Police ended his letters to her with the naïve and impudent formula: "Love and kisses."

Delphine de Custine had been one of the fair admirers who wrote to Chauteaubriand on the appearance of *Atala*. She met him again at Mme. de Rosambo's at the time of *Le Génie du Christianisme*. He was ardent—she was yielding. Though a royalist at heart, she could be useful to him with those in authority, a consideration that he was not the man to overlook. His association with Mme. de Beaumont was known to her and lent him the added attraction of a man to be torn from a rival. It would seem that it was not till the early months of 1803 that their relations became wholly intimate, but that even towards the end of 1802 Mme. de Beaumont saw that her lover was leaving her. "The poor Swallow," she wrote to Joubert, "is in a sad state of numbness."

The poor Swallow would have been sadder yet had she known that when Chateaubriand left her in October 1802 for a journey in the Midi, he intended to return by way of Brittany. The avowed reason for his going was the seizure of a "pirated" edition of *Le Génie du Christianisme*, which had been published by a bookseller in Avignon. Yet Chateaubriand told Chênedollé, who had gone back to Vire, that he would go and see him ere long, beseeching him to say nothing in the Rue-Neuve-du-Luxembourg. This was because he proposed to go, not to Vire only, but to Fougères to meet Mme. de Chateaubriand. Why this visit to a deserted wife? There are several possible explanations. Céleste had been ruined by an uncle's bankruptcy and some provision had to be made for her. A candidate for a post at the Vatican must live, outwardly at least, a decorous life. It was to be hoped that Mme. de Chateaubriand, who had been hostile to her husband's first work, would be appeased by the title of the new, even if she had not read it. In any case a meeting would be useful for making sure that she should not become a stumbling-block at the crucial moment.

Hence Avignon, Lyons, Bordeaux, Nantes and Fougères—a circuit of six hundred leagues. All went well in the matter of seizing the pirated edition. At Lyons he got to know the bookseller Ballanche's son, a sickly and gifted youth who had written an odd book on feeling in literature and who was to become a life-long friend. He was chiefly astonished at his own renown. *To Fontanes:* "I must say I am overwhelmed by the reception with which I have met wherever I went. All Lyons is ringing with my fame—the newspapers, the societies, the prefectures. . . . My visit is heralded as that of a person of importance." After that, need it be said that he enjoyed himself at Lyons. "It is, I think, the town I love best in the world." He spent a whole week in Fougères with the Marignys. He saw his wife, apologised for being as yet unable, for lack of money, to invite her to Paris, and suggested that she should join him in Rome, in the event of his being appointed. It was an invitation which he also conveyed to Mme. de Beaumont, Mme. de Custine, Mme. de Marigny and even to poor Chênedollé.

The year 1803 opened without the appointment having been made and, as always happened when the external world betrayed him, Chateaubriand dreamed of escaping on another voyage. "I am swithering between a thousand plans. There is no desert solitude that I have not considered. Sometimes I want to set sail for Louisiana and see the forests of the New World once more, sometimes I think of Russia. Oh! could one but waft all that one loves to some unknown corner of the world and there, in some agreeable retreat, found a little colony of friends!" It was not merely by chance that he mentioned Russia as a possible refuge. Thanks to Mme. de Krüdener, whom he had met in Paris, his name was known at court and beautifully-bound copies of the *Génie* had been sent to "The Emperor and Empress of all the Russias."

In March there came out a new edition and, on this occasion, the author threw himself at Bonaparte's head in a dedication which was "short, simple and lofty, as befits one addressed to a hero." "Citizen First Consul, you have graciously taken under your protection this edition of *Le Génie du Christianisme*. It is a fresh token of your favour towards the august cause which is triumphing in the shelter of your power. None can fail to see in your destiny the hand of that Providence which marked you from the first for the accomplishment of its vast designs. The eyes of the nations are upon you; France, grown great through your victories, has set her hopes on you, inasmuch as it is on religion that you have grounded the foundations of the State and of your own fortunes. Continue to stretch forth a helping hand to thirty million Christians who pray for you at the foot of the altars which you yourself have restored to them."

Well-content, the Citizen First Consul was gracious enough to say that "he had never been better praised." Fontanes slightly increased the pressure on Talleyrand, who had to shew him consideration, having entrusted him with a highly compromising mission to the princes at the time of the 18th of Brumaire, and on May 4th, 1803 Chateaubriand was appointed Secretary to the Rome Legation. "I came to politics by way of religion. It was *Le Génie du Christianisme* which opened the doors." In London, Peltier was so unkind as to recall, in his paper, the fact that the dedication of the first edition to Louis XVIII had been worth a gratuity of three

Le Génie du Christianisme

hundred livres to Chateaubriand, while that of the second edition to Bonaparte had earned him a post with an income of fifteen thousand francs. *Chateaubriand to Fontanes:* "My very good Friend. Tell the best of women and noblest of patrons that my heart is brimming with undying gratitude and that I feel for her the reverent love we give angels. . . . Assure the Family that there is nothing it may not ask of me, so long as it accord with my honour."

The note that he had sent to the *Mercure* was curious: "We have it on good authority that M. de Chateaubriand is determined to publish nothing for some long time. We are inclined to encourage him in his resolution, for we are convinced that it is not by adding volume to volume that fame is increased. Besides, when a man has raised such a monument as M. de Chateaubriand has done in *Le Génie du Christianisme*, he has a right to rest." The attitude was high and mighty. The Vicomte de Chateaubriand had deigned to embrace the career of letters for the fulfilment of a great political and religious mission. His task accomplished, he left others to reap the fields that he had sown and dedicated himself thenceforward to matters of State.

His rejoicings at the appointment were tinged with melancholy, for he had to leave Mme. de Beaumont and, worse still, Mme. de Custine, whom he loved with all the freshness of novelty. How could such a thing happen when he was himself the only love of a woman as tender, as matchless and as fragile as Pauline de Beaumont? He had been cut off for so long from the delight of pleasing that he seemed incapable of resisting sweet temptations. He let his life shape its own pattern—his feelings chimed with his desires and partook of their fugitive and intermittent character. There was nothing ill-natured about him—indeed, when the sight of suffering struck him directly, he gave proof of great depths of goodness, yet he did infinite harm through his indifference and his incapacity for entering into the feelings of others. As Joubert said: "He never even passed judgment on his infidelities, for he pitted against the error of his ways his essential feelings, which were good." Occasionally the whim took him to make sacrifices for those who loved him, "but that is too contrary to his nature," said Mme. de Boigne, "for it to last long." Always allowing for that nature, he was pleasant and easy to get on with. "Save that he shattered your life, he was prepared to make it a sweet one." *To Mme. de Custine.* "You cannot imagine what I have lived through since yesterday—they wanted me to leave today. I vow I'm half crazy and think I shall end by sending in my resignation. The thought of leaving you is killing me. . . . It is five o'clock in the morning and I am alone in my cell. My window is open to the dewy freshness of the gardens and I can see the first golden flush of sunrise over the place where you live. I do not believe I shall see you today and my heart is heavy. It is all rather like a novel, but have not novels their charm? And is not all life a tale of sadness?"—"Yet another day in which I shall not see you. You will paint, make much of Trim and forget that there are people in the world who love you. How are you this morning? My cell is very cheerless. . . . But a holy vision which has appeared to me in my abode makes parting unbearable." It is hard to believe that the word "holy" is an apt description of what the apparition of one so kind as Delphine de Custine in the room of an ardent young man, head over heels in love, must have meant.

There remained to secure an advance from the Minister for Foreign Affairs before he could set out. Fontanes was given the responsibility: "The Cardinal has said that I may have six months' salary in advance. That is six thousand francs—plus expenses for the journey. Try to make Talleyrand generous." Fontanes extracted nine thousand francs from the Minister. Chateaubriand was off at last, shedding, in all sincerity, a few tears over Mme. de Beaumont, over Mme. de Custine and over himself, for he was in love and a man of sensibility, but he was also gazing, with all his eyes, at the lovely landscapes of the valley of the Yonne, for he loved nature and life.

5. Comedies

At Lyons he made the acquaintance of "his" Cardinal and had no doubt of having made a conquest. "I'm on the best possible terms with the Cardinal." He then preceded his superior to Italy and got in touch with the old legation before even the ambassador arrived. The legation consisted of the Minister, Cacault, who described himself as a "reformed Revolutionary"—a seasoned old diplomat, canny, astute, well in with the Pope and the Cardinal Secretary of

State, Consalvi, and the Secretary, Artaud, both of whom were strongly prejudiced against the amateur theologian who was coming to replace them. Chateaubriand could be charming when he pleased; his naturalness disarmed them and they were touched by his admiration for Rome. They were amazed to find him so likable and Cacault sent Talleyrand a word of reassurance: "Citizen Minister, Citizen Chateaubriand has arrived and seems to me a sound man, very interesting and incapable of laying down the law here. He will grow to like the work of the Legation, so all is well."

Citizen Chateaubriand himself was in the seventh heaven: "Everything goes right," he wrote to Fontanes. "Here am I installed in the house of M. Cacault, who treats me as his son. He is a Breton. Moreover, my job is delightful: nothing to do, master of Rome, I'm spoiled, belauded and made much of. The only thing I'm going to miss is money. I must have a carriage. My predecessor had one and it is customary. I shall spend the proceeds of my fourth edition on one, after which I shall have recourse to our patroness."

"Master of Rome"—he rather forgot that he was not the ambassador and, without waiting for the Cardinal, sought a personal audience of the Pope. The welcome he was given enraptured him. Pius VII, "the Pope of Sorrows," was pale, dignified and sad. He clasped the Secretary's hand, called him "My dear Chateaubriand," "shewed him his book open on the table" (as he wrote to Joubert) and "quoted the page he was reading" (as he wrote to Fontanes). It was all intoxicating and Mme. de Beaumont grew a little anxious over his letters to her. "It is a kind of delirium," she said. The coming of the Cardinal changed nothing: "I like the Cardinal very well, very well indeed." While the ambassador was settling in and paying his calls, the new secretary, with superb indifference, was going visiting likewise. Now there was in Rome a king—the King of Sardinia. Ought not the familiar of the Pope to be that of sovereigns also? Chateaubriand went to see the King of Sardinia.

There was no crime in that, but it was a mistake. The king, who had been deprived of part of his territories and was naturally embittered, had surrounded himself with political refugees and was thought to be conspiring against the new France. The Cardinal, who was under orders to walk warily in that direction, was furious when he learned what his secretary had done and the two men were soon in open conflict. There was no more question of "I like the Cardinal very much, very much indeed" as Chateaubriand had thought in the first flush of enthusiasm. He was vain, spiteful, miserly, bigoted and jealous. His secretary thought himself entitled to ask audience of the Pope directly. The Cardinal forbade it. Chateaubriand went above his head and took French pilgrims to see the Pope when they had not been presented to the ambassador. The latter banished the rebel to the attics of the palace and gave him, for sole occupation, the signing of passports. The unhappy Chateaubriand, beset by fleas, which swarmed over his white trousers, and with no other diversion than looking out of the window at the Roman washerwomen who waved to him from the houses opposite, thought himself back in his London "kennels." Before long, the government offices in Paris were reading alternate and conflicting complaints from the ambassador and the secretary.

The affair of the King of Sardinia had made a considerable stir. A secret note, on the Cardinal-uncle's avarice and on "the imprudent utterances which exposed him to public laughter," which Chateaubriand addressed direct to the First Consul, through the intermediary of his "wonderful patroness," may have interested and amused Bonaparte, but was certainly not calculated to leave him with the impression that its writer would ever become a disciplined official. "Chateaubriand," said he, "has his own ideas of liberty and independence. He could never enter into my system, as I conceive it." Bonaparte never saw cause to change his opinion and, on St. Helena, still spoke of "Chateaubriand's disloyalty in the business of the King of Sardinia." Fontanes, who was responsible for the appointment, had to bear the whole brunt of the matter, while Mme. de Beaumont, who was slowly dying, sent him notes begging that he would intervene on behalf of the culprit. "M. de Chateaubriand, who is loath to pester M. de Fontanes with his letters, has commissioned me to talk to him about an indiscretion of theirs and to beg his help in putting things right. The indiscretion lies in having paid a visit to the King of Sardinia. . . . I ask M. de Fontanes' pardon, I am so utterly exhausted as to be incapable of re-reading this scrawl." Fontanes saw Talleyrand, who received him well, and the Consul, who jumped down his throat: "Men who write," he snapped, "those who have gained any kind of literary reputation, are tempted to think that they are the centre of everything."

A long letter from Fontanes, full of administrative and worldly wisdom, went off to Rome: "Be on your guard against your heart and your habits. The open frankness of a Breton gentleman of ancient race goes for nothing at the Vatican. Cardinals in no way resemble Père Aubry. . . . I need hardly point out to you that, in our age, the Pope is rather the Vice-Consul than the Vice-God. . . . Statesmen sometimes make much of great writers, but they have little love for them. Let us link our destinies firmly with that of him on whom they all depend. In me it is not a question of policy, but of esteem and admiration." It should be remembered that the secret censorship was then functioning and that if the document were to be read by "him on whom they all depend," the blindest admiration could not hurt the author.

Fontanes' letter in no way appeased the wrath of its recipient: "All my life I shall repent of having got into this pother. . . . The briefest blunders are the best. I count on your friendship to get me out of the mire. Nay, I will go further—now that I am in it, I see that the post of Secretary to a Legation is beneath me. All my colleagues are young nobodies with no authority, men who are on the threshold while I am near the finish." Once more, as he always did when disappointed with public life, Chateaubriand returned to his dreams of a rural existence: "A hut in the neighbourhood of Paris, no matter where, on the hillside at Marly." His Parisian friends, who were not saints, were rather amused by the discomfiture of the "dear and illustrious Crow." What! Only a few weeks ago he was the "Master of Rome," more powerful than the princes of the Church, the Pope called him his "dear Chateaubriand," and now . . .

Even Joubert was growing severe. With all his virtues, he was a man. He had suffered on being supplanted with Mme. de Beaumont and how could he be as lenient towards a friend whose fame was beginning to echo as towards his shy protégé of two years ago at Savigny-sur-Orge? Joubert was incapable of running a man down, but he had ceased to be partial and his sense of justice, sharpened by his slight exasperation, was matchless in its penetration.

It was in a letter to Molé that he set himself to analyse the character of "poor Chateaubriand." He accused him first of writing for others, to impress them with sounding phrases and well-drawn images, rather than of striving to satisfy himself. "It is for their suffrage rather than his own that he is ambitious; hence it comes that his gifts will never make him happy . . ." Then Joubert marvelled at their friend's egoism. "He writes only for others and lives only for himself." Even in love, Chateaubriand never really let himself go: "Transparent as he is by nature, he is reticent by policy. He never contradicts and is always ready to make mysteries of everything. Though he is open-hearted, he not only keeps other people's secrets (as should we all) but his own. I believe that, in his whole life, he has never told them fully to a soul. Everything goes into him and nothing comes out." The great danger of such circumspection is that it deprives his friendships and even his writings of some of their charm. The friend and the author in Chateaubriand are always in the limelight, always busy in arranging a period or a pose. It is of this inability for self-expression, of this constant separation between the person and the personage that ennui is born. "An undercurrent of world-weariness, which seemed to spring from the vast abyss that yawned between himself and his thought, forever drove him in search of distractions which no activity and no companionship could give him as he would have had them, and no wealth suffice to cultivate unless, sooner or later, he learned wisdom and discretion."

The picture is dark enough, but the conclusion was less severe: "If it seems to me inevitable that such a man should commit a few follies, I do not think it possible that he should be guilty of serious errors. . . . There is, and always will be, in him a depth of childhood and innocence which render him as incapable of grave wrongs as of sustained kindness. There is one essential point—guilty or not guilty—we shall always love him. In the former case we will champion him, in the latter, console. Once that is granted let us judge him without mercy and speak of him without reserve." Clearly Joubert had no hesitation in doing so.

Le Génie du Christianisme

6. Tragedies

From the time of Chateaubriand's departure, Mme. de Beaumont had shewn herself resolved to join him in Rome. Not that she did not know him faithless: "I judge myself," said she sadly, "as a wholly indifferent person would judge me and I see my friends as they are." Yet she loved him, she knew that she was dying and she longed at least to see him once again. Nevertheless, before going to Italy, she wanted to go and take the waters at Mont-Dore. Little Guéneau de Mussy, who saw her before she left, felt that there was no hope. "Her mind, with every virtue, every grace, was like the faint flame, the shining haze that mounts from a dying pyre." The journey, which she undertook in a rattletrap conveyance, gave the finishing stroke to her exhaustion. The cure at Mont-Dore was too short to do her any good: "I am coughing less," she wrote, "but I think it is so that I may die noiselessly."

Chateaubriand was alarmed by her letters and gently reproached Joubert with having let her go alone: "The letters that our friend writes me from Mont-Dore rend my very soul. She says she feels there is no more oil in the lamp and speaks of her heart beating its last. Why was she allowed to make this journey alone?" He went to Florence to meet her, accompanied by Bertin, one of his new friends in Rome. This Bertin was a French exile, rightly suspected of royalism—Mme. de Beaumont, as everyone in Rome knew, was the daughter of one of Louis XVI's ministers. The unhappy Secretary of the Legation had compromised himself finally in the eyes of his government. It must be said to his credit that, the moment he saw how ill Mme. de Beaumont was, he had no thought but for her. He was distraught to see her so weak, for she had no longer the strength even to smile. In Rome he had taken her a house, near the Piazza di Spagna. It was very quiet and secluded, set between a garden with espaliers of orange trees and a courtyard where grew a fig tree. He never left her side. Because strong and thick coming emotions were necessary to his being, he was more capable of constancy towards a dying woman than towards one who was gay and carefree. "I love all that is dear to me with the same passion as in my earliest years. Grief is my element. It is only when I am unhappy that I really find myself." True, naught save a keen sorrow could, as summer-lightning momentarily links the dark thunder-clouds with earth, leap the yawning abyss of which Joubert spoke, the gulf which, in Chateaubriand, separated the personage from the person.

Sickness sanctified their association. The Pope sent to enquire for M. de Montmorin's daughter, the cardinals followed the example of His Holiness. Even Cardinal Fesch gave Mme. de Beaumont tokens of pity and regard such as his secretary did not expect from him. The end came with alarming rapidity. In the last lingering days of October, Chateaubriand was still trying to take his friend about Rome, but she had no more zest for anything. She seated herself in the Coliseum on a stone facing the altar, "let her gaze wander over the archways and the ruins softened by trailing briars and columbine, all saffron for the autumn, then lowered it slowly down from step to step to the arena where it came to rest upon the altar. 'Let us go,' said she, 'I'm cold.' " He took her back to her little house, where she was put to bed, never to leave it again.

She thought, at first, that she would die on All Souls' Day, November 2nd, and, seeing tears in Chateaubriand's eyes, stretched out a hand to him. "What a child you are," said she, "weren't you expecting it?" Throughout her agony, which was heroic, she never ceased to express her surprise at the strength and sincerity of her lover's grief. Because he had loved another woman, more beautiful and strong than she, she had doubted whether he really cared. She thought she was a burden to him and wished to go away so that he might be rid of her. When she saw his tears, she died anguished and content.

If, far more than ever he knew, he had brought her suffering in life, he honoured her dead. The funeral rites, at St. Louis of France, were beautiful and moving. The Cardinal, who had diplomatically absented himself, sent his livery and his carriages. The account of the ceremony and of their friend's dying moments which Chateaubriand wrote him, brought tears to Joubert's eyes. "One worships the creature as one reads and—as for her—I feel she would have given ten years of her life to be so mourned." It was Chateaubriand, too, who thought to raise a white marble monument to Mme. de Beaumont in one of the chapels of St. Louis of France.

Le Génie du Christianisme

He sold all that he had to pay at least a part and himself composed the inscription:

D. O. M.

Having seen all her family perish,
Her father, her mother, her two brothers and her sister,

PAULINE DE MONTMORIN

consumed by a lingering sickness
came here to die in a strange land.
F. A. de Chateaubriand has raised this monument
to her memory.

In common with many great voluptuaries, he could speak nobly of death and the tomb. He excelled in casting over a woman's light and crumbling dust the lofty pall of solemn language. The worst of which he could be accused was that his regret was fraught with pride to find it so richly arrayed. He could not check a sense of drear and aesthetic pleasure on going "from the tomb of Cecilia Metella to the bier of a woman acquainted with grief." "You would never believe," he wrote to his friends, "how my grief and my behaviour on this occasion have made me loved and respected here." We might, perhaps, love him the more if he had not been so conscious of that respect and so greedy for the pleasure of pain.

After the death of Mme. de Beaumont, he found life in Rome more irksome than ever. He could feel its tragic beauty and it was then he wrote Fontanes the wonderful letter on the Roman campagna which is one of the glories of French prose. Yet he no longer desired to stay in Italy. The strong emotions he had just gone through and a revulsion against the vanity of action had reawakened his taste for writing. It was in good faith that he told Fontanes of his longing for retreat. Already he spoke of devoting the remainder of a wretched life to compiling his memoirs. He wished them to be worthy of all that was best in him: "I will not give posterity the details of my failings. I shall say of myself only what befits my dignity as a man and, I venture to say, the loftiness of my heart. Only what is well and fair should be offered to the world; it is not lying to God to disclose only so much of our lives as may breed noble and generous sentiments in our peers. There is no lack of example when we would master our poor human nature. There is but one point on which I am hesitating, that is to say whether I shall go and bury myself in Brittany or with Joubert, at Villeneuve."

Fontanes, the wise, besought him to wait. Had not a man to live and eat? "I know that your gifts, your name and your work will never leave you at the mercy of man's primary needs, but I can see more fame than fortune in that direction. Your culture, and your aptitudes demand a measure of expense; reputation alone is not enough to provide the necessities of life and the painful science of keeping the pot boiling overshadows all others when one would fain live carefree and independent."

Just at that moment there arose an unlooked-for opportunity of obtaining a post as leader of a diplomatic mission. The Canton du Valais had been proclaimed independent because Bonaparte wanted a military road to Piedmont. A French chargé d'affaires was therefore needed at Sion and, despite the stubborn opposition of the Cardinal-uncle who maintained that "this intriguer was likewise a bad man," the First Consul was well-disposed towards a writer whose style he admired and inclined to appoint Chateaubriand. Fontanes besought him to accept. "If I am offered the appointment," replied Chateaubriand, "I shall respect the Consul's command and the wishes of my friends. I shall go to the Pays de Vaud. But, for God's sake, deliver me from Rome quickly. It is killing me." Then came a flash of pride: "I laugh pityingly when I hear fools remark that I can do nothing but write books. Is it nothing to make a book that the public will read? It needs more order and more sound sense to put two worth-while ideas together than to sign all the passports in the universe and give a diplomatic dinner as well."

On his return to Paris he found that Fontanes had become one of the most powerful men in the government and President of the Legislative Body, with a princely train. Sancho, the realist, was making more success of things than the Knight of La Mancha. Yet the statesman was as much a man as ever and the most faithful of friends. He took Chateaubriand to see Talleyrand, who was pleasant and told him what rejoicings there were among the Catholics of the Canton du Valais. The new chargé d'affaires was not over-enthusiastic. He had found Paris in a state of turmoil and threat. The empire was imminent and the idea of a new dynasty provoked Monarchists and Jacobins alike. "Daggers were in the air." Chateaubriand knew that by rallying to Bonaparte he had incurred the blame of his former friends. He had again seen Mme. de Custine, who was as royalist as ever in spite of Fouché, and—though he had a few bones to pick with her—he thought a good deal of what she and her circle felt and said. Chateaubriand's own feelings towards the government were no more kindly than theirs, for he felt that he had not been treated with the gratitude which his adherence and his powers deserved.

Among the pieces of advice which Fontanes showered on him there was one which Mme. de Beaumont had already given him as she lay dying—it was to effect a reconciliation with his wife. It was the clear duty of the "all-but-ambassador," not to speak of the Christian and the husband. He saw the point and sent for Céleste to Paris. Husband and wife met in an unpretentious hotel in the Rue de Beaune. Mme. de Chateaubriand was thirty, she had had smallpox and had lost her one and only attraction, the freshness of her youth. Sickly, sarcastic, angular in mind and body, she had less chance than ever of winning her husband. Nevertheless, they both made their preparations for going to the Valais and Chateaubriand got Talleyrand to advance him twelve thousand francs, which he spent on buying plate and linen for the embassy. He hoped that he would not be at Sion for long and was already looking for a house in Paris.

On March 19th he was present at the reception in the Tuileries and saw the First Consul, who seemed preoccupied and did not address a word to him. On March 21st when, doubtless for the pleasure of rending his heart, he went out to feast his eyes on a cypress that Mme. de Beaumont had loved, he heard the newsboys crying: "Verdict of the special military tribunal convoked at Vincennes, pronouncing sentence of death on the so-styled Louis-Antoine-Henri de Bourbon, born August 2nd, 1772, at Chantilly." The announcement came as a thunderbolt. "That sentence changed the course of my life," said he, "as it did Napoleon's." Louis de Bourbon, Duc d'Enghien, the last of the Condés, did not deserve to be shot as a traitor in the ditches of Vincennes. He had been arrested illegally, condemned secretly and executed mercilessly. It was the first ignoble act of a government which had sought to be one of reconciliation. Chateaubriand went home, burning with indignation. He found his wife there and before long they were joined by his monarchist friend, Clausel de Coussergues. With their approval he decided to send the Consul his resignation.

To Talleyrand: "Citizen Minister, The doctors have just informed me that the state of Mme. de Chateaubriand's health is such as to arouse fears for her life. As, in the circumstances, it is utterly impossible that I should either leave my wife or expose her to the risks of a journey, I beg that Your Excellency will permit me to return the letters of credit and the instructions sent me for the Valais."

Though couched in moderate terms, this letter was in itself an act of courage when sent on the day following the execution. "For several days," says Clausel, "all Chateaubriand's friends were in perpetual dread of seeing him carried off by the police. I went to see him two or three times a day and always with the same shiver when I reached the porter's lodge." Mme. de Chateaubriand says that Fontanes was appalled on hearing of the resignation. "He was already picturing himself being shot in company with M. de Chateaubriand, and all our friends after them. I went to see him in the hope of quieting and reassuring him. It was useless. He had lost his head and ended by infecting me with his fears, not for him, but for my husband." Céleste was spiteful and, if Fontanes was indeed afraid, it was not for long, since, through the mouth of Elisa, he pleaded the cause of the friend who gave him so many and harassing anxieties. Even Talleyrand, to give the storm time to blow over, kept the letter of resignation some days before giving it to Bonaparte. When he read it, Napoleon merely said "Very well" and never referred to it again. To the eternal credit of Chateaubriand, it should be added that his courage found no imitators and that he was the only man to leave the Consul's service as a result of the assassination of the Duc d'Enghien.

Through this gesture Chateaubriand found himself thrown into the opposition. What was the inward significance of his action? Was it the Christian who could not make himself accessory to violence? Was it the royalist who could not endure a crime against

Le Génie du Christianisme

the royal family? The man who had so longed to serve Bonaparte and the author of the dedication of the *Génie* could not have been a very ardent royalist. It would be more true to say that it was the resignation itself that turned Chateaubriand into a militant monarchist. A great artist, striving to make the pattern of his life a work of art, he had struck, in his new-found loyalty to a family, an attitude which satisfied at once his craving for aesthetic unity and his feudal honour. By this letter alone "he washed away a three years' infidelity and justified, after the event, the exile he had not willed." Was it even impossible to give a coherent picture of apparently contradictory actions? Alive to the danger that would follow on cleaving the history of France in two by a blood-soaked trench, Chateaubriand had been for the Consul so long as he appeared in the guise of a liberator. Was it not natural that he should retire on the day when the Vincennes commission reopened that trench to shed the blood of a Bourbon?

Did he really regret all that he was putting behind him? He had believed that he loved action but, like all men of strong imagination, he was apt to weary ere long of a recalcitrant reality. Did he but meet the least obstacle, he took wing and soared above facts into the realm of fiction or of memory. From the outset of his battles with Cardinal Fesch he had sought a way of escape. The death of the Duc d'Enghien "gave him one that was fine and splendid, an arresting exit such as he loved." How should he have resisted the temptation of striking so brave an attitude, the excuse for such noble lamentations, when already his thoughts were set on the figure he would cut beyond the tomb?

It should be added that his resignation saved him from leaving for the mountains of the Valais with none for company but a woman with a long nose and pock-marked face.

CHAPTER V

Journey from Paris to Andalusia

1. The Lady of Fervacques

THE attitude had been struck. Confronted with the unconquerable master, Chateaubriand was thenceforth to represent the unconquered soul. Yet, among those about the Master, he had staunch supporters. Fontanes, a star of the first magnitude in the imperial constellation, remained faithful to him, and so, thanks to the same friend, did the "adorable Elisa." Fouché, sounded by Delphine de Custine, seemed by no means hostile. Though they had rallied to the Empire and hoped for honours and promotion from Bonaparte, Molé and Pasquier had not the least intention of breaking with Chateaubriand. "Under the Empire," writes Mme. de Chateaubriand, "people of contrary opinions could meet without tearing each other's eyes out, a state of affairs which became unthinkable under the Bourbons."

Chateaubriand's best champion with the Consul was, however, Bonaparte himself. A few days after the resignation he said to his sister: "Were you in very great fear for your friend?" The great reader of *Cinna* or *La Clémence d'Auguste* thus enjoyed shewing his forbearance. Not that he had more use than of old for writers who dabbled in politics: "They are," he remarked to his brother Joseph, "coquettes with whom one must flirt up to a point, but would never dream of making either one's wife or one's minister." Yet he was a man of letters and had that instinct for style which so often goes hand in hand with a genius for action. He had imitated Rousseau; he had a real feeling for Corneille; in Chateaubriand alone, among the writers of his time, he recognised "the sacred fire." If he had failed to "annex him to his system" he was not the man to persecute him.

Man must live, however, and the Chateaubriand household had now but scanty possessions. The sum which the Minister for Foreign Affairs had advanced on account of Sion had to be refunded. Sad to say, it had all gone on plate and linen. The Chateaubriands' only other resources were the royalties on *Le Génie du Christianisme* and the few government stocks remaining to them. They took a small house in a district which was then almost country, at the corner of the Rue de Miromesnil and the Rue Verte (subsequently the Rue de Penthièvre). Almost at their doors was a wheat-field where Chateaubriand, who always pined for country sounds and was all too often cut off from them, used to listen to the song of the larks, a waste land called the Butte aux Lapins and the deserted Parc Monceau, where he would go for lonely strolls among the statues and the firs, "talking to three crows about the Duc d'Enghien."

He was feeling rather depressed. His great rival in renown, whose head had been turned by "the admixture of Roman republic and Charlemagne" dropped in his ears by Fontanes and Lucien, had newly made himself emperor on May 2nd, 1804. Fontanes had amused Mme. de Chateaubriand with a comical description of the cavalcade, which he said was not unlike those which follow the Shrovetide Ox. Mounted on horseback and resplendent in knee-breeches and silk stockings, he had nevertheless been one of its most notable actors, while Chateaubriand, a slave to his sceptical loyalty, paced his little garden alone. If his solitude had been but complete, he might have found some sweetness in such lofty aloofness, but his wife was with him now and, if there was one thing on which she was determined, it was that she was not going back to Brittany.

Twelve years of peril and misfortune had strangely matured the fair-haired child of the wind-blown, pink pelisse whom Chateaubriand used to watch on the Sillon at St. Malo. Céleste de Chateaubriand had become an energetic and combative little person with a very sharp tongue. No sooner did she see him again than she grew dangerously attached to her illustrious husband, but realising that he was unfaithful to her and always would be, she accepted the situation with a mocking gaiety which hid the bitterness of her grief. Dreading what she might find there, she had taken the course, not of avoiding reading her husband's books, but of saying that she never opened them. There was to come a time when Chateaubriand himself dipped freely into Céleste's notebooks for, once he had clothed it with a few adjectives, the swift brilliance of her style could be interwoven with his own without shewing too marked a join. Taken all together, she was an original, bitter and amusing woman in whom the most hard-to-please of critics found a certain vinegarish charm, but she lacked the beauty, the sadness and the unreasonableness which might have brought Chateaubriand to love her. She teased him, goaded him and sometimes even influenced him, for, when honour was not at stake, he was still oddly docile and did his best to avoid quarrels. What it was not in her to give was the daily bread of poetry, without which he could not live. She amused him "and captivated him not." Above all—and it was her worst defect—she was his wife. "God!" he wrote to Mme. de Custine, "how little I was created for all that! What a poor captive bird I am!"

In that household, Delphine de Custine played the part of consoler. Though, in 1803, she had bought Fervacques, the beautiful castle near Lisieux which had seen the loves of Henry IV, she took a house in the Rue Verte, directly opposite the Chateaubriands'. When one is married to a woman for whom one has little love, it is agreeable to have at one's very door a Queen of Roses, pretty, shy and rather giddy-pated, who prattles engagingly of birds and flowers. Alas! the mistress's character was not much improvement on that of the wife. Chateaubriand had christened her "Princess Forlorn" since, if there were two days' silence, she was persuaded that her friends were all dead, or had gone to China, and that she would never see them more. It must be admitted that he made her wait long for his visit to Normandy, being vexed by certain of her remarks, which may have been tactless, on the matter of the loan he had requested at the time when first Mme. de Beaumont's illness, and afterwards her monument, had cost him so dear. Mme. de Custine had regarded such an appeal to his mistress, made on behalf of another woman by a heartbroken lover, as unseemly; he had pitied her failure to understand the nobility of the trust he had shewn in her. Poor Princess Forlorn felt that she was deserted by a man who, in his incurable boredom, invariably preferred the vicissitudes of courtship to the sureness of possession. Nevertheless, after a visit to Champlâtreux, where he stayed with Mathieu Molé, now one of his most intimate friends, he at last set off for Fervacques in August. To that green and well-watered Norman valley he summoned the doleful Chênedollé, perhaps with intent to cut short the reproaches of the lady of the house. "I shall be at Fervacques next Monday. Do you mind my inviting a neighbour of ours, my close friend M. Chênedollé, to meet me there, for we have things to discuss? He is a wit, a poet and so forth. . . . You see how dreadfully I have given the lie to your prophecies. Heavens above! when will you learn to believe me and to have some common sense? 'I love to love you.' It was Mme. de Sévigné who said that."

It was a pleasant stay. The castle was moated and, from his window, Chateaubriand could see the meadows bordering the river. The soft-hearted Chênedollé was touched by the interest that a gentle and kindly woman was ready to shew in his sorrows. "The Enchanter" elected to sleep in the vast bed where Henry IV "had spent the night with some Florette" and doubtless thought, as the Béarnais had done in his time, that "the lady of Fervacques was worth lusty attacks." He christened her "Cross-patch"; she called him "Colo," there is no knowing why (perhaps because he called her "Colombe") and, quite often, "The Genius." It seems that she kept unforgettable memories of what befell in one of the grottos, and of a little arbour framed by two superb myrtles. His "bread-and-butter letter," on the other hand, was somewhat cavalier for a man very much in love. "I miss Fervacques, the carp, you, Chênedollé and even Mme. Auguste. If only I could come back to it all in October as I long to do. Are you as eager to see me again? If so, try to have the billiard-table levelled, the weeds pulled up so that we may see the pike, the gamekeepers told to bid our neighbour of Vire and her of Caen to a meeting, to have the calves fatted and the hens instructed to lay fresher and less brown eggs. When all is done, let me know and I will see if it is possible to get to Fervacques for fifteen twenty-franc pieces." The wit in these letters serves well enough for hiding the cracks in the feeling.

On his return from Fervacques, he set off for Burgundy to stay with the Jouberts, who had adopted Mme. de Chateaubriand. They liked her sense of fun and her patience and, when her too seductive husband left her to run after some faithless lady or other, they admired her longsuffering. In their house, Chateaubriand was lodged in the green room where Pauline de Beaumont used to sleep and sometimes he dreamed of the Swallow. Joubert, who had gastric trouble, or thought so, was now living entirely on liquid food, but he none the less enjoyed the good spirits of his visitors. "His wife and he seemed to be really in their element here. . . . I wish you could see him to judge of what matchless goodness, of what perfect innocence, of what simplicity of life and manners and, amidst it all, of what inexhaustible gaiety, of what peace and of what happiness he is capable when there are no influences about him but the seasons, and none to rouse him but himself."

Joubert's young brother, who was then living at Villeneuve, also was surprised to see how charming and natural Chateaubriand could be when friendliness set him free from the constraint of vanity. "I shall never forget how happy we were during the six weeks spent in the company of such guests. We worked all morning, and after dinner indulged in all the madcap sports inspired by the gaiety of another age amid the hills which alternate with laughing meadows about Villeneuve-le-Roi. A sage and serious person, who knew M. de Chateaubriand only through his books, would have been amazed to see the author of *Le Génie du Christianisme* and the singer of *Atala* lend himself, with perfect freedom and good-humour, to almost childish games, but he would have ended by saying: 'This man of genius must be the best of fellows. . . .'" The fact was that, in the presence of Joubert and Céleste, Chateaubriand thought all poses useless and dropped the mask of René, for he realised that they had read him through and through, yet loved him none the less.

Two painful dates, however, were drawing near—Mme. de Beaumont's "year's end" (November 4th) and the moment of the Emperor's crowning. "I leave for Paris a week today. I shall stay a fortnight and then come back to Villeneuve for November 4th, a memorable day in Joubert's life and my own. My wife will await me here. We shall return to Paris only towards the end of December when all these celebrations, which for me are occasions of mourning, are over. . . . I am thinking of complete retirement. My thirty-fifth year has just struck (the 4th of this month) on that clock which never tolls the same hour twice. It is borne in upon me that I have, at the most, only a like number of years to languish in this world, that they are quickly sped and that all my present afflictions will be as nothing to me at the ending of the play."

In point of fact, it was not to Paris that he was going to spend the last fortnight of October, but to Fervacques, in response to a fretful summons from the Queen of Roses. Women never will understand how often reproaches and lamentations have wearied lovers who, left in peace, would gently have accustomed themselves to the comfortable tedium of fidelity. This time, however, the bread-and-butter letter which reached the eternal scold was most winning: "It was a great grief to me to leave your castle of owls. I should be sorry to see it very often, for I feel that I should grow more attached to it than I ought. Try to leave at once and return to the land of the living. Remember that you will be my neighbour and that you can see me as often as you wish. . . . Yours, while life lasts . . ."

Thereupon he returned to edify the Jouberts by his goodness and sweet-temper, but hardly was he arrived at Villeneuve than there reached him the terrible news that Lucile was dead.

2. Death of Lucile

Here, from various moments in the past, we must pick up the scattered threads of Lucile's story and weave a more closely-knit tale. It was the opinion of many of the men who came near her, her illustrious brother in particular, that Lucile had genius. It would seem that the beauty of her eyes and the "heavenly fire" of her expression beguiled their literary judgment, for what neo-classical work of hers has come down to us is ingenuous and commonplace. Still, her letters are beautiful, for she had strong imagination and a heart so burning that, in the end, it consumed her reason. As a child, she had believed herself persecuted by her parents; later, at Fougères, she mistrusted her sisters; though at first passionately devoted to her sister-in-law Céleste, the latter eventually inspired her with fear and, she imagined, hate. Thus she headed straight for that loneliness of the spirit which, when it grows complete, is madness.

Her life had been a strange one, and wasted. Though she longed to take the veil, she had—during the Revolution—consented to marriage with an old man, for she thought there was no danger of its being consummated. A few days later she had to flee from her husband's roof. Then came her widowhood. At the time of her brother's return she attached herself to Mme. de Beaumont, as much from real admiration as from a reaction against Céleste. Among the little society of the Rue Neuve-du-Luxembourg she had met Chênedollé and the sadness of the Crow of Vire touched the recluse of Fougères. She found in him what her brother had once meant to her at Combourg, a being on whom she was all-powerful and one who shared her taste for dejected and sentimental poetry. Yet Chênedollé, because he was a lesser poet, "lived" what Chateaubriand transmuted into literature. His retreats were real and his tears authentic. "Unperceived, there grew in him a secret worship for this sorrowful and fine-strung soul" and he asked Lucile to marry him. She refused, but promised never to marry another. It was one of those gently destructive pastimes in which she delighted: "There is a charm for me in my pledge never to marry, for I think of it as a bond, as being somehow a way of belonging to you." In his eagerness, Chênedollé had pursued her to the castle of Lascardais, where she was staying with her sister Bénigne de Chateaubourg, a managing woman. Lucile had gone to meet her friend at Fougères and, as they returned in the carriage, said beautiful and sad things about the consolations of Nature. Driving up the avenue of oaks, he pleaded with her again. "I will not say no," she murmured. Wild with joy at her half-promise he took his leave and on his return to Vire wrote: "I am persuaded that you are the only woman whose feelings are in harmony with mine and with whom I can find my everlasting rest. Write to me then and say that you still love me a little." There was no reply to his letter. Worried and heartbroken he waited a month and then wrote to Mme. de Chateaubourg, who replied in a courteous but frosty letter that her sister had gone to Rennes, adding: "I am wholly ignorant of the reasons for my sister's silence with regard to you. Perhaps what seems to you inexplicable may have a very simple and natural cause."

There was indeed a cause, but it was neither simple nor natural. Lucile's family, and afterwards herself, had learned without a shadow of doubt that Chênedollé—the loving, wise and doleful Chênedollé—was already married. While an exile in Hamburg in 1796, in the course of a grave illness he had married Mlle. Marie-Victoire Bourguignon, the daughter of a Liège printer. A Catholic priest had performed the ceremony. In 1797, when his wife was with child, Chênedollé decided that their temperaments were wholly incompatible and deserted her. On his return to Vire he had confessed to his father that he was married. The latter, an old Norman lawyer, skilled in pressing texts into the service of his interests, had declared that a union contracted in exile was null and void, since émigrés were dead in the eyes of the law. These ingenious grounds for nullity were accepted by the son, who was struggling to forget an unhappy marriage, but his false position was partly responsible for his hopeless gloom. Less honest than Chateaubriand had been with Charlotte Ives, he had sought to make Lucile the second wife of a bigamist. When she learnt the truth, she had fled—wounded to the quick.

He sped to Rennes. "The despairing and passionate things I said to her and the reproachful tenderness of her replies were such as may not be expressed." She ended by being kind and treating him with a sad and forgiving gentleness, but told him that she could never be his. When he found himself out in the street and the rain, it struck him that he had just seen her for the last time and there seized on him a fierce anguish. She, on her side, seemed to have been wounded to death. None was left to her now but her brother and Mme. de Beaumont: "In the thought of you," she wrote to them, "I found refuge from my weariness and grief of heart. My only occupation was to love you." Then Mme. de Beaumont herself disappeared and Lucile saw, with dread, the reconciliation of the two Chateaubriands.

She was ailing, she was nervously exhausted, she had sold her last farm to her Chateaubourg nephews and had now no possessions. Chateaubriand sent for her to Paris and installed her in a convent, giving Saint-German (Mme. de Beaumont's old servant) the delicate task of looking after her, of paying her bills and deceiving her on the price of things in order to quiet her scruples. There, in her loneliness, Lucile lived only for her brother, reading his letters over and over again and recalling their childhood. "God cannot make me suffer save through you. I thank Him for the precious, dear and good gift that He has granted me in your person and that He has preserved my life without stain. Those are all my treasures. I might take as the emblem of my life a cloud-barred moon, with this device: 'Often darkened but never tarnished.'" (This seems a sad and far-off disavowal of the aberrations of René). "Good morning, my dear. What colour are your thoughts this morning? . . . There is nothing like the thought of death for ridding us of the future. . . . Since yesterday I am rather pleased with my courage. I pay no heed to my grief or to the kind of inward weakness that has come upon me. I have forsaken myself. Do not fail to deal lovingly with me always. It would be an act of charity nowadays."

Her hallucinations presaged madness: "My Dear, There are a thousand conflicting ideas in my head of things which seem to exist and not to exist, which give me the impression of objects seen in a glass and of which one cannot therefore be sure, distinctly as one sees them. I don't want to bother about such things any more. From now on I give myself up." Only her brother's visits quieted her somewhat. "You spoke," she wrote to him, "and all my inward being grew ordered once more." Seeing how ill she was, he suggested that she should come and live with him at Villeneuve, with the Jouberts, but a presentiment of Céleste's wrath may have lent hesitancy to his invitation, for the perpetual martyr was conscious of his embarrassment: "My dear brother, do not weary yourself either with my letters or with my presence, when you will soon be forever delivered from my importunities. My life is flickering to its close. Remember that we have often been nursed on the same lap and lain on the same breast, that you wept for my tears, that—from the earliest days of your life—you have watched over and protected my frail existence, that we played together and that I shared your first lessons. I will not speak of our youth, of the innocence of our thoughts and joys and of our mutual longing to be always together. Yesterday, when you spoke of going to stay with you, you seemed grave and anxious though your words were affectionate. What! my dear, shall I cause you trials and estrangement? If you have changed your mind, why not have said so frankly? I lack courage to face your courtesies."

The last visits were painful. She had a slight convulsive twitching of the lips and was making visible efforts to gather her thoughts together. She spoke of various little things on which she wanted to begin working again; then Chateaubriand left for Villeneuve. A few days later a note from old Saint-Germain broke the news that Lucile had died on November 10th, having left the convent for a boarding-house on the evening before. "A terrifying thought had struck me," said Chênedollé when he heard the news, "I fear that she may have attempted her own life. Great God! Grant that it may not be so!" It seems likely, on the contrary, that it was so, for not a single church in Paris has any record of a religious funeral and only suicide can explain why Chateaubriand did not even return from Villeneuve, why Lucile left the Augustinian convent on the eve of her death, why she was buried in the common grave and why Mme. de Marigny, who had "paid the last tributes of respect" to her younger sister, did not follow the bier.

To Chênedollé, Chateaubriand wrote: "We have lost the fairest soul and the most lofty spirit that ever lived." And he added— for even in his deepest griefs he could not stop thinking of himself as the centre of the universe and the favourite butt of destiny: "You see that I was born to all sorrows." There followed a painful business correspondence with his sisters, for they refused to accept the estate save on condition that they were not liable for debts beyond the assets descended. At the time of her brother's emigration, Lucile had stood his security for ten thousand francs and they feared that the responsibility might devolve on them. As for Mme. de Chateaubriand, he tells us that "still smarting from Lucile's imperious whims, she saw in her death only a happy release for a Christian gone to her rest in the Lord. . . . But I cannot enter," he concluded, "into the consolations of Mme. de Chateaubriand."

From the month that followed, the guests of Villeneuve had other cause for sorrow and anger so that they forgot the tragic death of Lucile. Céleste fumed to see the Pope come running, like a private chaplain, to his master's call. "Pius VII's speech proclaiming that he would anoint Bonaparte is incredible," said she. He calls him "this powerful prince," "Our good and well-beloved son." In Paris, on the way from the Tuileries to Notre Dame, the cheering had been enthusiastic and almost unanimous. "All the former royalists of the little society," said Céleste ironically, "Molé, Pasquier and the rest swore fealty, one after the other, to all the powers present and to come." During Pius VII's residence in Paris, Chateaubriand neither sought audience nor reminded the Pontiff of those in Rome. "He bowed respectfully," he said, "before the gracious condescension of the Church towards the Empire, remembering that in the fifth century the Pope, St. Gregory the Great, had hallowed with his praises Phocas, the bloody successor of the emperor Maurice." Yet he prophesied to Fontanes that "a day might come when the mouth of the anointing Pope would pronounce the anathema." On a planet where all things die or draw to their end, how could Cassandra be deceived?

In January 1805, when the last of the coronation celebrations were over, Chateaubriand felt he could return to Paris, see his dear "Cross-patch" once more and send an invitation to poor Chênedollé, against whom he bore no resentment, although his was a hanging matter: "I am expecting you. Your bed is ready . . . We will muse on the past and groan over the future. If you are sad, I warn you that I have never been in darker depths. We shall be like two Cerberuses barking at the human race." It was one of the many moments in his life when only an escape into a world of his own creation could console him for a momentary setback.

3. TAEDET ANIMAM MEAM VITAE MEAE . . .

To Mme. de Custine. "So you are very sad! Why? Because your birds are dead? Well! What is there that does not die? Because your blackbirds are flown? You know that all things are fleeting, beginning with our days. This seems rather like poetry and I am obviously scribbling. I will bring you the first two volumes of certain *Martyrs de Dioclétien*. You haven't an inkling of what they are to be about. There is a young pagan girl, such as are to be found everywhere. There is a young man, once very corrupt and now very Christian who converts the young woman. The Devil takes a hand and, in the end, everyone is roasted by the worthy philosophers of the Age of Diocletian, always full of humanity."

This delightful letter is dated June 18th, 1804. From then on, all through the dramatic winter of 1805, he worked at *Les Martyrs de Dioclétien*. The idea had come to him in Rome. Having maintained, in *Le Génie du Christianisme* that the Christian religion was more favourable than paganism to the play of epic passions and that the wonders of Christianity could hold their own with those of mythology, he thought that the most natural demonstration of his argument would be to add example to theory in his work. There was no difficulty about the note to be struck. A great reader of Genesis and Homer and the translator of Milton, he set those sublime examples before him. There needed to find a subject which allowed of a historical parallel between the two religions, and the age of Diocletian exactly met the case. The study of manners and customs? That was a question of learning and just the kind of work he liked. "When you are devoured by imagination there is nothing like turning it onto dusty tomes and the interpretation of tongues."

He had still to invent a plot and heroes. In creating characters, Chateaubriand rarely went outside himself. For Eudore, "the young man once very corrupt and now very Christian," he made use of the recollections of his youth; for Cymodocée, "the young pagan girl," of the Protestant, Charlotte Ives. As for pagan philosophers, he had suffered enough at their hands in the time of the *Génie* to take a savage delight in portraying them. During his peaceful stay at Villeneuve he had written a fragment of *Les Martyrs* in which the scene was laid in heaven, for never were place and theme better accorded. The following volume brought him to a description of the court of Diocletian and the conduct of the Empire. There could have been no better opportunity for saying, in discreetly transparent terms, some good of Napoleon, a great deal of good of the Christians about him, and a great deal of ill of the sophists "who preached republicanism in the bosom of the monarchy." In short, the struggle between Fontanes' neo-Christian party and the survivors of the Revolution was transmuted, in *Les Martyrs*, into a drama of the third century.

It was then the fashion among the monarchists to seek apologies and examples in ancient histories. "Tacitus is everywhere the rage and, so it is said, ladies do not find him too strong meat." Chateaubriand found encouragement for his scheme among all the pretty women of the loyalist nobility. His resignation had made him the hero of right-thinking drawing-rooms. No sooner did he return to Paris at the beginning of 1805 than the great country-houses began fighting over him. Delphine de Custine was the first to have the benefit of his near neighbourhood in the meadows of the Plaine Monceau. "Since my arrival here not a day has passed without his coming to see me. He is not yet all that I would have him, but he is improved. I am not happy, but I am a little less unhappy." Alas! ere long the house in the Rue de Miromesnil was sold and the Chateaubriands gone to live in the Place Louis XV in the attics of the Hôtel de Coislin. Mme. de Laborde had again invited them to Méréville and Molé to Champlâtreux, while Mme. de Custine renewed her lamentations in her letters to her confidant Chênedollé: "Our friend says that he will spend six weeks at Fervacques, but I am not the woman to be cozened. I am crazier than ever and more unhappy than I can tell you. The Genius is glad to see you once more. He shares in all your sorrows and, when he speaks of you, one could almost believe that his heart is in the right place." Was she indeed unaware that it is easier to have one's heart in the right place in friendship than in love?

To Chênedollé: "The one thing certain is Colo's grumpiness. To my sorrow I have re-read his letters from Italy and found them kind and tender. Doesn't he love me any more? Or less? No, he does not love me at all!"

Nevertheless, in July the Genius did go to Fervacques, while Mme. de Chateaubriand kept old Mme. de Coislin company at Vichy. Unfortunately, once two people begin bickering there is no help. The visit was one long succession of scenes. Mme. de Custine seized a gun and "narrowly missed sending a bullet through her heart." It was long before anyone dared tell her that Chateaubriand was proposing to rejoin his wife at Vichy and make a trip to Switzerland *with her*! The idea was almost unbelievable. A friend of Delphine's, the Duchesse d'Arenberg, tried in vain to preach counsel. "This journey to Switzerland is not only useful, but vital. . . . Paris is his death-trap. I would gladly banish him from it for some years; the most I should allow him would be a few months at Fervacques, the rest of the time I should like to send him to the Swiss mountains or the American deserts. You see that I love him neither on my own account nor on his, but solely for his renown to come! My soul is all Roman in its feeling for him. I want him to live for posterity even more than for his friends. Whether he will be grateful to me for such heroism I do not know, but if there is one thing sure, my dear Delphine, it is that you will not share it."

No, Delphine de Custine in no wise shared that renunciation. She lamented having been bewitched, abandoned herself to "that sadness which encompasses all thought" and "would have liked to murder sleep lest she should no longer think of her love." To all this the wise Mme. d'Arenberg replied: "Delphine, my dear, how that sentence hurt me. There is such an intensity of passion in your letter that I tremble for you. I would not have you do other than love him, but I would fain see you his friend. Love him a little less, so that you may love and be loved by him always. He has given us the clue to his character in his books. Make the most of it, my dear Delphine, to temper your emotions." It is always easy to temper emotions one does not feel. Chênedollé, who had become the indispensable *tertium quid* in all this coil, was summoned to Fervacques, where he came with his heart on his sleeve, to suffer through his dead love for Lucile and his newborn love for Mme. de Custine. She shewed him the grotto and the little arbour with its two superb myrtles. "So it was there," said Chênedollé, "that he was at your feet?" "It was perhaps I who was at his."

In August 1805 Chateaubriand could at last go to Vichy for his wife, thence to Lyons to see his friend, the faithful Ballanche, thence to Geneva, where he had a whirlwind visit from Mme. de Staël and finally to the Mer de Glace and the Grande Chartreuse, where they all but lost their lives in a storm—Mme. de Chateaubriand scampering through the torrents while her husband, "who could not see that there was the slightest danger," said there was no cause for alarm. It was an idle journey. Mont Blanc disappointed him: "I have come home ill-pleased with the mountains. I do not like the sense that my frail being is crushed between those heavy masses. Mountains are only beautiful as a horizon. . . . Their fate is that of all greatness; they should be seen only from afar." Why the devil should he have wanted to see them nearer? To bestir himself, to be up and doing, to fill that weary inner emptiness of his. In that year, when the Other was going from victory to victory, Chateaubriand was meditating on his life with the utmost gloom: *"Taedet animam meam vitae meae. . . ."* The short conjugal journey did nothing to cure him of his disrelish.

He found himself reflected all too strongly in *Les Martyrs*: "Poor Eudore laments his failings so gently that he has only rooted me the deeper in my own. I cannot speak authentically of those demons whom the angels have set on earth without everywhere giving away the secrets of my inmost heart." He would have liked to see his beloved Italy once more and to go to Greece and Palestine to seek colours for *Les Martyrs*, as he had once sought those of the *Natchez* in America. To do that there was needed money and, as he had none, he could only wander from Fervacques to Méréville. It must be admitted that there was a great charm about Méréville, not only by reason of its studiously wild and beautiful park, designed for the financier Laborde by Hubert Robert, a past-master in artificial grottos and ruins shrouded in weeping-willows or topped by poplars, but by reason of the young women and girls who enlivened its gardens with their grace and wit.

Among these young women there was one who found especial favour in Chateaubriand's sight. This was M. de Laborde's daughter, the Countesse Charles de Noailles, afterwards Duchesse de Mouchy. She had a charming face, framed in curls, great eyes that spoke a childish sadness, a dazzlingly white throat and the prettiest frocks in the world. A famous portrait depicts her as a huntress with a little gun on her shoulder, a man's hat planted on her lovely hair, pleasingly dressed in a greatcoat with fur collar and cuffs—the masculinity of the costume relieved by an embroidered front. Like Mme. de Beaumont and Mme. de Custine, she was one of those women whom ill-fate had clothed with poetry, with daring and secret despair.

She had been married at fifteen to the elder son of the Prince de Poix, Count Charles de Noailles. At the beginning of the Revolution her husband had emigrated. She had seen her father mount the scaffold and had herself been imprisoned throughout the Terror. When the 9th of Thermidor set her free, her one thought had been to rejoin her husband in England, for at that time she loved him passionately. On her arrival she found him harnessed to the chariot wheels of an aged mistress of the Prince of Wales. To be rid of her, he sent her to live in the country, in Norfolk, and charged one of his friends, Vintimille, to pay her court. As she resisted, Vintimille confessed to being sent by her husband and the shock, coming on top of a trying journey, sent Natalie de Noailles half crazy.

Thereafter she had not lacked for consolations. "Coming back to Paris at the time of the saturnalia of the Directory," says Mme. de Boigne, "she took all too active a part." Vintimille, by a just revenge of feeling, had fallen madly in love with her and she treated him not a little harshly. At the time when Chateaubriand met her, she was witchery itself. "She was Armida," writes Molé. "Her grace outrivalled even her beauty. Whether she spoke or sang the charm of her voice was irresistible. . . . Gifted with a phenomenal memory for learning everything, she had even more promise than she had talent. Adapting herself at will to the character of the person she wished to attract, she borrowed every form and took on every tone. With my eighteen-year-old self she had the candour and the ingenuousness of my years, with the Comte de Melzi she had the wit, the brilliance and the yielding softness of Aspasia, while with the blind classical scholar Portalis she construed Virgil. . . . Chateaubriand she liked to bewilder by out-adventuring his taste for adventure and by the inexpressible riot of her imagination. Her coquetry was almost a mania. She could not endure that a man's eyes should rest on her indifferently. More than once, at table, I have caught her anxiously scanning the faces of the waiting servants to see what impression she was making on them."

It was at Fervacques that she met Chateaubriand for the first time and it was poor Delphine de Custine herself who rashly introduced them. Among the men who were paying her court he was far from being the most influential or the most handsome, but his books, his resignation, his legend and his love affairs assured him of an almost irresistible prestige. A young woman who saw him at Méréville about that time has described him as he was when he and Natalie de Noailles met: "M. de Chateaubriand was short and rather ill-made. . . . There was nothing amiable about his character. An undercurrent of bitter sadness lent his conversation a natural melancholy which was not without its charm." He was given good grounds for hope and the hapless Queen of Roses was thenceforward nothing but a stumbling-block in his life. She knew that her fall from favour was final when, as an excuse for not going to Fervacques, he advanced his wife's high temperature and the scenes she would make if he left her. When a faithless husband falls back on conjugal scruples, his mistress realises that she has ceased to attract. Delphine de Custine grew bitter and ironical—never a good method of holding men: "To return to Paris only to see you for a day or two, after which a thousand social obligations would involve you in a like number of calls, hardly seems to me worth while. Hence I shall stay here till December, yet I cannot but think that, when you are only just back from a journey as costly as the one you took in your wife's company, it would be an even greater folly to come here in the bad season for the sake of meeting a fortnight earlier. I hardly imagine that you are even thinking of it. You have travelled enough. Stay peacefully and maritally at Villeneuve. Spend part of the winter there even, get on with your book, build up your reputation—it is dear to you, as it should be. Let everything else slide and, as your example should inspire another, I too will do what you find so easy." That was the time when, speaking of Chateaubriand, the wise Duchesse d'Arenberg wrote to her kinswoman, Delphine: "I see that he really is not good to love."

Was it true? Was he a cruel and dangerous Don Juan? It is a fact that he made nearly every woman he loved unhappy, but was that not partly because they were unhappy before ever he met them? It is easy to accuse love of driving poor women mad; would not the sensible thing be to wonder whether it may have been madness which first drove them to love? Chateaubriand liked fickle and sensual women, perhaps because fickle and sensual women are easier of approach than the others. It should not be forgotten that, like most Don Juans of his imaginative and intellectual type, he was rather shy. He might doubtless have said with his younger disciple Byron: "I have been more ravished myself than anybody since the Trojan War."

Yet Mme. d'Arenberg was right in thinking that he was not "good to love." However sincere his devotion to a mistress, he always preferred his work. In every woman of flesh and blood he sought the imaginary woman, the Sylph who haunted his dreams, and in the successive companions of his emotions he saw only the successive incarnations of the single phantom, fashioned of his desires, that he bore within himself. Interested in nothing but his own dreams, he hardly attempted to know or understand a Delphine de Custine. She was merely a walker-on in his inward drama, a partner of his boredom. Not a word in any of Chateaubriand's love letters (save much later, in the time of Mme. Récamier) shews any striving towards that lofty form of love which is friendship more endeared. He seemed indifferent because he was absent-minded, exacting because he compared the real woman with her whom he had once drawn from his thigh, amazed by the lamentations of his victims because, existing in a world of imagination, he had no need of living beings. In short, he was not good to love because he was himself incapable of loving.

However, while Delphine de Custine and Natalie de Noailles vied with each other for that "buttoned-up" heart, Mme. de Chateaubriand, imperturbable, on the surface at least, held her salon every evening in the attics of the Hôtel de Coislin. An odd mixture of favourites and opponents of the government was to be met there, from Fontanes, the man in power, to Bertin, suspect of royalism, and Clausel de Coussergues, an avowed monarchist. Between the long and dearly loved Mathieu Molé (whom the Emperor was about to make a Commissioner of Audit to the Council of State) and the Hôtel de Coislin a coolness had sprung up since Chateaubriand, reviewing a volume of his friend's essays in the *Mercure*, appeared to reproach him with too ready a submission to despotism. Strangely enough Chateaubriand, the hostile, was still a contributor to the Bonapartist *Mercure*, even going so far as to publish in its columns an article in praise of Charlemagne, which—in the jargon Fontanes and Lucien had made the fashion—was tantamount to homage to the Emperor.

It was in the *Mercure*, too, that he wrote an apologia for the man of letters which betrayed at once his desire to be caught up into the sphere of great action and his rankling memories of his brief incursion into active life. "It is said that men of letters are not fitted for the handling of affairs. It would be a strange thing," said Chateaubriand, "if the genius necessary for giving birth to the *Esprit des Lois* were incompetent to run a ministerial office." He maintained that literary fame marched hand in hand with that of great kings and heroes: "Let us go further and say that the glory of the Muses is the only one that owes nothing to outside circumstance. Military successes may always be laid at the door of the soldiers or of fortune—at least in part. It was with the aid of the Greeks that Achilles vanquished the Trojans, but Homer created the Iliad alone and, were there no Homer, we should know nothing of Achilles."

Was it a way of inviting the Achilles of the age to bid for the good will of a modern Homer? The author himself could not have said. He knew only that he was not happy, that this great noise of victories with which his name was not associated saddened him, that he suffered in not being able to reconcile his honour with his ambition and, lastly, in that he longed to escape from Paris and from France. Where was he to go? Mme. de Noailles, who was interested in Moorish customs and antiquities, was making ready for a journey to Spain, and he was greatly tempted to follow her. But what would Mme. de Chateaubriand say? One thing was certain—a journey to Greece and thence to the tomb of Christ would have the double advantage of promoting a discreet meeting in Spain on the homeward journey and of putting the best of finishing touches to the figure of the great Christian traveller. In Greece (as he had once found those of the *Natchez* in America), the author of *Les Martyrs* would find those lively impressions of colour which he needed to illustrate his book—every chapter of which now existed in rough draft. The explorer would turn pilgrim and, for the second time in history, a Chateaubriand would visit the Holy Sepulchre. The man of the open air would once again experience the bliss of nights spent beneath the stars. It would all be wonderful, only— it would all take money. In May 1806 this was suddenly forthcoming, probably from the Empress Elizabeth of Russia, the wife of Alexander Ist, a romantic, melancholy and dreamy person who, at Mme. de Krüdener's request, gave the needful 40,000 francs.

Before he left in June, he at last went to spend a fortnight at Fervacques. It was a visit of farewell, tender and peaceful enough. Mme. de Custine knew her fate and was resigned to it: "This vision of Greece is realised at last. He is leaving for the fulfilment of his vows and the wrecking of all mine. Everything in this last fortnight has been perfect, but equally all is over."

It was true that his love was at an end. Mme. de Noailles had promised him her favours if he came to join her at Granada. She had broken the heart of M. de Vintimille, who had gone to Naples to die for the woman he had once sought to seduce in sport. Some of Natalie's friends went the length of maintaining that he had killed himself and it was partly to escape their tittle-tattle and reproaches that she wanted to take so long a journey. At that time she was very depressed. "It is essential to keep busy," she wrote to her brother, "or my mind would weaken under its endless cycle of sorrowful thoughts. Once the spirit is wounded, the senses break free and it would be better to die a thousand deaths." Chateaubriand himself admitted the real object of his pilgrimage with complete cynicism: "Was I going to the tomb of Christ in a spirit of repentance? Only one thought absorbed me. I counted every moment with impatience. Aboard my ship, I kept my eyes fixed on the evening star, praying that it would send winds to waft me more quickly home and fame to win me love. I hoped to meet with some in Sparta, in Memphis and in Carthage that I might bear it back to the Alhambra."

4. THE SECULAR PILGRIM

Mme. de Chateaubriand, whose health was frail, rather dreaded journeys. On the other hand, she was devout and was prepared to make valiant efforts to reach the Holy Sepulchre. When she suggested it, her husband's anxiety was obvious. Would she not irretrievably spoil his fine homecoming to Granada and love? He painted the toils and dangers of the expedition and—to make sure that she should be convinced—loaded himself up with pistols, carbines and even blunderbusses—admirable word. He girt his loins with a belt stuffed with gold, dressed his cook's brother in an icoglan and blue turban, and assumed the part of an explorer with as much enjoyment as he had in America. Mme. de Chateaubriand, alas! more understanding than affrighted, realised that her presence was unwanted and contented herself with taking him on his road as far as Venice.

The start was in the grand style. A superb carriage called a "dormeuse" was "the pilgrim's staff." At Lyons one of the firearms went off of its own accord. It was a bad scare because of the powder in the carriage. Mme. de Chateaubriand fainted and, when she came to, had powder and weapons alike thrown into the Rhône. Neither cared much for Venice. Chateaubriand declared that as a town it was against nature since you couldn't go a step without taking boat. Mme. de Chateaubriand, on her side, wrote to Joubert: "I am writing to you aboard the *Golden Lion,* for the houses here are really only ships at anchor. There is everything to be seen in Venice except dry land. However there is one tiny patch called the Piazza San Marco, where the inhabitants come in the evening to dry."

Then came the time for goodbyes. The pilgrim set off for Trieste. Céleste, all forlorn, awaited the coming of the trusty Ballanche, who was making the journey from Lyons solely to escort her home. Hardly was she alone when she fell into the depths of despair. She was too delicately perceptive not to realise that her husband, after a seemly detour, was going to join the most bewitching of his "Madams" and though, up till the very moment of farewell, she put a brave face on it, she suffered. It was on the gentle Ballanche that she vented her spleen.

Chateaubriand, meanwhile, standing in the darkness near the helmsman, was tasting the joy of that freedom which he sought sometimes in journeyings, sometimes in love, and sometimes in literary creation. Above his head glittered the stars that Mme. de Beaumont had taught him to name. Many a time in the course of his life had he thus spent his nights in watching amid the sound of the waves. As of old he paced the quarter-deck alone, going from time to time to pencil a note by the glow of the lamp over the steersman's compass. Yet on this occasion he was not going beyond the seas in search of a primitive and natural life. It was no longer the student of Rousseau, but of Homer and the Bible who sought in time-hallowed spots imagery to which he might pin his dreams. The forests of America, the sough of the wind in desert places, the roar of a far-off cataract, "all these things bring content at twenty, for then life (so to speak) is sufficient to itself, and our first youth has about it something restless and hesitant which forever drives us back on dreams and visions, *ipsi sibi somnia fingunt*; but, at a riper age, our mind turns to more enduring tastes—fain to feed on memory and historical example. Gladly still would I sleep beside the Eurotas or the Jordan if the heroic shades of the three hundred Spartans or the twelve sons of Jacob should visit my rest, but never again will I go out for to seek an undiscovered country whose soil is yet unravished by the ploughshare. Now I must have deserts old as time which, at my pleasure, give me back the walls of Babylon or the legions of Pharsalia, *grandia ossa!* of the fields whose furrows teach me what I am and lay bare the blood, the sweat and the tears of man."

When he caught his first sight of the shores of Greece, he fell under such a spell of beauty as nothing could ever after break, for he was sincere. The love of fame was strong in him. Since he longed to fashion for the generations to come a fair image of his own destiny, he reverenced the heroes of the past who, though men, had cast giant shadows into these our days. When, in the desert places that had once been Sparta, he cried to all the echoes: "Leonidas!" it was not an idle pose, but a means of drawing to him that sweet sadness which he found in contrasting human greatness with the nothingness of eternity.

Some of the eye-witnesses of his journey reproached him with being casual. An Italian doctor, who took him to see Argos, was indignant at his heedlessness and reminded him that the true scholar should scan every stone and each single inscription. Chateaubriand replied that "a landscape or even a glance was enough to bring into his mind the pleasing fictions of legend and the memories of history." It was true that he saw swiftly and saw rightly. Nothing could be more beautiful than his descriptions of Greek horizons:— "From the height of the Acropolis I have seen the sun rise between the twin peaks of Mount Hymettus; the rooks, which nest about the citadel but never venture beyond, were wheeling above us, their sable-shining wings frosted with rose by the first faint streaks of dawn; columns of blue and aery smoke mounted from the shadows about the flanks of Hymettus, giving token of parks or beehives. Athens, the Acropolis and the ruins of the Parthenon grew dyed with the loveliest shade of peachblossom; the sculptures of Phidias struck by a ray of level golden light, took life and breath until they seemed to move against the marble, so mobile were their shadows in relief. Afar off, the sea and the Piraeus were one pearly whiteness, while the citadel of Corinth—reflecting back the splendour of the new-born day, gleamed on the horizon of the sunset like a rock of purple and fire." After a space of twenty years he had found yet again the eye and the language of the great colourist— those gifts which he had so carefully trained in the forests of the New World.

It would doubtless be true to say with Père Garabed that, "in going to seek impressions in the East, he was mainly bent on leaving his own there for ever." It would be easy to smile at his third-hand learning and at his description, borrowed from the Abbé Barthélemy, of a rock-hewn staircase which had been destroyed fully seventeen centuries before his coming, easy to be amused by the magic style which translates innkeepers into patriarchs, by the insistence on the careless courage of a man who had lived among American savages and, finally, by the contrast between the poet's account of his experiences and the flat, prosaic notes of his valet, Julien. It all matters very little and he forestalled criticism with a sound reply: "Where the rest is concerned, I do not know why I should be so bent on justifying myself on a few points of learning. It is doubtless just as well that I am not at fault, but—even if I had been—there would still be nothing of which to accuse me. I have said from the first that I had no pretentions to being either a scholar or a traveller. My *Itinéraire* is the swift ranging of a man who sets out to see the heavens, the earth and the seas and comes back to his own fireside with a few impressions the more in his mind and a few feelings the more in his heart."

Rather, he was accused of having swamped his somewhat meagre recollections of too brief a sojourn in the Holy Land in a flood of information re-hashed from others. This "passionate pilgrim" paused only three days in Jerusalem and substituted for the real *genius loci*, which seems hardly to have touched him, the study of two hundred dreary accounts of Judea. He hardly took time to drink the waters of the Jordan as he had drunk those of the Mississippi, of the Thames, of the Rhine, of the Po, of the Tiber, of the Eurotas, of the Cephissus, of the Hermas and of the Granicus. He so loved fame that even that of rivers moved him and he was conscious of a need for symbolic communing with their memory-laden waves. Between Palestine and Spain his voyage was slow and dangerous for, at that time, navigation in the Mediterranean was difficult. Chateaubriand took ten days to go from Venice to Pylos and thirteen from Constantinople to Jaffa. In order to get from Alexandria to Tunis, he had to wait ten days for fine weather and was nevertheless caught in a storm on November 23rd so that it was January 12th before he reached Goletta after a fifty days' crossing. Finally, in the spring, he had a further eighteen days from Goletta to Gibraltar. On his way he had naturally drunk Nile water, which he found to be salty and of a fine red bordering on violet, the colour of autumn mist. Gazing on the Pyramids, he reflected that "the idea of vanquishing death by a tomb, of forcing generations, customs, laws and ages to break against the foot of a bier could not come of a vulgar soul. If it is pride, it is a great pride."

On March 30th, 1807, he at last disembarked at Algeciras, whence he went overland to Cadiz. He found there, not Natalie de Noailles, but a man who talked of her. It was the valiant royalist Hyde de

Neuville who, banished from France, was with his wife in Spain, awaiting the moment when they should embark for America. A pattern of loyalty and courage, he had defended his king during the Revolution and it was leaning on his arm that Malesherbes left the Convention after his plea for Louis XVI. That alone would have given him a great claim on Chateaubriand's affections. Ten times he had been a conspirator, had been imprisoned and had been condemned to death and ten times he had escaped. In Spain he encountered the fair Natalie, who—in that country—insisted on being called Dolores, and their monarchist ideas drew them together. Like all truly noble souls, Hyde de Neuville saw generous spirits everywhere, and brought out all that was best in Dolores— a gracious and cultured woman. Together they spent hours of high communing in the cathedral of Seville and vowed eternal friendship. So vividly did she describe Chateaubriand's charm that Hyde recognised him immediately on his arrival in Cadiz, and—as their friendship progressed—found him to be the same lovable creature as Joubert knew.

Why was Mme. de Noailles herself no longer in Cadiz to welcome a friend who had been all round the Mediterranean only to prepare the way for their meeting? Mme. de Boigne maintains that during her long sojourn in Spain she had allowed the assiduous attentions of an English colonel to soothe her anxieties. While in Granada, awaiting the pilgrim from Jerusalem, she learnt (according to Mme. de Boigne) of the colonel's death, so Chateaubriand came back to find a mourning woman, weeping for his rival. Is it to be believed? And did a great Portuguese nobleman likewise play a part in the Spanish adventures of Natalie-Dolores? True, she left Cadiz shortly before Chateaubriand's arrival, but how could she foresee the date of her lover's coming? He was several weeks late; in France it was already rumoured that he was dead. It may have been that after so long a stay in Spain, she had to leave for home.

Nevertheless she did meet Chateaubriand in Spain. On April 18th, 1807, she wrote from Aranjuez to her cousin Mme. de Vintimille: "My dear, you are sure to have all the news of M. de Chateaubriand by now, but I will give you some notwithstanding. He is very well, rather tanned and has filled out, but he is as gay and fresh as though he had done nothing out of the way. He talks of Jerusalem as if it were Montmartre, and wants to go to Toboso because he thinks they go rather well paired. He has been to Granada, though he has a profound contempt for Europe. He is due here in two days, but I shall not wait for him, since I am in such haste to leave as to be loath to delay even for a day. Besides, he hasn't the least need of me, for he is so used to living among people he cannot understand, to sleeping on the ground and to living only on dates and rice, that he finds Spain a land of superfluities. I think he enjoyed his journey. In Tunis he saw the ruins of Carthage; by the time he leaves here, he will have seen everything worthy of his attention— Granada and Cordova. It was a great pleasure to be with him again, for I had been anxious on his account. He ran into many a danger in the various countries he has traversed, especially in Palestine; hence he wears a fine big sabre by his side. I, my dear, long only to be back at Méréville and to see you all once more. I'm feeling very depressed and not too well, so it will need the utmost tolerance of friendship to put up with me."

This letter has been taken as a proof that, despite their mutual wishes and the legend to that effect, Chateaubriand and Mme. de Noailles did not succeed in meeting at the Alhambra. But a woman does not always tell another woman the truth, especially when there is a man in question, and that man her lover. A little earlier she gave her brother Alexandre very different news. "I have had news (don't speak of this to anyone, I beseech you) of M. de Chateaubriand. He tells me that he is crossing the Peloponnesus overland and that, if he has a chance of landing in Spain, he will pass through Granada on his way back to France. You know that the plan was already in his mind when we discussed it with him at Méréville. I should be very sorry if this were known in society, or even if it came out that I hear news of him, for there would be a great deal of envious tittle-tattle and there is nothing I so much desire as to be forgotten by the whole world. . . ."[1]

When, after his return, Chateaubriand wrote a short story, *Le Dernier des Abencérages*, depicting, against the magical background of the Alhambra, the birth of a mutual love, he made no concealment of the fact that Natalie de Noailles was the real heroine of

[1] Unpublished letter.

the tale. In the Blanca who sings the Zambra in a lightly veiled voice which stirs the depths of the soul, and who dances to the sound of the guitar with a strange mingling of gaiety and sadness, it would be difficult not to recognize the lady of Méréville. In life as in fiction, after their wanderings among those lacy galleries, those fountains and those marble runnels bordered with lemon trees in flower, the lovers wished naïvely to link their names with the melting yet warrior beauty of those cloisters of love. "The moon, as it rose, spread its fitful light through the abandoned sanctuaries and the deserted courts of the Alhambra. Its pale beams patterned the grassy lawns and the walls of the great chambers with the tracery of an aery architecture, with the arches of the cloisters, the moving shadow of the leaping waters and the shrubs swaying in the breeze. A nightingale was singing from amidst a cypress that pierced the domes of a ruined mosque, and the echoes gave back his lament. By moonlight Aben-Hamet wrote the name of Blanca on the marble in the Hall of the Two Sisters, tracing it in Arab characters so that the traveller might come upon one mystery the more in this palace of mysteries." Sainte-Beuve maintains that, towards the middle of the nineteenth century, those two names might still be read on a column of the Alhambra and that it was not in Arabic they were written. It was Adrien de Laval, the chaste Montmorency, who afterwards effaced them.

One thing is certain—Chateaubriand kept an undying memory of "those spell-bound days of rapture and delirium." "I went from one end to another of Spain, the country of dreams, and even now I seem to see its great deserted roads. I loved to listen to the songs that were made only for me. When I touched France and tore myself away from the witchery of those melodies, it was of her alone I thought in crossing the Pyrenees. As I drew near Paris, I took the road leading to the château which had been the beginning, as it was the end, of all my wanderings." That château was Méréville, but he went but slowly thither. He broke the journey at Bordeaux and did not reach Paris till June 5th, 1807. The Jouberts were eagerly awaiting the traveller who was to tell them of "the things of far countries." He came back strengthened both in his royalism by the discourse of the kindly Hyde and the fiery Natalie, and in his liberalism by the horrors of Turkish despotism. *To the*

Journey from Paris to Andalusia

Marquise de Pastoret: "I believe, Madam, that you will find me somewhat changed. Ten months of perils and fatigues, the sight of the greatest ruins in the world, the sun, the East, the gravity of the peoples among whom I lived, all these have weighed on my spirits and it is natural that I should feel more sad and sober. . . . Ah, Madam! What a theme for reflection is the grinding tyranny of the indescribable wretchedness I have witnessed. I should advise those who preach absolute government to pay a visit to Turkey." To a friend whom he saw on his way through Bordeaux he added: "My one desire is to own a corner of earth where there is a little shade."

CHAPTER VI

The Valley of Wolves

I know perfectly well that I am nothing but a book-machine.
—CHATEAUBRIAND

1. THE ARTICLE IN THE *Mercure*

AT THE beginning of 1807, between Eylau and Friedland, there was a brief period in which the Emperor's enemies once more looked forward to his fall. The continental blockade was too vast a design and imposed on France the necessity of dominating Europe. Every year armies had to be recruited in greater numbers, and the campaigns were growing more murderous. In the cemetery of Eylau, among the wounded and dying, Napoleon had been "gentle with everybody, as he always was when things were going wrong." The letters that went to Paris from the army were most discouraging. "In four months we have not made the slightest headway against the Russians," wrote Caulaincourt,[1] "and God knows when we shall meet them." The Emperor himself, realising that France was in a state of nerves, grew anxious for the effect that Paris chatterers might have abroad. "The mere belief that I was experiencing the least set-back in France would make several powers declare against me."

Now in France, he was experiencing more than one set-back. In Brittany and in Normandy there was still a latent Chouannerie. Émigrés from London or Jersey occasionally came to fan the flame, bringing English gold for the cause. Though, in Paris, many of the former royalists were rallying, though Molé and Pasquier were Commissioners of Audit to the Council of State, though

[1] Quoted by Madelin, *Le Consulat et l'Empire*.

The Valley of Wolves

Fontanes as Grand Master of the University, was nominating Bonald and Joubert to the highest posts and had made the "Crow of Vire" an Academy inspector, the underground struggle between the ex-royalists and the ex-jacobins associated in the administration of France went on. Had the Empire been founded "on the ruins or on the institutions of the Revolution"? It was a sign of weakness that the question could still be asked, and that so weighty an edifice could rest on so frail a compromise.

At the time of his return from the East, Chateaubriand believed prematurely in the possible success of a monarchist opposition. He came back ill-informed. The Emperor's difficulties were exaggerated abroad and the semi-victory of Eylau was translated by the émigrés into a defeat. While in Spain, that fair rebel, Mme. de Noailles, had given him her own version of the state of feeling. She had rekindled in this passionate pilgrim the ancient flame of Breton chivalry and, for his lady, he was ready to challenge the dragon. Who could tell? Perhaps the Emperor was already tottering and the glory of his overthrow might be reserved for the poet?

Mme. de Chateaubriand, whose "devoted but rarely approving severity" seemed unchanged on his return to Paris, was not too pleased to find him in such a frame of mind. Where her husband's sudden political frenzies were concerned, she experienced the natural reactions of a legitimate wife against the passions fanned by his mistress, and, for some time, had been surprised to find herself growing Bonapartist. The Emperor had treated her rather well in her husband's absence. When a courtier announced that the ship on which Chateaubriand sailed had gone down, Napoleon said: "Chateaubriand has a wife here. It would be a pity to cause her unnecessary distress. Wait till there can be no doubt before publishing anything in the papers. . . ." "Would our Bourbons," said Céleste, "have done as much for their friends as Bonaparte thus did for an enemy?" She put not the faintest trust in the princes and prophesied to her husband that, if ever the king came back, it would be the royalists who fared the worst. Mme. de Chateaubriand had no use for a traditional and sentimental loyalism, but her good sense was powerless over her husband. "In politics," said he, "if Mme. de Chateaubriand has opposed me, she has never held me back."

On this occasion also, she did not hold him back, and, in order that he might write thenceforward what he and Mme. de Noailles wished, he bought the *Mercure* for twenty thousand francs. Where on earth did he raise them, considering that on his way through Bordeaux he had just lamented his poverty to a visitor? It is probable (but not proven) that he was helped by royalist propaganda, which was again growing active and hopeful. Be that as it may, he was not slow to give pledges to that party for, as early as the beginning of July, under the cloak of a review of the *Voyage pittoresque et historique de l'Espagne*, written by Mme. de Noailles' brother, Alexandre de Laborde, the *Mercure* published a ringing article over the signature of Chateaubriand: "When, in the silence of abasement, no sound is to be heard save the voice of the informer and the dragging of slaves' chains, when all tremble before the tyrant and it is as dangerous to incur his favour as to deserve his disgrace, comes the historian, entrusted with the vengeance of the nations. In vain does Nero flourish, Tacitus is already born within the Empire; he grows, unknown, besides the ashes of Germanicus; and even now a righteous Providence has delivered up to a humble and lowly child the glory of the master of the world."

Following these fine and daring phrases, Chateaubriand attacked the despotism which his friends Bonald and Molé held too dear. "If, in common with men whose gifts and character we admire, we had held that absolutism is the best of all possible forms of government, a few months' stay in Turkey would have wholly cured us of that opinion." Then, in inflammatory and allusive terms, he recalled the revolt of Sertorius against Sulla: "He fell in his attempt, but—in all likelihood—he never counted on success. He thought only of his duty and of the holiness of the cause in whose defence he stood alone. . . . Magnanimous actions are those in which the ends envisaged are ill-fortune and death. After all, what matter reverses, if our name, spoken among the generations to come, should cause some generous heart to beat two thousand years after we are dust? We have no doubt that, in the time of Sertorius, pusillanimous souls, who count their baseness reason, thought it madness in an obscure citizen to dare to strive alone against the power of Sulla. Happily, posterity judges otherwise the actions of men. In the last resort, it is not cowardice and vice that pass sentence on courage and virtue."

Don Quixote, rising in his stirrups, was hurtling—lance in rest, against the despot. The onlookers admired, but not without affright. Mme. de Chateaubriand, who had the unhappy power of foreseeing the consequences of violent gestures, was seriously alarmed, but the actor—enraptured with his own performances—was enjoying the stir he caused. "If Napoleon had done with kings, he had not done with me. My article, falling into the midst of his prosperity and his marvels, shook all France. Innumerable copies were distributed by hand; many subscribers to the *Mercure* tore out the article and had it bound separately; it was read in drawing-rooms; it was peddled from house to house. One would have needed to be alive at the time to conceive the effect of one lonely voice echoing through the silence of the world."

Such was his later version of events. In actual fact they fell out somewhat differently. At the time when the article was conceived and subsequently written, Napoleon seemed to be by no means "done with kings"—very much the contrary. It was the time when victory was trembling in the balance, when the anxious Emperor was wondering what Austria and Russia would do, and when Jomini murmured: "If I were the Archduke Charles . . ." It seemed as if the hero were badly hit and a vigorous attack would end him. When the issue of the *Mercure* came out, however, the victory of Friedland had newly restored all the lustre of the imperial star, and, two days later, the Peace of Tilsit gave Napoleon "the happiest moment of his life." The master was about to turn home, all-powerful in France and Europe. The act of courage became no less than suicide.

For a time it was hoped that, in the joy of his return and of his victory the Emperor might not see the number of the *Mercure*. Alas! Cardinal Fesch, in spite, took care that it should meet his eyes. "Eventually," says Joubert amusingly, "the thunder growled, the cloud burst and the lightning-bolt in person said to Fontanes that if his friend began again, he would be struck." Fontanes has described the storm. "Does Chateaubriand imagine," said the Emperor to him in one of his worked-up rages, "that I am a dolt or that I do not understand? I will have him put to the sword on the steps of my palace." Fontanes (if he is to be believed) pleaded: "After all, Sire, his name gives lustre to your reign and, in the future, will be more in men's mouths than yours. There is nothing of the conspirator about him; he can do naught against you; he has only his gifts. Yet, by reason of those gifts, he will be immortal in the chronicle of the age of Napoleon. Would you have it said, one day, that Napoleon caused his death or sent him to languish in prison for ten years?" Napoleon would not. Despite every cause for complaint, he had a strong and lasting taste for Chateaubriand. He liked his work and knew that he was in high favour with the Faubourg Saint-Germain, whose suffrage mattered to him. Besides, after a sound drubbing from his wife and his official friends, the culprit had made honourable amends. The August number of the *Mercure* sang the praises of the "saving government which made victims forget even the memory of their wrongs."

Nevertheless, the storm did not wholly spare "M. Chateaubriand and his clique." In a letter to Chênedollé Joubert gives a delightful description of what befell: "It was all very fierce—violent even—but it didn't last long. Today everything has calmed down, only—it hailed on the *Mercure* . . ." Chateaubriand had been ordered to give up the editorship of the paper and had been replaced by Esménard and Legouvé. "During the storm," went on Joubert, "gold rained on the ousted, so I do not advise you to be in the least sorry for them." The Emperor, in short, had withdrawn the *Mercure* from Chateaubriand's control, installing censors and writers of his own choice, but, as far as money went, it had been no bad business for the culprit. It is a fact that on the day following the hailstorm which turned to a rain of gold, the Chateaubriands, who had been hard up till that moment, were able to buy a country house at the gates of Paris.

The estrangement from the Emperor seemed complete enough to debar Chateaubriand for ever from a life of action. Was the fall from favour of his own choosing? He had not lost his involuntary admiration for the man who had "cleft the rocks of the Simplon, planted his banners on the capitals of Europe and raised up Italy from the dust in which she had been prostrate for centuries." Yet he was too concerned for cutting a consistent figure, and for the aesthetic value of his life, to humble himself and capitulate. Though in far less measure than his preoccupation with public opinion, there was the desire to content himself. As, to a great painter, the lines of a first sketch suggest the finished picture, as, to a great writer, the movement and tone of chapters already written dictate the sequel, so to Chateaubriand, the passionate sculptor of his own life, bygone acts prompted actions new. Because he had written *Le Génie du Christianisme* he could conceive of no other possible subjects than *Les Martyrs* and the *Itinéraire*. Because he had sent in his resignation at the moment of the Duc d'Enghien's assassination, he owed it to himself to remain an adversary of the Empire. For him, as much and more than for the spectators of this first half of his life, there emerged a figure—a figure with hair blown back by the wind of tempests, with fine eyes dark with defiance and a hand slipped, almost imperially, beneath the lapels of his coat. Henceforth he was to seek to accentuate that figure and to fix its traits.

2. The Valley of Wolves

"It is four years since, on my return from the Holy Land, I bought, near the village of Aulnay in the region of Sceaux and of Châtenay, a gardener's cottage, hidden among the wooded hills. The rough and sandy ground belonging to the house was simply a kind of wild orchard with a ravine and a chestnut copse beyond. That narrow room seemed to me meet to enclose my long hopes; *spatio brevi spem longam reseces*." Mme. de Chateaubriand, in her turn, describes a cottage as primitive as any to be found in the mountains of Auvergne, and Joubert: "I have seen this Valley of Wolves. It forms a wooded hollow rather like those you see in Brittany or even Périgord."

The unique charm of the valley was that, though only a few leagues from Paris, it offered a retreat as quiet as heart could wish. The trees which shut it in on every side seemed only a part of that stillness. When Chateaubriand bought the land, it was an orchard of barren apple trees. He pulled them up and helped by M. Benjamin—"the most rascally of gardeners"—with his own hands planted the fine trees which surround the lawn today. The women among his admirers gave him seeds and shrubs. To bring back memories of his travels, he had cedars of Lebanon, of Virginia and Louisiana, pines from Jerusalem and Judas-trees. "I was in a state of endless delight. Without being Mme. de Sévigné, I trudged in a pair of clogs to plant my trees in the mud, to pace up and down the same paths, to go back and back to all the little corners, to hide wherever I found a bush, thinking to myself that it would be my future park, for there was a future then." A botanist, thanks to M. de Malesherbes, trained during his English exile by a race of gardeners, he had clear and individual ideas on the design for a park. Mme. de Chateaubriand who, for her part, had ideas on everything, could only give in.

He made some additions to the house. "I adorned its brick wall with a portico upheld by two pillars of black marble and two female caryatids of white, for I remembered that I had passed through Athens. My intention was to add a tower at the end of the summer-house, meanwhile I built artificial battlements on the wall which separated us from the road." As for the Gothic windows they recalled the fact that "the master of this dwelling had thrown open the doors of the churches and sounded the trumpet before the temple." Park and house were a kind of symbolic summary of the life and thought that conceived them. Vigny, on visiting the Valley of Wolves in after days, was very hard on those symbols. "A feeble, low-built house, concealed without by hypocritical battlements and adorned within by caryatids in the depraved taste of Louis XV, an English garden and a tower with a chapel to the Virgin."[1] It was all there, but seen through the eyes of ill-will. To say sooth, there were two ways of regarding Chateaubriand and his hermitage. That which ignored the greatness of the man and the beauty of his park was not the better.

When first he took up his abode in the Valley of Wolves, Chateaubriand hardly went out at all except on Sundays, when he went to Mass at Châtenay. Lamartine, who was then a boy, came with some friends to watch for a glimpse of their admired author. Hidden among the leaves, the lads spent two days without seeing anyone, but at last—on the second evening—the door of the little house opened. "A little man in a black coat, with powerful shoulders, spindle legs and a noble head, came out, followed by a cat to whom he threw pellets of bread to make him gambol on the lawn;

[1] Vigny—*Journal d'un Poète*.

man and cat alike were soon deep in the shadows of a path and the shrubs hid them from our sight." It was an apparition nearly as mysterious as the ghost who, likewise followed by a cat, had haunted the vaults of Combourg.

This retreat was naturally conducive to work. It was in the Valley of Wolves that *Les Martyrs* was finished, the *Mémoires d'Outre-Tombe* and the *Études historiques* begun, the *Itinéraire de Paris à Jerusalem* and the tragedy of *Moïse* written entirely. Yet, though he worked with that sustained ardour which comes of incurable ennui, Chateaubriand was enchanted when a neighbour's visit gave him an excuse for tearing himself from his labours. "Often we would find him," says Mme. de Boigne, "writing on the corner of the drawing-room table with a worn-out quill that would hardly dip into the neck of the wretched little phial that held his ink. He would give a cry of joy as he saw us pass the window, stuff his papers under the cushion of an old armchair which served both as his portfolio and his desk and, with one bound, would come to meet us, as gay as a schoolboy set free from class." Like most writers, Chateaubriand never had enough ink and paper to get on with. "I've even used the cook's memoranda to scribble *Moïse*," he tells us. Étienne Pasquier, after he had been made Prefect of Police, could not resist the temptation of pulling some unfinished manuscript out of the sofa-desk if ever he were left alone in that drawing room. But Mme. de Chateaubriand had her eye on him.

Later, her husband took to working in an octagonal tower which stood solitary in the park, half-hidden among trees. His friends called it "Velléda's tower" because the Gallic prophetess of *Les Martyrs* long had her abode within its walls. There he could find some hours' escape from an exhausting wife. "She has plenty of wit," observed Mme. de Boigne, "but she uses it to extract the wormwood and the gall in everything. She has been really hurtful to her husband by making his home-life unbearable. He has always had the utmost consideration for her, but he cannot get peace by his own fireside." Ever mistrustful, Mme. de Chateaubriand accused friends of betrayal, governments of injustice and servants of theft. When, tired of being regarded as a rascal, the gardener Benjamin gave notice, Chateaubriand said: "My dear good Benjamin, I don't take any notice of all that flow of language, yet all day long she words me, Benjamin, she words me!"

He was indeed worded, for the pessimistic Céleste de Chateaubriand prophesied great misfortunes. "Only evils," said she, "can come out of Pandora's box." Her carping accentuated the failings of friends and the attacks of enemies. "She was a good hater," said Vitrolles, "and kept her husband in a state of perpetual exasperation with the world." Probably, if he had been left to himself, he would, despite his grievances, have found refuge in the indifference which comes naturally to men of powerful imagination. "M. de Chateaubriand is so stupid," said Céleste, "that if I were not there he would speak ill of no-one."

Though their shared passions, their friendships and their grudges might have brought the two together, their tastes kept them apart. He luxuriated in his sorrows; she hid hers, and her classic good sense was pitiless in its mockery of the romantic storms so dear to her husband. "As I am not in the least melancholy," said she, "and as I have passed the age when one enjoys sighing, I love neither the wind nor the moon. The only things I like are rain for my grass, and sunshine to bask in."

With all her faults, she had droll humour, gaiety and even affability. She greatly enjoyed seeing her friends and knew how to win their affections. The devout royalist Clausel de Coussergues had become her "minister" and servant. On October 4th, the feast of St. Francis, it was Clausel whom she entrusted with recruiting guests "more particularly among the clergy." She laid siege to the Jouberts by a good table. "My Cat is no use for anything, not even for eating mice. Yesterday he was supposed to start the Stag and summon him to come and eat the choicest of calves' livers. Not a bit of it. He went running from Madam to Madam till five o'clock and only remembered his errand at the moment when my wrath broke on him and on your faithless spouse. Listen—I array myself all in red like the Caliph Haroun and I proclaim 'If the Stag does not come and share Frisell's burden with us tomorrow, I will have his house rased to the ground so that I may never set foot in it again.'"

Only to Mme. Joubert, "the person whom she loved best in the world," did she ever speak of her husband's "Madams." She put

The Valley of Wolves

up with their existence, since she could not away with them and, though rather sadly, found them a source of amusement. Chateaubriand's admirers waited on her hand and foot. If ever she had a cold, there would come as many as five gifts of beef-tea, accompanied by affectionate notes. Within the species "Madam," Céleste distinguished varieties. There were the favourites—Mme. de Custine had filled the part, but from the time of the Spanish journey she was ousted by Mme. de Noailles. Delphine de Custine remained Chateaubriand's friend; he wrote to her—especially if he had any favour to ask of Fouché; she did him the service he asked, bewailed herself sadly, grumbled and, sometimes at Fervacques, sometimes abroad, fled society, which "intimidated, bored and irked her." Natalie de Noailles, ever bewitching amid her enchanted gardens, through her melting caprices and that shadow of melancholy-madness which Chateaubriand adored, was loved, but not indulged. When she said she felt unwell, all Méréville fussed round the couch where she lay half-fainting. Chateaubriand alone, with the dreamy smile on his lips, went on reading the papers "without putting himself out in the least."[1] Yet it was for her sake and in memory of "the spell-bound days of rapture and delirium" that the walls of Velléda's tower were covered with mementos of Granada and Cordova. Perhaps, through a little door pierced in the wall of the park, she may sometimes have come there to meet the pilgrim. The second class of "Madams" was that of the Egerias. Sometimes they too became temporary favourites. Chief among them were the Duchesses de Duras and de Lévis and Mme. de Bérenger (later Duchesse de Châtillon). Mme. de Bérenger was very much in the good graces of Mme. de Chateaubriand, who described her as the gentlest, the best and one of the most beautiful. "Come, come," she wrote to Joubert, "she is one of the best of women. I am determined that you shall love her and I want the Wolf [Mme. Joubert] to love her too, although she is a lamb." If Mme. de Boigne is to be believed, Mme. de Lévis scored a complete success and this was a great grief to Mme. de Duras, who mistrusted her own charms, not alas! mistakenly.

Yet she was a friend worthy of love. *Née* Claire de Kersaint, the daughter of a famous sailor who, like M. de Malesherbes, had begun

[1] *Souvenirs de Mme. de Ségur.* Published by the Comtesse Jean de Pange.

by believing in the principles of the Revolution, had been a Conventional, a friend of the Girondins and had gone to the scaffold for refusing to connive at the massacres of September, she had lived in England during the Revolution. In London she had married Amédée de Duras, Gentleman of the Chamber to the princes, who—by reason of her considerable fortune—had forgiven her her father's opinions. On his return to France, the Duc de Duras had taken up his abode in the Château d'Ussé, had avoided rallying to the Empire and came but seldom to Paris. His wife tried her hand at writing, produced little novels that were not without merit and in conversation aspired to wit—a pretention which made men find her tiresome. It was at Méréville that Mme. de Duras met Chateaubriand, for whose work she had a lofty admiration. She heard the reading of *Le Dernier Abencérage*. The speaker hummed the song of the Cid in a strong Breton accent which gave his verse a quaint originality. When he ended:

"*Il préféra, disait-il, à la vie
Son Dieu, son roi, sa Chimène et l'honneur.*" . . .

a mischievous young girl murmured: "And what else?" Chateaubriand who overheard her, laughed wholeheartedly[1] but Mme. de Duras was not amused. Like many another, she had lost her heart to the Enchanter, and was too honest a person not to be aware of her own plainness.

She did what a shy society woman in love may—invited him to dinner with twenty others. He refused: "It is extremely kind of you, Madam, but I really dread unknown faces. I am such a recluse that I dare not answer for my humour. Happy as I should be to spend with you the moments you are so gracious as to grant, I should be loath to trouble your company with my silence and hangdog face. In the evening especially, I am not of this world." Later, with that chaste and delicate tenderness men show towards the women who do not attract them, he constituted her his "sister" or, as they were both old inhabitants of London, *my good sister*. When she voiced her fears that their friendship might wound her fair cousin Natalie (now Duchesse de Mouchy), he recalled her sharply enough to good sense and to his brotherly attitude: "My

[1] *Mme. de Ségur.*

The Valley of Wolves

dear Sister, how utterly absurd! Mme. de Mouchy knows that I love her and that nothing shall ever come between us. Since she has this confidence, Mme. de Mouchy forbids me neither to see nor write to you, nor even to go to Ussé without her. Were she so to command me, she would doubtless be instantly obeyed, as I have told you a hundred times. You do not object—rather you esteem me the more. . . . It was Mme. de Mouchy who inspired the *Abencérage*. "I am very glad that you like it so much."

Claire de Kersaint considered the matter settled and fell back on the rôle of sister and patroness for which the author of the comedy had cast her. Her acceptance was free neither of revolt nor regret but, the moment she betrayed a twinge of jealousy or sought to offer more than services, she was promptly put in her place: "There are times when my sister passes belief. I love Adrienne dearly. I love Mme. de Bérenger well enough. I love Mme. de Mouchy passionately. Yet, has my sister not a place apart, where she reigns unrivalled and undisturbed?" It was true, but the place was a minor one and the office of a sister dearly bought. Claire de Duras, a generous person by nature, grew embittered and ultimately developed a mortal complaint of the liver. Was it ever to be hoped that nobility of feeling and powers of intellect could suffice to rank with the bodily incarnations of the Sylph?

The "Madams" came but rarely to the Valley of Wolves, and to keep them away from Velléda's tower, where isolation might have gone the length of guilt, as much as to exorcise the pagan deities of a spot consecrated to *Les Martyrs*, Mme. de Chateaubriand eventually had a chapel fitted up above her husband's study. Mme. de Chastenay, Mme. de Boigne and that delightful Mme. de Vintimille, who had assumed in Joubert's life the rôle of platonic friend, left vacant by the death of Mme. de Beaumont, were, however, often to be seen in the Valley. The Jouberts were old friends—so, naturally, were Fontanes, Pasquier, the Englishman—Frisell, Molé and Clausel. All the "original members" of the little society now held important office in the imperial administration. Molé, a Councillor of State, was in charge of the Highways Department. Fontanes, as Grand Master of the University, had made Joubert an Inspector General and their academic conversations bored Mme. de Chateaubriand to tears. It may be imagined that her husband also grieved to see that he alone was out of the stream which was sweeping his friends to fortune. Even the Academy failed to beckon to him, for it was still under the domination of Jacobin philosophy. Time was passing, life was fleeting, money was lacking. In his black moments he dreamt once again of shaking off the dust of France and "going to die upon a foreign soil."

They were only moments, however. "I know perfectly well," said he, "that I am nothing but a book-machine." When the machine was running smoothly his temper was of the sweetest. The Valley of Wolves saw the last years of the Chateaubriand Joubert had held dear—the lovable creature with the mirth of a child. No writer has ever taken his friends' criticisms in such good part. When, one Sunday, he read them the *Druidess* (that is to say the Velléda episode from *Les Martyrs*) and saw from the expression of his listeners that it was not going down too well, he wiped away a tear and said that he would try to recast his text. On the following Sunday the amended version was enthusiastically received.

When there was nothing to read, Joubert and Chateaubriand lost themselves "in the most delightful of brown studies," while their wives amused the gallery by the droll way in which they recalled the dreamers to the workaday world. Chateaubriand's coat was threadbare; he anxiously awaited the end of every month; all his ambitions seemed fated to failure, but the long days sped in the hope of seeing Natalie once more, for she was lonely as he in her lovely valley. "How often, in imagination, have I left the woods behind me, always to take the same road! I pictured myself setting forth, turning home, shutting myself up in my tower to dream of her and of *Les Martyrs*, persecuted by the tyrant, glorying in his hate, dreaming of masterpieces conceived amid alarms, loving, inspired, unhappy and content." For, in the union of honourable ills and lofty loves, he found a climate tempered to his heart.

3. The Book-Machine

Never, since the English exile, had the book-machine been so prolific as during this exile in France. In the Valley of Wolves Chateaubriand finished *Les Martyrs*, which he published in 1809, wrote the whole of *Le Dernier des Abencérages*, *L'Itinéraire de*

Paris à Jerusalem and the tragedy of *Moïse* and finally began the *Études historiques* and the *Mémoires*.

They were vast undertakings, but he loved breadth and even painting larger than life size. That is clear from *Les Martyrs*, which was an Iliad for guilds and sodalities. Chateaubriand loved Homer to the point of playing the sedulous ape and the beginning of *Les Martyrs* is more or less a translation. "It is second-hand antique," said Saint-Beuve and it must be admitted that the epic machinery, the descriptions of Heaven and Hell, the catalogues and the invocations are hard to stomach. Yet the general plan of the work is simple and beautiful. A young Christian Greek, Eudore, loves a pagan girl Cymodocée, the daughter of the priest Demodocus. In her presence he tells the story of his life, which had been a stirring one. Born of an old Messenian family, the Lasthenes (the Chateaubriands), he is sent to Rome (Paris) in his youth. There he succumbs to the promptings of the demon of pleasure and forgets his religion (influences of Guingené and Parny). As a soldier in the armies of the Emperor Diocletian, Eudore fights in the army of the Rhine (the Princes' Army) and takes part in a battle against the Franks. Following military successes, he is made Governor of Armorica. There he meets the fair Druidess Velléda, who tells her love and dies. Thereupon Eudore repents and returns to his first faith. Cymodocée, greatly moved by this recital, falls in love with Eudore and for his sake becomes a Christian. After a long separation, the lovers meet in Rome, where Eudore is condemned to the lions. Cymodocée determines to share his fate and dies in the arena, "lying light in her husband's arms as a snowflake on the branches of some Maenalian or Lycaean pine." The martyrdom is graciously conceived.

Since the days of Cardinal Wiseman, of Bulwer-Lytton and of *Quo Vadis* the theme of *Les Martyrs* may seem threadbare, but at that time the subject was new. All the passages in which Chateaubriand had been able to draw on his recollections or the impressions of his travels, were fraught with a real beauty—the camp on the Rhine for instance: "Never have I heard without a certain warrier joy the fanfare of trumpets caught up by the reverberant crags, and the whinnying of the steeds as they greeted the dawn. I loved to see the camp sunk in sleep, the folded tents from which a few soldiers emerged half-clad, the centurion pacing before the piled arms with his vine-stock in his hand, the motionless sentry who, in the struggle against sleep, kept a finger raised as though enjoining silence, the horseman splashing through the river coloured like fire in the dawn, the victimary drawing water for the sacrifice and, often, a shepherd leaning on his crook watching his flocks at drink." It is easy to see that this delightful picture was drawn from notes taken while with the Princes' Army.

The druidess Valléda, according to the author, was intended to recall Natalie de Noailles. "She was an unusual woman. There was something capricious and attractive about her, as there is in all the women of Gaul. She had a darting glance, her mouth was slightly disdainful and her smile singularly sweet and unearthly. Her manners were sometimes haughty, sometimes melting. Her whole personality radiated goodness and dignity, innocence and art. Pride was the dominant characteristic of this barbarian, while the ecstasy of her emotions often bordered on frenzy."

The proconsul of Achaia, Hiéroclès, was recognisable as an unflattering portrait of the dread Fouché. "A Greek by birth, Hiéroclès was suspected of having been a Christian in his youth, but the vanity of human letters having corrupted his mind, he threw himself into the sects of the philosophers. No trace of his early religion was discernible save, perhaps, in the strange delirium which the very name of the God he had forsaken roused in him. . . . His sententious and decisive speech and his air of pride and self-importance rendered him odious to our open-hearted simplicity. Even his person seemed to repel confidence and affection. His low and glowering brow betokened obduracy and party spirit. His eyes were false and furtive like those of a wild beast, his glance at once timorous and fierce; his thick lips were nearly always parted in a hungry and cruel smile; his thin and bristly hair hung in disorder, as though it had nothing in common with those locks which God has cast as a veil about the shoulders of the young, and as a crown of glory about the head of the old. Something indefinably cynical and shameful emanated from every feature of the sophist. It was obvious that his ignoble hands were ill apt to grasp the soldier's sword, but that they might easily wield the atheist's pen or the hangman's knife." In the joy of painting, the author had doubtless forgotten that the original was the Minister of Police.

Les Martyrs was by no means a dull book. The public of the Empire read it with pleasure. A whole school of young historians believed it to be a pattern of historical reconstruction. Guizot and Augustin Thierry praised it highly. Yet it cannot, like *Le Génie du Christianisme*, be said to be a great book. Chateaubriand had written *Les Martyrs* as the complement of an attitude and as a literary exercise. Learning is an impassioned state; for the novelist it is a rejection. Unable to express the real strength of emotions on paper, he heaps up ramparts of facts to conceal his passions. On reading *Les Martyrs* one is reminded of some vast historical picture, painted to order, which yet—because it is the work of an artist of genius—has fine highlights. These correspond, too, with the moments when the author has at last dared to be himself, whether he is describing the campaigns of Eudore or the vileness of Fouché, or again, when he paints in Hell that demon of pleasure who remained his familiar spirit.

Le Dernier des Abencérages, a memento of the Alhambra and of Natalie de Noailles, was written at the Valley of Wolves but for reasons of decorum not published till 1826. "A masterpiece in the Troubadour style" it is a well-constructed short story, clearer in outline and freer of useless ornament than the rest of Chateaubriand's romantic work. The plot is the same as in all his tales—the love of two beings who are divided by an insuperable obstacle. In the *Abencérage* it is religion which comes between a young Christian and a young Mussulman. The feelings of all the characters are equally lofty, equally simple and equally symmetrical. After the capture of Granada by the Spaniards, the household of the Abencérages has had to seek refuge in Tunis. Much later, the last of its descendants, Aben-Hamet decides to go on pilgrimage to the land of his ancestors. There he meets Blanca, a Christian of the lineage of the Cid. "If Aben-Hamet turns Christian," says Blanca, "I will marry him," and Aben-Hamet: "If Blanca turns Mussulman, I will serve her with my dying breath." Together they visit the Alhambra. "By moonlight Aben-Hamet wrote the name of Blanca on the marble in the Hall of the Two Sisters, tracing it in Arab characters so that the traveller might come upon one mystery the more in this palace of mysteries." Twice again, Aben-Hamet returns to Granada. The third time Blanca introduces her brother Carlos and Lautrec, a knight who is in love with her. Carlos provokes the Moor. Aben-Hamet, the victor, spares the life of Carlos. Thereafter they all live together and sing ballads which, alone among Chateaubriand's verses, have remained famous.

> Combien j'ai douce souvenance
> Du joli lieu de ma naissance!
> Ma soeur, qu'ils étaient beaux les jours
>   De France!
> O mon pays, sois mes amours
>   Toujours! . . .
>
> Ma soeur, to souvient-il encore
> Du château que baignait la Dore,
> Et de catte tant vieille tour
>   Du Maure,
> Où l'airain sonnait le retour
>   Du Jour!

And again:—

> Prêt à partir pour la rive africaine
> Le Cid, armé, tout bouillant de valeur,
> Sur sa guitare, aux pieds de sa Chimène,
> Chantait ces vers que lui dictait l'honneur.

The Abencérage is naturally too loyal to turn convert, Blanca too sublime to marry him. She cries to him: "Go back to the desert," and falls senseless. To all alike Chateaubriand lends his own taste for striking attitudes and his own ethic, which has no other springs than honour and faith. Hence they are chivalrous puppets, as unreal as they are charming.

L'Itinéraire de Paris à Jerusalem occupied Chateaubriand from 1809 to 1811. Joubert would have done well to remind him of his advice at the time of *Le Génie du Christianisme* and beg him not to smother his memories and impressions under masses of documents. All through the first part, the scene of which is laid in Greece, the genuineness of Chateaubriand's feeling for Athens and Sparta (for he was a traveller of profound classical culture), the

The Valley of Wolves

mocking portrait of the pilgrim himself, of his servants and of the landscapes "drawn from nature in the nude" enliven and throw light on the account. Chateaubriand has been accused of figuring, as always, in the rôle of no less than three characters—the pilgrim, the lover of the glory that was Greece, and the great traveller. Yet he cared for glory and antiquity with all his heart and there is no disputing that his narrative, which was then wholly original in character, has made him the ancestor of the author-explorers of today.

It was in the Valley of Wolves, too, that he wrote the whole of the tragedy of *Moïse*—alas! wholly without merit. He was far from suspecting the fact. "I am very pleased with it. . . . It is the Bible in all its purity, in all its greatness and in all its nobility, as in *Athalie*, and does not fall far short of Racine. What do you think of my tragedy? Have I not told you scores of times in my letters that I was writing one, that it was called *Moïse* and that I had two acts finished? I will even add that I think those two acts excellent. Now and then I must brag. Don't worry, however. If my tragedy is not a masterpiece and fails to place me in the front rank, I shall have no hesitation in putting it on the fire since, after all, it is not on it that I have set my renown. Now you are reassured. Remember, too, I spent twenty years of my life in writing verse before ever I penned a line of prose, so I am no novice where the instrument is concerned." His more perspicacious friends long restrained him from having *Moïse* performed.

About 1809 he took up another idea, which had come to him in Rome after the death of Mme. de Beaumont, that of writing his Memoirs and carving for posterity a statue of himself which should arrest for all eternity his favourite attitude: "A gentleman, I think, may well wait until he is dead to speak his whole mind from the shelter of a tomb weighted and sealed at last with a heavy stone." The *Itinéraire* did not leave him much time, however, and—at the Valley of Wolves—he got no further with the *Mémoires* than the Breton schools. Another scheme which occupied these years of retreat was that of a reasoned analysis of the history of France. It was a fine enterprise and he took it seriously: "I am working contentedly at the history, and *Moïse* has done naught but good to the long-gone tragedies of the most Christian

Kings. I shall treat our friends magnificently. Already I have brought before me a few Durases, La Trémoilles, Montmorencys, etc., but now I must be reverenced from afar and woe to him who looks at me askance. Poor Philip the Fair! What a dressing-down I've given him for his States General! It's odd that the history of France still remains to be written and that no one has ever suspected it."

In the midst of such work, the time passed peacefully enough. From time to time, the reading of a few pages gave the "Madams" a chance of proving their devotion. The sun of a little universe of his own, Chateaubriand forgot the lustre of the Other and would not have been too unhappy if his enemies had left him in peace. There were some among them, however, who were not disarming.

4. HE AND HE

"At the moment when *Le Génie du Christianisme* appeared, envy had not yet had time to take steps. The public likes to flatter talent in its dawn. Later, it revenges itself on an established reputation for the enthusiasm and admiration with which it built it up." The remark is Chênedollé's—it is bitter, but true. For Chateaubriand, every publication that followed the triumph of the *Génie* was to give rise to a battle. Even a battle may be waged from a point of vantage and with sound allies, yet—if, at the time of the *Génie*, Chateaubriand had the Consul, the great bell of Notre-Dame and all the chimes of France for him, at the time of *Les Martyrs* the reigning powers and even the Church itself were inimical.

It was not that Napoleon really nursed a grudge against him. He continued to think Chateaubriand unfitted for affairs of state. "There are men," said he to Metternich, "who believe themselves universally competent because they have one quality or one talent. Among such men is Chateaubriand, who goes in for opposition because I will not employ him. The man is a reasoner in the void, but he has great powers of dialectic. If only he would use his powers within the lines laid down for him, he might be useful, but he will do no such thing, and so is no use at all. A man must either know how to govern himself or submit to orders. He can do neither the one nor the other, so he must not be given employment. A score of times he has offered himself to me, but rather as though to bend me to his imagination—which always leads him astray—than to obey me. I have refused his services; that is to say, I have refused to serve him."

Politics apart, "M. de Chateaubriand was always an object of rare predilection for the Emperor, who never wearied in his desire to see him an ornament of his reign and never lost hope. Momentary persecutions on his part were merely signs of annoyance." When Girodet's portrait of Chateaubriand was hung in the Salon, Denon—to curry favour—relegated it to a place where it would not meet the eyes of the official procession. The Emperor asked that the picture should be produced and looked long at that sallow face, that storm-tossed hair and those hands slipped, almost imperially, beneath the lapels of his coat. "He looks," said Napoleon, "like a conspirator who has just come down the chimney." It was a feeble witticism, but there was no malice in it and any sign of interest from the Master was a favour. Then again, the friends of both men saw to it that their relations should not be poisoned. Fontanes had everything that might have stirred up the *Mercure* episode eliminated from the manuscript of *Les Martyrs*. "It does not do to sharpen the teeth of the lion." Fouché, favourably disposed by Mme. de Custine (who, for a few days, had almost as many ardent notes from Chateaubriand as in the old days of Fervacques, but only on this subject), received the author and assured him that he would not have it censored. He left it to him. Chateaubriand, wild with delight, gave thanks to the Queen of Roses: "No censorship, loud praises, honours, flattery—things could not have gone better. A great friend, a divine person! Till tomorrow, my Dear." On friends' advice, the book was carefully pruned. They even went the length of suppressing a few words on the origin of Diocletian, who was the son of a registrar, because the pamphleteers had given out that the Emperor was the son of a registrar in Ajaccio.

Alas! the friends' counsels were too concerned with Diocletian and not enough with the sophists at his court. It may be remembered that the portrait of Hiéroclès, proconsul of Achaia, bore a dangerous likeness to Fouché himself. There was certainly some indelicacy in publishing the caricature in a book which its prototype had exempted from the censorship. Provoked by this offence, Fouché's hostility was to rekindle the zeal of the sceptical set against the work for, though defeated in 1802, the philosophers were again raising their heads in 1809.

By a grievous blow of fate, at the very moment when *Les Martyrs* was about to appear, a terrible storm broke upon Chateaubriand. Armand, the cousin with whom he had played on the Sillon as a child and who had gained him a welcome among the recalcitrant émigrés of the Princes' Army, had gone on living in Jersey, where he had married and where he was still one of the most active emissaries of the Chouans. There were a few such poor devils whom the princes' agents occasionally launched on some hopeless enterprise. Their aim was to keep the English government on the alert and to wring a little gold out of it. After a succession of contrary adventures (everything conspired against him—storms at sea, ambushes on land, the ocean, Napoleon, compromising papers thrown overboard and washed ashore by the tide), Armand had fallen into the hands of the police; his identity (at first concealed under a false name) had come to light and his mission had been all too clearly established. He had been charged with obtaining secret information on the situation in France and the chances of a restoration, and with taking back a detailed plan of the port of Brest. The espionage could not be denied. Would Fouché incline the Emperor to clemency? It was very unlikely. By reason of his political position he was hostile to the royalists and disposed to exaggerate the importance of their plots. This was more true than ever in January 1809 when, on his return from Spain, the Emperor was hustling Talleyrand and Fouché severely. If, over and above these circumstances, Fouché had just read the cruel description of himself in *Les Martyrs*, he could not have been feeling very tenderly towards the name of Chateaubriand.

No sooner did the writer hear of his cousin's arrest than he intervened in his defence and called on Fouché in the company of Mme. de Custine. Fouché temporized craftily. He began by maintaining that no Chateaubriand figured among the prison entries. That was true, for the prisoner had been committed under a false name. When, at last, the Minister admitted the facts, it was merely to say "with the cool unconcern of the revolutionary" that he had seen Armand, that Chateaubriand might set his mind at rest, that his cousin had promised to make a good end and indeed seemed steadfast in his resolution. Chateaubriand behaved as well as possible, busying himself over the least details. *To the Comtesse de Marigny:* "I am sending you my greatcoat, my hat, my breeches, my waistcoat and a pair of stockings. Have them all sent to the gaoler and buy some shoes if you see need. I am putting in my black stock as well. I do nothing but haste on this wretched business. Even now I am not without hope, but remember that this is the day when they are to appear before the Tribunal and he must be dressed early."

He wrote the Empress a letter which Mme. de Rémusat promised to deliver. Napoleon threw it on the fire saying: "Chateaubriand asks for justice; he shall have it." On March 29th, the opening day of the trial, he addressed a second letter to the Emperor: "Sire, Armand de Chateaubriand appeared this morning before his judges; tomorrow sentence will be pronounced. Allow me to plead a second time with Your Majesty for the lives of my cousin and his unhappy companions, in the event of their being condemned. Deign, Sire, to let your clemency redound on behalf of a family which, for centuries, has shed its blood for its country; it is the first time my name has ever appeared on the list of the enemies of its native land. Of myself, Sire, I dare not speak to you. Had I won more repute in the field of letters, I might perhaps have some claim to appeal to your renown. But, to the foot of your throne, I bring only a nameless grief and the tears of a faithful subject.[1]

Hoping for an audience, he did not undress all night and was still in his court clothes when, on the following morning (Good Friday, March 31st) he learned that the tumbril was bearing the condemned to Grenelle. He arrived when all was over. Though he saw the body, he could not recognise his cousin, for the lead had left nothing of his face. To Mme. de Custine he carried back a handkerchief steeped in the blood of the hapless Armand. Never afterwards did he cross the parade-ground of Grenelle but he

[1] Letter published by Mlle. Daremberg (*Bulletin de la Société Chateaubriand*).

stopped to look at the scars of the bullets on the wall. He loved to gaze out on dark horizons.

He was accused of seeming rather exasperated than grief-stricken after this tragedy, and of wearing his weeds with "insulting ostentation." The fact remains that he gave proof of courage, and that, in the circumstances, none could have saved Armand—who was guilty—from the web of that spider, Fouché. *Les Martyrs* had not escaped his eye. Despite his fair promises to Mme. de Custine, "the great friend" had seen to it that the book should be pilloried in the official gazettes particularly by the critic Hofmann, who shrewdly attempted to array against the author the very forces which had made the success of *Le Génie du Christianisme*—that is to say the Catholic public. He all but taxed Chateaubriand with having—by opposing Jupiter to Jehovah—rewritten the unseemly *Guerre des Dieux* which he had strongly condemned in the past. "It would be grievous," said Hofmann hypocritically, "to so estimable and religious an author if he should find himself accused of having corrupted the public taste or of having been no other than a philosopher in sheep's clothing." The indictment told. "We saw," said Mme. de Chateaubriand, "people who called themselves royalists, priests even, who could not say enough ill of us. It was one way of currying favour." Chateaubriand challenged the "literary mountebanks" in the pay of the police with contempt, but he feared that his book might be doomed. The eagerness of the public soon reassured him, for *Les Martyrs* sold as many copies in a few days as *Le Génie du Christianisme* had sold in months.

5. Lull

Suddenly, after Wagram, "the wind turned." The Emperor, who had long hesitated between the revolutionary and monarchist camps, decided to play the game of the Kings. Joséphine was sacrificed and Napoleon married Marie-Antoinette's niece. When, in her palace of the Tuileries, Marie-Louise played whist with Fouché and Cambacérès, Talleyrand remarked that there was a dead man at the feast. To appease that importunate shade, the regicide Fouché, Duc d'Otrante, was dismissed. The Catholic party triumphed. Fontanes was translated to the Senate, Pasquier to the Council of State. The new Minister of Police, Savary, had orders to treat the Faubourg Saint-Germain with the utmost consideration, since its support was vital to the new Court, and to ensure the co-operation of writers. "Treat men of letters well," the Emperor told him. "They have been prejudiced against me by the report that I disliked them—a rumour spread of set purpose. If I had not so much to do, I would see more of them. They are useful men and must be singled out for distinction since they bring honour on France."

Of all French writers of the age, the most illustrious was Chateaubriand. His courageous retirement had only increased his renown and no more flattering conquest could have been made. The Emperor desired it. It is even possible that, through the instrumentality of La Valette, he helped his adversary financially. About that time Mme. de Chateaubriand noted in her diary that, in their absence, the gardener of the Valley had an odd visit. Two gentlemen, the shorter of whom seemed to be the master, asked to see the garden and Velléda's tower. When they left, they gave Benjamin five napoleons. That evening, on going to lock up the tower, he found a laurel branch planted in a handful of new-turned earth and a wash-leather glove which he treasured. " 'Deed Ma'am," said he, "I thought it was Bonaparte." She liked to think so too, and her Bonapartism revived. Fontanes, who thought that his friend's hour had struck, took his stand by his side, not more faithfully, but more overtly. He sent him some fine stanzas on the woes of Tasso, ending with the promise

> Du prix qu'un nouvel Alexandre
> Promet à l'illustre écrivain . . .
>
> Que le mérite se console,
> Un héros gouverne aujourd'hui;
> Des arts il veut rouvrir l'école,
> Et faire asseoir au Capitole
> Tous les talents dignes de lui.

What was this prize, created by the new Alexander, which Fontanes offered to Chateaubriand? He was referring to a longstanding plan of Napoleon's; for, readily persuading himself that if the Empire had no literature "it was the fault of the Minister of the

Interior," the Emperor had founded, for writers, scholars and artists, decennial prizes of ten thousand and five thousand francs, to be awarded on the recommendation of the various classes of the Institut. The first distribution had been fixed for November, 1810. When the choice of the second class (the Académie Française) was made known, public opinion and the Emperor were hotly indignant. Chateaubriand, who was the bête noire of Marie-Joseph Chénier and of the Abbé Morellet, had been passed over, though to neglect—among the publications of the last ten years—*Le Génie du Christianisme* and *Les Martyrs* was a crying scandal. The Emperor, who had counted on the lustre of the prize to effect a reconciliation between himself and Chateaubriand, was deeply vexed and ordered Montalivet to ask the class its most explicit reasons for passing over *Le Génie du Christianisme*. The Emperor had to be answered. The Academy appointed a commission. M. Népomucène Lemercier declared peremptorily that so imperfect a work as the *Génie* could not, "without a hint of the ridiculous," take up more of the Academy's time. Fontanes sprang to the defence of his friend and stirred up incredible outbursts of rage. "After a great hullaballoo" the class stated that the work was faulty, but that it yet had beauties of the first order and, though it could not be awarded a prize, the author should be recommended to His Majesty for special distinction. *Chateaubriand to Mme. de Marigny:* "By order of the Minister I am to stand for the first vacancy in the Institut and I shall take it by storm."

Such indeed was the Emperor's will. By the irony of fate, Chateaubriand's chief enemy at the Academy, Marie-Joseph Chénier, died at that moment. Chateaubriand's friends took it into their heads to see him elected to Chénier's vacant chair, for such a posthumous revenge appealed to them. The hero of the comedy proved less enthusiastic. He admitted that, for a man exposed as he was to the pestering of the police, it might be necessary to enter "a body powerful by reason of its renown and membership, and to work in peace in the shelter of such a buckler." However, the oration on Chénier seemed to him a danger-point. Marie-Joseph had been a regicide. Could a royalist deliver his encomium? If he submitted to doing so, was he not bound in honour to proclaim his fealty to his kings and his abhorrence of the crimes of 1793? Did that not

The Valley of Wolves

constitute yet another provocation to the Emperor? Fontanes, an expert in imperial diplomacy, reassured him: "My friends replied that I was mistaken, that a few of those praises of the head of the government which are obligatory in an academic oration (praises of which, from one point of view, I thought Bonaparte worthy) would make him swallow all the truths I was bent on uttering, that I would at once have the honour of maintaining my opinions and of calming the alarms of Mme. de Chateaubriand." Eventually, so that he might protect his forthcoming *Itinéraire* from the hostility of the government press, he consented to stand.

Invitus invitam. . . . Against his will, he sought the suffrage of an Academy which was loath to give it, but the Emperor's personal candidate had to be elected. "Such are the paradoxes of the age." At least they meted him the scantiest possible measure. Twenty-three members only were present at the meeting and, on a second ballot, Chateaubriand was elected by no more than thirteen votes. In the evening, at the Emperor's club, Napoleon seemed in high good humour, congratulating M. de Fontanes with that smile which could be so winning: "Ah, ha! You are begging the question, gentlemen of the Academy. You have been foxing with me; you have taken the man instead of the book." It was pleasant mockery. He knew perfectly well that, save for the strict orders of the Minister of Police, they would have taken neither the one nor the other. He added: "I must see whether there are no means of giving the new member some distinguished literary post, the controllership of the libraries of the Empire, for instance." Fontanes repeated the remark to Chateaubriand who, ever sanguine as in the days of the embassy and Rome, spent a few weeks picturing a great career of action in that Empire which an empress of royal blood now linked with the House of Bourbon.

6. The Fall of the Rival

Chateaubriand's friends had thought that his election to the Institut would bring about the reconciliation of the Emperor and the poet; it became the cause of their final estrangement. "It matters little," said Fontanes, "that you should have to make Chénier's panegyric, provided that you make the Emperor's and I know that, from many points of view, you can do it with genuine admiration."

But Fontanes, a born academician and the soul of tact, failed—despite twenty years' intimacy—to conceive of his friend's violence. "I do not know," said the latter, "how to measure the dose of academic praise." He avoided the possibility of mistake by leaving out the ingredient.

The commission whose duty it was to listen to the reading of the speech was left gasping. The encomium was an indictment. Not the regicide only, but the cruel brother and the enemy of religion found themselves held up to judgment. True, the bonapartist peroration on which Fontanes had insisted was there: "Caesar ascends the Capitol. The nations shew forth his wondrous works—the monuments of his raising, the cities adorned, the borders of the Fatherland laved by those distant mains which bore the vessels of Scipio and by those far-off seas on which the eyes of Germanicus never looked. As the Victor marches on, with all his legions about him, how shall the harmonious children of the Muses do their part? They will go forth to meet his chariot that they may twine the olive branch of Peace with the palms of Victory." It was not bad, but it was not enough to pass off a tirade on liberty, nor on the raising of sacrilegious hands against dynasties, nor—above all—the condemnation of the Jacobin Chénier.

Caesar himself, when the text was communicated to him, fell into one of his towering rages. It was a feigned and official fury, for—in his heart—he was content to receive his whiff of incense from such hands, but he, the Conciliator, could not endure that the quarrels of the Revolution should be reopened: "Monsieur," said he to Ségur, "are the men of letters bent on setting all France ablaze? I have done all in my power to pacify the parties and to restore calm. Now the ideologues must needs wish to set up anarchy once more! How dare the Academy speak of regicides when I, who am crowned and should have more cause to hate them, dine instead in their company?" When Chateaubriand's manuscript was returned to him, it had been slashed by the imperial pencil. The author was no more aggrieved in reality than the Emperor had been. "The lion's claw," said he proudly, "had been dug all over it and there was a kind of pleasurable irritation in thinking that I felt it in my side." In the emotions which held these two high-souled enemies apart there was something not unlike a lover's spleen.

The Valley of Wolves

The affair raised a question of academic etiquette—how was Chateaubriand to be received? Daru suggested alterations and when, with true Breton stubbornness, Chateaubriand refused to change a single word, advised him to write another speech. Again he refused and wrote to the president of the class that "as his many occupations and poor state of health forbade his devoting himself to work, it was impossible to fix the date on which he would request the honour of being received into the Academy." Would he be allowed to take his seat without an official reception? It was not possible. Would there be reprisals against him? The Minister promised that there should be none. *Chateaubriand to Mme. de Marigny:* "For the moment I am quit of it all. I have flatly refused to write a second speech. It seems that no harm is to befall me. I do not know whether my name will be struck off the roll, but this much is certain—I shall not have the right to attend meetings and hence cannot become a member of the Institut—a circumstance which delights me and enraptures everyone else." He came out of it with flying colours. Public opinion (that section, at least, which he heeded) was for him and for "his tripled fame." Yet, once calm was restored, he felt his isolation. In *Les Martyrs* and in the *Itinéraire* he had bidden farewell to letters; at the time of his election he had believed that an honourable reconciliation with the Empire was about to restore him to an active career as Director of Libraries or of Belles-Lettres. Instead, he found himself back in the Valley of Wolves, poorer than ever and cumbered with a wife who, despite her wit and her good qualities, bored and irritated him. Moreover, if the Empire were to outlast his life time, he had no hope of change. Wandering by night in his garden, he followed the track of the comet which, in that summer of 1811, arched the horizon of the woods. "She was beautiful and sad, and—like a queen—trailed her long veil about her path." With this starry queen, there came to him the fallen Empress. Joséphine sent for him to Malmaison and gave him magnolia plants for his garden. He donned his dress-coat and those two great ruins consoled one another. It was scant consolation! Then, as nearly always happened when he was passing through a crisis of dejection, he believed himself to be seriously ill, developed palpitations and attributed the pains in his side to an aneurism. His sceptical wife regarded the sickness as purely moral and the great Laënnec confirmed her diagnosis.

So illness, too, betrayed him. Meanwhile, the bonds between him and Mme. de Mouchy, whom he had loved with passion, were slackening. Poor Natalie was charming—but depressingly capricious and rattlepated. Mme. de Duras was made the confidante of the approaching break: "The Rue de Cerutti is back at its storms. Yesterday I was given my formal dismissal and I accepted it for, when all is said and done, there is an end to everything. Whether I shall be recalled I do not know, but one thing is certain, I can stand it no longer." Then, ten days later: "The Rue de Cerutti is always the same story over again. I was indeed recalled, but matters have in no way changed and will never change again. I have returned all I had and not a trace remains of that which has gone to make the joy and grief of my life. I believe I shall be happier, though perhaps a trifle sadder, too. But time is hasting and will bear me away with all my futilities and all my follies.'

Though Natalie de Noailles was out of the picture, the battalion of "Madams" was no less strong in numbers. Mme. de Lévis, Mme. de Bérenger, and Mme. de Montmorency, whom he called "Adrienne" because her husband was Adrien de Laval-Montmorency, "the dearest little person imaginable," continued to vie with each other for visits from the "Genius" and were unfailing in their attentions to Mme. de Chateaubriand. None, however, found the way of his desert heart and he was bored to death. "In the perfect freedom I enjoy, I long only for solitude and rest. The passion which has supplanted all others in my heart is my garden. When a man's old, he must dodder about something." To Claire de Duras who taxed him with unsociability: "My sister wants me to have friends. Are they of our own making? Is it in our character to change? At heart I'm a real hermit. If I were free, I should certainly live in absolute solitude. Once a man has an overmastering taste, it's all he's good for. I know perfectly well that I am nothing but a book-machine, but I am neither exaggerating nor romancing when I say that the things I need, or rather have needed, are a desert, a library and a miss." The picture was still that of the happiness he might have tasted with Charlotte Ives. There is no

The Valley of Wolves

Don Juan but spends his life lamenting the tender and faithful being he has slain within himself in youth.

Money troubles followed on the frets of love. At every fresh alarm Mme. de Duras, who never wearied, took the field bravely. Sometimes she lent a few thousand francs, sometimes she founded a society which advanced Chateaubriand the bulk of the money he needed, in exchange for the royalties on some of his books. In such societies Mme. de Duras was always the chief shareholder, but Adrien de Montmorency also subscribed, as did some of the "Madams," the Tocquevilles, the Rosambos and Chateaubriand's nephews. *To the Duchesse de Duras:* "My nephews are providing four thousand francs and I think I can easily raise two thousand more among the family. That leaves only six thousand to be found between you and your friends. It shouldn't be difficult. Hence, if all goes well, I shall have twelve thousand francs a year and I shall be a high and puissant seigneur."

The elder of his nephews, Louis—the heir of Combourg—had lately married Mlle. Zélie d'Orglandes, and the uncle, who had gone to the wedding despite his horror of that "gloomy ceremony," set everyone weeping by his ingenuous and melancholy diatribes. "It's done now. They're on the high road to all sorrows, and it's quick walking. When I saw the poor orphan and his brother seeking foothold in a family of strangers and heard him address a person whom he had seen hardly a dozen times as 'Mother,' I was really moved. It reminded me of the death of all my kin, of my loneliness on this earth and of the tombs that are rising about me. But a few years and I too shall be numbered among them that rest."

Thus marriage, equally with death, brought him back to the centre of his thoughts—his own tomb. "My forehead is growing bald; I am beginning to dodder; I bore other people and I bore myself. Fever will come and one fine day I shall be borne to Chatenay. Who will be found to remember me? My dear sister, tell me that. A few musty tomes that I have left behind me and that none reads more will arouse a brief controversy at the time of my passing. Some will say that they are worth nothing and have died with me. Others will maintain that there is a something in all that lumber. They will leave it at that and close the book—then go their way to dine, to dance, perchance to weep. . . ."

. . . .

Envy and cowardice go ever paired. No sooner did Chateaubriand's enemies know him to be under a cloud than all the campaigns began again. At first they were confined to sneers and more or less harmless parodies. Under the title of *Saint-Géran ou la nouvelle langue française* the chemist Cadet Gassicourt published a parody of the *Itinéraire* which aimed at being droll and succeeded in being dull. Until then, the *Essai sur les Révolutions* had been almost unknown in France. Following the episode of the Academy oration it was denounced and the "philosophers" set out to prove first that, in his early works, Chateaubriand had attacked religion more violently than ever did Marie-Joseph Chénier and secondly, that he had lied in the preface to *Le Génie du Christianisme*, that the death of his mother and sister had in no wise determined his feigned conversion, which had been sheer hypocrisy. Warned in time, he could muster his defences. *To the Comtesse de Marigny:* "My dear Child, if it is in any way possible will you please let me have by return of courier, the exact dates of our poor mother's death and of Mme. de Farcy's. Try to remember the month—the day even—but especially the year. I hope once more to triumph over the ills that dog my steps." Gladly would he have published the complete *Essai*, for the impartiality of the work would have been its best defence. The censorship forbade, however, and he had to content himself with getting a young writer to take up the cudgels in a pamphlet which included those pages of the *Essai* most favourable to his thesis. All things considered, the incident redounded to his credit.

In September 1812, following some indiscreet remarks, Chateaubriand was invited (with the utmost courtesy) by his friend the Prefect, Pasquier, to try the air of Dieppe for a few days. The prospect of once more beholding his old foster-mother, the sea, and the pebbles on which he had learned to drill with the Royal-Navarre, was by no means unpleasant. Pasquier, knowing how Mme. de Chateaubriand clung to the feast of St. Francis and her dinner-party, made no difficulties about allowing the exile to be

The Valley of Wolves

home for October 4th and may even have been at the dinner himself. Because it was efficient, the imperial police could afford the leniency of strong powers.

It was yet a time when, foreseeing the possible fall of the Empire, all were preparing a line of retreat, a time "of surface greatness and inward anguish." Chateaubriand spent the winter of 1812-13 in Paris. Owing to the position he had taken up, to his celebrity and to his past, he had become the recipient of many confidences, some of them extremely grave. Not only did his fair friends of the Faubourg and such monarchists as Clausel de Coussergues keep him informed of the hopes of Louis XVIII, but government officials told him of their fears. The clergy, who had long been favourable to Napoleon as the restorer of religion, began to fall away when, in 1809, the Emperor was excommunicated and the Pope led prisoner to Fontainebleau. Wise and peaceable men such as Fontanes and Pasquier were alarmed to see that their sovereign could not free himself from the vicious circle of his wars. Already they prophesied the inevitable consequences. Napoleon himself was beginning to lose faith in his star. From the beginning of his incredible adventure he feared that the edifice of his building was founded upon sand. In an attempt to strengthen it, he had tried to raise it upon the buried pillars of the past. The Roman Church, the Austrian Empire and the nobility of France—all those forces which he regarded as more enduring than force—had been called to his aid. At the first reverses those coerced and rebellious allies escaped him. Since the Russian campaign even his marshals stood out against their chief. By 1812 Mallet's conspiracy, feeble as it was, came near to succeeding. "A breath had all but overthrown the Empire." It seemed that the Emperor was lost and many Frenchmen, dissociating the cause of their country from that of its sovereign, rejoiced.

Amid such chaos, "each and all were preoccupied with the part they would play in the approaching catastrophe." Chateaubriand's wish was to see the return of the Bourbons, not that he had any enthusiasm for Louis XVIII, who was old and gouty, but that "when there is no refuge from a storm save a tumble-down building, one shelters even among its ruins." The difficulty was that the rising generation, educated under the Revolution and the

Empire, had scarcely even heard the name of its kings. When, in 1814, a general of the Empire mentioned to the young Chevalier de Cussy the possibility of a Bourbon restoration, he said: "It was the first time that ever I heard of that illustrious and ill-fated family. At school their name was never mentioned. Only once did the chaplain refer to the memorable fall of the Bourbons, stricken by the hand of God who, in his divine wisdom, was making ready the way of the great Napoleon." If the French were to accept the king's return, the first essential was to make him known to them. Hence, in October 1813, while Napoleon—slowing down the march of the European powers arrayed against him—was winning "his last and mortal victories" and while the long thunder of the distant guns died above the lonely woods of the Valley of Wolves, Chateaubriand sat down to write "pages as stirring as the events of the day."

. . . .

The pamphlet was entitled: *De Buonaparte et des Bourbons*. It was made up of three parts. The first "Of Buonaparte" was an unvarnished picture of the Revolution. "Then there crept out of their lairs all those half-naked kings, grimed and besotted by poverty, grown ugly and deformed through toil, their only virtue the insolence of wretchedness and the pride of rags. . . ." There followed a portrait of "Buonaparte the foreigner," who—after this Revolution—had become its supreme head. The time had been when Chateaubriand granted him qualities of greatness but, in 1813, he had not a good word to say for him. He thought him a little lower than the vilest of Roman tyrants: "Absurd as an administrator, criminal as a politician, what had this foreigner done that he should beguile the French? Was it his military glory? Well, he is shorn of that. True, he was a great winner of battles, but—apart from that—the least of generals is cleverer than he. . . . He knows only how to march straight forward, score points, bustle to and fro, carry off victories by man power (as has been said), sacrifice everything for one success—careless of reverses—and kill off half his soldiers by forced marches beyond the power of human endurance. He has been thought to have perfected the art of war, but there can be no doubt that he has reduced it to its second childishness. . . ."

The poet stamped upon the head of his rival: "Buonaparte is a pseudo-great man. Of magnanimity, which makes true kings and heroes, he knows nothing. . . . That vast head of his is the realm of chaos and of night. . . . He is something of a mountebank and a player. He is forever acting, even the passions he does not feel. . . . On every occasion he tries to speak what he believes to be a memorable word or to do what he imagines a notable deed. Under the mask of Caesar and of Alexander there looks out the man of naught, the son of nobodies. His contempt for men is sovereign, for he judges them by the pattern of himself." Then, in a brutal apostrophe to the Emperor, he bids him "Come down from that heap of ruins of which you have made your throne. As you cast out the Directory, so do we cast out you. . . . That is our message to the foreigner. If we then thrust out Buonaparte, who shall take his place?—The King."

Part the second: "Of the Bourbons." King, magistrate and father, for the Frenchman these three ideas are one. He does not know the meaning of an emperor. He knows neither the nature, the form nor the limits of power attached to that foreign title, but he knows the significance of a monarch descended from St. Louis and from Henry IV. . . . "Louis XVIII, who should be the first to reign over us, is a prince famed for his enlightenment, inaccessible to foreign prejudices as to vengeance. . . . Not only has he the moderation and good sense needful in a monarch, but he is a princely patron of letters, a broad and enlightened mind, a man of firm and philosophic character." Under the sway of the Bourbons all would grow smooth and lawful: "Their very presence will restore that order of which they are for us the principle."

Part the third: "Of the Allies." This section was the most discreditable of the pamphlet, for in it Chateaubriand welcomed with unbounded enthusiasm the invaders of France. "They are liberators," said he, "not conquerors." He ended: "Friends, men of France, companions in misfortune, let us forget our quarrels. . . . Let the cry of our salvation resound throughout the land, that cry which our fathers sent echoing in defeat as in victory, the signal of our joy and peace to come: Long live the King!"

None of all Chateaubriand's political writings is so difficult to judge as this. It is painful enough to see Chateaubriand heap scorn on the Emperor, who was even then defending the bounds of France, but it must needs be admitted that it was Bonaparte who was responsible for the invasion. The text might more truly be described as an act. Chateaubriand wanted to achieve results, to wean the French from Napoleon and bind them once again to the Bourbons. Come what might, it needed considerable courage to write such a pamphlet at a time when the Empire was still unconquered. Had it been confiscated Chateaubriand might well have been sent to the scaffold or to Vincennes. He knew it, locked the door on himself while he was working and, at night, hid the papers under his pillow. In the daytime, Mme. de Chateaubriand, who was terrified at her husband's daring (which she did not altogether approve) and dreaded his carelessness, wore the manuscript beneath her dress. One day, while walking in the Tuileries, she realised that it was no longer there and decided that she must have lost it by the way. Already, in imagination, she saw her husband arrested, and fell senseless in the middle of the garden. Kindly bystanders took her home. She went straight to bed, raised the pillow and saw—the roll of paper. "Never in all my life," she wrote, "have I known a moment of such joy."

It was Chateaubriand's hope that his pamphlet might pave the way to the return of the Bourbons, but so swiftly did the fall of the Eagle trace its "lightning furrow" that events outran the prophet. By the end of March 1814, the Cossacks were at the gates of Paris. On the 30th the town surrendered and on the 31st a handful of royalists, in order to shew that France desired the return of the Bourbons (for it had been doubtful until then), went out to meet the allied sovereigns wearing white cockades. "No sooner," wrote Mme. de Chateaubriand severely, "was it certain that the lion was in chains and that the sovereigns were entering Paris than there were no curses too loud and deep for him who had known the breath of their incense. Every individual who went to meet the foreigners might have been returning from Coblenz. Mme. de Talleyrand (the divorced wife of Mr. Grant) drove through the streets in an open carriage singing hymns in praise of the godly family of the Bourbons. She and her following of ladies waved as many flags as they had handkerchiefs—all with infinite grace. Fifty carriages brought up the rear and took the cue from their leaders, so that the Allies, who debouched at that moment in the Place Vendôme, gained the impression that there were really as many lilies in the hearts of the French as there were white flags in the breeze. In another moment the air was filled with cries of 'Long live the King.' The signal was given. In France people would be ready to shout 'Off with my head' if they but heard their neighbours take up the cry. Houses were invaded in search of white ribbons and even petticoats to tear up for cockades, for the shops could not keep up with the demand. The red and blue were trampled underfoot, by the Bonapartists above all, while every tricolor to be found was carried to the cellars of the Luxembourg there to await its coming round once more. A friend of ours came to ask whether he might pillage my wardrobe, but he found me little disposed to hymn the victory before I knew the outcome of the strife, and I kept my petticoats."

For that he was a man of honour, Chateaubriand (despite the violence of his political passions) was more ashamed than triumphant when he saw the troops of the Emperor of Russia and of the Prussian king march past on the boulevard. "Numb and disquieted within as though the very name of Frenchman had been reft from me, to give place to the number by which would thenceforth be known in the mines of Siberia, I was conscious of a growing exasperation against the man whose glory had brought us to this shame." In that phrase, Sainte-Beuve can see only a feigned sorrow, worked up after the event. He maintains that Chateaubriand's one emotion at the time was a delirious ecstasy of joy. What can he know of it? May not a man be torn between two conflicting loyalties?

Whatever the truth of the matter, it was the psychological moment for publishing the pamphlet as soon as might be and, on March 31st, the walls of Paris were plastered with a white handbill: "*De Buonaparte et des Bourbons et de la nécessité de nous rallier à nos princes légitimes pour le bonheur de la France et celui de l'Europe*, by François Auguste de Chateaubriand, author of *Le Génie du Christianisme*. The work will appear tomorrow, or the day after tomorrow at latest, and will be on sale at Mame's and all booksellers."

Meanwhile, at Fontainebleau, the Emperor had tried to poison himself and, having failed, was at last making up his mind to abdicate. When he kissed the vanquished Eagle, there was not a dry eye among the soldiers of the Old Guard. Could he have done so without betraying his whole life, how Chateaubriand would have loved to make of these heroic tears and of a great man's fall the theme of noble periods, scattered with lofty imagery! But, eleven years before, he had chosen the camp of the Bourbons—and bravely chosen—at a time when he stood alone. Now, for the first time in his life, he found himself on the winning side, but his satisfaction was tinged with surprise, with anxious remorse and with a hint of melancholy. In those days of triumph and defeat, he may have tasted no joy more sincere than this—the knowledge that before he went from France, the Emperor found time to see his pamphlet and weighed it without anger, saying only: "That is true— That is mistaken," for, though he had just done his best to bring about the ruin of Napoleon, Chateaubriand yet admired Bonaparte in his heart.

CHAPTER VII

The Partisan

> What concern had I with all these futile troubles, I, who have never believed in my own era, I, whose roots are in the past, I, who have no trust in kings, no faith in nations, I, who have never cared for aught but dreams, and those only when they endure but for a night?
>
> —CHATEAUBRIAND

1. THE FIRST RESTORATION

THE King was about to return. Chateaubriand had been among the first to foresee or welcome a restoration. He was persuaded that his pamphlet had done more towards the crowning of Louis XVIII than an army of a hundred thousand men and, by dint of repetition, had come to think that both Napoleon and Louis XVIII said the same. At the time of the Consulate, it was a masterpiece of his that linked France with her religious past. Why should he not also be the writer to restore her to her monarchist traditions through the instrumentality of some new magnum opus? Once he had been the chosen spokesman of the Catholic party; now he aspired to become the director of conscience of the royalist. On the publication of the *Génie*, Chateaubriand had been given admirable publicity by the *Mercure* and by Fontanes. It was the *Journal des Débats* and Bertin who had to do the same for *De Buonaparte et des Bourbons*. Hardly a day passed but an article extolled "the Tacitus of the age"; compared the success of his pamphlet with that of the *Satire Ménippé*, and stressed the author's claims on the gratitude of the King and his long past of political loyalty. In that month of April 1814, he lived in high hope. Had he not the right to be sanguine and was it not hard to rust "at the age when a man is fit for anything? . . . We shall find consolation for the lost illusions of our youth in seeking to become citizens of credit and renown," he wrote. "What have we to fear from time when we may grow young through glory."

Meanwhile, the Emperor Alexander, the guest of M. Talleyrand in the Rue Saint-Florentin, was busy constituting a provisional government until such time as the French princes should return. Chateaubriand, who had not been invited to share their counsels, was justly indignant. "I, the coming man of the likely restoration, had to wait beneath their windows in the street while Talleyrand found places for his whist-partners in the provisional government." It leaked out that the maker of ministers had chosen the Abbé de Montesquiou, the senator Marquis de Jaucourt and a few others. In despair, Chateaubriand tried to see Alexander.

Through Mme. Krüdener, he had, since the beginning of his career, been in touch with the Empress Elisabeth. It was not long since she wrote to her mother, Amelia of Baden: "I am a great admirer of M. de Chateaubriand; there is something magical about his style. . . . When I read the *Itinéraire*, I'm often tempted to tell him of my flame." The Emperor was less warm. Chateaubriand, who had been granted an audience through the good graces of Mme. de Boigne, waited in a drawing-room with M. Étienne, the author of a play the Emperor had seen the night before. When Alexander passed through the apartment he stopped to say a word to M. Étienne about his play, admitted to Chateaubriand that he had not yet had time to read his pamphlet, "preached mutual peace between the two gentlemen, assured them that it was the business of men of letters to amuse the public, never to dabble in politics, and passed on without letting him get a word in edgewise." Chateaubriand left in a rage.

The famous pamphlet may have been itself to blame for such a welcome. Its attack on Corsicans was far from prudent: "Through what shameful caprice have we given the heritage of Robert the Strong to the son of an usher of Ajaccio?" Now the chief adviser of the Emperor Alexander was a Corsican—Pozzo di Borgo. Apart from this, Chateaubriand had offended the Duke of Wellington by making no mention of the English in his praise of the Allies, and had wounded his friend Fontanes by accusing the imperial university of teaching young Frenchmen "debauchery to the sound of the drum." When such errors of tact were pointed out, he corrected them with the same brusqueness as had led to their commission, brought out a new edition, introduced an encomium of Corsica, sang the praises of England and even went the length of writing: "We are too sensitive to glory not to admire that Lord Wellington who so strikingly reincarnates the virtues and the talents of our own Turenne." Thereafter he rehabilitated the school-drum, which Fontanes had hastened to replace by a bell. These sops to men in power and praises of the enemy were accompanied by further strictures on the fallen Emperor. There was nothing heroic about it all, but Chateaubriand, though anxious and disappointed, still believed that his destiny as a statesman was at stake and, since he had spent fifteen years in playing a losing game, dared take no further risks.

The 12th of April arrived bringing, not the King—who was laid up at Hartwell with an attack of rheumatism—but his brother the Comte d'Artois. Three or four hundred horsemen went out to greet him, Chateaubriand among them. He was presented to that affable and gracious prince, who (naturally enough) had no recollection of one day seeing at the court of Louis XVI a certain cadet from Brittany, and had never in his life opened *Le Génie du Christianisme*. An astute adviser, however, had constrained him to skim the pamphlet *De Buonaparte et des Bourbons* and Chateaubriand went home charmed with the prince's affectionate compliments. It wore off somewhat when he learned that, on his arrival, the new Lieutenant-General of the Kingdom had dined, not with a royalist among royalists, but at the inevitable Talleyrand's with the bonapartist Caulaincourt.

It was not long before Chateaubriand was like a bear with a sore head. His "proconsul Hiéroclès," the loathly Fouché, was received by the Comte d'Artois; Pasquier, who had been Bonaparte's Prefect of Police was made Prefect of Police under the Bourbons; Fontanes, one of the pillars of the Empire, remained Grand Master of the University. Going to call on Monseiur he remarked gravely: "We have been through difficult times, Your Royal Highness." There could be no doubt about that. "As for us, poor devils of legitimists," growled Chateaubriand, "no doors were open to us. We went for nothing. Sometimes word was sent out to us in the street to betake ourselves to bed; at others we would be recommended to hush our cries of 'Long live the King!' since the shouting had been entrusted to others." He forgot that, for success in politics, those "others" had two qualities in which he was entirely lacking—slipperiness and patience.

At long last came the King. All those who hoped to form part of the new Court rushed to Compiègne to meet him, the Duc de Duras, First Gentleman of the Chamber, among the van. The "dear sister" went with him, though Louis XVIII had refused to receive the daughter of the Conventional Kersaint. In the intoxication of the return all such things were forgotten. "The castle was soon packed with people from Paris, who saw to it that they were warmed, fed and lighted at the King's expense." With the old nobility there mingled the field-marshals of the Empire, notably Marmont and Ney, whom the courtiers treated with hypocritical respect since they were needed to make sure of the army. In order to witness that spectacle, which he thought partly of his contriving, but to which he was not invited, Chateaubriand had to get the *Journal des Débats* to send him to report it.

He admits that his account of the arrival at Compiègne was idealised. "The King wore a blue coat, relieved only by his epaulettes and the star of an order; his legs were encased in long gaiters of red velvet, edged with a narrow gold cord. . . . When he seated himself, his old-fashioned gaiters and the cane between his knees gave him a remarkable likeness to Louis XIV at fifty. . . . He stepped from his carriage, leaning on the arm of a young woman; he stood before captains who had never seen him and grenadiers who scarce had heard his name. 'What man is that?' 'It is the King.' Everyone fell at his feet." So ran the article in the *Débats*. Later, when Chateaubriand was compiling his *Mémoires*, he added: "What I said was true of the leaders, but with regard to the soldiers I lied." Having then outlived all hope and all ambition, he could give rein to a secret satisfaction in describing the lowering faces of the Old Guard, who looked like thunderclouds as they lined the route of the obese and gouty sovereign who had come to take the place of their Emperor.

For the King on whom so many hopes were fixed was an invalid.

The Partisan

In the white waistcoat which reached to his knees and gaiters that bagged like a petticoat, he inspired stupefaction rather than awe. "The King," remarked someone at the time, "has something of the old woman about him and something of the capon, of the son of France and of the schoolmaster." It was sound observation. With the pedantry of the schoolmaster, Louis XVIII united the riggish imagination of the capon, the senile affections of an old woman, but the dignity of the son of France to boot. During his long exile, he had been capable of majesty even when in dire distress. An absolutist at heart, he believed in his divine right. "Apart from that right what am I? A sick old man." One gift he possessed in the highest degree—and it made him a sovereign much to be desired at such a time—"the tact of possibilities," and he knew that, for the moment at least, absolutism was doomed as a political theory. His people and the allied sovereigns were about to demand of him a constitution on English lines. He was resigned to granting the Charter which such parliamentary royalists as Chateaubriand desired—the question was to discover whether those about him would sanction conciliation. He had always been surrounded by favourites, and the minion of the moment, the Duc de Blacas, was an émigré with a long memory for a grudge. "The rabble must sweat," said he. But the rabble still had the guns. There were those who forgot the fact.

Would Chateaubriand be less harried by the new master than by the old? If the glories of the monarchy and of the Empire were to be fused in the person of the new king, if such a reconciliation of all her splendours were to effect the moral unity of France, then a poet and historian such as Chateaubriand would indeed be useful. So much grew clear when, in July 1814, the flower of all parties and all nations met at Mme. Récamier's house to hear him read *Le Dernier des Abencérages*. Yet he saw two of his friends, Fontanes and Clausel de Coussergues, appointed to the commission which was to draw up the Charter, while there was no mention of him. Why? The reason was that Fontanes and Clausel were opposed to the freedom of the press and fairly determined that the constitution should grant the French people only the minimum of rights, whereas Chateaubriand, who relied on the support of the *Débats* (to which the liberty of the press was vital) and on his "dear sister"

Mme. de Duras, whose family traditions were liberal, passed—in politics—for a dangerous Anglomaniac.

Strong in her husband's eminent position at the new court, Claire de Duras promised to take Chateaubriand under her protection. But the ministries had already been assigned. On June 4th, when the list of peers came out, there was no mention of the author of *De Buonaparte et des Bourbons*. "The way in which the men who had suffered most for the Bourbon cause were treated in 1814," said Mme. de Chateaubriand, "was a lothly sight to see. . . . Up to a point, we were made much of in the hope that M. de Chateaubriand would put the dreams of those Hartwell ghosts into good French, for it was indeed another world from which they came. Seeing that every office was being filled, my husband thought fit to ask whether he would not be pressed into the service of those masters to whom he had sacrificed fortune, honours and repose. M. de Blacas turned a deaf ear to every plea on his behalf, and to a person who remarked: 'So it comes to this—M. de Chateaubriand must go into exile when the exiles return, since there is no way of living nobly in France,' that impertinent lackey replied: 'Let him go.'" Mme. de Chateaubriand handled her husband's enemies without gloves.

When Chateaubriand threatened really to leave for Switzerland, Mme. de Duras too became "stormy." She went in search of M. Talleyrand, Minister for Foreign Affairs. Every embassy, save those of Sweden and Constantinople, had already been allotted. "He put them both at our disposal," said Mme. de Chateaubriand, "marvelling that my husband should need to have recourse to him. 'I imagined,' he remarked to Mme. de Duras, 'that since M. de Chateaubriand had nothing, he had wished for nothing. The first day of the princes' arrival they should have offered him everything, the second would have been over-late and the third useless.'" Chateaubriand chose Sweden. Louis XVIII approved, adding kindly, "What I am giving you is a ring for your finger." He was glad to be able to play such a trick on Bernadotte, who would doubtless be furious to see a partisan of legitimacy at Stockholm, but he could not like Chateaubriand. The King was a Voltairian, a classic and a sceptic, the writer a student of the Bible, a romantic and a Catholic. "Beware," said the King, "of ever letting a poet into your counsels. He will upset everything. Such people are no good at all." For different reasons, Louis XVIII held the same opinion as Napoleon. He liked witty and amusing people; this needy author, with his pride and his high-flown language, bored him.

It was a grave error of judgment, for Chateaubriand's influence on public opinion, at a time when it stood in great need of direction, was indisputable. In 1814 France was complex and divided against itself. Men of Coblenz and men of Valmy, Conventionals and nobles were vying for power. On the Right were the passionate royalists whom the public nicknamed "Louis XIV's Light Infantry." Those among them who formed the little court of the Comte d'Artois, known as the "Pavillon de Marsan," longed to see an absolutist reaction and cried their loudest: "There is only one constitution—'What the King wills, that the law wills.'" They went about maintaining that the granting of the Charter was a feint intended to lull the nation's suspicions, but that the King was resolved to quash it as soon as might be. "Considering the state of public opinion in the nation and in the army," wrote Sismondi, "and remembering where the real power lay, such imprudence was little short of madness."

In the other camp there was growing discontent among the men of the Revolution and of the Empire. In vain did their spokesmen attempt to defend the honour and glory of the country in the face of a government restored by foreign intervention. A bald memorandum of old Lazare Carnot, who—though an ex-Conventional and a regicide—had helped to organize the victory, reminded the King that public opinion was no negligible force and that there could be no enduring legitimacy unless France were behind it. Louis XVIII, more open to reason than his followers, was ready to take his meaning. Though he had no liking for either Chateaubriand's work or his person, he was pleased when, in October, the latter replied optimistically to Carnot in a shrewd and useful article published in the *Débats*. To the vanquished he pointed out the excessiveness of their demands, to the victors the impossibility of a reaction; on all alike he counselled acceptance of the Charter. Such timely wisdom won almost unanimous approval. *Chateaubriand to Mme. de Duras:* "Behold my fate! Had you and M. de

Duras been here, I believe I should have found myself a peer. I wrote an unsigned article, published in the *Journal des Débats* of October 9th. It was such a success and so pleased the King that the Chancellor and the Minister of Police sent to thank me. The former gave me to understand that the King wished to entrust me with something else. Do come back and labour to keep me here. You could have made the most of this episode, for it must now be perfectly clear, even to their eyes, that I am the one writer to whom the public will listen today. Why then should they deprive themselves of the very weapon within their hands? By evening the papers with my article were selling for half a crown. All parties and all shades of opinion were pleased. They were at one on that."

Already he was bubbling over with confidence. After the publication of the article, the King gave him the Cross of St. Louis and created him a colonel of horse, whereupon he tricked himself out with a huge sabre. *To the Duke of Fitz-James:* "The King, Your Grace, has deigned to give me hopes of the cross of St. Louis. In the event of his conferring such an honour upon me, may I make bold to solicit another? It is that Monsieur would make me Knight. As a Knight of the Holy Sepulchre, I was girt with the sword of Godefroy de Bouillon at the tomb of Jesus Christ. Was it not only that I might be the worthier to receive the order of Saint Louis from the hands of the illustrious brother of our Most Christian King? I beseech Your Grace, obtain this favour for me. You know that, in all that touches the Bourbons, I am without fear and without reproach." Had Chateaubriand been capable of sacrificing petty ambitions to great, his career would have been both nobler and happier, but, alas! the natural effect of injustice is to put a keener edge on vanity. Success makes it lie quiet, waiting goads it; scorn of honours is a virtue habitual only to those who have known them all.

Louis XVIII informed Chateaubriand of his gracious pleasure that he should continue to write in the same strain. Within a short time he published the *Réflexions politiques* which were also conciliatory. "All Europe seems disposed to adopt the system of moderate monarchy. France, which supplied the first impulse, must needs follow it now. Let us rally about our government. Henceforth, let us be of one mind in our love of King and country and in our loyalty to the Charter! To the King, and to the King alone, we owe it that all the France of Louis XIV is ours today. . . . Why should we not say so openly? True, we have lost much through the Revolution, but is there nothing gained? Are twenty years of victory, are so many heroic actions, so many generous sacrifices nothing? Have done then with our self-calumnies, with saying that we know naught of liberty; we discern all, we are ready for all, we understand all. . . . Set before us now an example of justice and order, as we set that of glory."

Once again the King expressed his satisfaction. He told Jaucourt that he had corrected Chateaubriand's proofs and that it was now generally thought that he would not leave for Sweden, but would become the champion of constitutional monarchy, and that a great political career lay before him. Just then the Chancellery of the Legion of Honour fell vacant; his name was mentioned in that connection and he was already in the seventh heaven when the "matadors" of the emigration reverted suddenly to the attack. His enemies had been burrowing into his past and what could they not find there in the way of political opinions? A petty official, M. Bail by name, published the *Rêveries de M. Chateaubriand* in which he recalled the dedication of the *Génie* to Napoleon. True, Mme. Bail—who came to make excuse for her husband—was pretty and, in compensation for his calumnies, graciously offered favours which were as gallantly accepted. The harm was already done, and the *Essai sur les Révolutions* dug up once more. Swift to lose heart, Chateaubriand fled to the Valley of Wolves. There he looked out upon the autumn woods—"bare ruined choirs where late the sweet birds sang"—and fell to dreaming of those long past days when his hope was set on "an instant's sight of Natalie, lonely, as he, in her fair valley." Those were the times that had been good, the times when he was persecuted by the tyrant, glorying in his hate, loving, inspired, unhappy and content. *To Mme. de Duras:* "Today Ambassador to Sweden, ah, what an end is there! To leave all—work, dreams, and all besides. Poor valley! When shall I return? It may be never . . . I should have died the day the King entered Paris."

He had not a halfpenny in the world and urgently needed a

hundred thousand francs. He besought Mme. de Duras to obtain them of the King. Fontanes, the Bonapartist Fontanes, had been better treated than he. True, he had been retired, but on a considerable income and with the Grand Cross of the Legion of Honour. Yet who had more claims on the King's goodwill than Chateaubriand? Once again he got M. Bertin to enumerate them in the *Débats*, but Bertin's articles and Mme. de Duras' efforts were alike vain. The attacks had affected the king and aroused his prejudices. "M. de Chateaubriand," said Barante, "was literally and politically one of his antipathies."

Paris has always been a restive city, and during this time its blood was rising. When the parish priest of Saint-Roch re-enforced the excommunication of players and refused to receive the body of Mlle. Raucourt within his church, he stirred up nothing short of a riot. Helped by the crowd, a whole army of young half-pay officers forced the doors of the building and bore in the actress's bier. "Look at that, my friend," said an English onlooker to Villemain. "It's a rehearsal for revolution. Given a leader, it would need only such another riot to change your government."

The leader was not far off. From the Isle of Elba, where they kept little guard, he was watching his opportunity for return. In Paris, when the veterans of the Old Guard met, they murmured: "Do you believe in Jesus Christ?—Yes, and in his resurrection." Fouché, a stony-hearted police officer who knew his job, prophesied disaster: "If our coasts are left as unguarded but a few months more, Spring will bring us back Bonaparte with the violets and the swallows." Meanwhile, the ministers continued blind and deaf.

"Suddenly the telegraph brought to staunch and to incredulous alike the news that the Man had landed." Chateaubriand was moved by the greatness of that lonely conquest, by the epic style of his proclamations and by the beauty of their imagery. He could have wished that the King too would take up an attitude worthy to be sung by a poet. In the conferences then held, he was one of the very few to counsel resistance. "Protected by the will of Louis XVI, the Charter in his hand, our aged King should stay quietly on his throne in the Tuileries. Let us resist but for three days and victory is ours. The king, if he defends himself in his castle, will arouse universal enthusiasm. If, in the end, he must die, may he die worthy of his rank." Louis XVIII seemed somewhat unresponsive to the beauty of such an end. In public he stated that he would not leave his arm-chair, but in private: "So you want me to die on the curule chair. I am not in the mood." Sickened and chagrined, Chateaubriand was fuming: "Why have I been a royalist against all my instincts, at a time when a miserable race of courtiers would neither hear nor understand me? Why should I have been thrown amidst a band of mediocrities who took me for a rattle-pate when I preached courage, and for a revolutionary when I preached liberty?"

It was obvious that the King "was planning a skedaddle." The ministers were already dividing out the funds in the Treasury in preparation for his flight and theirs. Dreading betrayal, the Court informed no-one of their intentions. Chateaubriand met the Duc de Richelieu in the Champs Elysées. "We're being hood-winked," said the Duke, "so I'm mounting guard here as I don't want to await the Emperor alone at the Tuileries." Mme. de Duras, indignant that her great man should be kept in ignorance of what was in the wind, ran to M. Vitrolles, the Minister of the King's Household, pointing out the danger that the Emperor's return would bring upon Chateaubriand and the shamefulness of leaving him to vengeance. In the course of the interview she fainted in a ministerial arm-chair and, thanks to the fright thus occasioned, extracted a sum of 12,000 francs which would finally allow of the Chateaubriands' departing with the King.

Mme. de Chateaubriand had posted a servant as sentry at the Carrousel, with orders to return as soon as the King's flight was a certainty, but, on March 20th, when Chateaubriand had just gone to bed, Clausel came to tell his friends that the King had started for Lille and to bring them the 12,000 francs Mme. de Duras had wheedled out of the Chancellor. At four o'clock in the morning, Mme. de Chateaubriand thrust her husband into the carriage. "I was in such a fit of rage," said he, "that I knew neither where I was going nor what I was doing. We left by the Porte Saint-Martin. At dawn I saw the crows flapping peacefully down from the elms on the highway." Those birds of ill omen were ever there to wheel about his flights.

2. The Hundred Days

Throughout a night of pitch darkness, horses and carriages that lost their way, ran into each other and grew bogged in the mire, blocked the roads to the North. Voices called from the mirk: "Where are we going? Where is the King?" Chateaubriand fumed as the berline jolted him against his wife, who was as ironical, as witty and as ailing as ever, remembering that twenty years earlier he had taken this same road to exile. Amiens, Lille, Tournai—the stages were identical. But then he had been young and high in hope as he set off in search of the Sylph. Now he was forty-seven. He dragged after him an angular spouse and what was he? Naught—save the Minister to Stockholm of a sovereign without a realm.

The favourite, Blacas, and the Duc de Duras, who accompanied the King, advised him to go back to England. Louis XVIII was wise enough to halt at Ghent. There he formed a ministry and, in the absence of the Abbé de Montesquieu, Chateaubriand found himself temporarily appointed Minister of the Interior. As the entire territory of France was in the hands of the usurper, it was difficult to see what the Minister of the Interior could control, but the post gave Chateaubriand his first opportunity since the Restoration of coming into any sort of personal contact with Louis XVIII. He summed him up with illusions and without injustice. The King wanted peace at any price. Though temperamentally cold and insensitive, he formed "affections which bordered on passions" and gave in to his favourites to a dangerous extent. "He did not go out to meet events, he let events come to him." That was just what Chateaubriand was incapable of doing.

In Ghent, he was several times invited to the royal table and, as he laughed more humanly than the courtiers at the stories the King had a gift for telling, did not wholly fail to please. The "lovable creature" in him was more likely to find favour with Louis XVIII than the personage. Unfortunately Mme. de Duras was there and her efforts to push him, her intrigues with Talleyrand on his behalf, only succeeded in being compromising. In Ghent, where no-one had anything to do and where, save for the gentle Mme. de Lévis, most of the "Madams" were absent, Claire de Duras had hoped to have her great man to herself. Yet, even in exile, he escaped her. When she asked him to go with her to Brussels, where her mother, Mme. de Kersaint, seemed to be dying, he snapped at her for her anxiety: "Don't, for the love of God, behave like that. Come and see Mme. de Chateaubriand and decide for yourself whether I am the master of my own time. The great pressure of work on the Interior takes all the rest. It is important, for it is my first chance of proving my capacity for administration. Don't scold! Don't go! A moment more and all will be well!" The day following the "all will be well" Mme. de Duras told him that her mother was dead. "Dear God! What a news! What is this our life! Poor woman! God bless our souls!" The profusion of exclamations made up for the coldness of the regrets.

The great pressure of work was not wholly imaginary. Lacking instructions from non-existent prefects, the Minister of the Interior was drawing up a "Report to the King on the State of France on May 12th, 1815," afterwards published in the *Journal universel*, for the indispensable Messieurs Bertin had even come to Ghent, where they founded that émigré gazette. This report, on which Chateaubriand was counting to establish his reputation as a minister, went almost unnoticed. Once it was finished, its maker grew bored and was happy only when he visited the Béguinage, where he was given a welcome befitting the author of *Le Génie du Christianisme* and recaptured a breath of his renown.

Round about him life went on. A crowd of foreigners brought bustle and animation to Ghent—soldiers, gunners, dragoons, vivandières and politicians gesticulated along the quiet canal beside the motionless fishermen. Every afternoon the King drove out in a coach drawn by six horses, precisely as though he had been in Paris, and when he met the Duke of Wellington, gave him a patronizing nod. The Comte d'Artois, who had reassembled his little court of the Pavillon de Marsan in Ghent, gave excellent dinners, notable for the abundance of ices and the delicacy of the pastries. In that set, Chateaubriand was not taken seriously. "He was a Constitutional, a man with a bee in his bonnet," moonstruck on the subject of Westminster, a reformer, a visionary. At this juncture the Pavillon de Marsan pinned all its hopes to Fouché. There were whispers of "a man who, it had to be admitted, was behaving splendidly, who was foiling all the Emperor's plans and becoming the saviour of the Faubourg Saint-German."

There was no mistake about it. At that time, Fouché was holding himself in readiness to leap into the victor's camp—whichever it might be. He was ever willing to render services to those royalists who had remained in Paris, and established relations with Ghent at the self-same moment as he was intriguing with Talleyrand in Vienna, sometimes for the benefit of the Duke of Orleans, sometimes for Napoleon II. Meanwhile he never ceased to swear loyalty to the Emperor, who knew just how much reliance to place in his protestations, but had never, now least of all, been able to do without the Duc d'Otrante.

The news of Waterloo was late in reaching Ghent. On June 18th, 1815, Chateaubriand had gone for a solitary walk along the highroad to Brussels, browsing in Caesar's Commentaries, when he heard a distant sound of muffled thunder. He stopped beneath a poplar to listen and the south wind brought him more distinctly the roar of artillery. Clearly a great battle was in progress. Not a living soul passed him on the road; in the fields one or two women were peacefully hoeing their furrows of vegetables. A courier whom he stopped told him that Bonaparte was the victor.

He sped to the King. Ghent was in a state of general stampede. The English were rumoured to have sustained a crushing defeat; the wagon that carried the crown jewels was harnessed; Chateaubriand stuffed his ministerial portfolio with the silk handkerchief he wound round his head at night. It was, he said, the one important document of the Ministry of the Interior. He had been richer at the time of his first emigration, when it was the manuscript of *Atala* that lay in his haversack. Louis XVIII did not go to bed. He spent the night at his window, eagerly watching for news and thinking his own thoughts. It was then, it seems, that the King measured the mistakes of the last six months, especially the émigrés' ignorance of public opinion in France, and that he promised, if his throne should be restored to him, to bind up the wounds of the Revolution. Next day, the court of Ghent learnt of the Emperor's defeat. There was wild joy. "We could not have been prouder," said Mme. de Chateaubriand bitterly (for she had a patriotic soul), "if Bonaparte had been defeated by a son of France." Her husband,

The Partisan

in the *Journal universel* of June 21st laid the Emperor's defeat at the door of Providence. "A great reverse has shattered his hopes, a great punishment is laid upon him, and the unseen hand which is leading him to his doom at the same time, makes as though to avert from us some of those calamities with which his resistance threatened the nation."

In Paris, Fouché had formed a provisional government. Louis XVIII's decision was quickly taken. Without waiting to know the advice of the Allies, he resolved to march on Paris so that none might dispute his throne. Talleyrand, newly arrived from Vienna, hoped to be able to handle the King and keep him in Belgium until he himself could reach the French capital and become the arbiter of the situation. He was none too well pleased to discover that the Court had already set off, but he caught up with them at Mons where, full of spleen at the neglect of his counsels, he replied to those who advised him to go to the King: "I am never in a hurry. Tomorrow is time enough." Louis XVIII, conscious that—sorely as it went against the grain—he must rid himself of M. de Blacas, who was detested by the public, had just said affectionately to Chateaubriand: "I am about to part with M. de Blacas; the place will be empty, Monsieur de Chateaubriand." It was tantamount to offering him the Ministry of the King's Household.

Thanks to Mme. de Duras, however, Chateaubriand had some weeks before thrown in his hand with Talleyrand. Now "The Cripple" prouder than ever, refused to believe that the King could do without him. When at last, he did seek the presence, His Majesty said ironically: "So you are leaving us, Prince of Benevento? The waters will do you good. You must let us have news of you." Whereupon, without waiting for a reply, Louis XVIII was gone. In this pass, Talleyrand had no-one to whom to turn save the Chateaubriand whom he had once cruelly scorned. He begged him to intervene. For Chateaubriand such revenge was sweet. "M. de Talleyrand was tenderness itself. He leant on my shoulder." To taste that exquisite but fleeting joy, he committed the fatal mistake of remaining in the background at the moment when everything was being settled.

Those about the King made it a grievance against him. The "chameleons" were laying siege to the victor anew. On his way through Le Cateau the King issued a first proclamation threatening traitors. By the time he reached Cambrai he had already been wheedled into pardoning all save "those men whose reputation is a theme of sorrow for France and of dread to Europe." This clearly referred to Fouché, but the Duc d'Otrante had succeeded in convincing Wellington and Blücher that he alone was capable of effecting the King's entry into Paris without riots and without bloodshed. The Allies advised the King to keep him on as a Minister. Chateaubriand, who had finally come back into the foreground, protested vehemently and was upheld both by Talleyrand and the King. A regicide the Minister of Louis XVI's brother! "That's neither here nor there," replied Wellington coldly, and the entire Faubourg Saint-German came to intercede for Fouché. No sooner did he see the strength of his rival's position than Talleyrand turned trimmer and came to terms with him. "Ah, my unhappy brother!" sighed the King, but he signed the decree appointing Fouché.

Then, Chateaubriand having been set aside, this "miry ministry" was gathered together—M. de Talleyrand (Foreign Affairs), the Abbé Louis (Finance), Pasquier (Keeper of the Seals), and Fouché (Police)—three defrocked priests and a Bonapartist. Chateaubriand had missed the greatest opportunity of his political career. He had been faithful to a pact with Talleyrand and true to his honour in rejecting Fouché. He was beaten. At Saint-Denis, where it was the hardest work in the world to prevent the little girls of the Legion of Honour from crying "Long live Napoleon!" he betook himself to His Majesty the King. He was admitted to an antechamber, where he sat down in a corner to wait. "Suddenly a door opened and there came in silently Vice leaning on the arm of Crime; M. de Talleyrand supported by M. Fouché." Chateaubriand went home in a state of consternation. "At the castle they talked of nothing but the expediency of yielding, that is to say of flaunting the tricolor cockade, of worshipping Fouché and dismissing the Musketeers." The King agreed to everything save the cockade. Next day Louis XVIII sent for Chateaubriand. His first remark was: "Well, Monsieur de Chateaubriand?"—"Well, Sire, it seems that Your Majesty is disbanding his regiments and taking Fouché?" "Yes," replied the King, "needs must. . . . What do you think?" "Alas! Sire, the thing is done. Allow me to say nothing." "No, no.

The Partisan

Speak. You know how I've held out since Ghent. Tell me what you think." "You will have it, Sire. I can tell you nothing but the truth, and, since Your Majesty pardons my free-speaking, I believe that it is all over with the monarchy!" The King was silent. Chateaubriand was beginning to be rather alarmed at his own temerity when His Majesty rejoined: "Well, M. de Chateaubriand, I am of your opinion."

He was left with nothing but the office of Minister of State without Portfolio, which carried an income of 24,000 francs a year. The vilest of the "chameleons" was better provided.

3. The Minister of State Becomes Leader of the Opposition

In July 1815 the King convoked the electoral colleges, and the Vicomte de Chateaubriand was named president of that of Orléans. The mission was by no means unimportant. The president would doubtless be the first of his college to be returned; he was responsible for directing the electors (about five hundred to each college) and for seeing that they should vote for royalists. Orléans especially was in the public eye, for the town was situated on the borderline of the zone occupied by the allied troops and the district to which those which remained faithful to Bonaparte had retired. Chateaubriand set off, accompanied by a secretary who was none other than Pauline de Beaumont's former confidential servant— old M. Le Moine. Him he now made his "First Gentleman of the Chamber."

Mme. de Chateaubriand, who was half-dead with fright over the proximities of that "frontier," bombarded M. Le Moine with questions. "Tell me frankly, Monsieur, is there any danger to fear for him at Orléans? I much prefer to know; this uncertainty is making me really ill." It was her husband himself who sent her reassurance: "Your letter was pure Bedlamism. None could be more loved and fêted than I." In point of fact he had every reason to be delighted with Orléans and with himself. As he journeyed, he had composed an opening speech in which he evoked Louis XVI, "the murdered king of sorrowful and sainted memory," pointed out that Europe's estimate of France would depend on the result of these elections (the people of France will see kings at the bar of its counsels), and inhibited "the authors of our troubles" from the right of representing France. "Do those who brought these strangers within our walls deserve to obtain your suffrage?" Mme. de Duras, to whom the speech had been submitted, thought it too intransigent. She besought Chateaubriand to omit "the murdered king." He snapped: "I will change the word *murdered*, but I will not promise to leave out the *sorrowful and sainted memory*. . . . If you were in this part of the country, you would see how royalist it is and that there is need for discretion touching liberalism." The electors indeed, were more royalist than the King. They applauded Chateaubriand's speech and even made him re-deliver it on the following day. In all the streets there were cries of "Long live the President" and he would have been the first to be elected had he not learned at the last moment that the King had newly created him a peer. Was the honour a matter for rejoicing or should he regret his commission as a deputy? The peerage was hereditary, but how should that matter to him, who had no children and who would wholly die? Nevertheless, he accepted. *To Mme. de Chateaubriand:* "Send for the tailor Le Bon and order my peer's robes so that they may be ready for my coming. Try to ensure that the fleur de lys may not look too paltry." Meanwhile, the elections could not have gone better. The four returns were excellent and he even had a nephew of Talleyrand's nominated. "The Cripple should be pleased with me," he wrote to Mme. de Duras, begging her to "puff" the speech, the success and all else. A period of activity had delighted him. For the first time he had lifted up his voice before the multitude; he had even improvised a few brief harangues and discovered a naïve joy in playing on the vibrant nerves of a responsive public.

Since his spirits were as swift to rise as to fall, he was enraptured by the thought of his entry into public life, convinced that he would play a momentous part in the Chamber of Peers. *To Mme. de Chateaubriand:* "Now, will you believe me? Now will you let me be? Will you at last cease egging me on to become this, that and the other thing? Peer and Minister of State—the first rank both in the political and social order—what needs there more? Money? It will come. I was sure of being elected here, I was sure of the peerage. You have been most unreasonable. I have steered a good course, in my own fashion—true—but every man to his character. Work, our Valley, ease—we shall be very happy. . . . Come, pluck up some gaiety and cheer—no more of this crazy ambition. Leave me a little independence if you wish me content."

The stay at Orléans was important in that it led Chateaubriand to believe, wrongly, that all France was hostile to liberalism and that if he wished to succeed in political life (for he now brought to a career of action that ardour of desire which he had ever shewn in love) he must howl with the wolves. The devil of it was that the magic of his style made his howlings more sonorous than those of the rest of the pack. On September 4th, 1815, he presented "his" deputies to Louis XVIII: "Sire," said he, "you have twice saved France. . . . You have seized that sword which the Monarch of the Skies has entrusted to the princes of the earth that they may give rest to their peoples. . . . Sire, this justice (alas! all too needful) but adds to the clear-shining of your goodness. With tears of gratitude and awe, your subjects are telling of all that you have done for France, and your fatherly chastisement is extolled as the chief among your lovingkindnesses."

It was regrettable that the champion of the Duc d'Enghien should set chastisement among the number of lovingkindnesses at a time when chastisement meant death. The bodies of La Bédoyère and Ney were soon to punctuate his periods. The explanation of his inhumanity was to be found in Chateaubriand's natural wrath at seeing the team of Revolutionaries remain in office even after a second restoration. Fouché, who for fifteen years had played with him as a cat plays with a mouse, was still all-powerful. His old friends among the Bonapartists—Pasquier and Molé—had more influence with the King than he. That the anger with which he was convulsed was shared by the electorate of the country he knew. As at Orléans, the elections had everywhere been more royalist than the King. France (as represented by those country squires and bourgeois who alone had the right to vote) had despatched Louis XVIII an "indiscoverable Chamber." In the South and in the Vendée the mob was massacring the men of the Revolution and the Empire. In Paris, the Gardes du Corps, incited by the provincial electors, were merciless in their endeavour to stamp out every vestige of those régimes. The "runaways of Ghent" were clamouring for punishment on Bonaparte's generals. "We're going to hunt the field-marshal," said the Duc de Berry. Alone of all his family, the King refused to be carried away and murmured sadly: "They are implacable." *They* were his brother, his nephews, Chateaubriand, (despite Mme. de Duras) because he was disappointed, a few society women whom fear had rendered bloodthirsty, and that little court of émigrés which held Louis XVIII himself to be only a crowned Jacobin, desired to replace the scaffold by the gallows, and revelled in the grisly watchword: "It is time to put an end to mercy."

A Talleyrand-Fouché ministry could not weather such a storm. Talleyrand undertook to exile Fouché, but his betrayal did not save him. Chateaubriand wished that the King would play the constitutional game according to English rules and call in the leaders of the opposition, of whom he was one. The real France, however, seemed a country still too divided against itself to put up with a ministry such as the electorate desired and Louis XVIII chose the Duc de Richelieu, a wise and unambitious man of simple bearing, who made it his first task to clear the ground. Was there any likelihood of Richelieu's offering Chateaubriand an active ministry? No, for he had no liking for a man whose money matters were never straight, who had to appeal to the privy purse and who had too many women eager to advance him. Chateaubriand did all he could to win him round, even to reading the Duc his tragedy of *Moïse* one day when they were at Mme. de Boigne's. Richelieu fell asleep and bore him a lasting grudge. He took as his chief collaborator young Élie Decazes, the son of an attorney in Libourne and former secretary of Mme. Laetitia. Appointed Prefect of Police in June 1815 and promoted Minister in September, this intelligent if ambitious official had proved his mettle and his capacity for work, becoming a great favourite with the King. Though wholly justified by his merits, the rapid rise of the ex-Bonapartist Decazes fanned the flame of the ultra-royalists' wrath. "I will raise him so high," said Louis XVIII, "that the greatest lords must envy him." Meanwhile, they loathed him heartily.

Once more passed over for office, Chateaubriand was eating his heart out. Failing a ministry, he would have accepted the Roman embassy, but it had already been given to M. de Blacas. Through Mme. de Montcalm, Richelieu's sister, he tried to compass "a little freak department which should concern itself with religious worship, the arts, public instruction and the theatre." He was offered only Fontanes' former post—Public Instruction, without a seat in the Council. Wounded, he declined and decided to attack where he could not charm.

How could a Minister of State, drawing his salary as such, become one of the leaders of the opposition? He set himself to explain in a political pamphlet: *La Monarchie selon la Charte*. "As a Minister of State, I owe the King the truth, and I will speak it. If the Council of which I have the honour to be a member were ever to meet, I might be told to 'speak in the Council,' but it never does meet. Hence I must find means of making my humble remonstrances heard and of fulfilling my charge as a minister.... What! If I see France threatened with fresh ills and legitimacy itself in peril, must I keep silence because I am a peer and a Minister of State? My duty is far other. It is to point out the reef, to fire the distress signals and call all hands to the rescue."

He then expounded his doctrine—which was far different from that preached at the same time by Bonald, Maistre, and Ballanche. These three writers were supporters of absolute monarchy; they maintained the natural inequality of man; they wished to see the country governed by the clergy, the great landed proprietors and the corporations—in short, they desired to erase the Revolution from the history of France. Chateaubriand, faithful to that "ancient alliance of honour and liberty" which he had observed in England, defended parliamentary monarchy, the alternation of parties and the liberty of the press. He was alive to the dangers of liberalism, but they seemed to him less than those of despotism. Besides, how could the Bourbons inflict on France a tyranny which Bonaparte himself had been able to maintain only with the aid of six hundred thousand devoted soldiers?

To this doctrinal and somewhat conciliatory opening there succeeded so belligerent a close that it was said: "Chateaubriand claims to pour oil into our wounds, but it is boiling oil." He once again deplored the unworthy treatment of the royalists. The King attempted to justify it by saying that he could find able administrators only among those men bred in the school of Revolution and trained by Bonaparte. It was a prejudice which the "revolutionary interests" exploited to the full for the attainment of office which would afterwards bring opportunity of betraying the white cockade. "Faction is laying hold on all the posts . . . It has invented a new jargon to achieve its end. Where, at the outbreak of the Revolution, it spoke of *Aristocrats*, it speaks today of the *Ultra-royalists*. The papers which are stranger to its pay and to its interests write simply: *Ultras*. We are then *Ultras*—we, the sad heirs of those *Aristocrats* whose ashes now rest at Picpus. . . . Devotion is the eternal theme of such men's pleasantries. The journey to Ghent they call 'the sentimental journey.' 'Where are your certificates?' they ask the best of royalists who humbly solicits the least of offices. For twenty-five years he has suffered for the King; he has lost all—family, fortune, all. Such claims are not enough. Enter a Bonapartist. Furrowed brows grow smooth. His papers were in the keeping of the police. Sad to say he lost them when M. Fouché was dismissed. They take his word for it. 'Welcome, my friend, here are your letters-patent.'"

Chateaubriand held that the chief government appointments should be entrusted only to the supporters of the legitimate monarchy. "Does it need so many to save France? I ask only seven for each department: a bishop, a commandant, a prefect, a King's procurator, a president of the summary court, a commander of military police and a commander of the National Guard. Let those seven men stand for God and the King and I will answer for the rest. . . . As for those able men whose minds have been warped by the Revolution, who cannot realise that the throne of St. Louis must be sustained by the altar and buttressed by the ancient customs and traditions of the monarchy, let them go cultivate their fields. France may recall them when their powers, weary of rusting in idleness, are sincerely convert to religion and legitimacy." The ostracism was explicable, but not applicable.

Should this "liberal catechism which ended as an Ultra tract" be published? During the whole summer of 1816, Chateaubriand recast and polished his pamphlet, awaiting a favourable occasion.

The Partisan

To Mme. de Duras: "My work is almost finished. If I publish it, I think I shall do an immense service to France. I may, perhaps, save it from doom, but it will be at my own expense. . . . My grey hairs are beginning to make me cantelous." Thereafter he remembered that he had once vanquished that Other, who was now languishing in Saint Helena, and reflected that he could easily bring to heel the pigmies who had succeeded the giant.

On September 5th, 1816, the Indiscoverable Chamber was suddenly dissolved. It was Decazes who persuaded the Duc de Richelieu and the King of the need for this measure. "Otherwise," said he, "the intolerance of the Ultras would provoke a further revolution." Hastily, Chateaubriand added a postscript to his pamphlet: "I foresaw the upshot and have prophesied it time and again. . . . To dissolve the only assembly which, since 1789, has shewn itself purely royalist in its sympathies seems to me a strange way of saving the monarchy! . . . What is the King's aim? Were it lawful to penetrate the secrets of his high wisdom, might it not be presumed that by leaving full constitutional liberty of thought and action to his responsible ministers, he was looking beyond them? . . ." He was seeking to embroil Louis XVIII with Decazes. When, a few days later, the pamphlet was published on September 17th, the King's indignation knew no bounds, and he expressed it openly. Mme. de Montcalm had warned a frenzied and despairing Mme. de Duras of the inevitable consequences of such a publication, but her warning had been in vain.

Chateaubriand carried his daring to the point of insinuating that instead of regarding the ordinance of September 5th as a free expression of the King's personal views, it should be considered a lamentable proof of his favourite's credit. An order was inserted in the *Moniteur:* "The Vicomte de Chateaubriand, having in a printed publication cast doubt upon Our personal will, as manifested in Our ordinance of September 5th, the Vicomte de Chateaubriand will cease, as from today, to be numbered among Our Ministers of State." It was war at last. Deprived of office, ruined, hurled by the impetuosity of ambitious women into ineffectual opposition, this royalist was to contribute more than any other towards the downfall of the legitimist monarchy.

4. JULIETTE AND RENÉ

In his *Mémoires*, he treats his disgrace with arrogant lightness: "By nature I was careless of the loss of my salary. It cost me no more than taking to shanks' mare and, on rainy days, driving to the Chamber of Peers in a hired cab. In my plebeian equipage, under the protection of the rabble which seethed about me, I entered into the rights of the proletariat of whom I made one." In a posthumous work such phrases are most effective. In April 1817, when bills payable on demand had to be met, taxes paid, and household expenses somehow provided, all on the 12,000 francs appertaining to the peerage, his courage was mingled with the bitterness of anguish.

How were so many obligations to be faced? The sterling M. Le Moine, who trotted about Paris from morning till night trying to extend the date of bills and to obtain abatements, could see no other means of safety than selling the Valley of Wolves and, as a start, Chateaubriand announced that his library would be put up to auction. The only thing he wanted to keep was the pocket Horace covered with his marginal notes and translations. *To the Duchesse de Duras:* "Here, my dear sister, is the catalogue of my books. An author who sells his books is like a merchant who sells his stock—and all for the greater glory of our Most Christian King." After the auction he wrote: "The library is sold. I have also permission to put the Valley of Wolves up to lottery. Hence I am well and truly stripped. Like Job, naked I came from my mother's womb and naked I shall return thither." The sacrifice was painful, but the attitude sublime, and the victim could not but find in it some consolation.

The sale by lottery of the Valley of Wolves was secured by M. Denis, a solicitor, who issued ninety tickets at a thousand francs. Bertin published the most enticing and well-worded of descriptive notices in the *Débats*, whereupon the Chateaubriands went on long visits to their friends' châteaux till such time as subscribers should make their appearance. It was as good a way of surviving as another. First they went to Montboissier to stay with Mme. de Colbert-Montboissier, Malesherbes' grand-daughter. His temper frayed by royal ingratitude, Chateaubriand would have proved a trying guest had not the memory of a lovely face and eyes that boded unknown bliss companied with him on his lonely walks.

The face was Juliette Récamier's. He had once met her at Mme. de Staël's, you remember, at the time of *Atala*, when the young author hardly dared raise his eyes to the loveliest woman of the age. Thereafter, with hosts of others, he had admired from afar that irreproachable and adventurous existence. During the Consulate, the sight of Juliette dancing in those diaphanous white frocks which half-betrayed her perfect body and "swirled about her like faint wreaths of mist," had conquered Lucien Bonaparte, Bernadotte and everyone else who was worth the conquering. In each and all it had been her good pleasure to kindle love and even desire, only to bring them, with angelic coquetry, "the consolations of goodness." Faithful to an ageing husband, whom she regarded as a father, but to whom she wrote: "It is to you I owe all the happiness I have known in this life," she had lived surrounded by worshippers who, beneath the spell of her simplicity, her gift of listening wonder, her loyalty, modesty and gentle pity, asked only to be her willing slaves. All had found in her "strangely woven, the twofold enchantment of the virgin and the lover." A rebel to the passions of love, she had a genius for friendship and that "sweet ambition of the heart" which made her disdain no conquest. Succeeding generations within one family had loved her with equal ardour. "My father was in love with you," the Duc de Laval (Adrien de Montmorency) told her. "Whether I too love you, you know. It is the fate of all the Montmorencys." And indeed his cousin Mathieu, a godly and sober man, had much ado to hide his love for Mme. Récamier under counsels of religion.

Prince Augustus of Prussia had desired to marry her; Metternich courted her in vain; the fascinating Prosper de Barante met with a rejection. It was the same with women. Mme. de Staël and Queen Hortense had attached themselves to Juliette with a passionate devotion akin to love. During a stay at her native town of Lyons she had annexed Ballanche, for she spurned no success, and that shy mystic saw in her "his Beatrice." "She was a very witch," says Saint-Beuve, "in transmuting love all unperceived to friendship, yet left the fragrance of that erstwhile flowering. She would have had it forever April. Her heart was still in that first springtide of the year when the orchard-boughs are white with blossom, but have yet put forth no leaves." She was the Sultana of a thousand and one dawns.

Under the Empire, partly, no doubt, by reason of her friendship for Mme. de Staël, she had taken up with the opposition. In 1806 her behaviour under the stress of Récamier's ruin had aroused universal interest. Though she no longer went into the world, she not only kept all her friends but remained the centre of the society of her age. Exiled in 1811 to a distance of forty leagues from Paris, she came back with the return of the Bourbons. In 1814 Chateaubriand consented to give a reading of *Le Dernier des Abencérages* in her drawing room. The goddess of reconciliation gathered about him Bernadotte, the French general who had become King of Sweden, the marshals of the Empire, the Duke of Wellington, who was as much in love with her as everyone else, the Duc de Doudeauville, Mathieu de Montmorency who, righteous and starchy as he was, devoured her with his eyes, Metternich, Benjamin Constant and Prince Augustus of Prussia. So lofty was the rank of her divers worshippers that, when she called them together, she appeared to have summoned a congress of the Powers.

Though, in 1814, she was thirty-seven, her face and form were still those of a young girl. It was even rumoured that her marriage had never been consummated and that she was yet a maid. As she drew near forty, however, she began to find her long succession of barren victories wanting. Beneath her mask of still serenity the more perceptive of her friends caught glimpses of her emptiness of soul. "I am afraid," said Prosper de Barante, "that her way of giving herself with both hands may prevent her from ever knowing the keener edge of happiness." "You are devoured by the need to spend yourself," Ballanche wrote to her, "yet you have no one to whom to consecrate your thoughts, your actions, your very life itself. You are burning out in loneliness." She herself confided to a Swiss friend: "I have never been happy, and I think I never shall." On her return in 1814 there were probably moments when she contemplated a closer friendship with

Chateaubriand, for we know that in the years which followed she endeavoured to be of use to him, intervened several times with Richelieu and somewhat disturbed Mme. de Duras, who was alarmed to see her most dangerous and equally platonic rival take an interest in her great man.

During all this period Juliette Récamier yet continued to fetter hearts. "I need to be loved," she said, "no matter by whom." She had taken it into her head to make Benjamin Constant care for her, though he was then forty-seven. "Dare," she said to him tenderly, as she had to many another. He left her house head over heels in love, but for her it was only a game and he was soon the most unhappy of men. "I had never known a coquette. What a scourge! . . . She delights to attract, but pity for the harm she has done, or balm to sain it, she has none. . . ." Later: "Faith, I give it up! Today she has made me go through an inferno. She is a feather-brain, a cloud, with neither memory, discernment nor preferences." It took him two years to grow cured. Ballanche, meanwhile, had a wary eye on Constant, while Wellington bewailed Juliette's redoubtable coquetry to Mme. de Staël.

In 1817 she was forty and doubtless more than ever conscious of the hollowness of friendships that no bond of the flesh linked with her inmost life. The commonplace-book she kept at the time has interesting extracts from her reading: "It should be remembered that there is but a short time to be beautiful and an age to be it no more." "The 'nays' of Chastity, says Montaigne, leave no wounds." "The reign of beauty is soon over and gone. It is known as a brief tyranny." On May 28th, Mme. Récamier was to dine with Chateaubriand at Mme. de Staël's, but their hostess, who had one of her attacks, was obliged to send apologies to her guests. Chateaubriand and Mme. Récamier, seated side by side at a table where the near presence of a dying woman made conversation difficult, fell into long silences. Only towards the end of dinner did she address a few words to him concerning Mme. de Staël's illness. "I turned my head slightly," says Chateaubriand, "and saw my guardian angel standing on my right. Today I dread to profane with the lips of age a feeling that has been ever-young in my memory, and has grown more endeared with the ebbing of my life." Their eyes met. A woman's glance may sometimes be itself a solemn vow of oblation. From that moment he knew (or believed) that she loved him. Hence it was for her that, as he paced the park of Montboissier, he framed the Memoirs he was fain to write that Juliette might hear the tale of his beginnings.

"I was roused from my meditations by the whistling of an ouzel in the topmast branches of a birch. All at once the magic of that sound brought my father's house before my eyes . . . Swept suddenly back into the past, I saw those dear remembered fields where oft I heard the throstle's pipe. . . . In the woods of Combourg that bird-song spoke to me of a bliss beyond my reach; the selfsame song, in the park of Montboissier, brought up into my mind days frittered without recall in pursuit of the felicity I might not win. . . . Let me not waste the rest of my brief day; let me make speed to limn my youth while yet I may follow its flying feet. . . ." Next day he began Book III of the *Mémoires*: *Révélations sur le mystère de ma vie*.

That same day Mme. de Chateaubriand, shivering with fever, had to take to her bed. *To the Duchesse de Duras:* "Misfortune dogs me, Mme. de Chateaubriand has measles. I am completely taken up with my duties as a nurse, and, where Mme. de Chateaubriand is concerned, they are no joke. Pity me, love me and write to me." And to *M. Le Moine*: "I am so battered by the storm that I've given up counting the waves. One more, one less, what does it matter! I am leaving everything to Providence. . . . Such is the fruit of the persecutions through which I have lived. The burden has fallen on a poor wretched woman. When shall I be free of this accursed earth and escape a race of cowards and ingrates?"

A few days later he learnt of the death of Mme. de Staël, while Mme. de Chateaubriand's attacks of dizziness caused him serious alarm. He nursed her with the utmost devotion. His natural masochism bound him more readily to others through suffering than through happiness; he so loved opportunities for self-pity that he was grateful to his wife for giving him good excuse. She herself was greatly touched by the "Cat's" attentions. "My blessed Cat is at Mass. There are times when I dread his flying straight to heaven, for he is really too perfect to dwell on this wicked earth and too pure for death to touch him. What care he has lavished on me since my illness, what patience, what gentleness!" She was soon to sing to a different tune.

When she was a little better, the pair left Montboissier for Montgraham, where lived Mme. de Montboissier's sister, Mme. de Pisieux, a pretty woman whom Chateaubriand pursued on horseback down the avenues of her park. There was not enough distraction in that. He was sunk in the deepest slough of despond. The news of the lottery was disastrous. Only four tickets of all the ninety had been sold! Three to the dowager Duchesse d'Orléans and one to M. Lainé. . . . It was laughable. "I must pay back the money. What is to become of me?" Leaving his patient, not without a sigh of relief, he set off for Paris to "busy himself about the sad state of his affairs." Whatever happened, he had to raise money, find somewhere to live and perhaps see a few of the "Madams" for—if it is creditable to nurse one's wife, it is delightful to love others'. Chateaubriand's kindliness was real but intermittent and, during this stay in Paris, he hardly wrote to Montgraham. *Mme. de Chateaubriand to M. Le Moine:* "I am ill and depressed. Many things combine to make me so. I do not know where I dug up so many anxieties during my illness; my death would have left no void on this earth and might have spared me many a grief. If M. de Chateaubriand is still in Paris, on no account shew him my letter. It is not cheerful enough to amuse him."

When he returned to her, money matters had been miraculously settled. It would have been impossible to find a lender without security, but one of Chateaubriand's nephews had offered to give it. This Christian de Chateaubriand was an officer and a mystic, fiery as were all the Chateaubriands and ready to give his last farthing to his brother Louis, to his uncle or to anyone else. *The Duchesse de Duras to Mme. Swetchine:* "His money matters are settled, I am profoundly glad to say. He is independent at last for—thank heaven—there is nothing political in the arrangement. The thing that has really done him good is working on his memoirs. They make delightful reading, but I hope he will not be tempted to let other eyes than mine see them. I should be sorry for many reasons. . . ." Those reasons were called Lucile and Juliette.

It was in that summer of 1817 that Mme. de Duras brought him heartbreaking news—Natalie de Mouche, whom he had so passionately loved, was shewing alarming signs of mental derangement. Always odd, unstable and brilliant, she had been loved since their parting by Adrien de Laval, whose worship was purely platonic, and by the less reverent Molé, who willingly followed Chateaubriand's furrow if he might glean his mistresses. Her sadness and unsociability never lifted. Molé, who had stayed with her and Claire de Duras at Vichy, found her disturbingly strange, with nothing left of all he once admired. Sunk in gloom and heedless of her appearance, she spent her days in aimless walking at tremendous speed. Molé tried reading Benjamin Constant's *Adolphe*, which was newly published, but she heard him with utter indifference. "She seemed," said Molé, "to be listening with her inward ear to memories and old, unhappy secrets very different in their poignancy from the heartbreak betrayed by Benjamin Constant's pen." When any spoke to her of tenderness or goodness, the sardonic curl of her lips shewed clearly enough what she was thinking. "She had given up reading; books, science, the arts—all seemed to her lies and vanity. She wandered from hostelry to hostelry, from province to province, concerned only about her health and everywhere seeking healing that she nowhere found. The immense activity of her mind was concentrated on her sufferings, she was forever exaggerating them, and with the spectre of death always before her, spent her days in devising a stranger progress to the tomb."

By the time she came back from Vichy, she was wholly out of her mind. She was convinced that everyone was trying to poison her and at last "she whom nature had created for the adornment of the earth, she to whom no sin was forgiven because she had never loved" had to be shut up in a house in the Rue du Rocher. It was the ingrate Molé who passed so unjust a judgment on her. Mme. de Duras, in writing to Mme. Swetchine, was kinder. "Had it not been for that fatal journey to England, which left her sore wounded, with all her illusions in shreds, she might never have taken so disastrous a road." Her pride had been humbled to the dust, first by her husband, then by her lovers. Chateaubriand "had indeed sought to raise her up in her own eyes and in those of the world, but he was incapable of persevering in his concern for another's fate, being too absorbed in thinking of his own."

There was nothing violent in poor Mouche's madness; rather it was heart-rending. "In that state where there are no disguises, one sees her gentleness of soul and the extent to which she must have suffered," Mme. de Duras told Chateaubriand. "Dear God!" he replied, "poor Natalie. What fatality treads upon my heels. Have I not told you that all that ever I have known, loved, or sought, has run mad and I shall come to a selfsame end. There is nothing I would not have done or given to see Mouche happy. I hope her head may be cured. Perhaps the derangement is only temporary. Despite all the happiness she has given me there is nothing I can do for her in return. Dear Sister, how pitiably helpless human friendships are."

He spoke truly, though we may sometimes wonder whether that helplessness does not mainly depend on lukewarm feeling and whether a more strong and gentle affection might not have saved poor Mouche.

5. A Moment's Happiness

During the winter of 1817-18, Chateaubriand often went to Mme. Récamier's house in the Rue Basse-du-Rempart. She was touched by his assiduity and doubtless tempted to yield to his entreaties. Like him, she had sought to make her life a work of art. What better change could she work in the spirit of her dream than, having refused all alike, to give herself to the most illustrious and best-loved man of his age? As for him, all his life he had gone in pursuit of the Sylph and had been disappointed in real women. Mme. de Beaumont, though touching and subtle, had lacked beauty; Mme. de Custine, tender and retiring, had irritated him by her scolding tongue; Mme. de Noailles, with all her charm and follies, had worn him out with her whims. In Juliette Récamier he found united for the first time beauty, purity and a tact beyond understanding. It was natural that he should do as she had done and abandon himself with joyous confidence to a love it seemed the gods themselves approved.

Alas! Once more it was "the irruption of a hawk into an aviary where birds twittered in peace and harmony about a dove." In vain did the trusty Ballanche, Juliette's moral mentor, adjure her to distract her thoughts from so dangerous a liking by literary work and advise her to translate Petrarch. In vain did he urge that by so doing she, alone among women, could give understanding of the truth that beauty is a moral thing—a mirror of the soul. He had to admit the vanity of his counsels and the unbelievable change that had come over Juliette. "Today I was deeply grieved and ashamed, both in regard to others and myself, by the sudden alteration in your manners. Ah, Madam! What rapid strides this sickness, which makes you fear your most faithful friends, has made in a few weeks!" Chateaubriand's character made him afraid for her, since he knew Chateaubriand to be spoilt and as intoxicated with himself as are all sovereign despots.

The devout Mathieu was no less anxious. At Juliette's request (for she wanted to help Chateaubriand unobtrusively), he had consented to buy the Valley of Wolves for 50,000 francs and spent a whole summer there in her society. It took all M. de Montmorency's saintliness to prevent this abduction from causing a scandal. "I can picture your little household in the Valley of Wolves as the most pleasing one imaginable," wrote the Duchesse de Broglie, "but when Mathieu's biography comes to be written in the *Lives of the Saints*, you must admit that this tête-à-tête with the loveliest and most admired woman of her age will make an odd chapter. To the pure all things are pure, as St. Paul rightly says." Saint though he was, Mathieu wrote to Mme. Récamier on buying the house: "I count on your perfect discretion not to be at home to its former owner too often." But she would promise nothing and performed no more than she promised. She was defeated. In vain did she try to flee Chateaubriand, to go to spas and to restore a health that had been undermined by her struggle against herself. The Invincible was to be vanquished by the Enchanter.

It would seem that it was in October 1818 that she yielded—at Chantilly. A friend of Récamier's had a delightful country-house there and for the rest of his life Chateaubriand remembered the evenings spent on the terrace of the castle, with its steps leading down to a wood full of shadow and mystery where, far from all eyes, he walked at night with the divine Juliette. Before long he was to say in his every letter to her, "Do not forget the forest of Chantilly." They fell into the habit of writing to each other every morning and the police, who kept an eye on Chateaubriand's correspondence, preserved a few of their notes for us.[1]

Mme. Récamier to Chateaubriand: "Love you less! My Dear, you don't believe it in the least.... Till eight o'clock.... Don't believe in what you call conspiracies against you. Neither you, nor I, nor anyone else can ever now prevent me from loving you. My love, my life, my heart—all are yours." A woman who writes in that strain is a mistress, and Juliette had never penned such letters to any man.

Till then she had always lived in the same house as M. Récamier. Timely circumstances were about to allow of their separation without any stain on her whiteness. It was about the moment when Récamier, a daring banker, came to his final ruin. They had to leave the town-house in the Rue Saint-Honoré and that garden where Chateaubriand had often waited for her by the moonlight which filtered through its clump of limes. She sought refuge in a little apartment in the Abbaye-aux-Bois, a convent on the Left Bank which extended its religious hospitality to a few lone women. There, in her uncomfortable tiled rooms on the third floor, she could live at small expense and even contribute toward her husband's. Chateaubriand has described that cell: "The bedroom was decorated with a bookcase, a harp, a piano, a portrait of Mme. de Staël and a view of Coppet by moonlight. There were pots of flowers in the windows. When, breathless from climbing three flights of stairs, I entered the cell as evening was closing in, the view held me spellbound. The windows looked out on the abbey garden—a basket of greenery where the nuns were taking their walk and the schoolgirls running about at play. The crest of an acacia reached to the level of my eye; pointed steeples cut the sky and far on the horizon could be seen the hills of Sèvres. The setting sun gilded the picture and streamed through

---

[1] They have been published by M. Maurice Levaillant.

the open windows. A few homing birds came to sleep among the slats of the undrawn blinds. Above all the noise and tumult of a great city I grew one with the lonely silence of the distance."

To simplify life is to attain strength. Mme. Récamier was more powerful in her cell in the Abbaye-aux-Bois than ever she had been in her fine town-house. "It was there," said Sainte-Beuve, "that her gentle spirit, freed from too great a pressure of circumstance, made its kindliness increasingly felt. . . . Party spirit was then at its height. She disarmed wrath, smoothed away rubs, charmed away ungraciousness and implanted tolerance." A woman, if she is beautiful, has a touch of the coquette and knows how to listen, can do what she will with men's passions. Everything is granted her because she makes no demands. "To be the protégé of Mme. Récamier was, for over thirty years, the most infallible of recommendations." She reigned over the Academy, the faculties and the ministries—"and there was no one, even to her apothecary's and her porter's bastards, but this essentially good and obliging woman found means to settle in some suitable post in government offices."

At the Abbaye-aux-Bois the loves of Chateaubriand and Mme. Récamier took on a ceremonial and public character reminiscent of the days of the great king. The reason was that they were both sovereigns in their fashion and neither was unaware of what they owed to their glory. Every day Chateaubriand made his appearance at three o'clock and such was his punctuality that the people of the neighbourhood set their watches by his passing. Naturally unsociable, he admitted no one, or practically no one, at this hour. *Mathieu de Montmorency to Mme. Récamier:* "When, after two days' absence, I come with very sincere interest to enquire news of you for the second time, I cannot inure myself to your shutting the door in my face and sending your maid with a perfect fairy-tale so that you may more easily enjoy your tête-à-tête with M. de Chateaubriand." To her friend Mme. de Boigne, Juliette said in explanation of her new-found submission: "It has perhaps the piquancy of novelty. The others were interested in me, while he demands that I should be interested in him."

Chateaubriand, for his part, had sacrificed the other "Madams."

The Partisan

Claire de Duras bewailed her sad lot and, torn between love and ambition, sought solace in writing novels. Mme. de Boigne, ever hostile to Chateaubriand, assured Mme. Récamier that he used, rather than served, her and that one day she would find him leaving the little cell for gilded drawing-rooms. It is true that character rarely changes and, even in love, Chateaubriand remained ambitious and sensual. Gradually, however, Juliette strove to hush the storms, and allay all rancour. In her sweetness was such art that there slowly grew up in him unaccustomed feelings of reverence and affection which, though they could not wholly eradicate, tempered his egoism and his pride.

6. The Gilded Drawing-rooms

"The Cat is burning to get to Paris and fling himself madly into politics," wrote Mme. de Chateaubriand during the "stormy holidays" of 1817. The fact of the matter was that the great man could not think of politics without ramping. After only a few weeks there had succeeded to the Duc de Richelieu Decazes himself, more than ever in the king's good graces. Throughout the country the spirit of the eighteenth century and revolutionary interests were renewing their strength. The partial elections were returning more and more advanced Liberals to the Chamber. This was due to the support of the Ultras who, in adopting the policy of the worse evil, which—to protect a house—fills it with incendiaries, proclaimed: "Better Jacobin elections than ministerial elections."

For the better carrying on of the struggle against Decazes, Chateaubriand and his friends founded a paper, *Le Conservateur*, for the support of religion, the king, liberty, the charter and honest folk in general. Meanwhile they were organizing their party. Chateaubriand, the leader of the opposition in the Peers, got in touch with M. de Villèle, who led the movement in the elective Chamber. The two men were not made for understanding. Villèle, who had been a naval officer at the outbreak of the Revolution and Mayor of Toulon in 1815, was a member of the lesser Gascon nobility, puny and lacking in brilliance, but a hard worker with plenty of tenacity and shrewdness. He had a head for finance and those pedestrian qualities which in Chateaubriand "broke bounds, got soaring room." "During a discussion he would listen and summarize, but offer no conclusions. He was a great business promoter. A prudent sailor, Villèle never put out to sea during a storm and, though he could steer skilfully into familiar harbours, he would never have discovered the New World." It might justifiably be wondered whether the old fox from Toulouse would get on for very long with the Breton corsair whom chance had made his ally.

Chateaubriand has described with pitiless realism the meetings of the opposition leaders at that time: "We all arrived looking extremely ugly and seated ourselves in a circle round a drawing-room lit by a smoky lamp. I left those meetings rather more of a statesman, but rather more persuaded of the poverty of the entire science. All through the night, between sleep and waking, I saw before me the various attitudes of those bald heads and the divers facial expressions in those shabby drawing-rooms. . . . It was doubtless all very venerable, but I preferred the swallow which awakened me in youth, and the muses who filled my dreams." It is a haughty page which clearly betrays the artist who has outsoared his own party and his own activity, who quits it in the very instant of pursuit and who, perhaps despite himself, is concerned rather to draw men than to direct them.

The thing that makes politics to have no laws is the violence of the emotional storms which some unforeseeable accident may let loose upon a nation. On February 13th, 1820, Louvel, a saddler attached to the king's stables, "a sly snarling cur who walked by himself," stabbed the Duc de Berry, the heir to the throne, and —with the same thrust that killed him—gave the death-blow to the liberalism of Decazes. Chateaubriand was already in bed when the Marquis de Vibraye came to tell him of the outrage. He hurried to the Opéra in his peer's robes. All Paris was already thronging in that direction. "Men love anything spectacular, especially death, when it is a death that strikes in high places."

There was no reason why the crazy attack of an individual should affect the policy of the kingdom, but since his marriage to the hot-blooded Marie-Caroline, the daughter of the king of the Two Sicilies—the Duc de Berry had become the great hope of the Ultras. The duchess his wife, the Comte d'Artois and the more violent of their friends, pretended to believe the hapless President of the Council responsible for the crime. "Take that man away! I can't bear the sight of him! He is repulsive to me!" said the Duchess, when she saw Decazes near her husband's body. In Parliament, Clausel de Coussergues, Mme. de Chateaubriand's pious friend, dared to say—and he a magistrate of the Supreme Court: "I have the honour to propose that the Chamber lodge accusation against M. Decazes, the Minister of the Interior, for complicity in the murder of Mgr. le Duc de Berry." Villèle and Chateaubriand, "not more scrupulous but more circumspect," blamed Clausel for his imprudence, but were equally determined to make the most of the incident. Chateaubriand wrote in *Le Conservateur*: "The hand that struck the blow is not the most guilty—the real assassins of Mgr. le Duc de Berry are those who for four years have been setting up democratic laws within the monarchy . . . those who have rewarded treason and punished fidelity, those who have yielded up office to the enemies of the Bourbons and the creatures of Bonaparte . . . . Those are the true murderers of Mgr. le Duc de Berry."

The article enraged the king, who wrote to Decazes: "As a rule, my dear son, I tend rather to skip M. de Chateaubriand's works, but today I read the whole as a self-imposed penance. It has filled me with indignation. I should like to go and see the author, who is certainly a scallywag (all slanderers are) . . . and force him to sign a recantation of his infamy." The letter was that of a courageous friend but an unwise monarch. "Chateaubriand is a man to be feared," said Fontanes to Villemain. "They should have made peace with him, but that is what ministers—even parliamentary ministers—are like. They soft-soap a fool and wound an implacable man of genius."

On this occasion the man of genius was to triumph over his sovereign. The Comte d'Artois and the Duchesse d'Angoulême, in deep mourning, refused to go near the Tuileries if there were any likelihood of meeting M. Decazes. Against the unanimity of his family, against the Gardes du Corps' threats to kill Decazes and against the almost united stand of royalist opinion, Louis XVIII found himself powerless. He yielded, but not without softening his "dear son's" fall to the best of his ability, for he created him

Duke, ambassador to London and Minister of State with an exceptional salary of 300,000 francs.

After the fall of Decazes, the issue of the strife between Royalists and Liberals hung for some time in the balance. Chateaubriand, still imbued with the principles of British monarchy, would have liked his friends and himself to succeed to the party they had defeated. However, the division among the Ultras allowed the king to summon honest Richelieu back, and Chateaubriand might be seen defending the liberty of the press in the Peers while his confederate Villèle was attacking it in the Commons. As they could not come to an agreement on policy, the *Conservateur* team soon gave up publishing the paper. The Comte d'Artois offered Chateaubriand 100,000 francs to write a memoir on the life and death of H.R.H. Mgr. le Duc de Berry and this task occupied the writer for some weeks in 1820. When, on September 29th, Henri, Duc de Bordeaux, the posthumous child of the murdered prince, was born, Chateaubriand offered for his christening the flask of Jordan water which hung on one of the trees in the Valley of Wolves. He was becoming at once the historiographer and "the pontiff of legitimacy."

The elections of 1820 were such that Richelieu could no longer do without the support of the Ultras. He would gladly have made Villèle a member of his ministry, for he appreciated his competence and apparent modesty, but not Chateaubriand whom the king would not accept at any price. How were they to be rid of this insufferable man of genius? Mathieu de Montmorency called into play the soothing influence of the great conciliator—Juliette Récamier. Manoeuvring with her customary skill, she wrought miracles. By reason of her promise to effect a reconciliation with Louis XVIII, provided he would take up an attitude of moderation, Chateaubriand agreed to conduct in person the negotiations between the two parties and to prevail on Villèle to accept a ministry without portfolio. It so happened, however, that Villèle had a Siamese twin, Corbière, a rough diamond from Rennes as Villèle was of Toulouse. In Paris, Villèle and Corbière were spoken of in the same way as Orestes and Pylades or Nisus and Euryalus. In order that Richelieu might get hold of Villèle, Chateaubriand had to advise him to take Corbière too. He consented. *Chateaubriand to Richelieu, December 20th, 1820:* "I have had the honour to call on Your Grace to give you a report on the present state of affairs. Everything is going splendidly. I have seen the two friends and Villèle is at last willing to join the Council as Minister-Secretary of State without portfolio, provided that Corbière agrees to enter it in like capacity with the charge of Public Instruction. Hence there is no more difficulty."

Creating ministers had tickled Chateaubriand's vanity but he expected a reward to follow. The post of Minister plenipotentiary to Prussia was offered him. Should he take it? Berlin was then a very second-rate legation and, for his honour's sake, Chateaubriand could have wished to see his Ministry of State restored to him. Mme. de Chateaubriand, still seething with indignation, said that Ghent had nearly been the death of her and that an exile should be at least healthy and agreeable. However, Mme. Récamier, who thought that the one important point was reconciliation with Louis XVIII, besought Chateaubriand to accept and sent her willing servant Mathieu de Montmorency to the castle to obtain pledges from the king touching this purely honorary ministry. Mathieu believed that his errand had been a success, and the diplomacy of the Abbaye-aux-Bois triumphed over Céleste's wrath. *Chateaubriand to Mme. Récamier:* "All is over. I have accepted in accordance with your commands. I am to go to Berlin. The Ministry of State is promised me. Therefore, sleep well. At least the rack of uncertainty is over." He was returning to the field of action, but by a postern door.

Minister to Berlin, so that was where he had attained after six years of restoration, he who, in 1814, might have believed himself one of the masters of France. Chance had gone for much in that misapprehension. It is unfortunate for anyone ambitious when, at a turning-point in his career, he comes up against a powerful man who, rightly or wrongly, can neither understand nor like him. By a queer mimicry we become what people think us and Louis XVIII, who misunderstood Chateaubriand, could never get anything good out of him. After his earlier disappointments, due partly to this royal antipathy, partly to the rancour of the ex-Bonapartists in power and partly to Mme. de Chateaubriand's sharp tongue and Mme. de Duras' officious zeal, Chateaubriand's capacity for doing the wrong thing was bound to grow. It is a fact that injustice breeds injustice. A man who, time and again, sees the posts to which his deserts entitle him refused, becomes —unless he is a saint (and saints are few and far between)—harsh, embittered and ambitious.

Had he been at the head of affairs from 1815 onwards, Chateaubriand would doubtless have been swift to realise the need for moderation. His earlier articles and his reply to Carnot shewed that, while France was divided, he was capable of understanding and forgiveness. Thrown back upon opposition he had lost sight of the interests of the country since he was not their administrator, while his very grievances and disgust had bred in him all the faults that, after the event, were to justify his disgrace. He had proudly extolled his own merits because others were blind to them. Modesty in success is easy. Modesty when things gang agley calls for a rare wisdom such as Chateaubriand did not possess and Mme. de Chateaubriand trampled beneath her feet.

As a matter of fact, if he had been left to his own devices, he would probably have contented himself as early as 1815 with some honourable and well-paid post, such as would leave him time for his dreams and his writing, but he was easily influenced and, writes Mme. de Montcalm, "he was dominated by his soured and ambitious wife and by women-friends who, by tickling his self-love, made themselves mistresses of the only kind of excitement to which he was susceptible. Left to himself, he united with a fine imagination the friendliness and simplicity of a child, the more charming in that they were remote from the impassive bearing which the rôles he adopted sometimes imposed on him. His self-esteem gave him a great desire for praise, with no taint of disdain or disparagement, but—once finally persuaded of another's admiration—he never boggled at listening to home-truths. He never brought a heart to his relationships, only that natural pliancy and love of praise which—he had the grace to admit—invariably made him the tool of stronger-minded people than himself, who knew how to flatter his vanity that they might use his gifts." It is a penetrating portrait which helps to explain how, under the influence of women and grievances, a liberal poet tended to become a cross-grained partisan. Only Mme. Récamier, when she had gently salved his quivering self-conceit, could still lead her friend by the footpath-way to power.

CHAPTER VIII

The Upward Climb. The Dizzy Heights. The Fall

> "My ambition—alas! where is it now? Where my gift of feigning? Where my capacity for enduring shackles and boredom? My power of lending importance to trifles light as air; what has become of them?"
>
> —CHATEAUBRIAND

1. MINISTER TO BERLIN

HE LEFT on the 1st of January, 1821, feeling rather pleased with himself. The weather was cold and the Seine frozen, but His Excellency travelled warm in his comfortable coach. With him went his private Secretary, Hyacinthe Pilorge, an oddly coarse man, red-faced, red-haired and red-whiskered, who—from 1816 onwards—had followed the fortunes of that proud and chaotic existence with unfailing devotion.

The conscious victim of grave injustice, who knows that it is in his power to take vengeance and yet abstains, finds the turmoil of his feelings rather enjoyable than otherwise. Chateaubriand was going into voluntary exile for the appeasement of political passions. The artist in him saw how fine a sketch the nobility of his attitude added to his portfolio, while his delight in travel and escape found satisfaction in this departure. Berlin offered a refuge from the strife of parties, from creditors, from the "Madams" and from his wife. The wound to his ambition was healing.

As he journeyed, he re-read Mirabeau's letters on Berlin and was again struck by the ineptitude of Louis XVI's government, which—despite such admirable correspondence—had failed to realise that only such a man could save the monarchy. The constant pricking of senseless humiliations had driven Mirabeau into the opposition camp. "All our misfortunes," meditated Chateaubriand, "are due to such-like follies." Then came the mental recoil. "I foretold a five years' future for France," he said to himself. "Till the very last I found that facts were denied, yet Mirabeau, disgracefully as he was wronged in public esteem, is avenged, while I shall not take vengeance." In this he was honest. For him, to cross the Rhine was to cross Lethe.

The French Embassy in Berlin stood in Unter den Linden. The vast and dilapidated building was ice-cold, with the result that the Minister's rheumatism grew worse. *To Mme. de Duras:* "You want to know what I am doing? Nothing. What I see from my windows? A tree-lined street, rather like our boulevards, and four or five large crows to whom I throw crumbs every morning at eight o'clock, when I breakfast with none but my private secretary for company. At half-past four I dine with my 'family.' Though much perturbed by my arrival, it took heart on finding that there was nothing more to it." For this family (the group of young attachés at the Legation) he had the tolerant kindliness of a father. "They do as they please. Since I never use it, my carriage is theirs rather than mine. I do my best to keep a good table. I live as one of themselves. If they run short of money, I have always a little at their service."

He won the hearts, not of his secretaries only, but of the Court. The simplicity of the Prussian family was proverbial. Often Chateaubriand would meet King Frederick-William, well-muffled against the cold in a grey overcoat and cap, driving his own carriole through the streets of Berlin. In the life of the exiled poet, the princesses—especially the enchanting Frederike of Prussia, Duchess of Cumberland, played the part of Sylphs. They were eager rivals in reciting passages from his works, in accepting his arm for a polonaise, and in chance meetings when he took his walks in the park. In the company of the Duchess of Cumberland he would visit the sick-poor. Together they would listen to the music of Glück and Rossini, or watch a performance of Schiller's "Joan of Arc." An old Don Juan, he could be at once reverent and tender with a woman, melancholy yet tireless to do her service. So delicate, indeed, was his art of pleasing that, when he left, the Royal

The Upward Climb. The Dizzy Heights. The Fall

Lady wrote him feeling letters in which she was wont to recall, as Mme. Récamier had the forest of Chantilly, "the dear little wood, which—lacking his presence—could nevermore know charm."

He was careful never to speak of such successes to the jealous "Madams" in Paris. Mme. de Duras bewailed the rarity of his letters. While Mme. Récamier was in no haste to answer the countless outpourings of the exile, Mme. de Duras was forever in need of reassurance. "All your tittle-tattle about the Abbaye-aux-Bois, the Pole, and heaven knows what besides, is but the outcome of the loneliness of your existence. Your old diplomat is past his youth, but his affection for you will outlast his life." To Mme. Récamier, on the other hand, it was he who was the suppliant: "At long last there comes my first news of you. . . . Though I grant that I am not unknown here, the men are temperamentally cold and what we call enthusiasm is unknown. They have read my works, more or less appreciatively. I arouse a momentary flicker of curiosity, but no one shews the least desire to improve the acquaintance or even to have some private talk. My only resource is Hyacinthe. We talk of your all-too-brief notes. What else is there to tell?" He besought them both to look after Mme. de Chateaubriand, whom illness had kept in Paris, but who was none the less determined to uphold the rights and privileges of a complaisant wife and so commented acidly on his fair friends' neglect. Meanwhile he confided his political ambitions to them both. These were great. He despised the men whom he had left in power in France, for he regarded them as his creatures and believed that he could overthrow Richelieu's ministry whenever he chose. Hence his despatches to Pasquier were by no means those of a devoted functionary. He would end them:—"I have the honour to be, M. le Baron, your most humble and obedient servant," but the text was neither humble nor obedient and shewed scant consideration for his former friend of "the little society," now his Minister. It is customary for a diplomat to ask his government for instructions. Chateaubriand gave orders instead. He asked whether or no he was to be sent to the congresses of Troppau and of Laybach as the representative of France. "M. le Baron, kindly send me an immediate reply." Would they grant him leave to visit Mme. de Chateaubriand in Paris? "If it is refused, I shall take it." Would they, finally, give him his promised ministry? "M. le Baron, spare me, I beg, petty details. If my services are no longer welcome, you could give me no greater pleasure than the saying so frankly. I neither solicited nor desired my present mission. My country is crying out for me. My wife is ill and needs my care. My friends are clamouring for their leader. I am either above or beneath an ambassadorship or even a place in the Cabinet."

Harsh as might be the tone of his letters, their substance was often excellent. Mme. de Duras nevertheless reproached him with devoting his despatches to high politics rather than to matters touching his post. She pointed out that his shots were fired too high and whistled harmlessly over the heads of the little men at whom they were directed. "I take aim at my own level," he replied proudly. "I have tried to raise diplomacy above gossip." Why had he not devoted as much time as Pasquier to the affairs of Europe? "Did not Dante, Ariosto and Milton make as great a success of politics as of poetry?" All things considered, his views were reasonable enough.

In matters of home policy he remained loyal to the formula "The King and the Charter." His advice to his friends was always:— "Welcome the constitutional government openly, drop the laws of exception, but give office to none but royalists." Where foreign affairs were concerned, the most serious problem was the conflict in Spain, Naples and Piedmont, between the absolute monarchies— backed by the Holy Alliance—and the peoples which demanded constitutional guarantees. Austria and Russia were for stamping out revolutionaries everywhere. Through fear of the Liberals, the French government hesitated to fall into line, yet dared not openly refuse for fear of the Ultras. Chateaubriand condemned so vacillating a policy.

He held that the monarchies should give their peoples the desired guarantees while taking firm action against the rebels, that they should at once uphold liberty and authority, but that the one thing that mattered was vigorous action. "Statements of principle are the province of writers, action that of governments. If a government speaks, it should be only to command." He would have rejoiced to see the French troops enter Savoy. The white banner could do with a little glory. "The Royalists will be delighted and the Liberals cannot but applaud a stand worthy of our strength. We should experience the double joy of crushing a demagogic revolution and of re-establishing the triumph of our arms."

Such a policy was by no means absurd. True, he propounded it to the Premier somewhat baldly, but that was only natural. He had met with neither justice nor consideration. He should have been a member of the Cabinet but was not. Richelieu had promised to give him back his ministry. It had not been restored. Chateaubriand was to have been sent to the congresses. He was not sent. While Villèle and Corbière, men whom he himself had made, took their seats in the Cabinet, Chateaubriand, in Prussia, frequented the balls of country squires or, in the bitter cold of Berlin nights, with only his rheumatism for company, would sit down to recall for the fourth volume of his *Mémoires*, the time of his presentation to Louis XVI and the gay suite of Marie Antoinette. The old Court of France was no more; the new, which owed him everything, heedless and ungrateful. He longed for leave. In April the Duke of Bordeaux, that child of a miracle, was to be baptised. Chateaubriand, who had sung his father and known the friendship of his mother, intended to offer as a christening gift his flask of Jordan water. His presence at the ceremony was indispensable. "I shall get my leave, for I am my own master." Pasquier hesitated, for he was not overeager to see a man whom he regarded as dangerous once more in Paris. The ambassador despatched him Mme. de Chateaubriand who obtained the furlough by main force.

Before he left Berlin there came the sad news of the passing of Fontanes, who died very suddenly with the fervent cry "My Jesus" on his lips. Though politically, the two men had often been in opposite camps, their personal friendship was unusually faithful. In Paris his death went almost unperceived. "Poor Fontanes! Already he is utterly forgotten. Even so, a moment saw the disappearance of Mme. de Staël with all her stir. Strive, then, for Fame."

Before he died Fontanes had found time to make a bonfire of thousands of papers. Probably he burned most of his unpublished verse. As a poet he had chosen a career very different from Chateaubriand's, but—in times of stress—he had shewn a moderation which his friend could respect though he could not emulate.

When Chateaubriand at last returned to Paris at the end of April, he received a gracious welcome from the King, who told him smilingly that he might now change his coat. In other words, he was restored to the Cabinet. A few days later, at the very moment when the founder of the order was dying at St. Helena, he was awarded the Légion d'Honneur. Chateaubriand would willingly have taken his seat in the Council as a Minister without Portfolio, but—though his enemies would doubtless have approved—his friends were watchful. Villèle and Corbière, who feared his prestige and perhaps his sallies also, put Richelieu on his guard. "If once you let that man get his foot on the ladder, there is no knowing to what heights he may climb." Richelieu had no reason for being more "Chateaubriandist" than the poet's political allies, and so refrained from offering him a place in the Council.

In the early summer of 1821 there came a split in the ministry. The Ultras, who had the majority in the Chamber, were weary of bolstering up a ministry of concentration. Heedless of all his promises, the Comte d'Artois threw over Richelieu. When the latter complained to the King, Louis XVIII said:—"What else did you expect? My brother conspired against Louis XVI, he has conspired against me; he will conspire against himself." At that time the King was under the influence of a favourite, Mme. du Cayla, and Zoë du Cayla was herself obedient to the dictates of the Congregation, of Sosthène de la Rochefoucauld and the Extremists. These forced Villèle and Corbière, "the two maggots" as Chateaubriand now called them, to resign, though much against their will. One went home to Toulouse, the other to Rennes. No better opportunity of exchanging a chill and dreary legation for the promise of advancement could have arisen. Chateaubriand went into retirement, following the example of friends for whom he had little love and less esteem. The summer was one of intrigues. It was becoming more and more evident that Richelieu must go and that the new ministry would be recruited from pure Royalists. Chateaubriand seemed predestined for the Secretaryship for Foreign Affairs. It remained for Mme. de Duras and, even more, for Mme. Récamier, to implant the idea firmly in the minds of princes and of men in office. While awaiting his triumph, he renewed old friendships with women and spent happy days at Fervacques, where Mme. de Custine and her son marvelled to find that he was as companionable as ever and that the years had dealt kindly with him. To her he wrote:—"I left peace and happiness behind me at Fervacques. Here I have met with all the ills that flesh is heir to, petty anxieties, sickness, politics and anguish. I am much to be pitied and the four days spent with you in quiet have but made my usual wretchedness the harder to bear. If there are moments when you miss me, there is never one but I miss you." Tender and sincere as were his feelings, they were fleeting.

In December 1821, following the successive strokes of the Congregation, of the "pavillon de Marsan" and of the favourite, Richelieu the staunch fell—abandoned by his king. Villèle, backed—as always—by Corbière, was called to office. The "two maggots" had triumphed. Because they lacked brilliance, Chateaubriand had always under-estimated them. Corbière was coarse and headstrong, a man who owed his strength to a capacity for brutal frankness. Villèle was a shrewd minister, intelligent, modest to the point of dulness and a sound administrator. Both morally and physically, his adversaries regarded him as a little man, more fitted to unravel small matters than to conceive of great. Yet his parliamentary skill, conciseness of speech and grasp of finance made him valuable. In politics mediocrity often triumphs over genius, for it knows how to bow to circumstance, while genius glories in creating it.

Had Villèle even seriously considered offering the Secretaryship for Foreign Affairs to Chateaubriand? Was it the King's opposition which restrained him? The truth seems to be that Villèle and the king were at one in their distrust of the poet. The Ultras thought him too liberal, and the Liberals too ultra. When the Ordinances were published in the *Moniteur,* it was to Sosthène de la Rochefoucauld's father-in-law, the devout Mathieu de Montmorency, that Chateaubriand's coveted portfolio was assigned. The presidency of the Council was divided between Montmorency and Villèle. The Court clique had won the day.

The Court, however, could not command a government majority and Villèle had to make terms with Chateaubriand, whose first reaction to this last betrayal was fury. "I am too easily duped and too good-hearted." When the government had the coolness to offer him the Ministry of Public Instruction, without a seat in the Council, he was mortally affronted. To Mme. Récamier he wrote:—"I, a departmental head under Corbière! The wretches! Never has my pride known such a wound. Mathieu is already beside himself for joy." And next day:—"I am shaking with anger as I write."

It must be granted that his friends' behaviour was crazy. If there was one man more than another who had made a royalist ministry possible, it was he, yet he saw himself excluded. Thanks, no doubt, to the kindly light of the Abbaye-aux-Bois, Mathieu finally saw his mistake and came forward with the offer of an embassy to appease the wrath of Achilles. "I shall accept none but London," replied the hero. London was the diplomatic plum, but—at whatever cost—it was essential to get rid of Chateaubriand without offending him. London was therefore offered and accepted.

2. The London Embassy

A comparison of Chateaubriand's daily letters to Mme. Récamier and to Mme. de Duras at the time of his departure for London is one of the curiosities of literature. From one point of view they are almost identical. The facts are very like, but they are expressed in differing strains. To Mme. Récamier he writes:—"Dear and good angel, you must not grieve. I love you for time and for eternity, with a love that knows no change. I promise to write. My return shall not be long-delayed and its occasion, as always, is at your command. All this is but for a time till I can be with you for ever. Goodnight. The day after tomorrow you may look to hear from me at Calais." Meanwhile he wrote to the Duchesse de Duras:—"What would you have me do? Your porter can bear witness that the Secretary for Foreign Affairs was my guest. In stirring times it is a mistake to make friends of ambassadors if you would not have them embroiled in matters of state. The only moment at which I am free to see you is after dinner, at eight o'clock and, even then, it can be but for an instant, since I leave tonight." As for Mme. de Chateaubriand, a masterpiece of conjugal diplomacy had painted the English climate in such alarming colours that she was cured of any desire to play the ambassadress in London.

The Upward Climb. The Dizzy Heights. The Fall

Thus, during the fourteen-hour crossing from Calais to Dover amid heavy seas, the noble passenger was the soul of gaiety. A true son of St. Malo, he rediscovered his youth at sea. He broke into song, skipped to and fro and climbed the mast with as much zest as he had years before on the voyage to America, laughing at his sea-sick fellow-travellers. In his calmer moments he was lost in wonder at his adventure. To return as ambassador to a country, which he had left twenty-three years before as an unknown and impoverished exile, was a mighty destiny and his vanity found solace in the thought that he alone had shaped his ends. "I owe it only to what I bore within myself when I passed this way before." At Dover, the salute of guns which heralded his arrival, the eager greetings of the ladies, and the sentry at his door—all delighted him. In London, he rejoiced in the contrast between his fine house in Portland Place and the attics which had known him of old. As he was going, splendid in gold-trimmed coat, to present his credentials to the king, he pointed out to his secretary, Marcellus, the house where his friend Hingant had attempted suicide. "There," said he, "my friend tried to kill himself and I came near to dying of hunger." One evening when his chef, the great Montmirel, had surpassed himself, he exclaimed:—"The weight in gold of but one of the gastronomic masterpieces on which Montmirel is expending such genius today would have sufficed, thirty years ago, to save me from starvation and Hingant from suicide. O fortune!"

A great talker, loving antitheses and composition in art, this reader of Seneca and Cicero could not fail to be moved by such incessant contrasts. Of old, the Literary Fund had advanced him a pound or two. He was now its patron and guest of honour. During the years of exile, vague longings had come upon him as he gazed from afar on the fair unknowns of Kensington Gardens. Now, as Ambassador, he fled from lionising hostesses, eager for a moment of his time. Where once he had thirstily emptied jugs of water, Rothschild poured him brimming goblets of his finest Tokay. And, as he loved laments no less than triumphs, he meditated on the nothingness of glory and chewed the Dead Sea fruit of success. *To Mme. Récamier:* "I cannot take a step without meeting something which recalls my youth and my sufferings, the friends I have lost, by-gone worlds, vain deluding hopes, my earliest works, my dreams of fame—all, indeed, that goes to body forth the future of a young man, conscious of his high destiny. On some of those visions I have laid hold, others have escaped me. Not one of all has been worth my labour. I am a little unwell, thanks to fresh paint, charcoal and fog."

The Court made him welcome. At the close of his first audience, George IV personally conducted him to the drawing-room where the diplomatic corps was assembled. "Gentlemen," said he, "I introduce a new colleague." "We are proud and happy to see him among us," replied the Austrian ambassador, Count Esterhazy. Lord Londonderry, the Foreign Secretary, invited him to his country house. Though Chateaubriand gave him credit for a pretty wit, he found the Secretary's reserve, his chilly good-breeding and his capacity for silence somewhat disconcerting. Among others, he saw the Duke of Wellington, who was then the most popular man in England. The Duke's admiring fellow-countrymen had subscribed towards a monument whereon he was to be represented, semi-clad, as the young Achilles. The tribute irritated Chateaubriand, since it was the reward for a defeat inflicted on France. "No," said he to Marcellus as they were passing the famous statue—"No, he did not vanquish the Invincible. All he did was to beat Maréchal Soult and, at Waterloo, he was merely the instrument of divine justice."

With Canning he struck up a friendship the more easily in that they had both come to politics by way of literature. Together they bewailed the royal distrust of poets and men of feeling. "When once they have accepted our ideas," said Chateaubriand, "they ought, in justice, to accept our persons." Canning, however, vowed that he would not exchange the pleasures of poetry for the helm of state. "Literature," said he, "is the best respite from the chances and changes of life." "Literature," replied Chateaubriand, "was the staff of life in the days of my poverty and I am persuaded that it will not fail me in old age."

An unexpected visit from his first love, Charlotte Ives, at first delighted the ambassador. Years earlier, the sudden flight of the Chevalier de Combourg had caused her such deep suffering that she fell seriously ill and, for a long time, would not hear of marriage. Eventually, however, she became the wife of a naval officer, since promoted admiral, and was now Mrs. Sutton. She called on the ambassador ostensibly to return a manuscript which he had left at Beccles, twenty-five years before: in reality, because she was glad to see him again. Young Marcellus decided that she had fine features and that, though she had grown plump, her skin was remarkably white. "But Spring was over, the hey-day of Summer passing, and Autumn drawing on."

The ambassador was kindly, courteous and distant. "Can I be of any service to you?" Such haughty civility was cruel enough. She faltered, had no answer ready, and did not go again. A few months later she wrote him a letter, touching in its humility, asking that he would put in a word with Canning for one of the young Suttons, who was a candidate for a post in India. "Wrapped up in the cares of empire and placed so high as hardly to conceive the anxieties of a humbler existence, Your Excellency cannot easily imagine with what painful intensity the mind of a private person may become absorbed in a single thought. . . . That, my Lord, is what I would ask of you, and you will never know what the request has cost me. With every good wish for your health and happiness and kindest regards, in which Admiral Sutton joins me, I have the honour to be Your Lordship's most humble and obedient servant."

Your Lordship. . . . Most humble servant. Thus, then, ended the most delicate of idylls. It seemed, indeed, that destiny found sport in re-evoking, in that house in Portland Place, all the old loves of an already long life, for the ambassador received there Astolphe de Custine, the son of the Queen of Roses, and Léontine de Noailles, poor Mouche's daughter, both of whom he had known as children, one in the park of Fervacques, the other in the gardens of Méréville. On Sundays, in the solitude of his vast house, the ambassador took up the thread of his *Mémoires*. What stage had his emotional life reached? In boyhood he had pursued a phantom and dreamed visionary loves. Charlotte Ives had been no more than a virginal and lovely shade. In Pauline de Beaumont the nymph had begun to take flesh, but in how frail a vesture of the soul, how quickly fled. Then came real women and with them those moments "when one strives to prison all being in a word or look." None of his mistresses had given him the supreme happiness of his imagined bliss. Love, as fame, had left a savour of ashes in his mouth. "And my soul, what was it? A little by-gone grieving, lost upon the wind. . . . And I would think within myself: 'Ensue happiness before it is too late. But one day more and you can be loved no longer.' "

In London, then, he sought happiness and there was no lack of women ready to collaborate in the attempt. The attachés at the French Embassy had painted him to Englishwomen as a romantic hero. They told how one duchess had died for love of him and another run mad. When the hero appeared in person, a country of giants was somewhat disappointed in the little man. The Princess de Lieven, "of the sharp and forbidding face," decided that he looked like "a hump-back without a hump." She describes him as affecting in drawing-rooms "a dreary and sentimental pose, and wearing on his sleeve an outworn heart that was for sale though it no longer found bidders." When he confessed to boredom, she offered to introduce him to intelligent women. "Madam, I do not like intelligent women." "You prefer them stupid?" "Far and away." It was a thinly-veiled way of saying that he did not like Mme. de Lieven, whom he labelled "dried-up and tiresome."

If Marcellus and Chateaubriand himself are to be believed, others proved more kind. Lady Fitzroy, "as pretty as all Venus' Loves," was among the most assiduous. It was also rumoured that he had "thrown the handkerchief" to Mrs. Arbuthnot. Above all, there were the Frenchwomen. Mme. Laffont (the actor's wife), who had the finest eyes in the world, received frequent invitations to the embassy with her husband. Now and again she would disappear at moments when, oddly enough the ambassador was also nowhere to be found. "He is keeping her," said a scandalised Mme. de Lieven, "and she does the honours of his house. . . . He spends his evenings in her company and discourses to her for hours of fame, of enthusiasm and even of virtue."

There was also a Mlle. Le Vert (or Leverd) who so perturbed Mme. Récamier that she departed from her usual reticence to remonstrate. "Come!" replied Chateaubriand. "I would rather know just how absurd you are than read too much into the hints in those hurt notes of yours. I think I have it. The trouble must be the woman of whom the Queen of Sweden's friend spoke to you. Be fair! Can I prevent Mlle. Le Vert from writing me declarations and a score more stage-folk, male and female, from coming to

England to try to make a little money. And, even if I were to blame, do you imagine that such passing fancies could ever touch you or take from you one jot of what is yours for ever? You really deserve that I should be a little unfaithful. I remember a time when you were bent on knowing whether I had any mistresses, yet hardly seemed to care."

It was unusual for him to write to the Abbaye-aux-Bois in this strain. Nearly always he was tender:— "If only I could be in the little cell. . . . Isn't it idiotic of me to love you so? And the forest? do you ever go there? . . . My one thought is to order my life for you." To Mme. de Duras, who was jealous of Mme. Récamier, of his idle fancies and even of Céleste, he wrote more unsympathetically. "Your answers to my letters are torrents of absurd reproaches. Unless tomorrow's post brings me a handsome apology, I shall not write again. . . . You would try the patience of a saint! . . . I am incapable of affection! I do not trouble to read your letters! and a thousand accusations of the sort. Intent on your obsession, you stab to the heart, heedless of consequence." And, when, he was in the most charming of moods:— "You tell me that you will say nothing, since whatever you had to say would be disagreeable. I know it all in advance—That I love no one, that I am the complete egoist, that I must be the sole centre of interest, that I am a base deceiver. My dear Sister, ransack the dictionary for terms of abuse; you will not make me love you the less."

As for Céleste, he saw to it that Mathieu de Montmorency should invite her to dinner whenever English notabilities were on their way through Paris. "She is murmuring and, indeed, has cause." To Pilorge, his fat, red-faced private secretary, was entrusted the duty of keeping Mme. de Chateaubriand informed of the ambassador's life—a task which he most prudently performed. It is through him we know that Monsieur "rose at nine, that he had adopted the English habit of taking something solid with his tea, read seven or eight English newspapers, all very long, very wide and very closely printed, gave a few audiences, strolled in the park, worked, read and yawned. . . . With it all Monsieur is in the best of health. On Tuesdays and Fridays, the days when the courier arrives, despatches and private letters take up the time usually given to walks, visits and boredom."[1] The *time given to boredom* is rather funny; it would seem that Hyacinthe Pilorge developed a sense of humour while in England.

It is to Pilorge, too, that we owe the account of that great ambassadorial dinner which Chateaubriand determined should be a triumph, even seeking to inveigle George IV to his house. The dessert was superb, the porcelain dinner-service magnificent and the chef Montmirel, the great Montmirel, inventor of the pudding à la Chateaubriand (afterwards pudding Diplomate) and of beef-steak Chateaubriand, cooked between two slices of sirloin, worked wonders. After his dinner and the reception that followed, Chateaubriand believed that the pomp and splendour of the French embassy roused the jealousy of all English hostesses; Mme. de Lieven maintains that he had no gift for entertaining, that his luxury was that of a parvenu and that, in his house, good society was always swamped in a crowd of nobodies. Behind the illustrious ambassador, Mme. de Lieven doubtless divined the little Marquis of Carabas who, fifty years earlier, had arrived at Combourg, with bells a-tinkling, in a coach drawn by horses bedizened like Spanish mules. When the evidence is well weighed, it seems that Chateaubriand did not get on too well with the English aristocracy, that he was nettled by their coolness while his aloofness irritated them and that the only happy days of his embassy were those on which, surrounded by French visitors of no importance, he could be as laughter-loving as a child. On his return to Paris in 1801 his English manners had been a nine days' wonder. In the London of 1823 he reverted to the man of Paris, of Villeneuve-sur-Yonne and even of Plancoët.

"The French embassy, so long forgotten in this country, should once more take a leading place in pleasures as in affairs. The influence of society extends to politics and, where diplomacy is concerned, balls are by no means useless to the king's service, but that part of my job is not the one I like best." The part he liked best was high politics. His despatches, written and carefully corrected by his own hand ("Take care of the epithets," he told Marcellus), dazzled his young secretaries by their accuracy and

---

[1] Quoted by Mme. Pailleron. *La Vicomtesse de Chateaubriand.*

intelligence. English statesmen, though he imagined that he had some ascendancy over them, did not care for him, but that was chiefly because his ideas ran counter to their plans. He desired that in Spain, a country torn by civil war, Europe should intervene on behalf of King Ferdinand VII. England was opposed to any such intervention.

A congress was about to be held at Verona for the discussion of this and the Italian question. Chateaubriand was bursting to go there as the representative of France. It would give opportunity for proving his diplomatic talents and would be a kind of stepping-stone to the Ministry. Once more he set his Egerias—the Duchesse de Duras and Mme. Récamier—in motion. To Juliette he advanced sentimental arguments: "This Congress has the immense advantage of bringing me back to Paris, and all this talk of politics no other meaning than that I am dying to see you." Love and ambition rubbed shoulders in his letters: "To be loved by you, to live quietly and peacefully in some little retreat with you and a few books, that is my heart's desire and the goal of all my longing. . . . Remember the Congress." With Mme. de Duras he was more outspoken: "To have in their own ranks a friend who has achieved, who knows the kings and ministers of Europe, whom even the opposition in England honours, and yet go in search of such tools as enemies with no aptitude for the task and hostile nonentities! However, my dear sister, settle it all with Villèle."

As he also laid claim to the blue ribbon of St. Louis (since it was "ridiculous and unseemly that an ambassador should be reduced, like a war veteran, to the cross of the Legion of Honour") poor Claire de Duras ended by lamenting that ambition of his which, she said, now overshadowed every other feeling. "I do not know whether, as you say, my ambition has become a great tree; but I can say of it what my poor sister used to say of joy touching herself: 'It is no plant that grows on mortal soil.' And believe me, those of my first forests please and suit me better." It was true, but only intermittently.

Would he be given a seat in the Congress? For long Mathieu and Villèle kept him in suspense. The entire diplomatic corps wanted to be sent on the delegation: Mathieu himself, Adrien de Laval, Blacas. "Mathieu and Villèle say *yes* and *no, no* and *yes*. . . .

If that is how they intend to reward me for my loyalty, they have not heard the last of it. . . . No one shall be suffered to make a laughing-stock of me."

Suddenly, while the Ambassador of France was working on his *Mémoires* and, for a few hours daily, stifling his disappointed ambitions by amusing himself, in his great house in Portland Place, with describing the garrets of his adolescence, the head of the Foreign Office, Lord Londonderry, cut his throat. Once again there flashed across Chateaubriand's life the sinister lightning of madness. "It will be long before I cease to see the great coffin wherein lay that man slain by his own hands at the very height of his prosperity. There is nothing for it but to become a Trappist." Such monastic aspirations in no wise hindered him from thinking of his Congress. *To Mme. Récamier:* "I know what you're going to say: Are you so terribly set on this Congress? Not a bit of it, but it is the road that leads most naturally home to the little cell. There is all my secret." Finally on September 3rd: "The matter is all settled, but with what bad grace on Mathieu's part! But tell me, couldn't you come to meet me at Chantilly? . . . I should see you before anyone else, we could talk and talk. There are so many things I have to tell you and I've bottled up so much in my heart in the last five months! My heart beats faster at the thought of seeing you."

If he had returned from his first stay in London a complete Anglomaniac, on this occasion the impressions he bore back were inimical. The frivolity of high society, the discontent of the masses had left him with a sense of decadence. He no longer believed in the stability of England. It was this superficial judgment which partly explained Chateaubriand's later policy.

3. The Congress of Verona

The problem which confronted the Congress of Verona was the same which, since 1815, had been occupying the attention of the princes of the Holy Alliance: how to deal with the disease of Liberalism? How were the infected countries to be purified? More especially, how should they intervene in Spain to save King Ferdinand VII from the rebel Cortes?

There seemed to be three possible solutions. The first, non-intervention, found favour with England, which saw in the Spanish disorders great advantages to her trade with South America. The second, Metternich's, was for sending the Russian and Austrian armies to intervene in Spain, with the help of France, which would grant them free passage. The third left to France the responsibilities, but the glories too, of a campaign. This last was Chateaubriand's, but he was careful not to say so, for he would not have had the support of his government.

He had been sorely disappointed to learn that his Minister and friend, a Mathieu de Montmorency, would himself head the French delegation to Verona. Chateaubriand disliked playing second fiddle, especially by the side of Mathieu, whose virtues he held in greater esteem than his intelligence. Hence he was in the seventh heaven when, in Montmorency's absence, Villèle was created prime minister by the king, thus becoming the superior of a discomfited Mathieu, to whom he sent instructions by Chateaubriand. They were prudent: France was to enter into no engagement.

At Verona Mathieu no more enjoyed being under Chateaubriand's eye than the latter enjoyed being under his orders. The Emperors of Austria and of Russia were there, the King of Prussia, the Grand Duke of Tuscany and the Duchess of Parma, Napoleon's widow. "We found her looking very well," said Chateaubriand. "We told her that we had encountered her soldiers at Piacenza and that there had been a time when she had more." She replied. "I never think about such things now." Chateaubriand held that she was in the wrong. In his opinion, the kings to whom he was presented did not treat him with the respect due to his renown. The Queen of Sardinia asked him amiably whether he was related to the M. de Chateaubriand who wrote tracts. He was shocked. Metternich, who feared him, tried to make bad blood with Alexander. Pozzo di Borgo called him "an old child of fifty." These old campaigners of the congresses Chateaubriand antagonised by a clumsiness, compact of pride and shyness. He was incapable of assuming a suitably passionate interest in Metternich's exposition of the proper way to make macaroni. "He is a mediocrity with neither depth nor vision," he wrote to Mme. de Duras, "and has no ascendancy save over Mathieu de Montmorency's weakness."

Ousted from the chief debates and refusing invitations to the little suppers, Chateaubriand spent his time at Verona in the company of "his young folk," the secretaries to the French delegation, for only among them did he find that warmth of admiration which he craved. He went to Mantua to see Virgil's tomb, took walks in the sunshine, spoke little, and now and again captured a fine image. "This evening they are giving a fête in the Amphitheatre. The ruins will be illuminated. It is reminiscent of many things." Mathieu de Montmorency wrote to Mme. Récamier: "I don't much care for the general position in which he is placed. . . . His starchiness, his unsociability make people ill at ease with him. . . . I can't help feeling that he must be very bored by the kind of life he has elected to lead, and I do not know whether he finds his great desire to come to the Congress altogether justified."

That sad state of affairs changed completely on the day when Mathieu de Montmorency decided to return to Paris. The Minister for Foreign Affairs had two very strong reasons for wishing to get away from Verona. (a) He had pledged himself to Metternich to make France the soldier of the Holy Alliance in the Spanish business, whereas Villèle and the King wanted to temporise, and he felt that he ought to explain himself in Paris. (b) His wife had set off to meet him and he dreaded her arrival in this mocking little town where, for a few weeks, all the courts of Europe were concentrated.

The Vicomtesse de Montmorency, née Hortense de Luynes, was a strange person. A loveless marriage and long neglect on the part of her husband had thrown her back on religion which, perhaps in chagrin, she carried to the point of taking a vow of chastity. At the age of forty-five a succession of deaths in the family had suddenly constrained her to apply to Rome for dispensation from her vow, in order that there might be an heir to the name of Montmorency. Awakened to the realities of love through duty and late in life, she had unexpectedly developed a strong taste for them and tended to display an unbridled passion for her old husband, who had not lost "the spell of youth upon a half-bald brow." It is understandable that he should have had no desire to stage this St. Martin's honeymoon for royal groundlings.

Who would succeed to the leadership of the French delegation? Villèle nominated Chateaubriand, partly because the Minister wanted to give pledges to the royalists, but mainly because he thought Chateaubriand in favour of his own policy of agreement with England and non-intervention. Therein he was badly mistaken, for—at that very moment—his ambassador was writing to Mme. de Duras: "If hostilities, and not very dangerous ones at that, with Spain should result in our recovering our military rank in Europe and in making us forget the tricolor cockade, we shouldn't have much cause for complaint."

Chateaubriand, who was eclipsed in the second rank, shone in the first. In a few days he won the respect of the Congress. "I shall leave behind me in Verona the reputation of an able man and one to be feared. I am much sought after at present, but these people are too feeble to like me." Thanks to the beneficent influence which Claire de Duras exerted from afar, the Princess Tolstoi had patched things up with the Emperor Alexander and these two men of imagination had found pleasure in discussing the affairs of Europe. In the course of their conversations, Chateaubriand had conceived far-reaching projects. With Russia behind her, why should not France hold out against England? Why should not Russia, in exchange for Constantinople, give her the left bank of the Rhine and effect a revision of the treaties of 1815? The designs were vast, but they appealed to the Emperor. "I am very glad you came here," he told Chateaubriand; "we gain mutually from seeing each other."

England laid before the Congress proposals for dealing with the slave trade and with piracy in the American seas. Chateaubriand, in shrewd and ironical notes, pointed out that while these measures were doubtless inspired by humanitarian considerations, they would indirectly serve British interests and pave the way to recognition of the revolutionary republics of South America. Metternich, seeing that he was opposing England, believed he had found an ally in that direction and began to treat him with more regard. "Our face and our language must be very deceptive," wrote Chateaubriand, "or else the Arch-Chancellor's perspicacity is not such as is supposed." The truth of the matter was that Chateaubriand, a secret and reserved man, had determined in his heart to make war on Spain and to make it alone for the greater glory of the white banner and of Chateaubriand; meanwhile he wheedled Alexander and lulled the suspicions of Metternich. It was not a bad stroke.

In France, he followed the fortunes of Villèle. "He is, after all, the only man capable of office and I would a hundred times rather have him than the canting, scheming, jealous stupidity of Mathieu." Villèle, indeed, backed him because he imagined him a convert to his ideas. As a citizen of Toulouse, the President of the Council was determined, at whatever cost, to avoid war on the southwest frontier of France. He disclaimed the pledges made to Metternich by Montmorency, who thereupon seized the first excuse for sending in his resignation, receiving in compensation the title of Duke, which delighted his wife.

Who would become Minister for Foreign Affairs? Chateaubriand longed passionately for that portfolio; Villèle seemed ready to give it him; there remained to overcome the prejudices of the king. Eventually Louis seemed to yield and the offer of the coveted ministry came. Though he was in ecstasies and determined to accept, Chateaubriand felt that his behaviour towards Mathieu might seem dubious and he feared the judgment of Mme. Récamier. Torn between those two men, the friend of the setting and the lover of the rising star, she played her impossible game without the slightest error of tact. "I hear," the Duc de Laval wrote to her, "that you are coming through all your difficulties wonderfully, that you are trusted by all alike, that everyone is content and no-one betrayed." A more passionate woman, judging this impeccable negotiatrix with a trace of irritation, might perhaps have thought that if no one was betrayed, it was because everybody was.

When the portfolio was offered to Chateaubriand, he began by refusing, and advised Villèle to take it himself for the time being. *To Mme. Récamier:* "Mathieu did not deserve this sacrifice, considering his behaviour to me, but I owed it to you and to my loyalty. . . . I can no longer be said to be ambitious." To Mme. de Duras he admitted his dread of seeing his disinterestedness taken at its face value: "Monsieur, instead of urging me to accept, clasped me in his arms and said that I was behaving like a hero. . . . Who is being hoodwinked?" Who, indeed, was bamboozled? Certainly not public opinion, which was not for a moment deceived by this comedy. "When the ministry was offered him," said Pasquier, "he put on all the appearance of a man who dreaded its labours and difficulties. . . . They had almost to resort to violence to make him accept the power of which he was burning to possess himself."

The King eventually overcame this fragile modesty. "Accept," said he, "I command it you." Never was there an order sweeter to obey. Chateaubriand was so afraid of seeing the King go back on his decision that he put Villèle on guard against every possible danger. "You realise, my dear friend, that the appointment must be announced at the same time as the resignation, otherwise the papers of the Right will go up in smoke and the King will draw back," and—almost at that very moment—*to the Duchesse de Duras*: "The King has ordered me to accept, I have obeyed, but as a man led to the slaughter." Great as her indulgence for him was, Claire de Duras must have smiled as she read that note.

On moving into the ministry, he wrote to Juliette Récamier that nothing would be changed and that she would see him every day at his accustomed hour. "Tonight I shall lay me down in that ministerial bed which was not made for me, where there is little sleep to be had and where none stays long. It seems to me that with every bridge I cross I am further from you and that the journey I must take will be a long one. It breaks my heart but I will give the lie to such foreboding. I shall see you every day and at our hour, in your little cell." It was a promise he did not keep for long.

4. THE MINISTER

"My private correspondence is written by my own hand and goes to the four corners of Europe. I entrust it to no-one else." It was a fact that, on becoming a minister, this writer worked as hard as the most active of his predecessors. Despatches, private letters to ambassadors, to Canning, to the Czar Alexander—he sometimes spent nights in penning, in that large haughty script of his, those precise and forceful documents which always bore the imprint of his style. He wanted war in Spain, convinced that it would be an easy undertaking, that it would discourage the European revolutionaries, unite the French armies and stabilise the monarchy.

On his road, he met with several obstacles. The first was Villèle, his President of the Council. Villèle had chosen Chateaubriand at a time when he was yet unaware that the new minister's plans were even further from his own than those of Montmorency. When he discovered his mistake, his spleen was great. To all appearances he was conciliatory, for he needed Chateaubriand's friends in the Chamber and the latter went on proclaiming to all and sundry that he was on the best of terms with Villèle. He was alone in that belief.

Second group of adversaries: Mathieu de Montmorency and his son-in-law Sosthène de la Rochefoucauld, the leading spirits of the Congregation, whose secret though bitter grudge was only awaiting an opportunity for revenge. Third obstacle: the French liberals, who, from doctrinal and political necessity, supported their brethren, the Spanish liberals. Fourth obstacle: the Holy Alliance, which was vexed to observe that France could do without the other powers and dreaded that the contagion of the Spanish revolution might spread to the French armies. Fifth and last obstacle, which seemed the most insuperable: England—whose government, though Tory, was encouraging the Spanish revolutionaries, both because the City was anxious to capture the market of the South American colonies, and because the Foreign Office feared to see, once more, on the thrones of France and Spain, monarchies that were too closely bound to each other.

All these enemies Chateaubriand faced fearlessly. "France will have an answer for everything," he wrote to Marcellus, "and she is afraid of nothing." And to the Comte de la Garde, the French ambassador to Madrid: "I suggest, M. le Comte, that you should raise the tone rather than lower it." Finally to Canning himself, January 14th, 1823: "War, you say, might overthrow our institutions while their foundations are still not very secure? Possibly, but, for a government there are two ways of dying—one through reverses, the other through dishonour. If revolutionary Spain can boast of having made monarchical France tremble, if the white cockade retreats before the *descamisados*, the power of the Empire and the triumphs of the tricolor cockade will come back to mind. Think what that memory will mean for the Bourbons. Ours is a nation of soldiers. A success would bind the army to the King for ever and would make all France run to arms. You would not believe what can be wrought among us by the very word *honour*." This letter intensified Canning's ill-humour—a result which might have proved dangerous. "If Mr. Canning had equipped a score of ships with arms and sent them to Cadiz, he would have put us in an extremely difficult position." But the English prime minister contented himself with a hostile speech, and those break no bones.

The Upward Climb. The Dizzy Heights. The Fall

If France were to act, it had to be speedily. To maintain inactive, on the frontier of a revolution, an army of a hundred thousand men, many of whom—both officers and privates—were ex-Bonapartists or republicans, was to expose the troops to a most dangerous contagion. Chateaubriand had taken office at the beginning of January 1823; by the end of the month, on his orders, the French ambassador to Spain had asked for his passports. Canning's ill-humour turned to rage and fury. In London, the windows of the French embassy were pelted with stones, but, as Chateaubriand had foreseen, the reaction in England was not military. *To Mercellus:* "Let my honourable friend Canning fume as he pleases. . . . He has dreamed of war and is powerless to make it. That is the secret of his ill-humour. . . . One thing I do impress upon you: from now on, go and see Mr. Canning only very occasionally. Let your visits be short and cold and do not have any talk with him; a man who has spoken publicly against France should have only the most indispensable contact with France's representative."

Ere long a speech from the throne notified the French of war with Spain. The Duc d'Angoulême was appointed Commander-in-Chief. With Maréchal Victor, the Minister for War, Chateaubriand busied himself in making ready his armies. He demanded that, in the choice of leaders, military experience rather than a man's political past should be the first consideration. "Every French officer," said he, "will be loyal in the face of fire." When General Foy, in the name of the Left, attacked him in the Chamber on the Spanish expedition, he replied on the 25th with a great speech, the first he had made before that assembly, and had a real success. He began by replying to the liberal orators who maintained that a nation has no right to intervene in the internal affairs of another country.

"In all ages," said Chateaubriand, "there has been a recognised exception to that rule—the one whereby a nation has the right to intervene when her own interests are at stake." That had been England's motive in making war on France at the time of the Revolution. "Never forget," he continued, "that if the war in Spain, in common with every other war, has its hardships and its perils, it will bring us one immense advantage—it will have given us an army. . . . Something, perhaps, is yet lacking to the complete reconciliation of the French; it will be brought about under canvas. Comrades in arms are soon friends. . . . The King, with generous trust, has given the keeping of the white standard into the hands of captains who fought for the triumph of other colours; they will teach it anew the way of victory; it had never forgotten that of honour." When he concluded, the whole of the Right rushed to shake hands with him and even fell on his neck. That speech was the occasion of the famous incident which ended with the expulsion *manu militari* of the deputy of the Left, Manuel. "Vicomte de Foucault, when you seized. . . ."

The country, however, remained calm. The army, held up while crossing the Bidassoa by a hundred and fifty French and Italian revolutionaries who shouted at the soldiers: "What are you out for here? To put a despot back on the throne?" replied with a salvo of guns which was enough to scatter the little detachment. The Spanish population welcomed the French troops with cries of "Long live the King!" There was no fighting—only "a somewhat jerky military route-march." No later than May 24th, the Duc d'Angoulême entered Madrid. Unfortunately the Cortes had fled in the direction of Seville and Cadiz, taking the King of Spain with them. "We must not conceal from ourselves the fact that nothing is accomplished so long as we haven't the King," wrote Chateaubriand to Marcellus, adding: "In my opinion we shall only get the King by striking a blow at Seville or Cadiz. Couldn't you find in London one of those enterprising men, such as grow like blackberries in that country, who might kidnap him for one or two millions? Think about it." The romantic novelist was collaborating with the minister.

If there had been any doubt of Chateaubriand's qualities as a man of action, the Cadiz affair certainly brought them to light. "Let us not hymn the victory yet," he said; "I'm desperately afraid of that baggage, Fortune," but he did his best to settle the affair. The Duc d'Angoulême was endeavouring to win over the Spanish rebels by his moderation, setting limits (by his ordinance of Andujar) to the vengeance of the monarchists let loose, and hoping to achieve the King's liberation without striking a blow. His policy brought an outburst from the Ultras in both countries. Chateaubriand was all for the strong hand. "My dear friend," he wrote to Villèle, "I believe it is today that you are to write to M. le Duc d'Angoulême on a matter of capital importance: he should beware of tipping the scale in the direction of the Spanish constitutionals. On all sides I hear rumours that the royalists are alarmed at this tendency in the prince. It is to the royalists, after all, that we owe our success today and if their generals, their soldiers, their parish-priests and the rest of the clergy believe that all the blows and the dangers have fallen to their share and all the favours to the generals of the Cortes, we shall be abandoned in the midst of Spain."

The man of letters was urging on the men of war. *To General Guilleminot, Chief-of-staff to the Duc d'Angoulême:* "If once you can succeed in bombarding Cadiz, all will soon be yours. You are surely not alarmed by the foolish idea that a shell might find its mark in the King. I hope that no harm may befall him, but after all it is a question of royalty. In time of war a king is merely a general. He must take personal risks. . . . Fears and pusillanimities hold everything up. . . . You may be sure that you will get no results save by striking suddenly and violently; speed and daring can alone bring you success. You know, when matters are critical, the price of a moment lost. . . . The day may be carried in the twinkling of an eye if you go about it quickly, and drag on six months if you shuffle." *To the same general:* "I have sailed those seas. It is not to me you should come with hair-raising tales of the equinox." And again: "I have told you once and I say it again—so long as I am a member of the Council, Cadiz shall not be abandoned. I would rather die a score of deaths than see a single Frenchman retreat. For the third time, I tell you Cadiz shall fall and the Spanish business succeed."

It was he who proved right. The fort of the Trocadero, the key to Cadiz, was taken in September, the Cortes defeated and the King set at liberty. Chateaubriand triumphed: "I have always been sure of the ultimate success of the Spanish war. I have remained in the ministry for the reason that I have that Breton stubbornness which never draws back, which circumstance may thwart, but never subdue. Believe me; when a man's will is inflexible, he is nearly always stronger than the event." The method is one which gives excellent results so long as events remain on the human scale.

Was it a final success? So far as Spain was concerned, the release of Ferdinand VII, a tyrant who had learnt nothing and forgotten nothing, was far from being a perfect solution. In the Duc d'Angoulême's despite, Ferdinand authorised the most cruel of reprisals on the part of his followers and, ere long, the general discontent was such that the English influence in Spain became more powerful than the French. "France," said Chateaubriand, "desires that Spain shall be peaceful and happy. She will oppose every dangerous reaction as she will any spirit of vengeance. We are concerned not to seem a party to stupidity and fanaticism. Rather would we abandon Spain than lend our weapons to those who prefer the shedding of blood on the scaffold to its outpouring on the field of battle." They are lofty thoughts but, when it came to facts, he was powerless to bridle passions.

In reality it was in France, rather than in Spain, that he hoped for great results from his victory. He attained them. Thenceforward the army accepted the white standard without demur. A contented country returned to Paris, in the December elections, a "rediscovered" Chamber. The victors were given a triumphal welcome on their return: salvos of guns, illuminations, a *Te Deum*, nothing was lacking. The Duc d'Angoulême, who was a modest man, thought it was all much ado about nothing. Such was not the opinion of Chateaubriand, who was vastly proud of his work: "We could admit to ourself," he said, "that we were of as much worth in politics as in literature, if worth indeed we have."

Yet over his exaltation there fell the shadow of grief, for Mme. Récamier had left Paris because he had earned her displeasure.

5. Angels, White and Black

Women love power and the triumph of love readily attends on the triumph of arms. For Chateaubriand, this year of diplomatic successes was also a year of personal conquests. The more he was overwhelmed by cares and toils, the more time and strength he seemed to find for new ties. Some among them were slender. Mme. Hamelin, a beautiful fashion-plate with raven hair and eyes of fire, who had taken him under her protection in the days of Napoleon's rages and had been grudging neither of her favour nor her favours, came in her turn to ask his help. Though no longer in her first youth, she was still alluring. He allowed himself

The Upward Climb. The Dizzy Heights. The Fall

to be tempted and more than once the minister was seen to leave the ministry with the fashion-plate.

Mme. Hamelin was past forty. Cordélia de Castellane, who was the great love of this *annus mirabilis*, was only twenty-five. A daughter of the banker Greffulhe, married to Colonel Count Boniface de Castellane, she had as much daring as she had charm and beauty. Chateaubriand has painted her portrait, in his *Vie de Rancé*, under the name of another Castellane: "The pallor which seemed the first layer of colour for the freshness of her complexion gave her the stamp of passion. She had wide blue eyes, an inheritance from her mother." Molé describes the angelic beauty of her face, her blue eyes, "her pale colouring, exquisite in its delicacy, her hair which had a fairness all her own. . . . When she smiled and her pearly teeth gleamed against the smoothness of her wild-rose skin, the dim gold of her hair and the matchless blue of her eyes, one wondered if she could indeed be mortal woman."

Yet again, Chateaubriand believed that he had found the Sylph. She yielded at once, for she was mettlesome and sensuous, and on the day following that first night of love suggested a runaway stay by the sea. He replied with an ardour such as neither Mme. de Custine nor Mme. de Mouchy had ever kindled: "My angel, my life, I know not what besides, I love you with all the madness of my untried youth. For you I have once more become the brother of Amélie; I have no memory of anything since you granted me to fall at your feet. Yes, come to the sea, where you will, so it be far from everywhere. At last I have laid hold on the dream of bliss that I have followed so long. It is you whom I have so long worshipped while yet I knew you not. You shall know all my life; you shall see what will be known only after my death; I will leave it in trust with him who shall come after us." For his first impulse, somewhat naïf but rather touching, when he wanted to seduce a woman, was to give her his *Mémoires* to read.

A week later, he was crazy with desire: "Never have I seen you at once as beautiful and as pretty as you were yesterday evening. I would have given my life to have you in my arms. Tell me, was it your love for me that made you even lovelier? Was it my consuming passion for you that made you so bewitching in my eyes? You saw for yourself that I could do nothing but look at you and kiss the little gold chain. When you left me, I would fain have fallen prostrate at your feet and worshipped you as a goddess. . . . Ah! if only you loved me half as much as I love you. . . . My poor head is turned. Salve with your love the hurt that you have done me. At eight o'clock I shall await you with a throbbing heart."

Sometimes he wrote to her in verse, the best he had ever penned, expressing the fears of so old a traveller in loving so young a woman and the sadness of feeling that, if she loved him a little, it was rather for his works than for himself.

> *Le talent ne rend point ce que le temps efface;*
> *La gloire, hélas, ne rajeunit qu'un nom.*
> *L'amant de Velléda, le frère d'Amélie,*
> *Mes fils ingrats, m'ont-ils ravi ta foi?*
> *Ton admiration me blesse et m'humilie.*
> *Le croiras-tu? Je suis jaloux de moi.*
> *Dédaigne, ô ma beauté, cette gloire trompeuse . . .*
> *Il n'est qu'un bien, c'est le tendre plaisir.*
> *Quelle immortalité vaut une nuit heureuse?*
> *Pour tes baisers, je vendrais l'avenir.*

At the moment of the taking of the Trocadero, this love blazed up in all its freshness. Chateaubriand, once again athirst "for glory to win him love," found delight in casting down politics at the feet of his mistress. Forced to remain in the ministry to await the news of victory, he went the length of cursing a triumph which deprived him of one night spent in Cordélia's arms. "Ah! I can write to you without constraint and tell you that I would barter the world for one of your caresses, to be able to hold you close to the beating of my heart, to grow one with you in those long kisses wherein I breathe your life and yield mine up to you. You would have given me a son, you would have been the mother of my only child. Instead, I am awaiting news of an event which gives me no joy. What is the world to me without you? You came, and, sensitive though I was to its laurels, your coming has reft me even of my pleasure in the success of this war, on which I alone was resolved. Today all has vanished from my sight save you. It is you whom I see in all about me, whom I seek in all about me.

The Upward Climb. The Dizzy Heights. The Fall

This renown, which would turn the head of any other man, cannot distract me for an instant from my love."

On October 25th she left for Dieppe; he was to follow her. "But a few days and I shall be at your feet, I shall hold you close against my heart. . . . Far from the madding crowd, you shall see how I love you. Take all my loves, my Love, and remember that you are the mistress of my worship. I kiss your feet and your hair." To safeguard this meeting and put their acquaintances off the scent, Chateaubriand announced that he was going to spend some days at Fervacques, with Mme. de Custine. She naturally awaited him in vain. Paris was beginning to talk of the escapades of the Minister for Foreign Affairs. His blood was up. "It's perfectly nonsensical. I had every intention of going to Fervacques. Just as I was on the point of seeing you I was recalled." Public opinion no more believed him than did Mme. de Custine. He had altogether lost his head, as men of ripe age do when they are intoxicated with love for a young woman, and his follies succeeded in compromising him more and more in the eyes of his colleagues and of his usual patronesses.

Save a post for her son-in-law, the Duc de Rauzan, Mme. de Duras had got nothing but snubs since Chateaubriand's elevation to the ministry, but she was used to those. Mme. Récamier, more sensitive and more spoilt, had asked and had obtained much, yet she grew daily colder and more distant. She liked her life and those of her friends to be peaceable, well-ordered and discreet. All this commotion, chaos and intoxication wounded her sensibilities. When several days had passed without Chateaubriand's coming to see her at the "little cell" she took the painful decision of going out at the sacred hour. He came, failed to find her and bemoaned himself plaintively: "I spent three quarters of an hour alone in the little cell, longing for you, calling on your name and yet happy to be in the midst of your books, your flowers and all the things that live with you. . . . How *could* you go out at our accustomed hour? Couldn't you have waited for me just a little while? . . . It is very easy for you to do without me. . . . I had left everything to come to you."

Saddened by the rumours that came to her ears touching Chateaubriand's private conduct, she also disapproved his policy.

"M. de Chateaubriand," she remarked shrewdly to the Duc de Broglie, "dreams plans of action as though they were those of his literary works and makes sounding phrases." She remained faithful to Mathieu de Montmorency; she even corresponded with Sosthène de la Rochefoucauld who, in the face of Chateaubriand, was conspiring to get a foothold for his father and himself in the ministry. She assuredly did not betray Chateaubriand, but she suffered to feel herself torn between so many conflicting loyalties and foresaw the dread approach of the moment when she would have to choose between her friends.

It was both to put off the evil day and to get away from Chateaubriand, now that he was in love with another, that she decided to leave Paris, making her niece's health the excuse. Early in November 1823 she set off for Italy, trailing in her wake the gentle Ballanche and young Ampère, two bashful, hopeless and ecstatic lovers. Chateaubriand was greatly upset by her departure. "If you go, you will soon come home and will find me just as I have always been with you, and as I always shall. . . . This was a very useless journey. I never grow tired and, though I had yet more years to live, my dying day would still be filled and radiant with your image. . . . Will you find me again on your return? It seems you hardly care. When anyone finds courage, as you have done, to make a complete break, what indeed does the future matter? . . . I wrote to you twice at Lyons and once to Turin, but you did not answer. Your note from Chambéry reached me safely and hurt cruelly; the *Monsieur* sent a chill to my heart. You must admit that I have not deserved it." Such are the great men who not only claim the right to call every woman they meet "angel," but are genuinely surprised when one among them takes umbrage.

6. The Tarpeian Rock

Nothing fails like success. Vastly proud of his victory, Chateaubriand regarded the Spanish war as his "political *René*," that is to say a masterpiece. He was intensely surprised when on running to the castle with his great news, he met with a bucket of cold water on his head. The King and the Comte d'Artois seemed to think the triumph due to their luck; the Duchesse d'Angoulême attributed it to her husband. The princes seemed hardly to notice Chateaubriand, who was naturally somewhat offended. At least he regarded his ministerial position as unshakable. Believing himself to be another Richelieu, he was only just prepared to tolerate an *Éminence grise* in Villèle. True, he was willing to leave him the presidency of the Council, but on condition that he had his hands free at the Ministry for Foreign Affairs, where he claimed to be achieving, with the aid of the Emperor Alexander, the greatest of ends—the reunion of the Churches, the creation of Bourbon monarchies in the New World and possibly even the annexation of the left bank of the Rhine. Such vast schemes demanded years of power; he was counting on them and would have been extremely surprised to learn that Father Joseph was thinking of getting rid of Richelieu.

Such, however, was the truth. For several months there had been nothing short of a conspiracy to undermine Chateaubriand's position. Sosthène de la Rochefoucauld, together with the Comte d'Artois and Mme. du Cayla, Louis XVIII's favourite, was bent on avenging the injury done his father-in-law and on finding his father a place in the ministry. Chateaubriand's enemies declared that he coveted the presidency of the Council and his conquering airs exasperated Villèle. The great man himself was not good at concealing the scornful indifference with which his colleagues inspired him. His self-sufficiency jarred. The ministers had found it hard to overlook his genius; they forgave him neither his military triumphs nor his triumphs in love, which—all too well known in Paris—scandalised the devouter members of the Congregation as much as they grieved the most faithful of Chateaubriand's women friends.

A Minister for Foreign Affairs should be above suspicion. Now there were slanderers who maintained that if Cordélia de Castellane had made Chateaubriand happy, it was because he had pledged himself to obtain from the Spanish government the recognition of certain of the Cortes' loans in which the Comte de Greffulhe, her father, had bought numerous shares. The story may not have been true, Villèle may have had far more to do with the matter of the loans than Chateaubriand, anyhow, there was talk and that was a mistake. Another grievance was that, at the time of the taking of Cadiz, a rain of decorations had descended on Chateaubriand—the Golden Fleece, the great cross of the Order of the Redeemer, the Annunziata—he had the noblest orders of Europe. The Czar's bestowal of the Order of St. Andrew on Chateaubriand and on Mathieu de Montmorency hurt Villèle and even Louis XVIII, who wanted to revenge himself by conferring the Order of the Holy Ghost on Villèle. Chateaubriand, in his turn, demanded the Order of the Holy Ghost and did his best to obtain in exchange the Order of St. Andrew for Villèle. It seemed as though a grave problem were thus settled and equality re-established, but a good deal of bad blood was left in ministerial hearts. Little things give rise to far more ill-feeling among men than great. "A secret weakness," wrote Chateaubriand, "often causes more flutter than the fate of an empire. In our inmost soul it is the trifling matter which assumes most seriousness. Could we but see the puerilities which cross the mind of the greatest genius at the very moment of his greatest achievement, we should be seized with amazement." He spoke from knowledge.

Grudging and irritated, Villèle laid stress on Chateaubriand's faults. He pointed out that his triumph was more apparent than real. In Spain, France had indeed set Ferdinand VII back on his throne, but Ferdinand turned a deaf ear to the counsels of France. In South America, while Chateaubriand was dreaming of Bourbon monarchies and diplomatic chimeras, England was making away with the earthly commerce of the new republics. "I do not drag poetry into matters of State," said Villèle perfidiously. "All those fine far-off countries will soon be nothing but an English market if Chateaubriand spends one more year in private correspondence with Canning."

The latent dissension which separated Chateaubriand and Villèle emerged into the light of open day when there came up for discussion a scheme, very dear to the heart of the President of the Council, for the conversion of government stock. The idea was to issue to holders of French stock, in exchange for their 5 per cent interest, 3 per cent bonds at 75 francs, and to allocate the money thus saved to indemnifying the émigrés whose possessions had been converted into national property. Chateaubriand, in common with his colleagues, had at first approved the plan, but he was swift to discover that it was unpopular. The stockholders felt that their interests were endangered, the press asserted that the bankers (Baring, Rothschild) would reap the whole benefit of the transaction and certain experts criticised the idea on the grounds that it would essentially increase the National Debt since the shares issued at 75 francs were redeemable at a hundred.

The Chamber of Deputies, which was partly composed of beneficiaries of the projected indemnity, had voted for the measure. In the Chamber of Peers the opposition seemed keen and it was freely reported that Chateaubriand was the inspiration and backbone of a campaign against the law. Presidents of the Council do not much care for coadjutors among their probable successors, especially when the latter are attempting to pave the way to the succession. On May 27th Villèle and his Minister for Foreign Affairs had a somewhat heated discussion, in the course of which Chateaubriand protested his good faith and even offered to speak in favour of the law. The offer was not accepted; there were too many people who desired his fall. On June 2nd the law was thrown out by the Peers with a majority of thirty-four, and Chateaubriand was so rash as to say to Villèle: "If you resign, we are ready to follow you." His enemies translated this into: "Resign; we are ready to take your place." If there was one thing the King would not hear of, it was that. "Villèle," said he to his President of Council, "do not abandon me to these rogues." He seemed to suspect some deep-hidden perfidy on the part of Chateaubriand.

During the days that followed, the distrust of the Foreign Minister was such that several members of the Council suggested getting rid of a man "whose behaviour was so dubious." Corbière was almost the only person to defend him and that not from liking, but because he feared his power. As early as May 27th the Baron de Damas wrote to Villèle to tell him that, in the event of its being offered him, the Duc de Montmorency would accept the Ministry for Foreign Affairs. The Comte d'Artois was in the plot. "I must admit," he wrote to Villèle, "that our trusty Corbière's hesitation is a great grief to me and that meanwhile another day has been lost. I hope that tomorrow you may succeed in prevailing upon Corbière." Mme. de Duras, however, still believed that her friend was secure. Several well-wishers told Chateaubriand that his dismissal was under consideration. "Dismiss me!" he replied, "this very moment, if they like," and he went to bed.

On the morning of Whit Sunday, June 6th, a swallow fell down the chimney of his room. He heard the sleepy murmur of water in his garden and the bells that were ringing in Pentecost. It was the anniversary of the day when, at Plancoët, he had been released from his childhood's vows. He set out for the Tuileries to hear the music of the chapel-choir. While he was absorbed in the lovely motets of the feast, a verger came to tell him that he was wanted. He followed and found his secretary Pilorge, who handed him a letter, saying: "Monsieur is no longer a minister." The Duc de Rauzan, director of political affairs, transmitted to him the following message, signed Villèle: "Monsieur le Vicomte, It is in obedience to the King's commands that I transmit to Your Excellency an order upon which His Majesty has newly decided." The order temporarily entrusted the Sieur Comte de Villèle with the portfolio of Foreign Affairs in the stead of the Sieur Vicomte de Chateaubriand. He was dismissed like a lackey, never to return to power.

When a man of genius fails, and fails seriously, in action, it is interesting to analyse the causes of his defeat. What did Chateaubriand lack to make him the political equal of the Villèles and the Corbières, when he was head and shoulders above them intellectually. His despatches are there to prove it. Knowledge of affairs? He knew his Europe better than they. His descriptions of Spain and of England are masterly and have not lost their truth today. Eloquence? His speeches would have done honour to the most illustrious of parliamentarians. Tenacity? At the time of the siege of Cadiz he had given more proof of it than any of his colleagues.

But it is with the virtues of a statesman as it is with the organs of the human body. The proper functioning of a sound heart, brain or stomach may be paralysed by some microscopic gland; the most dazzling gifts of a minister will prove vain and even dangerous unless they are accompanied by such minor qualities as modesty and patience. Chateaubriand had not a trace of humility, and his pride, though it was legitimate, offended men who knew themselves less brilliant, but who could have wished that he would not make his scorn of them quite so obvious. It is natural that great powers should beget great jealousy, but envy becomes virulent only when the man of parts lacks tact and moderation in his relations with his fellows.

Chateaubriand was not tactful. True, at the beginning of his career, during a period of engaging bashfulness, he had won the affections of Fontanes and Joubert, both of whom had remained faithful to him even while they were severe on his egoism. Pasquier and Molé, on the other hand, had passed from the closest friendship to open hostility. Chateaubriand's haughty indifference aroused the more disapproval in that it coincided in him with the most exacting of ambitions. He wanted at once honours and the right to look down on those who had them in their gift. Had he but taken the trouble to make a conquest of Sosthène de la Rochefoucauld and his friends, they would have chosen other adversaries. He believed that he was safe to neglect them; they avenged themselves by compassing his dismissal.

For long he had protected himself against the enmity of men by leaning on the friendship of intelligent and tender-hearted women. Mme. de Beaumont had made interest for him with Fontanes, Mme. de Custine with Fouché, Mme. de Duras with Villèle and Mme. Récamier with Montmorency. That method should have called at least for some fidelity. Once he had attained to power, Chateaubriand made the mistake of sacrificing his most stable relationships to the most fleeting of his pleasures. As a result, Mme. de Duras fell ill, Mme. Récamier took to flight, and he found himself with never a protectress at the time when he had most need of their friends and their advice. During his ministry, the figure he had cut both in public and in society was that of a lovesick quinquagenarian with neither dignity nor reserve. In 1723 France would have smiled; in 1823 she condemned.

Finally, the born statesman, when adverse circumstance lays him aside, knows how to disappear and be forgotten for such time as seems needful. It is silence which allows him, after a proper interval, to reappear as a peacemaker. But the man of vaulting ambition has but to see himself bereft of the power he thinks his due, and he falls into a rage. He makes violent attacks on those who have defeated him. He gives the impression of pursuing rather a personal quarrel than a conflict of doctrines. When the concerns of the country are at stake, it is a wretched state of affairs. If, at the beginning of his ministry, Chateaubriand had succeeded in fascinating some of the kings and ministers of Europe with his intelligence, he was soon to pass among them for an intractable and dangerous mind. Let us say rather that, like most writers, he was created to think and to live alone and that the team-work necessary to a life of action under any form of government was hateful to him. Now politics are not woven of dreams, but of men and of facts. Louis XVIII, Villèle, Corbière, Mathieu, Sosthène and Mme. du Cayla should have been regarded not as imperfect creatures to be moulded at pleasure, but as the data of problems that needed solving. Had he been more politic and more ready to yield to facts, Chateaubriand could have ruled his colleagues and his princes; he preferred to curse them, and it was that refusal to face reality, natural in a man of imagination, which explained his defeat.

CHAPTER IX

The Monarchist Against the Monarchy

> The world, as it is now being driven, is heading for a Republic. We have said so before, we say so again and this crime of lèse-monarchy is largely due to the monarchists.
> —CHATEAUBRIAND

1. THE MAN OF SPLEEN

CHATEAUBRIAND carried off the first shock of his disgrace with jaunty ease. Two hours after reading the letter which deprived him of office, he went to his home in the Rue de l'Université carrying his beautiful pair of cats. "The time for playing the great lady is over," said he; "now you will have to think about catching mice." The moral lesson was as germane to ministers as to cats. For that very evening he had arranged a dinner-party at the ministry; he sent apologies to his guests, told Montmirel to pack up pots and pans and fall back on his own little kitchen and, in the stead of the great ones of this world, invited Mme. de Chateaubriand and M. Le Moine.

The first day brought scores of visitors. Each and all believed that his disgrace would be of short duration and they were eager to claim the honour of having proved friends in misfortune, so long as it was at small cost to themselves. Bertin, the staunch, called on Villèle and informed him that unless he prevailed on the King to appoint Chateaubriand to the embassy in Rome, the morrow would see the launching of a campaign against the ministry in the *Journal des Débats*. Bertin reminded the President of the Council that the *Débats* had already overthrown Decazes and that it could easily overthrow Villèle also. "You overthrew Decazes," replied Villèle, by making royalist propaganda; to overthrow me you would have to make revolution."

Chateaubriand was not the man to "make a revolution," but his hate was sufficiently keen to spare him overmuch regret at seeing revolution made beneath his eyes. He was mortally affronted by the insult done him. "They threw me out," said he, "as if I had filched the King's watch from the mantelpiece." Forgive them? Forgiveness was not his strong point. "The ministers are my enemies; I am theirs. I forgive them as a Christian, but I shall never forgive them as a man." Besides, if he were thenceforth to attack the ministry, would he not be following English parliamentary tradition? At Westminster, a minister who lost his portfolio took his seat on the Opposition benches. That was what he proposed to do, unless . . .

He waited a fortnight to see whether reparation would be offered him in the shape of the coveted embassy. Then, on June 21st, 1824, as nothing happened, he opened his polemic in the *Débats*. In this duel with the ministers he was to discover the advantages of style. "I am not envious," said Villèle; "he has far more wit than I, but I have more sound sense than he and it is not wit that uses sense, it is sense that uses wit." Nevertheless, in a country where the electors belonged "to a cultured nobility and bourgeoisie, on whom poetry and eloquence had a strong hold," wit had it in its power to discredit good sense.

Chateaubriand had every opportunity for gibing at a pedestrian ministry. "It is always a mistake to transform business men into statesmen; their political councils are held at the Stock Exchange. As for literature, whoever writes is suspect. The first step to becoming a statesman is not to know French."

He described Villèle's endeavours to mimic the bearing of Napoleon, taking a score of little steps in imitation of one of the giant's. He pointed out that the new ideas were anything but dead. In point of fact he was busied with putting new life into them and was doing his best to unite both oppositions against Villèle's government, that of the Right with La Bourdonnais, Hyde de Neuville and Clausel de Coussergues, that of the Left with Royer-Collard, Benjamin Constant and Casimir-Perier. "To reject the tried servants of the monarchy, without adopting the ideas of the age, is surely to spurn every prop. Those who have no need either of devotion or of liberty must be rich indeed."

Ailing and spitting blood, Mme. de Chateaubriand, who had once been more quarrelsome, disapproved this controversy. During the period of the ministry, the "Madams," old and new, had put her out of all patience. To tear her husband away from their influence and to rescue him from politicians who compromised him as much as they pleased, she would have liked him to go into exile with her. Vainly did he attempt to smooth her ruffled feathers by buying (though he had not the money to do it) the little house next door to the Infirmerie Marie-Thérèse in the Rue d'Enfer and by promising to go and live there. Céleste approved of the purchase, accepted the house, but persisted in wanting to go to Switzerland during the removal. As Chateaubriand refused, she fled to Neuchâtel; he went after her but stayed only three days. In Paris, the political battle was once more in full swing and he was marching with the guns.

Villèle, exasperated by his enemies' sarcasms, had forgotten the prudence on which he prided himself and put himself at the mercy of the Ultras. He had given Foreign Affairs to the Baron de Damas, the King's Household to the Duc de Doudeauville and the administration of Fine Arts to Sosthène de la Rochefoucauld. Then, as the press criticised such a coterie, he re-established the censorship. The liberty of the press was Chateaubriand's hobby-horse. He wrote a stinging pamphlet: "What is the pass to which things have come? The minister has made mistakes, he has parted company with the royalists, in short he seems anything but capable and people are saying as much; those are the grave circumstances which compel him to steal from us the fundamental liberty of the institutions which we owe to the King's wisdom." Villèle was playing into the hands of his enemies.

On September 12th, 1824, Louis XVIII, racked by gangrene, entered upon his last agony. The heat was stifling and the stench of his sores nauseous. At four o'clock in the morning a Gentleman of the Chamber came to the Comte d'Artois, who was waiting in the next room, and said, "Sire, the King is dead." Then he announced, "Gentlemen, the King," and Charles X entered.

Though the Comte d'Artois had never treated him well, Chateaubriand saw in his accession an honourable opportunity for rallying to the monarchy. All men change. It is those who await favourable circumstances to proclaim that change whom we call constant. *Chateaubriand to Mme. de Castellane:* "You see how ready I am to forget the evil done me. It is so easy to be loyal . . . that I do not know why they should shew me so much gratitude." Charles X himself seemed desirous of a reconciliation. To the Archbishop of Paris who asked: "But, Sire, M. de Chateaubriand?" the King replied: "Oh! him—I miss him." It was he who asked Chateaubriand to write a pamphlet on the change of kingship. This tract, which was entitled *Le Roi est mort, vive le roi* was royally paid and, as its author proudly claimed, "did as much for Charles X as my pamphlet *De Buonaparte et des Bourbons* did for Louis XVIII."

In the course of the coronation ceremony which, by a return to tradition, took place at Rheims, Chateaubriand and the other Knights of the Holy Spirit had to kneel at the King's feet to do homage. Charles X had some difficulty in taking off his gloves to hold Chateaubriand's hands in his and said laughingly: "A gloved cat catches no mice." He expected some courtly expression of loyalty in reply, but the man at his feet had no gift of repartee and so kept silence. The reconciliation had failed.

Chateaubriand, moreover, was faithful to his renown and would support no policy other than one which appealed to the new generation—at once Catholic and liberal. Now, under Charles X, at the urging of an Ultra king, Villèle adopted a policy which was the exact contrary of the foregoing. When the so-called "law of sacrilege" punished the theft of sacred vessels with the same sentence as parricide, when there was talk of giving the clergy control of matters appertaining to the secular state, when the revival of the right of primogeniture was mooted, then Chateaubriand protested against the unwisdom of mediaeval methods of government at a time when everything foreshadowed vast changes in human societies. "Across the deserts of Kentucky there will travel on iron-roads seemingly magic waggons, driven without horses, carrying with extraordinary speed both enormous weights and five or six passengers. The isthmus which joins the two Americas will break its barriers to give ships transit from one ocean to the other."

The Monarchist Against the Monarchy

These and a myriad other changes, he said, would bring about the spread of progress among the lower classes of society and cause them to brook no power that was not founded on reason. He prophesied that if the monarchy continued to make mistakes, it would be succeeded by a republic. Foresight may keep its own counsel from party-loyalty or from the fear that a rehearsal of the evils it dreads may, in itself, serve to bring them about. Resentment and gall, by freeing him from such scruples, made of Chateaubriand the crusty and clear-eyed prophet of the woes which were to come upon the régime.

After a long stay in Italy, Mme. Récamier returned to Paris in May 1825. There she saw her faithless lover once more. There were neither explanations nor reproaches, but Chateaubriand was touched to see that Juliette's hair had grown white. Thenceforward there mingled with his love and friendship for her a new-found sense of regard. When, after a summer spent in the Valley of Wolves, she again took up her abode at the Abbaye-aux-Bois in October, Chateaubriand became the fixed centre of her salon, the only one in which Liberals and Ultras could meet on neutral ground. Cloaking her all-powerfulness with modesty, as she had once hidden her beauty under veils, Mme. Récamier was quietly edging one after another of her admirers into the Academy. In 1825 she had Mathieu de Montmorency elected and, on the occasion of his reception, Chateaubriand read his first speech on the History of France. Not long afterwards, on March 24th, 1826, a Good Friday, Mathieu died suddenly while at his prayers in Saint-Thomas d'Aquin, and Chateaubriand, though he had little love for the man, mourned him decorously. Thenceforward there was none but he to kneel behind Mme. Récamier's prie-dieu in Saint-Thomas d'Aquin. More than once, Lamartine watched him with no friendly eye as he leant towards his fair neighbour and whispered to her during the service.

Cordélia de Castellane had left for Italy, where she was travelling with the painter Horace Vernet, and Chateaubriand cloaked his desires, which had not yet lost their edge, in discreet and veiled terms when they wrote. Claire de Duras and Delphine de Custine, who were both very ill, gave him serious cause for anxiety. As for Céleste de Chateaubriand, she still enjoyed the tough fragility of valetudinarians. Grown resigned at last to Mme. Récamier's royalty, she enlisted the influence of this "Arch-Madam" on behalf of the Infirmerie Marie-Thérèse.

It was in 1825 that Chateaubriand, to protect the Infirmary against a contractor who wanted to set up switchbacks and kindred attractions on a neighbouring plot of ground, bought the site and the house in the Rue d'Enfer for the sum of 180,000 francs that he did not possess. To pay off his notes of hand, he got the bookseller Ladvocat to give him a contract promising the enormous sum of 550,000 francs for the complete edition of his works. Later the figure was slightly lowered, for the publisher came, with tears in his eyes, to tell Chateaubriand that to keep to such a contract spelt ruin. The whole edition was to be composed of twenty-six volumes, thirteen of them unpublished. In order to undertake so vast a labour of revision and composition, Chateaubriand took up his quarters in Lausanne, with Mme. de Chateaubriand. He began by working at a commentary on the *Essai*, the earliest work of his youth, with the intention of re-editing it for the first volume. Besides, it tickled his vanity to read it again.

On July 13th, 1826, he learnt that poor Delphine de Custine was dead. "It is over," wrote Berstoecher, the tutor who had himself been half in love with the Lady of Fervacques, "it is over, your friend no longer lives. She gave up her soul to God, with no pain, at a quarter to eleven this morning. As late as yesterday evening she could still go driving in her carriage. Nothing foreshadowed so near an end." From his windows, Chateaubriand saw the passing of the coffin that shrouded the beautiful bright hair he had so loved for a little space. Princess Forlorn was at last healed of her heartbreak, as once Pauline de Beaumont was healed.

He himself was growing old and his hair, though still tossed by an unseen storm, was turning grey. When he returned to Paris and the Rue d'Enfer he found builders and painters swarming all over the house. Amid the bustle, he set about revising the manuscript of the *Natchez* which, at the time of the Consulate, he had left in the keeping of friends in London, who restored it safely after the fall of the Empire. A poor English family had faithfully guarded the émigré's trunk. It was with considerable curiosity and some measure of admiration that Chateaubriand took up the manuscript from which he had already drawn *Atala* and *René* and found himself back among the American forests, the Indian encampments and the brown-skinned Céluta "with night in her eyes." This toil, evoking as it did fond memories, kept him amused and restored him to something approaching serenity. His desire to take up the political battle was no longer so keen. Villèle's blunders were to thrust it upon him.

If there was one subject which left Chateaubriand neither indifferent nor mum, it was the liberty of the press. There, his liberalism tallied with his respect for the Charter and his demands as a man of letters with his interests as a controversialist. It was, moreover, the only subject on which unconfessed republicans and constitutional monarchists were readily prepared to unite against the ministry. Villèle was rash enough to arouse the sleeping monster. By means of the censorship he had already muzzled the periodical press, even forbidding the papers to make mention of Chateaubriand's pamphlets. (On one occasion he went the length of blue-pencilling the epithet "wonderful," applied to the *Natchez* in an article.) He further wished, by a law which was ironically styled "the law of justice and love," to make the publication of pamphlets an impossibility. Chateaubriand rallied his friends to the defence of liberty and prevailed on the French Academy to address a protest to the King. In the Chamber, the opposition led by Chateaubriand and the Duc de Broglie, in conjunction with ex-officials of the Empire such as Molé and Pasquier, flared up so fiercely that Villèle had to withdraw his bill.

The man in the street was as hostile to the ministry as the men of letters. A review of the National Guard, when the King was cheered and his ministers hooted, proved as much. Before the review Chateaubriand wrote to Charles X: "What action will the King take? Will he deliver up his ministers to a cheering populace? It would mean the death of authority. Will the King keep his ministers? All their unpopularity would fall back on the head of their august master. . . . The ministers have lost their majority in the Chamber of Peers and among the nation. The natural consequence of this critical position would be their resignation." Villèle chose, on the contrary, to disband the National Guard. The hatred of him grew. When he held an election, Chateaubriand's monarchist friends and Royer-Collard's liberals formed a coalition against the government and obtained a crushing majority. The Left had 190 deputies, the opposition of the Right 70 and the minister only 170. Villèle had to resign.

Among the Royalists, it was Chateaubriand who best represented the mind of the victorious coalition. It would have been natural to call on him to form a ministry, while a request that he should join it was a necessity. He had, however, become the bête noire of the Monarchist and Catholic party. His mind, said they, was out of joint, he was a bad man, a revolutionary, a traitor. Even his liberal friends made fun of what they called his infidelities. "How is it possible," wrote the Duchesse de Broglie, "that his mind fails to save him from cutting precisely the figure of a tight-rope dancer." Villèle who, despite his resignation, remained all-powerful with the King, set secretly to work to form the new ministry and rule out Chateaubriand, "who," said he, "is more distasteful to me than any other." Through the instrumentality of Villèle, Chateaubriand was thus deprived not only of the presidency of the Council (offered to Martignac, a fine orator) which, strictly speaking, was explicable, but of any ministry soever, which was an affront. "He was so furious," said Mme. de Boigne, "that he thought he would suffocate; they had to give him a necklet of leeches. . . . Next day the bile had passed into his blood and he was green as a lizard." Mme. de Boigne was sarcastic, but it must be confessed that he was very badly treated.

Following a scrutiny, Martignac had soon to admit to the King that the ministry could not count on a majority in the Chamber unless overtures were made to Chateaubriand. The latter replied that he could accept a portfolio only if they took with him the other leader of the coalition, Royer-Collard, as the representative of the Left Centre. Once more he came up against those underground enmities and fermenting spites which lie in wait for genius, or even talent, when it has the misfortune to solicit what would willingly be granted to mediocrity.

Shewn the door, sick at heart, and past all patience, he was once more taken with that irresistible need of escape which comes naturally to artists and explains at once their discomfitures and their greatness. When, to be rid of him, he was offered the ambassadorship to Rome, he accepted almost at once. "I was seized with the longing to settle down, to disappear, if only for the sake of my reputation, into the city of tombs, at the very moment of my political triumph." Yet even that post was disputed him. France had already an ambassador in Rome, Adrien de Montmorency, Duc de Laval. Would he consent to giving up the post? At that point the great peacemaker intervened. Interpreted by the lips of Mme. Récamier, ambitions became pure and rivalries affectionate. "The language you attribute to your friend and the very words you quote are certainly widely different from those with which he is publicly credited," the Duc de Laval wrote to her. "In spite of appearances, it is you who must be right." And the Duke agreed to go to Vienna.

The consent of the Vatican had yet to be obtained. It was no easy matter at a time when the author of *Le Génie du Christianisme* had come to figure in the eyes of the bigots as an anticlerical, when he reminded his enemies among the Congregation of the "righteous M. Tartufe," when he denounced as violent and narrow-minded "the fanatics who are not less to be dreaded than the atheists" and when he went the length of writing that, if it could be proved to him that Christianity was incompatible with liberty, he would cease "to regard as true a religion which was opposed to the dignity of man." But the Church has infinite reserves of wisdom and the nuncio counselled the acceptance of the proposed ambassador. "Were the Holy See to refuse him now, M. de Chateaubriand—whose vanity is potent and whose self-esteem is very touchy—might wage ruthless war against us. I would add that many wise and godly people here among us believe that the choice would turn him into a writer full of zeal for the good cause."

Actually, the nuncio did not believe that Chateaubriand was anxious to stay long in Rome. "He aspires to the ministry, and, in my opinion, regards the Roman ambassadorship solely as a means to that end.... I ought also to point out to Your Eminence that M. de Chauteaubriand not only loves his wife dearly, but is as dependent on her as a child on its mother.... Now, as my letters have already informed Your Eminence, this lady is very devout and given to good works, but—like her husband—she has her share of vanity and is extremely sensitive to the good opinion of others. Hence, by laying yourself out to cultivate the lady and by paying her such attentions as seem expedient, I believe that Your Eminence would successfully obtain all you could desire of her husband."[1] This goes to shew that the Roman Church had a deeper understanding than the French ministers of the great man's weak points and of that compelling need of domestic peace which made him consent to anything rather than endure perpetual bickering.

The Cardinal Secretary of State followed this sensible advice and gave his approval to the choice of Chateaubriand, who was straightway appointed. *La Gazette de France* was not reassured by his departure: "M. de Chateaubriand is weary of seeing the fortunes of Caesar trammeled by the strife of the Girondins and his genius pale before the star of M. de Martignac. He will come back, with or without leave, and the ministry of conciliation will be ready for the day when he lands at Fréjus or at Golfe Juan." No praise had ever given him more pleasure than this attack, wherein he saw himself likened to the only hero he had ever envied.

2. The Roman Embassy

A journey towards Italy could not fail to revive the sad memories and satisfied pride which merged to make his joy. At every stage, a note left for the Abbaye-aux-Bois. Before leaving Paris: "Be persuaded that nothing in life can evermore separate us or put you out of mind. . . . I shall love you so, my letters will own it so often, I shall call you to me with such unswerving faith that you can have no excuse for forsaking me. Remember that we must and shall end our days together. It is a sorry gift I bring you in bequeathing you the rest of my life, but—take it."

From Fontainebleau: "I am writing from a little hotel bedroom, where I can be alone with the thought of you. You are well and truly avenged, if ever you wanted vengeance. I am going to that same Italy with a heart as full and as sore as yours was some years since." From Villeneuve-sur-Yonne he recalled the memory of Joubert and of Pauline de Beaumont. "On my arrival I saw the castle in which Pauline de Beaumont lived during the years of the Revolution. My poor friend Joubert used often to shew me the

[1] Quoted by M-J. Durry.

gravel path, visible against its wooded hillside, by which he used to go to visit his runaway neighbour. When he told me that, Mme. de Beaumont was already no more. We mourned her together. Joubert has disappeared in his turn. If you were not left, what would become of me?"

From the frontier: "I am writing in a mean and shabby cottage to tell you that in France as out of France, on the further side of the Alps as on this, I live for you and await you." *At the foot of the Simplon:* "I have just lived through two very dreary days; from Lausanne onwards I have followed steadily in the footsteps of two hapless women; one, Mme. de Custine, came to die at Bex; the other, Mme. de Duras, went to end her days at Nice. How all things pass. . . ." *Finally, from Rome:* "My memory for places, which is wonderful and cruel, had not let me forget a single stone." Yet, in twenty years, everything had changed. The house in the Piazza di Spagna, where Mme. de Beaumont died, had disappeared. Chateaubriand toiled up to the Villa Medici to see the director, at that time the painter Guérin—a man of discernment and a sensitive artist. "We opened a window over Rome and together gazed out at a horizon steeped in the dying splendour of the day. It is the only thing that still remains to me as once I saw it."

In Rome, as in London, Chateaubriand was to enjoy the contrast between a wretched past and a dazzling present. "In 1803 a young secretary, treated as a dog by his ambassador, had been relegated to a flea-infested kennel to sign reports; in 1828 that young secretary had himself become the ambassador, and his titles: peer of France, minister of state, Knight of the orders of the Holy Spirit, of the Golden Fleece, of Saint Andrew of Russia, of the Black Eagle of Prussia, of the Santissima Annunziata and of Christ of Portugal, took up several lines of the Roman papers."[1] In 1803 Cardinal Fesch had forbidden him to ask audience of the Pope; in 1828 Pope Leo XII did not even take time to dress for fear of keeping him waiting, refused to allow him to kneel and made him sit beside him. In the time of Cardinal Fesch, Chateaubriand had grieved over the niggardliness of the receptions and equipages; in the time of the Vicomte de Chateaubriand the French embassy was to leave Rome

[1] Marie-Jeanne Durry.

dumbfounded by the splendour of its *ricevimenti*, its fêtes, its illuminations and its banquets.

There were times when the ambassador wondered what was the use of all this luxury, this waste of time, this need for "giving up the last years of his life to the babblings of mediocrity." He vowed that Mme. de Chateaubriand and he pined for the solitude of the Rue d'Enfer, then let the taste for magnificence, the desire of upholding the prestige of France and the pleasure of annoying his colleagues by succeeding in a style of life in which each thought himself unrivalled, get the better of him once more. And what city could be more fitting than Rome for the *ricevimenti* of a Chateaubriand, who had her power of fusing ordered device with the noble simplicity of nature. "I had given balls and assemblies both in London and Paris, but I was far from suspecting what such junketings could be in Rome. They have something of that old-world poetry wherein death goes hand in hand with pleasure." As he watched wave upon wave of beauty, with its diamonds, its flowers and its feathers, swirl past him to the music of Rossini, he liked to think that this beauteous and lovely youth would all go down into some Roman sepulchre—a frail and lovely dust. Then, flushed with the sensuous and charnel musings in which he had dreamed away the evening, he would go to cool his fevered brow in the deserted Piazza San Pietro or amidst the loneliness of the Coliseum.

One of the last of these festivities was given in the gardens of the Villa Medici in honour of the Grand Duchess Helen. "We shall have music in the shrubberies," he wrote to Mme. Récamier, "folk-dancing, an improvisatrice and a balloon." At the last moment a sudden squall blew up to spoil the merrymaking out of doors. The ambassadress was dismayed, not so the ambassador. "The groups which were frolicking amidst the gusts, the women whose fluttering veils lashed against their faces and their hair, the improvisatrice who went on reciting to the clouds above, the balloon which sailed off awry with the emblem of the Daughter of the North—all these lent new character to those sports which seemed fraught with the wonted tempests of my life." As a matter of fact, the reception had been transferred to the inside of the villa and none save Chateaubriand observed these well-ordered squalls, but what matter? He described them with such art that they blow through our minds even yet.

Those were the red-letter days. On ordinary occasions the Palazzo Simonetti was no other than the dwelling of a little Breton household, unassuming and almost countrified. The ambassador rose at half-past five every morning; his social life did not begin till five in the evening. His greatest passion, apart from work, was walking —his gun under his arm and a game-bag slung across his shoulder. "I am never tired of wandering in the campagna. Not one of its lanes but is more familiar to me than the paths of Combourg. . . . I go botanizing to the tomb of Cecilia Metella; the ripple of mignonette and the blue-wind-flowers of the Apennines harmonize softly with the whiteness of the ruin and the soil. Often I make the circuit of the walls of Rome on foot. . . . My excavations are merely another form of the same pleasures. . . . It may be that I shall render my clay back to the earth in exchange for the statue she gives me." He could have wished to spend his eternity in a Roman tomb: "Rome is a fine place in which to forget all, to despise all and to die."

Sometimes he went to watch young Vaudoyer, a guest of the Villa Medici, at work upon the monument which Mme. Récamier and he had agreed to raise to Poussin. He wanted it to bear a bas-relief reproduction of the picture of the *Arcadian Shepherds* with the inscription: *F.-R. de Chateaubriand to Nicolas Poussin, for the glory of the Arts and the honour of France*. In the evening, if there was no reception, the embassy was a dreary place. The ambassador played chess or else planted himself in front of the glass with his legs astraddle, his back slightly bent and both elbows propped on the mantelpiece; with his fingers run through his hair and interlaced against his high forehead, he would stand thus for a quarter of an hour together looking at himself face to face.

What questions did he ask of the face he catechised so long? Doubtless they were those that men who have greatly loved women ask when they see themselves growing old: "Is it all over and done? Or may I yet, fame and fortune aiding, make myself beloved of some Sylph?" If Mme. de Chateaubriand were present she could not have misinterpreted that silence. Hence, in the Palazzo Simonetti

—for which she had little love—she grew more of a thundercloud than ever. If Chateaubriand complained of the heat, she rang for a servant to put another log on the fire; if, on the other hand, he were cold, she had all the windows opened. "She delighted to contradict, quietly but firmly, the somewhat hazardous statements of the author of the *Génie* and, when her husband's recollection grew too fanciful, pulled him up by quoting positive facts, uttered in a low and almost indifferent voice, but rather drily and decidedly bluntly." It was reality's revenge on poetry.

If ever she believed that, by leaving Paris, she would escape from the "Madams" Céleste was speedily disillusioned. Letter writers were as persistent as visitors. Not a day passed but a note full of endearments and protestations of fidelity was despatched to Mme. Récamier. He reaverred that his one wish was to end his life with her and he was sincere, for he could imagine no finer climax to his strange emotional history than that deathless relationship with a woman whose beauty bewitched him, whose reason flattered him and whose gentleness touched his heart. Everything drew him back to her, everything brought memories of the Abbaye-aux-Bois. "Tonight the wind and the rain reminded me of France: I pictured them lashing against your little window; I found myself back in your little room; I saw your harp, your piano, your birds; you played me my favourite air or else Shakespeare's; and I was in Rome—far from you. . . . Four hundred leagues and the Alps are between us twain."

Nevertheless, Mme. Récamier was not the only woman to receive tender letters from Chateaubriand. At sixty he had not lost his zest for new adventures and was still curious to meet his admirers. A certain Marquise de Vichet, who was bordering on fifty and the mother of a lieutenant, was so rash as to write him naïvely poetic letters of appreciation. At once he grew urgent and sought to bring about a meeting. The startled lady took refuge in her remote castle in the Vivarais. When he left for Rome, he wrote to her, as to everyone else: "Come to me."

Her answer was irreproachable, for it sprang of her candour: "You ask me whether I would journey to Italy in the event of your going there. If I were a bird, I might perhaps fly after you; if I were a boy, I might become your secretary or your page. . . . If

I were a friend or relation of Mme. de Chateaubriand, I would
leave all to follow her. But, being what I am, with what propriety
could I travel alone in a strange country?" And a little later "Mme.
de Chateaubriand's heart belongs to you; tell her that you have a
last sister, beg her to love me and she will, then I can make the
journey to Rome with you both." But Chateaubriand had a long
and painful experience of sisters, besides which he knew his wife
far too well to imagine that she would ever consent to play a part
in this comedy of three-fold bliss. He refrained from renewing the
invitation and continued, in his letters, to ask for a tête-à-tête.

Every old man who is at all famous has his young admirers.
Chateaubriand's Bettina was called Léontine de Villeneuve; she
was twenty-five and lived in the Southwest of France. It was in
1827 that, on reading *Le Génie du Christianisme*, she and another
young girl plucked up courage to write to the author. "I do not
really know, Monsieur, why I am writing to you; thousands of
others before me have wearied illustrious men with their nameless
letters. . . ." But he had been neither surprised nor shocked and
replied in that large untidy scrawl of his: "If ever we chance to
meet, Mademoiselle, I shall doubtless see a young and fair Westerner as full of grace and lofty sentiments as her letter; you will
see an old gaffer with a frosty pow, who has nothing knightly left
about him but his heart."

When ten letters had passed between them, they grew bold. "I
do not love you at all, you say, while you—for your part—love me,"
wrote the ambassador. "Do you want to take the word in its full
meaning? Then, to begin with, how would you have me voice my
feelings for a woman I do not know? Gratitude for your kindness,
fellow-feeling for a friendship touching in its simplicity and generosity, finally that undefinable attraction which attends on affectionate and trusting relations with a young woman—those, frankly,
are my feelings for Léontine." . . . "I can bring no one happiness,
for I have it not; it was not in my nature, nor does it belong to my
age." . . . "Religion, morality, order—all enjoin marriage; a gentleman can but talk in the same strain. So much my honesty com-
pels me to say; since, however, absolute independence is the essence
of my tastes and of my character, I shall always hold my peace
when I am questioned and refrain from saying to Léontine: get

married. . . . I can neither advise against a duty nor overcome an antipathy." And taking up the theme of the fateful being: "All who have ever grown fond of me have lived to repent it, all have suffered; all have died an untimely death; all have come near to losing their reason before they died. Hence I am terrorstricken when anyone wants to care for me."

The game was the more dangerous in that they had settled to meet at some spa among the Pyrenees and that Chateaubriand was becoming really infatuated. His departure for home had made the scheme impracticable, but they still corresponded and their letters were strangely ardent for two people unknown to each other. "Long live my grey hairs since they endear me to you. You dislike my mentioning marriage, yet you will still be talking to me about it. For my conscience' sake, marry; for the sake of my love, do not marry at all." . . . "Good morning, my lovely Léontine, my sylph, my unknown charmer, love me and write to me." . . . "Léontine, see you I shall, I care far too much for you, I'm an old dotard." All this was occasionally interspersed with a note of melancholy: "The meeting you have promised me on earth, I shall claim of you in heaven." It is the ultimate coquetry of an ageing poet to summon up such images of death when he would move the compassion of those he can no longer stir by the violence of desire.

Such were the unknown women whom imagination could clothe from afar with every beauty. Nearer home there were other fleeting fancies to beguile the noble ennui of the ambassador. Among the Roman patricians he had singled out a certain Contessa del Drago, to whom it was the duty of the young attachés to carry bouquets. Did she yield? There is no knowing. Hortense Allart, a Frenchwoman who was passing through Rome, was less discreet. She was a woman writer of twenty-three, pretty, intelligent, laughing, sensuous, experienced—in short, wholly worthy to tempt an old connoisseur and perfectly ready to be kind, for she held that "a woman does not really know great men unless they have been her lovers."

She came with an introduction from Mme. Hamelin. Chateaubriand, who gave her a coquettish welcome, proved "charming and charmed." She spoke of her admiration for *Atala*; he expressed a wish to see her again and the very next day, Easter Sunday, went to call at the Via delle Quattro Fontane. She was out. He read the inscription on her door: *Pens' all' eternità*. That day, he was thinking far more of the present. He went back, paid his court, offered to read a novel that Hortense had just written on the subject of a former liaison and, on the morrow, returned the manuscript, which he declared to be admirable. Hortense was shrewd enough to see that his regard for the book was chiefly desire for the woman, and that the desire itself was too unadvised and sudden to go very deep. "M. de Chateaubriand rather tended to act a part with me, as I was well aware; nevertheless, it was a genuine attraction, for he was very fond of women." *Women* rather than *a woman*. . . . Yet why should she demand what she had no intention of giving?

This well-groomed and illustrious old gentleman was by no means unprepossessing. Every day he arrived on foot, a flower in his buttonhole, dressed in the height of elegance and exquisitely dainty in his person. His teeth were perfection. He talked lightly and wittily of the power to which he might return, and laid France at his lady-love's feet. She, who was a woman of the Left and a friend of Béranger, picked a bone with him for his conservatism and his Spanish war. He defended himself with sweet tolerance and skill, developing his doctrine of liberty yoked with monarchy. These discussions, with their mingling of politics and caresses, were highly agreeable. Before long he was saying: "If Mme. de Chateaubriand wants to go to Paris by herself, I can easily spend my summer here. . . . I should miss Rome."

The pleasures of the Via delle Quattro Fontane did not cause him to forget the duties of the Palazzo Simonetti. The ambassador took his mission seriously and, on the whole, was successful. In France, the prime minister Martignac—a moderate with a bent towards liberalism—had to hold out against the encroachments of the priestly party and the counter-attacks of the Congregation. Hence it was vital to deter the Vatican from upholding the rabid Catholics in France. Chateaubriand found Louis XII sweetly reasonable. He ventured to talk to the Holy Father with a frank and audacious freedom that was very well received. He pointed out that the French clergy had been wrong in refusing to accept the new institutions, that there was a notable background of religion in France, even amongst the Liberals, and that the Church could attain a considerable degree of power if she had the wisdom to respect public liberties.

The Pope, who had listened attentively, replied: "I am of your mind. Jesus Christ made no pronouncement on forms of government. 'Render to Caesar the things that are Caesar's' merely means: obey the established authorities. The Catholic religion has flourished in the midst of republics as it has in the bosom of monarchies; it is making tremendous strides in America." Thus emboldened, Chateaubriand suggested to the Pontiff the reconstitution of Catholic unity and the reunion of schismatic sects by means of concessions on discipline. For, in the conception of vast designs, whether in ecclesiastical polity or European politics, he shewed the natural daring of those who are more versed in the joys of thought than in the difficulties of action.

To his minister and friend, La Ferronays, who asked his opinion on the liberation of Greece, he replied with a fine dissertation on the general policy of France. His argument was that the dismemberment of the Ottoman Empire was inevitable and even desirable; that the best course was to accept the idea of Russia's benefiting from such an event and to obtain from her, in return for French support in Constantinople, the left bank of the Rhine. This was but another expression of Chateaubriand's favourite thesis: the need for washing away the shame of the treaties of Vienna, the glory of putting the crowning touch to the work of Richelieu and Louis XIV, and the wisdom of relying on Russia for aid against Austria and England. The text sparkled with sound and statesmanlike maxims: "To gain time is a great art when one is not prepared. . . . One way to succeed with men is to spare their self-esteem, to give them a chance of elucidating their ideas and of escaping from a quandary with honour." There only wanted Goethe's observation: "Thought is easy, action is difficult; to act in accordance with one's thought is the most difficult thing in the world."

On February 10th, 1829, the Pope died, almost without warning. The rôle of the ambassador of France suddenly increased in importance. Was it possible to influence the Conclave and procure the election of a Pope well disposed towards France? The latter had the right of exclusion. Chateaubriand believed that millions were necessary if there was to be any positive action. "There are three things," said he, "which do not make popes: petticoat influence, ambassadorial scheming and the power of courts. Again, they do not spring from the general interests of Christendom but from the private interests of families and individuals."

His instructions touching the Conclave no longer came from his friend, La Ferronays, who had been obliged to resign on account of illness, but from Portalis, who had temporarily taken over the duties of the post—a man whom Chateaubriand disliked. Nevertheless, it was to Portalis that he had to explain the difficulties of his position: "I have to bring influence to bear on an invisible body, locked within a prison to which all access is strictly guarded. I have neither money to bestow nor posts to promise. The senile passions of fifty or so old men give me no hold over them. I have to struggle against crass stupidity in some, ignorance of the world in others; fanaticism here, craft and duplicity there; ambition, self-interest and political enmities in nearly all, and I am shut out by walls and mysteries from the assembly in which so many elements of discord are fermenting. From one moment to another the scene changes; every quarter of an hour conflicting rumours plunge me into new perplexities. It is not from any desire to take credit to myself, Monsieur le Comte, that I make mention of these difficulties, but that they may serve as my extenuation should the election fall out otherwise than it seems to promise and give us a pope such as you do not desire."

Against Cardinal Albani, the candidate favoured by Austria, Chateaubriand, on his own initiative, sent the Cardinal of Clermont-Tonnerre a letter of exclusion. In accordance with the usual custom, he addressed the Conclave, through a hole in the wall, in the name of the King of France. The speech was interesting in that he once more advised the Church to adapt itself to the progress of civilisation. On March 31st Cardinal Castiglioni was finally elected Pope, under the name of Pius VIII. His was among the five names drawn up by Chateaubriand, who made no secret of his triumph: "I have been completely successful. No-one can find fault with a single indiscreet word in my conversations with the cardinals.

Nothing escaped me. I descended to the most trivial details. My eagle eye saw that the treaty of the Trinità del Monte was an abuse and that neither of the two parties had the right to make it. Hence, mounting higher to the sphere of high diplomacy, I took it upon myself to exclude a cardinal, since a Minister for Foreign Affairs left me no instructions. Are you satisfied? Does such a man know his job?"

Portalis, who did not want any credit to accrue to Chateaubriand since he dreaded him as a rival for Foreign Affairs, chid him for the new pope's choice of Cardinal Albani, the man whom France had excluded from the pontificate, as Secretary of State. The tone of the despatch was mortifying; Chateaubriand's reply a studied insult. "This frigid despatch, written by some ill-bred clerk in the Ministry for Foreign Affairs, was not such as I had a right to expect after the services it had been my good fortune to do the King during the Conclave. Above all, he should have stopped to remember the person to whom it was addressed."

Chateaubriand was now as eager to leave Rome as he had been to see the last of Berlin and London. When he was cut off from Paris, he was always convinced that he must be missing golden opportunities. At the time of La Ferronays' resignation he had hoped for the ministry. No less than ten times he wrote to Mme. Récamier: "Shall I be summoned?"—but the King, who was swithering between Polignac, the Duc de Laval and Reyneval, ended by appointing Portalis. It was the last straw. "I have now come to the simplest, the calmest and the noblest of all decisions. I shall not send in my resignation; I shall make no to-do. Leave is due me. I shall use it to go peaceably to Paris with my wife when everything is over and there I shall lay my resignation at the King's feet. . . . I can be of no service to the government. . . . At the very moment when I succeeded in compassing the election of the Sovereign Pontiff desired by His Majesty, he saw fit to go outside all political eligibility in his choice of a minister. . . . It may be that I stood in need of this final lesson to quell the last gusts of my pride. I receive it in all humility and shall put it to good use."

True humility—was he capable of it? Perhaps by fits and starts. The last letter he wrote to Mme. Récamier from Rome expressed only a tender sadness. "My dear, I am coming to fetch you. I am going to take you back with me to Rome. Ambassador or no, it is there I would die hard by your side. At last I shall have a great tomb in exchange for a little life. Meanwhile I shall see you . . . What bliss." She, on her side, awaited him with all the impatience of first love. "M. de Chateaubriand's coming," she told her niece, "has rekindled my little flame of life when it seemed flickering to its close." What would this peerless friend have felt had she known that he had just won Hortense Allart to promise that she would join him in Paris?

3. The Return from Rome

May 1829. In France, Chateaubriand found a precarious state of affairs. The prime minister had to contend with the hostility of his own king, who went the length of launching an attack on Martignac in the papers devoted to the crown. In vain did wise counsellors warn Charles X: "Sire, you must not delude yourself. France is Left Centre." The King had only to make a journey to the country and hear rather more frequent cries of "Long live the King!" than "Long live the Charter" to exclaim naïvely: "If I had known that I was so popular, I should have kept Villèle." The wisest course would have been to keep the opportunist ministry which "served as a railing against the abyss" in office as long as possible. But wisdom was out of favour for the time.

Mme. Récamier, whose delicate feelers sensed storms afar off, saw how dangerous Chateaubriand's return might prove at such a juncture. If the prime minister were dismissed, if the King offered him Foreign Affairs in a ministry of the extreme Right, he might be tempted to accept and would thus risk not defeat only, but a crowning fall. If the portfolio were given to another, wrath might move Chauteaubriand to reckless utterances. "I am more worried," said Mme. Récamier, "by the position in which he is going to find himself than rejoiced at the thought of seeing him." There and then she set quietly to work to enfold Chateaubriand in her powerful protection, to put his mind at rest and lull his alarms. To win his consent to keeping the ambassadorship to Rome she promised that, if he returned thither, she would follow.

To turn his thoughts from politics to literature, she arranged to hold a reading of *Moïse* at the Abbaye-aux-Bois. There she gathered the flower of Paris and hatched "that conspiracy of flattery which was later to make the name and the work of Chateaubriand anathema to those who, like Sainte-Beuve, had been in the plot." Lamartine has given us a spiteful description of the occasion: "Under the picture of *Corinne*, M. de Chateaubriand figured as a kind of superannuated Oswald. He concealed the ungainliness of his lop-sided shoulders, his short stature and his spindle shanks behind the women's screens and arm-chairs. Only his virile bust and that Olympian head with its sparkling eyes came into view. A mouth, now solemn and tight-lipped, now smoothed into a fulsome rather than a friendly smile; cheeks as withered as the cheeks of Dante by the years which had furrowed their wrinkles with as many ambitious passions as they held days; an air of mock-modesty which counterfeited the bashfulness or rather the painted blush of renown, such was the leading actor who stood at the back of the drawing-room between the fireplace and the picture. He acknowledged and returned the greetings of every guest who entered with an embarrassed courtesy which was an obvious plea for indulgence."

Lafond, the actor who was to read the play, acquitted himself so badly that Chateaubriand ended by taking the manuscript from him. The listeners were disappointed. "It was an echo of Racine and of David, yet it was neither Racine nor David; it was their shadows, the pastiche of a man of genius, but a pastiche nevertheless." Mme. Récamier, who felt that things were not going well, seemed sad and there was a false ring about the compliments at the close. Chateaubriand, however, was as convinced of being a great tragic poet as of being an expert in finance and his friends' doubts passed him by.

Disheartened by injustice and soothed by praise, Chateaubriand was gradually growing resigned. The skies of France seemed to him cold and grey after those of Italy. Portalis, at the Ministry for Foreign Affairs, "seemed rather to be screening than filling the post." So be it! Chateaubriand would go back to Rome. He would end his days "in a cell near the room where Tasso breathed his last"; there he would finish his *Mémoires* and gather about Mme. Récamier a youthful court of talent and beauty. The new writers among his disciples, the Lamartines, the Vignys and the Sainte-

Beuves, would come thither on pilgrimage. Women, drawn by the sunset glory of his renown, would come flocking. Once more he would see the lovely Roman patricians, the Englishwomen touched by his melancholy and, in all likelihood, the Frenchwomen who were so faithful in writing to express their admiration. Mme. de Vichet and Mlle. de Villeneuve might even come to beguile the evening of his days in the ambassadorial palace—for, in his dreams, his cell straightway dissolved into a palace and he fed on the brightest hopes. "I will await in Rome the death of the King who, thank God, is in the best of health. There I will undertake my great work: *Une Histoire de France*. I do not say that I may not become a minister in my old age, perhaps at the accession, or during the minority of Henry V, for the Dauphin likes me no better than does Charles X. I am the bogey of their mediocrity."

Meanwhile, since he was in France and at leisure, he wanted to see his unknown correspondents, now that his old friends had disappeared. Delphine de Custine was lost to him and Claire de Duras had died at Nice in January 1829 without ever seeing Chateaubriand again. She had spent the last months of her life in excruciating physical pain, which she bore heroically, compiling *Réflexions chrétiennes sur les Passions*. There she wrote, in a meditation on forbearance: "Sorrow's crown of sorrow is to meet with inexcusable wrongs from those we love. Yet there is an excuse: They know not what they do. They may have rent our hearts, but they knew not what they did; they were blinded, their eyes were holden; your sufferings are the token of their unknowing."

Chateaubriand, as was his wont, treated her better in death than in life. "Since I have lost so generous a soul, I have not ceased, amidst my tears, to reproach myself with the moodiness which may sometimes have grieved faithful hearts. Let us keep watch over our character! Let us not forget that, however deep our affection, we may yet envenom existences we would redeem with our last drop of blood. When our friends go down into the tomb, how can we atone for the evil we have wrought? Our vain regret, our unavailing repentance—are these a cure for the hurt we have done them? They would liefer have had a smile in their lifetime than all our tears after they are dead." It was very well said, but could the hapless woman have returned with her demands and her reproaches, would she have fared better at his hands?

No sooner was he returned to Paris than the incorrigible philanderer sent an imperious note claiming a rendezvous with the sentimental Mme. de Vichet: "Tell me the hour and the day of the end of our illusions." He found a woman of fifty whose prudery could dally from afar with the poetic game, but who saw in the poet himself a dangerous libertine. "You are younger than I imagined. You look younger than you are, and our letters are unseemly." She bored him.

He much preferred to meet the young and oncoming Hortense Allart, whose proofs he had undertaken to correct. She herself has described those lessons in which he taught her by turns the art of love and the art of getting rid of conjunctions. "If I asked him the reason for the change, he gave me none, saying that it was a matter of taste, that these things had to be felt. . . . His corrections were very gay, very tender. . . . He brought to them all a kindliness, a goodness, a perfect good-nature, an innocent gaiety, a harmless mockery—all the likeable qualities of the mind joined with grace and courtesy. Often, when he talked of my youth, of the peace he found in me and the attraction of which he was conscious, though he declared that he had no illusions either of himself or the future, he told me that he was planning a novel in which he meant to depict such a love."

Hortense amused him, but he was also bent on making the acquaintance of Léontine de Villeneuve, the young girl from Toulouse to whom he wrote from Rome: "Léontine, see you I shall." She was to spend the summer in the Pyrenees, drinking the waters at Cauterets with her family. He decided to go there and, before calling at Nice to escort Mme. de Chateaubriand back to Rome, set off for the Pyrenees round about July 15th. He travelled by short stages, "strewing the way with joyful dreams." Hortense was requested to meet him on his road. At Étampes they took adjoining rooms. "As soon as he was left alone he came hurriedly to tell me that we should see each other, then he departed to dismiss the servants and order dinner, which was served in my room. He was back in no time, wholly at ease and bent on enjoying himself, whereupon we dined with the secrecy of young runaway lovers.

During dessert he was laughing and happy, laying himself out to say hosts of kind and tender things. . . . I was head over heels in love and as grateful as he, for—if he was beholden to my youth for loving him—I was beholden to his generosity in giving me so much of his time and talents."

He left her to meet Léontine, on whom he went to call as soon as ever he arrived in Cauterets, in the little apartment she shared with her aunt. He found a plain but fresh-faced girl of twenty-five, who wrote verses. He corrected the verse and talked to her with decorous tenderness. In the houses of the aristocrats who were taking the waters—the Duc de la Rochefoucauld, the Castelbajac, or the Broglie, the "Genius" was to be met with "the young friend of his declining years." The oddly-assorted couple went for walks among the firs and by the path which bordered the torrent, Chateaubriand talked of his enchanted palace in Rome and invited Léontine (as he had invited Juliette) to be its good fairy. There were moments when she was tempted. "There my literary talent would blossom under the direction of an old Master of Muses." Ingenuously, she also envisaged "the ideal of a life of friendship and of rigid virtue." In order that she might live near him without a whisper of scandal, she thought for an instant of shutting herself up in a Roman convent. Did she go the length of proffering her favours? Later, he was so indiscreet as to hint as much in his *Mémoires*. When she read them, she was indignant and recalled the fact that he could have been her father twice over.

Of this misunderstanding there sprang the first draft of a novel which contains some of the most moving and sincere sentences that ever he wrote. It was the manuscript entitled *Amour et Vieillesse*, a brief emotional autobiography, the confessions of a sexagenarian René with their passages of beauty and terror. "Before I went into society, I prowled around its outskirts. Now that I have put it behind me, I am as much cut off as ever; old and travel-worn, with no abiding place, I watch the homecomings at evening, when all shut to their doors, I see the young lover glide softly through the dark while I—seated upon a milestone—number the stars and trust not one of all, but await the dawn which has no new thing to tell me." He struggled wildly against the stealing step of age. "If you tell me that you will love me as a father, you will make me shudder; if you maintain that you care for me as a lover, I shall not believe you. . . . Yesterday, when you were seated beside me on the stone, when the wind in the pines brought us the distant sound of the sea, my heart failed for love and sorrow and I said within me: 'Is my hand light enough to lay on such bright hair? What can she love in me? A will o' the wisp that readily will destroy.' "[1]

With such alchemy did the Enchanter's crucible transmute the harmless walks he took beside a mountain stream with a pleasant and dumpy girl who wrote execrable verse. It was not long before politics put an end to the romance. On August 6th, 1829, Charles X dismissed Martignac, whose conciliatory opportunism, verging on the liberal, seemed to him cowardly and dangerous, and summoned in his stead his friend Jules, Prince de Polignac. Chateaubriand would never have believed that such a crazy idea could ever occur to the King. Polignac had charm, nobility and courage, but his obstinacy, his headstrong narrowmindedness and the ingenuousness of his absolutist creed could satisfy none in France save a handful of fanatics. Between the Monarchy and the Charter conflict was becoming inevitable.

With that generous ardour which men are wont to display when another's career is at stake, the bathers of Cauterets immediately bore down upon Chateaubriand to ask when he would send in his resignation. "The foxes enjoyed the situation. They were forever reminding him of his recent utterances, badgering him with premature congratulations and referring to him, in his presence, as a willing martyr." Léontine de Villeneuve advised him to keep his ambassadorship and not insult the King by throwing his resignation at Polignac's head. "Do not go back to Paris," said she. "Leave for Rome and see what happens."

During the days which followed, every post brought piles of letters adjuring him to send the King his resignation. "People whom I hardly knew felt called upon to prescribe my resignation. Such officious interest in my fair fame came as a shock. Thank God, I have never needed advice in matters of honour. . . . Where duty is concerned my mind works swiftly." His friends were merciless.

[1] Scholars are not agreed on the date and origin of *Amour et Vieillesse*. I shall endeavour to sketch the conflicting theories and to suggest reasons for my conclusions.

The Monarchist Against the Monarchy

"They were filled with abnegation on my behalf; they could not do enough to strip themselves of all that I possessed." It was heartbreaking to sacrifice the Roman embassy on which he had counted to end his days in peace. However, instead of setting off for Rome, he went to Paris, where he sought audience of the King. The audience was not granted and he saw only Polignac, who told him that neither he nor the King would accept his resignation and that he ought to return to Rome. "Am I not your friend? Your withdrawal may give rise to fresh strife. I beseech you, my dear Vicomte, do nothing so foolish." Chateaubriand replied that he was doing nothing foolish, that the Polignac ministry was unpopular, that France was convinced it would attack her liberties and that he, Chateaubriand, could only be their defender. "M. de Polignac swore that he had as much love for the Charter as I. But he loved it in his own fashion; he loved it from too close quarters."

When the ambassador's resignation was made public, the ministerial press attacked Chateaubriand while the triumphal liberal press sprang to his defence. "One of the finest geniuses of Europe has been false neither to himself nor to his renown." The liberals, Thiers and Mignet among them, came to him in person. Those who did not know him well would have liked to make him a political leader, but he was "a white banner rather than a chief. . . . At close quarters he was not very winning. An attitude of well-bred pride, often freezing in its effect, long silences and a kind of dreaminess or absent-mindedness, which was noticeable amidst the keen interest that stirred about him, were so many obstacles to the office of a political leader." In his lucid moments, he was more aware of it than any.

Mme. de Chateaubriand bore the loss of the embassy with a resignation the more meritorious in that she disliked a straitened household. They were now very poor. Chateaubriand owed the Duc de Laval fifty thousand francs for the appointments of the Roman palace; his publisher, Ladvocat, had gone bankrupt in 1828; despite his weariness and depression there was nothing for it but to set once more to work and take up the historical studies he had drafted in the Valley of Wolves. He had no joy in it all and that winter, dedicated to a long and laborious task, would have been very cheerless had it not been brightened by a few women's faces.

Nothing further was to be expected of Léontine de Villeneuve; she was about to marry and the thought gave him a touch of chagrin. "So you are going to change your name! Will your heart change likewise? Ah, well, for me you will always be the unknown Léontine. Farewell, my Léontine, my viewless fairy, my sylph, my angel of the mountain!" And on October 4th: "It is from the anniversary of my birth, of my feast day, of my entry into Jerusalem and of the death of St. Francis that this letter is dated. It is a sorrowful day which always finds me bereft of some good that was mine a year since! One year the more, the Léontine the less! Therein lies my final deprivation." But he had always flirted with despair and this was more feigned than real.

In the company of Hortense Allart, gloom became the handmaid of pleasure. "It was autumn," said she, "the season of tenderness and melancholy. He and I both loved the country and we used often to go long walks together in Paris. His talk was sometimes cheerless, but always friendly. If I forgot his age, he—for his part—never forgot. He often spoke of his death and liked to see my eyes brim with tears." While Mme. Récamier watched over his renown and Mme. de Chateaubriand made use of it to increase the sale of the chocolate that the sisters of the Infirmary manufactured for the benefit of her charities, the Genius would meet Hortense, sometimes in the museums they visited together, sometimes in the Champs Elysées and sometimes in the Jardin des Plantes. They would go and dine at the Arc-en-Ciel, a little eating-house where they were given a private room on the first floor. "He had an appetite and everything amused him." He would talk to her of his embassies, of the days of his youth and laugh for joy to find favour with her. He ordered champagne. Hortense used to sing him Béranger's songs—*la Bonne vieille, le Dieu des bonnes Gens.* "Then," added she, without any vain affectation of modesty, "he had his will."

Even more than the songs of Béranger, he liked her to sing the heroic ballads that he himself had composed. She knew that the best way to move him was to read him his own works. One day she chose a scene from *Les Martyrs* and read him the account of the tortures Eudore underwent in prison; before long he was shaken with sobs. "At those words he could no longer contain

himself, even if he would. It was feeling going back to its source;
he was in tears, enraptured, assailed in every part of his impassioned
soul. He let me see how touched and grateful he was; he said that
he had never known a like enjoyment." On her death-bed, one of
his old friends had already bequeathed him her copies of *Atala* and
René—It was perhaps a last and melancholy epigram.

There were times, too, when he dictated to his fair mistress a
few passages from the *Études historiques*. One day, following the
sentence: "The cross separates two worlds," he stopped and said:
"I shall die on your breast; you will betray me and I shall forgive
it you." He had always delighted to twine the idea of love with
that of death. She was touched by the nobility and gentleness of
his languor. "There is a greatness about that indifference and
world-weariness of his. The fulness of his genius comes out in his
ennui. He reminds me of the eagles I saw this morning at the Jardin
des Plantes, their eyes fixed on the sun and their great wings beating up against a cage too small to hold them."

Meanwhile the Polignac ministry was drifting rapidly towards
disaster. "Poor Jules," said Charles X, "he is so lacking in capability." And the Duchesse d'Angoulême, her unhappy memories
breeding painful presentiments: "This is a venture and I do not
like them. They have never brought us luck." Polignac vowed
that he would respect liberties. "I am sorry to hear it," someone
retorted. "Why?" "Because the only men on your side are those
who want a coup d'État, and if you do not make it yourself, you
will have no one."

When the Chamber met on March 2nd, the following address
was voted in reply to the speech from the throne. "The Charter
enshrines the right of the country to intervene in the discussion
of public interests. This intervention makes the lasting concurrence
of the political desires of the government with the desires of your
people a condition indispensable to the smooth running of public
affairs. Sire, our loyalty, our devotion, condemn us to inform you
that such concurrence does not exist." The gist of it was: "Get
rid of the ministry." Charles X replied: "I have announced my
decisions. They are irrevocable; my ministers will inform you of
my resolutions." Those resolutions were Ordinances, the first of

which abolished the liberty of the press, the second announced the dissolution of the Chamber, the third changed the electoral system and encouraged governmental pressure, the fourth made ready for new elections, and the fifth appointed friends of the government to high office.

Throughout the country, there was great and growing unrest. Matters had not yet come to civil war, but both camps were mobilising their forces. A "Breton Association" was formed to resist abuses of power. Chateaubriand was very proud of it. "My compatriots have often taken the initiative in our recent revolutions. There is, in Breton heads, something of the winds that lash the shores of our peninsula." At the time, there were certainly threatening enough clouds in his own.

At four o'clock on the morning of July 26th, 1830, he set off for Dieppe. There he was to meet Mme. Récamier, whom he found in an apartment the windows of which overlooked the beach where he had once learned to handle a musket. For some hours he talked quietly with her, as he once more watched the waves breaking on the pebbles with their rhythmic swell. Suddenly there appeared the red-faced Hyacinthe Pilorge, bringing the Ordinances. Chateaubriand read them. He could not believe his eyes: "Yet another government," said he, "which of deliberate intent hurls itself down from the towers of Notre Dame!" Not long afterwards, Ballanche confirmed the news and Chateaubriand bravely decided to go to Paris.

4. The Revolution of 1830

Access to the city was difficult. At the Étoile, students and workmen had set up barricades. The postilion went round by the Trocadero. From the gate, Chateaubriand saw the tricolor floating on all sides and reflected that though he had come for the protection of liberties, he would find himself obliged to defend the monarchy. There was a muffled sound of musketry and the clang of an alarmbell. He went straight to the Rue d'Enfer to hearten Mme. de Chateaubriand and to write to Mme. Récamier: "My position is painful, but clear. I shall no more betray the King than the Charter, the legitimate power than liberty."

Was his dual attitude defensible? Possibly, for the rebels were divided among themselves. The working classes wanted a republic; the middle classes, the Duc d'Orléans. By acting with authority and swiftness it might have been possible, if not to preserve Charles X on the throne, at least to bring about the acceptance of his and the Duc d'Angoulême's abdication in favour of the young Duc de Bordeaux, who would have reigned under the name of Henry V, while the Duc d'Orléans acted as Lieutenant General of the Kingdom. Yet how could any sensible decision be expected of Charles X, who had taken refuge at St. Cloud amid a crowd of flatterers and fanatics who, even under the fire of the populace, refused to believe that they were unpopular. And, if the Duc d'Orléans felt that the court was vacillating and powerless, what was to prevent him from stretching out his hand to grasp a proffered crown?

On the day following his return, Chateaubriand wrote to the King at St. Cloud asking to be informed of his wishes. Charles X sent to say that he had appointed the Duc de Mortemart prime minister and that he begged Chateaubriand to come to an understanding with him. But the noble Duke was nowhere to be found. Halted at the gate of St. Cloud by ill-informed troops, he had been obliged to make his way into Paris by going on foot through the Bois, although he was ill at the time. He arrived completely exhausted, his heel blistered, and straightway plunged into a bath. "M. de Mortemart's heel was the vulnerable point in which the last arrow of fate struck the legitimate monarchy."

Lacking royal instructions, what was to be done? Chateaubriand, summoned to the Chamber of Peers on the morning of the 30th, decided that he would go. First, however, he was eager to gather fresh news by taking a walk through Paris. He had never known fear, besides he discovered that "the town, by comparison with the Paris of 1789, was the very picture of order and silence." Respect for the law seemed to reign in both camps. On the Pont Neuf, the statue of Henry IV grasped a tricolor flag. Behind the colonnade of the Louvre, some students recognised Chateaubriand by his tempestuous hair and cried: "Long live the defender of the liberty of the press!" They then asked: "Where are you going? We'll carry you."

He protested, but half-heartedly. Actually, he was delighted.

When, after a first halt at the Palais-Royal, he admitted that he was going to the Chamber of Peers, a student thrust his head between the writer's legs and hoisted him on to his shoulders. By way of the Pont des Arts and the Rue de la Seine, the group climbed towards the Luxembourg, flanked by Hyacinthe Pilorge, who came in for his share of the republican embraces. People crowded to the windows to see the procession pass. "Long live the Charter," cried the students. "Yes, gentlemen," replied Chateaubriand, "long live the Charter, but long live the King." "Long live Chateaubriand," yelled the students. There were even some shouts of "Long live the First Consul." How Chateaubriand must have been delighted by those cries which seemed as though they would make him the heir, not of the Emperor whom he had hated and assailed, but of the young hero he had so admired!

Eventually, his bearers set him down in the courtyard of the Luxembourg. He entered it, thoroughly cheered by his adventure and convinced that it needed only a little courage for all to work out excellently. He found, said he, "dismayed faces, vacillating minds and trembling hearts." To tell the truth, the experiences of the other peers present at the meeting in no way coincided with his own. The students who, in Chateaubriand's imagination, set off three thousand strong numbered no more than three hundred when they reached the brains of his colleagues. "He was still intoxicated," writes Pasquier ironically, "by a sort of ovation with which he had just been honoured by about fifteen youths who helped him to pass the barricade at the end of the Rue de Tournon." In his enthusiasm, he let slip the reply to a few people who were anxious for the fate of legitimacy: "Set your minds at rest! You have only to preserve the liberty of the press, to leave me my pen, ink and paper and, if legitimacy is overthrown, I will have restored it again by the end of three months."

Did he really say any such thing? He certainly thought it. He even wrote it: "If Charles X had been overthrown by a conspiracy from without, I should have taken up my pen and—had I been left my mental independence—I should have engaged to rally an immense party about the ruins of the throne." Who knows? He might have done it. The game was not yet played. There were three opposing parties: legitimist, Orléanist and republican, and each of the three owed its chance of conflict to the other two. The Duc d'Orléans had been welcomed at the town hall by a republican mob and embraced by Lafayette. He, in his turn, had received a bantering and familiar crowd in his Palais-Royal, scared though he was. "The shouting and singing of the *Marseillaise* echoed even through drawing-rooms and made it very difficult to hear oneself speak. No-one dared shut the windows for fear of offending the mob. . . . It was more than triumph; it was the joyful orgy of a rabble populace, with no ill-will about it."

The nascent monarchy was keeping low company; the old was in flight, Charles X and the Dauphin made for Cherbourg and found the luckless Crow of Vire—Chênedollé—awaiting them on their road with a sheaf of lilies. Abandoned by their king, what could the royalist leaders do? The Duc d'Orléans urged them to rally to him. An emissary came to tell Chateaubriand that if he cared to go to the Palais-Royal, the Duchesse d'Orléans and the Duke would be delighted to see him. He went. The Duchess received him at once and made him sit beside her. "Ah! Monsieur de Chateaubriand," said she, "we are all in a sorry plight! If all the parties would unite, perhaps the situation might yet be saved. What do you think of it all?" He suggested his solution—Henry V king, the Duc d'Orléans regent. It was not at all what was expected of him. The princess sent to fetch her husband and Louis-Philippe arrived looking tired and shabby. "Madame la Duchesse d'Orléans has doubtless told you in what bad case we are. . . . I am of your opinion, Monsieur de Chateaubriand. To take the Duc de Bordeaux would certainly be the best thing to do. My only dread is that events may be too much for us." "Too much for us, Monseigneur? Are you not invested with full powers?"

The conversation left Louis-Philippe ill at ease. "I read on his brow," said Chateaubriand, "the desire to be king." He took his leave, rejoined his friends and said: "Well, he wants to be king and Madame la Duchesse d'Orléans, for her part, wants to be queen." "Did they tell you so?" "One talked to me of pastorals, the other of the perils threatening France and the irresponsibility of poor Caroline. Both wished to give me to understand that I might be useful to them and neither dared look me in the face."

When the Chamber of Peers held the meeting in which they were to take the oath to the new monarchy, Chateaubriand went —determined to refuse the oath and full of scorn for his colleagues. "From the republicans of 1793, translated to senators, and from Bonaparte's generals I expected only what they have always done. They deposed the amazing man to whom they owed everything; they were about to depose the king who confirmed them in the property and honours with which their former master heaped them." When Chateaubriand rose to speak, none—save a few peers who were determined to retire—dared raise eyes to him. His speech was shrewd. He pointed out that representative republics were probably the future state of the world, that the time was not yet ripe, that only the legitimate monarchy was strong enough to respect and preserve liberties, but that it had brought about its own fall through a conspiracy of hypocrisy and stupidity.

"It is not from any sentimental devotion that I plead a cause wherein all would turn against me anew should it triumph. I aim neither at romance, nor at chivalry, nor at martyrdom; I do not believe in the divine right of kings, but I do believe in the power of revolutions and of events. I suggest the Duc de Bordeaux simply as a sounder solution than the one under discussion. . . . An unprofitable Cassandra, I have wearied the throne and the country with my unheeded warnings long enough. Nothing is left me but to take my seat amid the ruins of the shipwreck I have so often foretold. I recognise in disaster every sort of power save that of loosing me from my vows of fealty. I ought also to make my life consistent. After all I have done, said and written for the Bourbons, I should be the vilest of the vile were I to deny them at the moment when, for the third and last time, they are on their road to exile." He himself has described the effect of his eloquence. "Many peers seemed overwhelmed. They sank so low in their chairs that I could no longer see them behind their motionless colleagues in front. The speech created a certain stir. All parties were stung by it, but all kept silence because I had set a great sacrifice beside great truths. I came down from the tribune; I left the hall; I went to the cloakroom; I laid aside my peer's robes, my sword, my plumed hat; I unfastened the white cockade; I put it in the little left-hand pocket of my black greatcoat, over against my heart." The sacrifice was ended.

The government of July had offered him wealth and honours. As in the time of the Duc d'Enghien, he chose honour and poverty. He had lost all that he might remain loyal to the princes who dismissed and persecuted him. The attitude was a fine one and must have delighted this sculptor of his own existence. Us it might touch more deeply if it had been less conscious.

As he had raised a monument to Pauline de Beaumont after making her suffer, as he had honoured Claire de Duras after snubbing her in life, so he leapt bravely to the rescue of a throne that he himself had shaken. He brought "to the concord of his mourning flutes one secret but invariable condition. He demanded that his dirge should be sustained, his gloom nourished on real calamities, on final and decisive ills, on falls with no hope of arising."[1] Even in shipwreck, he pursued with his indifference the dynasty he overwhelmed with his sacrifices. "After all," said he, "it is a fallen monarchy and many another will fall. The only thing to which it has a right is our faith—it has it." The faith fell like a blade.

Would any other behaviour have been possible? Should he have feigned admiration for Polignac's policy when he thought it not only imprudent but foolish? No. But he might doubtless have desired the peace of France more than the glory of Chateaubriand. Canning said of him that he had a taste for crises, and it is very certain that in politics he preferred fine rôles to useful actions. Lacking modesty, he easily identified his quarrels with those of God. "He is always Nemesis," said one of his adversaries, "speaking in the name of Jehovah." His vengeance had assailed in turn Napoleon, Decazes, Villèle, then Charles X. He had been a great destroyer. What had he built up?

At the time of the first restoration and afterwards at the moment of the Spanish war, his splendid intelligence had doubtless envisaged a monarchy, at once vigorous and just, which would entrust to royalists the adaptation of British institutions to French custom. Yet he had done nothing to win over to his ideas those who might have compassed their success. He had driven Louis

[1] Charles Maurras.

XVIII to give office only to Ultras; these in turn he had attacked without mercy from the day when Charles X gave them employment without summoning him. Now he gibed at those virtuous men who, on the pretext of putting France before all else, accepted high place and repudiated their past. Even though his suspicion of the purity of their intentions is understandable, it is permissible to believe that their resignation was of greater service to the country than his magnanimity.

Be that as it may, the July revolution had done him an immense service by allowing him to restore unity in his own mind. A disciple of Rousseau and an enemy of Robespierre, an admirer of Bonaparte and an enemy of Napoleon, a monarchist in revolt against his kings, a liberal and an Ultra, a man of sound sense and a visionary, Chateaubriand for forty years had been a man cruelly divided against himself and the two halves had never succeeded in coming together. The fall of the dynasty to which he had sworn fealty at last brought him a chance of reconciling himself with himself, of making a kind of inner coalition of his conflicting passions and of uniting the liberal and the feudal Chateaubriand in a common hatred of a bourgeois, usurping and craven government.

CHAPTER X

Towards the Grave

> Such as in himself at last . . .[1]
> . . . Death which I have always singularly loved. . . .
> —CHATEAUBRIAND

1. CHATEAUBRIAND, WHY FLEE FROM YOUR COUNTRY?

A REPUBLICAN by nature, a Monarchist by reason, and a Bourbonian from honour, I should more easily have come to terms with a democracy—if I could not preserve the legitimate monarchy —than with the bastard monarchy accorded by I know not whom." A sentence of this kind could content at once a journalist of the Left such as Armand Carrel and a legitimist such as Berryer. It was to Louis-Philippe that Chateaubriand's old age was to owe that fierce and leonine nobility which retirement and disgrace lend to the declining years of great men.

The disgrace, in point of fact, was wholly voluntary. Had he elected to rally to the July monarchy, no writer would have been received with more gratitude and respect. "I am indeed unhappy," said he, "I have done what I ought, I have reaped the esteem, yet I am sacrificing myself for a cause in which I do not believe and for fools who, could they understand me, would treat me even worse."

Indeed unhappy? Yes, no doubt, for he was once more as poor as a church mouse and, now that the time for embassies was over and gone, he could look forward only to long years of obscurity. Yet he had ever a secret joy in misfortune and the rôle of the

---

[1] On Chateaubriand's old age see, besides the works quoted above, Marie-Jeanne Durry's excellent work.

Chevalier of Exile was not without its bitter relish. With a gentle graciousness that delicate minds thought ostentatious, he whom the Bourbons had used so ill while yet they reigned made himself the kindly champion of the Bourbons dethroned. "He is thoroughly ridiculous," said the Duchesse de Broglie. "He always wants to be pitied for the ills he brings on himself. He fashions some great misfortune and tells us all about it." True, but the fashioning delighted him. Even on the threshold of age, the minister, the ambassador, the peer of France put off his broidered uniforms; he was left naked and old with service, poor and lonely, from loyalty to a child-king who—in all likelihood—would one day prove as ungrateful as his ancestors. The attitude seemed to him the loftier in that it was gratuitous and wholly vain.

However, man must live. The publisher of the *Œuvres complètes* had gone bankrupt. It was open to Chateaubriand to appeal to the Bourbons for whom he had lost everything. "But," said he, "rather than sit down to the banquet of kings I would choose to dine with Duke Humphrey, as in time past in London." Sell the house in the Rue d'Enfer? Mme. de Chateaubriand would not hear of it. Publish a new book? The only work that Chateaubriand could finish quickly was the *Etudes historiques*, which had been begun in the Valley of Wolves, laid aside, taken up again, copied in Mme. Récamier's small and delicate handwriting and even dictated, in the intervals of temporal pleasures, to Hortense Allart.

According to the original plan, six dissertations on the origins of Western civilisations were to adorn the substructure of a monumental History of France. Those notable dissertations were the only part written in the Valley. The History of France, which had been finished in haste, was simply "a reasoned analysis" interspersed with fragments of description. A preface written after 1830 linked the book up with the rest of Chateaubriand's work. "I began my literary career with a work in which I examined Christianity from the point of view of poetry and morals; I end it with a work in which I consider the same religion in its philosophical and historical aspects. . . . Hence, from the foot of the Cross to the foot of Louis XVI's scaffold, I lead up to the three truths which are the foundations of social order: religious truth, philosophic truth and political truth or liberty. It is my endeavour to shew that mankind follows a line of progress in civilisation even when it seems to retrogress."

In short, the author's purpose was to reconcile Religion and Progress or, as he said, "religious and political truth." He held that Christianity and monarchy had both been long corrupted by absolutism; both were about to realise at last the benefits of liberty. It was a strangely optimistic philosophy of history but, though serious objections might be advanced against it, it was impossible not to admire the immense amount of work that the author had achieved and the greatness of his purpose—that of linking France and Europe with their Christian origins.

There were many points on which Chateaubriand's keen intelligence had given him glimpses of new and great truths. For instance, he shewed ingeniously that it was the encounter of Christianity with invasions which gave the new religion a military force on which to lean and thus admitted of its triumph over the pagan world. It was he who first pointed out that the French monarchy had been elective until the time of Hugh Capet. Published at a time when the minds of the French were occupied with other things, the *Études historiques* were far from being welcomed with the attention and respect they deserved, but they were imitated and pillaged by a whole generation of young historians with a regularity which was itself an unworthy form of admiration.

To the *Études historiques*, published in 1831, then succeeded a pamphlet: *La Restauration et la Monarchie élective*, in which he again defended his favourite thesis: that only an hereditary monarchy can be a liberal government, since it alone is strong enough to have no fear of liberty. Thereafter he decided to go into exile in Switzerland, on the products of the *Études* and the pamphlet, and to work at his *Mémoires*. He could have wished that his departure was forced upon him by Louis-Philippe's government, but the authorities were wary of giving an illustrious adversary the prestige of persecution; yet there was no help for it but to leave Paris. Hortense Allart alone might, by the promise of pleasure, have withheld her old friend from going. But, for some months, she had been neglecting him for a young Englishman, Henry

Bulwer-Lytton, in whom she saw the double charm of youth and beauty.

Hortense no longer loved any but her foreigner, who—for his part—was interested in nothing but Parliament, and Chateaubriand grew jealous. "What!" said he, "You are leaving me for an Englishman, an enemy of our country, a member of that hostile race which cannot understand us! What has he said or done to have such sway over you?" He maintained that by going to England she would lose a gift that only he, Chateaubriand, was capable of fostering. "He told me that in the night hours he meditated death and even sought for weapons. He asked me if Atala, if Velléda, if René were lacking in passion. He said that I was choosing a man of no account. . . . He explored all the ways by which he might move me. . . . But I had caught a flash of the rapture of the flesh, a noble rapture for which I was born."

Hence Hortense was pursuing, in an English bed, her quest of noble rapture. Mme. de Chateaubriand was insistent on the journey to Switzerland. He gave in. To Mme. Récamier he wrote, in explanation of his departure: "I cannot reconcile myself to the yoke of a coward monarchy which allows France to be humiliated and will go and sing a *Te Deum* on the day when it has set an English prince on the throne of Belgium." The yoke was not very heavy, but Chateaubriand's grievances against the July monarchy were those of many Frenchmen; this half-way government, which relied on bankers and shopkeepers, exasperated aristocrats and proletarians alike. It could not be accused of any serious crimes, but there was scope for gibing at the mediocrity of its virtues.

Chateaubriand to Ballanche: "Here, as I not only foresaw but prophesied, the elections have taken us full in the middle. France is at present one big corporation and proud youth has been swallowed up in that swelling paunch. Much good may it do it. . . . Only one thing surprises me: it is the present lack of honour. I should never have believed that young France could want peace at any price, or that it would refrain from throwing out of the windows those ministers who send an English commissary to Brussels and an Austrian corporal to Bologna. It seems that all these contemners of our sage wigs, these future great men, had ink rather than blood in their fingertips." And in his pamphlet: "I doubt whether liberty will be content for long with the humdrum qualities of a stay-at-home monarchy; the Franks made the abode of liberty a camp; in their descendants it has kept its predilection for that first cradle."

In short, he was not yet recovered from his Napoleonic intoxication. "In the time of the Emperor, at least," said he, "France had honour and to spare." From Geneva, this champion of legitimacy was flirting with Bonapartists and republicans. Sainte-Beuve compared him to those husbands who keep all their ill humour for their wives. His wife in this case was the royalist party. He had sworn faith to it, but no more. It was for his adversaries, Armand Carrel, the journalist, and Béranger, the song-writer, that he kept all his graces.

Hortense Allart had once introduced him to Béranger. The author of *Le Génie du Christianisme* had given his academic vote for the author of *La Bonne vieille*; Béranger had promised Chateaubriand to dedicate a song to him. Mere trifling? Chateaubriand did not see it in that light. A great artist in his sensitiveness to public opinion, he knew the worth of a song by Béranger and more than once claimed the fulfilment of his promise. The *Études historiques* were sent to the song-writer with this imperious dedication:

> *Faîtes revivre au coin d'un feu paisible*
> *Mon souvenir en vos nobles chansons.*

In September 1831, Chateaubriand made a short trip to the French capital and dined at the Café de Paris with Arago, Carrel and Béranger, "all more or less discontented and disillusioned with the best of republics." During dessert Béranger recited the beginning of the promised song:

> *Chateaubriand, pourquoi fuir ta patrie,*
> *Fuir son amour, notre encens et nos soins?*

The last verses were not yet finished. Chateaubriand adjured their author to write them as soon as might be: "Well sir, my song? I am leaving. If you want me to return, I must take your commands with me."

Indeed, he was determined to make great use of Béranger's call.

He had it reprinted in a dozen newspapers, answered it himself in Armand Carrel's *Le National* and, since he was bored in Switzerland and weary of figuring in the official ceremonies of the town of Geneva as Mme. de Chateaubriand's inseparable companion, moved her to this tirade: "Two human beings who are incompatible should go their own ways. Well! for lack of a few pistoles they are forced to sit sulking opposite one another, fuming and eating their hearts out or quarrelling fiercely. The pinch of poverty squeezes them against each other and, prisoned in such tatterdemalion bonds, instead of mutually embracing, they bite." Then again, the boatmen on the lake irritated him by their over-enthusiastic descriptions of the storms braved by that Lord Byron who had been his rival in misfortune, in genius and in tempests—hence he proposed to make use of the authorisation of a song to return to France without ridicule.

The idea that he wanted conveyed to the mind of the public was this: Chateaubriand had desired to go into lasting exile, but Béranger had accused him of flight from his country, which seemed to him to be in an unhappy state. "Touched and tempted by its wretchedness, I reflected that it would always be lawful to leave it once it was happy." It was a thin but honourable pretext for putting an end to a wearisome exile.

To Mme. Récamier (for he had to make as much of the episode as was humanly possible) he wrote that "for love of her, he was capable of offering to a government for which he had no respect the hands that she had fettered." Such artifices were transparent and Victor Hugo set down gibing comments on the old master's sham exit in his notebook: "M. de Chateaubriand goes to Geneva, returns to Paris, is off once more for Geneva, leads us on, flirts delicately with us, leaves us a pamphlet and takes to flight. . . . *Et fugit ad salices et se cupit ante videri.*" There is no one to touch a coquette in seeing through another's wiles.

On leaving France, Charles X and his household at first found shelter with the Wells, a Jacobite family in Dorsetshire, who sought thus to repay the hospitality the Bourbons had offered to the Stuarts in the past. They then went to Scotland to stay at Holyrood. The Duc and Duchesse d'Angoulême were long accustomed to adversity and accepted their exile resignedly. But the Duchesse de Berry, the mother of the young king, Henry V, a mettlesome and unaffected Italian who had all the liveliness of her race, could not long endure such ceremonious isolation. She undertook to travel about, to enter into conspiracies and to regain her son's kingdom. To pave the way to that goal, she wished to create in Paris a secret Council of Regency and invited Chateaubriand to become a member. Of all the royal family, she alone had always felt sympathy and admiration for the writer. He, on his side, recognised that the duchess had something "whimsical, fresh and attractive" about her character, but did not hesitate, when occasion arose, to dub her crazy, eccentric and an "Italian tight-rope dancer." As he disliked underground scheming he refused to join the Council.

Suddenly there came cholera, a mysterious epidemic which carried off thousands of Parisians. The duchess begged Chateaubriand to transmit 12,000 francs to the victims' families in her name. On this occasion he accepted the mission. The prefect of the Seine and a few mayors refused the gift. It was a fine theme for an avenging letter. . . . Hardly was all the commotion dying down when the Duchesse de Berry landed in the Midi. There were no white banners flying "from steeple to steeple," enthusiasm was sparse, her following brave but scanty and she had to flee to the Vendée.

Grieved, despite its courage, by so rash and vain an escapade, the legitimist leaders—Chateaubriand, Hyde de Neuville and the Duc de Fitz-James—despatched Berryer to the Regent to beg her to abandon her design. Berryer was clumsy enough to get himself arrested and his indiscreet utterances successfully compromised his friends. At four o'clock on the morning of June 16th, 1832, the police arrived at Chateaubriand's house to arrest him. He found the experience rather diverting, but Mme. de Chateaubriand, who had not lost her terror of the Terror, was taken with a fit of shuddering. "Whoever knows her," said her husband, "must also know the tender affection she bears me, her affrights, the liveliness of her imagination and her wretched state of health." The affair was really rather funny than tragic, and the government put itself in the wrong by interfering with illustrious men who, though its declared foes, were no conspirators.

The Prefect of Police, M. Gisquet—a man of tact and intelligence—hastened to the cell of which Chateaubriand (entranced with his adventure and already busy in comparing his prisons with those of Tasso) had taken possession, and offered the prisoner the choice of every room in the prefect's private apartments. After much persuasion, Chateaubriand accepted Mlle. Gisquet's dressing-room, which opened on to a highly romantic English garden, and there found an almost Lotharian pleasure in recalling Anacreon's verses on a young girl's toilet.

His detention, which he thoroughly enjoyed and which was all too short for his liking, frightened Mme. de Chateaubriand nearly out of her wits. She believed that Louis-Philippe was bent on throwing her husband into prison and so sent Mme. Récamier into action. Mme. Récamier passed the word to Mme. de Boigne, who intervened with Baron Pasquier, the president of the Chamber of Peers (for, under every government, the indispensable Pasquier had obviously to preside over some assembly). But legal formalities took time. Mme. de Chateaubriand was made quite ill and had to take to her bed. No sooner was her husband set at liberty than she demanded that he again set off with her for Switzerland. To do that there was needed money. Despite their scruples, the pair had to apply to Charles X, who—through the Duc de Lévis—sent 20,000 francs. To these their nephew, Louis de Chateaubriand, added another 20,000. There was no longer any let or hindrance to their departure.

Before leaving Paris, Chateaubriand saw once again the cruel Hortense Allart, who—for two years—had so neglected him. As of old, after a stroll in the Jardin des Plantes they dined at the Arc-en-Ciel, in the private room that Chateaubriand called their cell and, once again, she allowed him to "have his will." Next day he wrote to her: "You see your power; you have restored the charm of all those places where I no longer went. What a crazy fool I am! . . . I am ashamed of my weakness, but I succumb all too readily. I am leaving, if not happy, at least wearing life more lightly. Farewell . . . and my dearest love to Your Infidelity. Who would have believed that I should come to that? Farewell most fickle, deceiving and beloved witch."

As he was to reach Switzerland before Mme. de Chateaubriand, he begged Hortense to join him there. "You will announce your coming as that of a faery. Tempests and snows, the loveliness and the unravished silence of the Alps will be a fit home for your mystery and for your magic. . . . I will give you more in a day than another could give you in long years." And, seasoned and disillusioned lover as he was, he sought to persuade the woman of letters by offering to listen among those alpine solitudes while she read him the novel she had just finished.

It was long since this passionate traveller had roamed the roads and mountains. Alone and free, with no definite goal, he took with him in a leather chest the papers he would need to work on his memoirs. Where should he make a stay? At Lugano? At Geneva? At Constance, where he had arranged to meet Mme. Récamier? He did not know. Hortense, crazy about Bulwer Lytton, who neglected her, and fully occupied in his pursuit, did not even reply to Chateaubriand's appeal and he soon found himself alone amid the Alpine peaks with his old age. In vain did the Lake of Lucerne recall the mere at Combourg, and the sound of chanting that drifted through the half open door of a chapel remind him of the litanies of his Breton home; in vain did the storm wind, as it had of old on the ocean or amid the seas of Greece, drench the paper on which he strove to write: "Readily would I paint Nature even yet, but why? Were I young, I should be solitary; being old, I am merely cut off. . . . How pitiful it is to drag across these mountains flagging steps that none is now fain to follow."

How he would once have revelled in these mountain storms and in the lightnings that struck against the rocks enfolding some hostelry in the St. Gothard; but, in his room, a second empty couch brought it home to the traveller that he had no more loves to lull asleep. Hortense was not come, nor any other, and he yielded himself to a meditation that is one of the loveliest and most lamenting he ever penned . . . the plaint of an old Don Juan: "These mountains, this storm, this dark are treasures lost to me. Yet what fierce pulse of life I still feel within my soul. . . . Never, when my heart's blood ran most hotly in my veins, did I speak the language of the passions with such vigour as now I could.

Meseems I descry my Sylph of the woods of Combourg gliding from the flanks of the Saint-Gothard. Art thou come to seek me again, fair phantom of my youth? Is it in pity of me? Thou seest I am not changed in aught save outward semblance; even now a dreamer of dreams, consumed by a fire that has nor source nor fuel.

"Come, sit thee down upon my knees; be not afraid of my grey hairs, caress them with the faery fingers of a shade that they may grow brown beneath thy kiss. This head, no sager for all its scanty locks, is still that same mad-cap as gave thee birth, first-born daughter of my air-drawn dreams, fair fruit of my mystic intercourse with my first solitude. . . . Come, together we will ride once more upon our clouds; we will go with the lightning to furrow, to illumine, yea to set afire the precipices where I shall pass tomorrow. Come. Bear me out of myself as of old, but bring me back no more. There is a knocking at my door; it is not thou. It is the guide. The horses are arrived and I must forth. Of this my dream there remain only the wind, the rain and I—unending dream and everlasting storm." As once the voyager on the Saint-Pierre, the pilgrim of the St. Gothard was "burdened with a superabundance of life," but now there was no Floridan eager to share his rapture. It was grim.

Next day he returned to Lucerne, still hoping that he might find news of Hortense's coming. Disappointed, he wrote her a reproachful letter: "It depended only on you to gaze with me upon those lonely heights of the Saint Gothard that must have proved an inspiration to your work. Far from the haunts of men, you would have read me your *Anglaise des Indes* as evening closed in upon the mountains. . . . Your excuse that a friend was leaving on Saturday is inadequate, as you very well know." It was hard to have been the man whom packs of jealous women once pursued with ardour and to find oneself alone at last, vainly offering to wholly indifferent young women hours they no longer cared to accept.

Happily there remained Mme. Récamier who, while he was awaiting Hortense, had quietly taken the road to Switzerland. For some weeks she too had been hesitant and anxious. Was it wise to break the magic circle of the Abbaye-aux-Bois to follow the

Towards the Grave

Enchanter into exile? Her friend Mme. de Boigne, who was always extremely sceptical where Chateaubriand was concerned, advised against it. "At our age it is so difficult to make life endurable that you should be wary of meddling where it has more or less settled down, above all when there is so little measure between what you give and what you receive." Mme. Récamier was aware of all that, but she felt that she was "drawn by fate." On the pretext of paying a visit to her friend Queen Hortense, she departed, leaving only the emptiness of loss to those in Paris from whom, as the gentle Ballanche was wont to say, "the Abbaye was the centre of the world, as the temple at Delphi had been for the Greeks."

Juliette and René met, therefore, on August 27th in the "tumble-down city" of Constance, where they lived in the same inn. "And the forest, have you forgotten?" Very likely the old lover urged the question eagerly and Juliette, the chaste, demurred. In the days of Chantilly she was only forty; here, in Constance, she was fifty-five, Chateaubriand sixty-four, and in the course of those fifteen years, thanks partly to his infidelities, love had turned to friendship. Nevertheless, it seems that on this evening she yielded once more to the Enchanter's spells. "M. de Chateaubriand," she wrote to a friend, "has been altogether lovable during his short stay in Constance." There is languor in the phrase and a kind of veiled gratification.

Next day they went for a wonderful sail on the lake. They landed in a park where they found gravelled walks along which to stroll aimlessly, then sat down on a bench by the water's side; from the shady groves there rose the sound of harps and viols; it was like a world of faery. There Chateaubriand read aloud the pages he had written among the mountains and their sadness, the intensity of their emotion made Mme. Récamier afraid. The temperate regions of her mind knew nothing of these burning storms; she dreaded them and sought to lead her friend to calmer thoughts. Handing him her tablets, she begged him to write a few lines in memory of this enchanted day. On the same page she had noted the last words of Rousseau as he lay dying: "Wife, open the window that I may once more see the sun." Chateaubriand wrote: "What I sought by the Lake of Lucerne, I have found by the

Lake of Constance: charm, intelligence and beauty. I have no wish to die as Rousseau; I want to see the sun for many a long year yet, if it is near your side that my life is destined to end. May its days ebb away at your feet, like those waves whose murmurings you love to hear. August 28th 1832." She alone among women could breathe into this exacting, fickle and untamed soul serenity, healing and a feeling for perfection.[1]

On their return to Constance they found Queen Hortense and her son Louis-Napoleon, who invited Chateaubriand to visit their castle of Arenenberg. The great legitimist got on admirably with the future Emperor of the French. Shortly afterwards they exchanged letters. "Whatever is Napoleonic," wrote Louis-Napoleon perspicaciously "finds an echo in your soul." "We meet," replied Chateaubriand, "in a common sympathy. You, with your youth, as I, with the evening of my days, desire the honour of France. . . . Ah! Monsieur, where is your uncle? Of others than yourself I would ask: Where is the guardian of kings and the master of Europe? Even while I defend the cause of legitimacy I have no illusions, but I believe that every man who cares for the esteem of the public must remain faithful to his oaths." And again: "You know, Prince, that my young king is in Scotland, that so long as he lives there can be no other king of France for me. But were God, in his impenetrable wisdom, to set aside the race of Saint Louis, were the customs of our country not such as to make a republican state possible, there is no name which better befits the glory of France than yours." He must have delighted to hover, as a final and spiritual arbiter, over the strife of dynasties in France.

Geneva. Again he found himself confronted with the sharp countenance of Mme. de Chateaubriand and again took to speaking of death, "which he had always singularly loved." However, when he began working on his *Mémoires*, he soon forgot his present ills. He raised the columns and the capitals of his building and promised himself that, as soon as the bulk of his work was finished and there was no further need to drag masses of material

---

[1] On the visit to Constance see Henry Bordeaux: *Amour ou amitié* and Maurice Levaillant, *op. cit.*

about with him, he would go and paint his interiors in Italy. Even Hortense, who was inflaming him once more, could not wean him from his beloved work. "I am making ready my tomb as the couch that is never betrayed by the faithless.... You talk of power and love. All that is over. I am keeping for myself alone the remainder of a life for which none has further use and which I desire to give no one."

However, he went for long and pleasant walks with Mme. Récamier, who had come to join the household at Geneva. One autumn day they went on pilgrimage together to Coppet. There stood the tomb of Mme. de Staël, at whose house they had first met; there Prince Augustus of Prussia had wooed Juliette, in rivalry with the passionate friendship of Corinne. While Mme. Récamier went to take new farewell of her friend's ashes, Chateaubriand, seated on a bench by the lake, mused on Rousseau and Byron, who had watched the same shores as he. When, pale and lovely, Mme. Récamier reappeared at the gates of Coppet, she seemed to him a shade risen from the grove of death. That evening Juliette and René talked long of "those aching and unforgotten days when passion is at once the bliss and torment of youth." When he went home, he made this note: "Now at the midnight hour, as I write this page while all about me is hushed and beyond my window I can see a few stars twinkling above the Alps, it seems to me that all that ever I have loved I have loved in Juliette, that she has been the hidden spring of all my tenderness, that, whether with true love or flighty, it was she alone whom I loved.... Her sway has brought ardor into my emotions as Mme. de Chateaubriand has brought order and peace into my duties." The Sylph, for an evening's space, had taken mortal flesh.

A little later, in October, Mme. Récamier left Geneva for Paris. He was wondering how he could follow her without laying himself open to ridicule when, on November 12th, he heard that the Duchesse de Berry had just been arrested at Nantes. He wrote at once to the princess to say that he desired to be her defender, sent copies of the letter to all the papers and set off for France. "No-one," said the cruel Mme. de Boigne, "was more delighted by Mme. la Duchesse de Berry's arrest than M. de Chateaubriand. . . . He was dying of boredom and could think of no way to come back. . . . He welcomed the Nantes arrest as the star of salvation."

2. THE LAST EMBASSY

Mme. de Boigne was as clear-sighted as she was spiteful. The imprisonment of the duchess gave Chateaubriand an opportunity to prove his courage and that in the most dramatic manner; it was the kind of thing he enjoyed and he did not let so fine a chance slip. To an admiring Mme. Récamier and a sarcastic Mme. de Boigne he read an *Hymne aux Vertus maternelles de Marie-Caroline*, and his own eloquence brought real tears to his eyes. Once again the Enchanter was caught in his own spells. "Your Highness, illustrious prisoner of Blaye, may your present heroism, in a land which is a judge of heroism, lead France to reiterate that which my political independence has given me the right to say: your son is my king." The sentence was terse, brilliant and moving; it became instantly famous. His enemies made fun of it. "M. de Chateaubriand," said Hugo, "has a self which he calls Henry V." And again, "What is Henry V to M. de Chateaubriand? An opportunity for style." Bands of young men nevertheless stationed themselves under Chateaubriand's windows crying, "Your son is my king." Suddenly—just as the prisoner's cause was making great strides in public opinion—there broke out an unpleasant and alarming scandal: the Duchesse de Berry, who had long been a widow, was with child.

Louis-Philippe's government covered itself with shame in outraging the modesty of one of his relations by forcing her to be brought to bed in the presence of her gaolers, but it thus succeeded in disqualifying the dangerous amazon and establishing strained relations between her and Charles X. Charles was now in Prague as the guest of the Emperor of Austria. In May 1833 the duchess entrusted Chateaubriand with the mission of going to Bohemia to explain to the royal family that she was secretly married to the Comte Lucchesi-Palli, to obtain the recognition of the marriage, the continuance of her title as a French princess and the right to see her children. He consented, for the mission seemed to him a worthy crown to his political life. "Yes, I shall depart on the last and greatest of my embassies, I shall go, on behalf of the prisoner of Blaye, to seek the prisoner of the Temple." Immediately he ordered Talleyrand's barouche to be made ready. "It was not accustomed," said he proudly, "to trot after fallen kings."

This journey across Europe, with none but Pilorge for company, gave him great pleasure. At every police post where customs officers examined his passport he was conscious of the radiance of his glory and delighted in its dazzling renown. German girls, wild flowers of whom he caught a glimpse at the edge of the fields as he drove by, flushed beneath the hot gaze of the old traveller. The moon, one of his oldest friends, herself went with him and it seemed as though she said: "Ah, there you are. . . . Whither away alone and so late? Are you not afraid of beginning your career over again?" At the castle of Prague, majestic and empty on its lofty heights, he felt as though he were again wandering in the awe-inspiring monastery of the Escurial. Charles X gave him a friendly welcome: "Good morning, good morning, M. de Chateaubriand, I am delighted to see you. . . ." The ambassador had been ready with daring remonstrances, but—confronted with this white-haired old man, who leant towards him with his good ear and said: "But my dear fellow, I have no grudge against anyone; everyone behaves as he sees fit"—tears sprang to his eyes.

The royal children were charming. Henry V was shy; his sister, Mademoiselle, chattered away: "Grandpapa said to us: 'Guess whom you are going to see tomorrow—he is a power in the land.' We replied: 'Then it must be the Emperor.' 'No,' said grandpapa. We thought and thought but we couldn't guess. He said: 'It is the Vicomte de Chateaubriand.' I beat my brow for not having guessed." The traveller was as old as a grandfather and as royalist as his Breton people. He was touched, but he disliked the little court at Prague.

The Dauphin, a straightforward but somewhat churlish person, thought himself dishonoured by the abdication and would see no one. The Dauphine, whom he saw at Carlsbad, was embroidering a length of tapestry. He was struck by the likeness between the princess's profile and that of her father, Louis XVI. She listened coldly to Chateaubriand's plea for the Duchesse de Berry. The Duchesse d'Angoulême had little love for her sister-in-law and felt towards Chateaubriand "the prejudices of the flock of hangers-on among whom she lived." In vain did he try to explain his policy: "Had I rejected the beliefs of the age, I should have had no grip on the minds of my contemporaries. I am striving to rally to the ancient throne those modern ideas which, from being adverse, grow friendly as they filter through my fidelity."

He left, having gained nothing but a frosty note and this ambiguous remark: "I am heartily sorry for my sister-in-law." However, despite the failure of his embassy, his mood remained triumphant. From this journey the artist was to draw two fine books of his *Mémoires*; he was aware of it and rejoiced beforehand. Throughout the return journey he continued to gaze at young girls with strangely passionate attention. When he reached Paris he failed to find the Duchesse de Berry, whom the government had shipped off to Italy. Before long, she sent for him and her summons was the occasion of a new journey in September. On this occasion M. de Talleyrand's barouche crossed the Simplon. The lover of mournful pilgrimages made a point of passing through Bex, where the Queen of Roses died, and Verona, where he called the roll of the kings and ministers he had known for the pleasure of answering after every name: "Dead." Venice, which held no appeal for him in 1806, was now full of the glamour of Childe Harold. He wrote to Mme. Récamier that "despite his extreme weariness he could not but be sensible of the sad beauty of so lovely and desolate a city." He went to the Lido to gaze out on the lonely sea by whose margin Lord Byron had ridden. Once again he looked on his faithful companions the waves which, "like young girls dancing in a ring, had surrounded his birth." Seated on the sand he yielded to "the whims of the age nearest the cradle." "I wrote a name on the ribbed sand just where the last wave came to die in foam. Slowly, one after another the breakers attacked the name that was my solace; it was only with their sixteenth ebb that they carried it out to sea, letter by letter as if in regret. I felt as though it were my life they washed away." What could the name of sixteen letters be, if not Juliette Récamier.

Meanwhile, the august princess whose orders he awaited sent for him to Ferrara. She asked him to escort her to Prague, where she dared not go alone. "*One* would not take the great journey without me. . . . *One* besought me to crown my work of reconciliation. That so much unhappiness, courage and fallen greatness should take refuge in my frail life overcame my resistance. . . . *One* insisted and I could only obey." They set off; Metternich's police arrested the duchess almost as soon as she started and Chateaubriand continued alone on a journey that was as vain as the first. "The journey has strengthened my doubts. I can do nothing for all these people. Prague outlaws Blaye, and I—a poor servant—am obliged to use my small authority to raise the hateful ban." He was disheartened, weary and resolved that, for the future, he would concern himself only with his own work. "I will serve no longer," said he, and this time he was sincere. Shortsighted ambitions were dead in him since he had found ones more lasting and he was determined, before he died, to fashion for the generations to come the Chateaubriand of the *Mémoires*.

3. OLD FOLK

1835. In his house in the Rue d'Enfer, next door to the nuns' infirmary, Chateaubriand felt as though he were living in a monastery. "In the morning, I am wakened by the sound of the Angelus. From my bed I can hear the chanting of the priests in the chapel; from my window I see a calvary that rises between a walnut and an elder tree, cows, chickens, pigeons and bees. Sisters of Charity in black frieze robes and white dimity coifs, convalescent women and aged ecclesiastics go wandering about the lawns among the lilacs, the azaleas, the spice trees and the rhododendrons, or among the rose bushes, the gooseberries, the strawberry beds and the vegetables in the kitchen garden. . . . From time to time there passes a procession which Mme. de Chateaubriand follows, telling her beads. Blackbirds whistle, warblers twitter, nightingales rival with the hymns. . . . From the theory of Christianity I have passed to its practice." With the stars that Mme. de Beaumont was wont to name, the evening brought back memories older yet. "When the constellations pierce the blue vault, I am reminded of that wondrous firmament at which I used to marvel in the heart of the American forests or on the bosom of the ocean."

In the eyes of the sisters at the infirmary, Mme. de Chateaubriand's husband was a strange and omnipotent person through whom they might obtain money and benefits for their patients. The Sister Superior knew that the greatest of ladies would bring their offerings if she promised to shew them a glimpse of M. de Chateaubriand. Fair legitimists were ready to pay their weight in gold for the stumps of pens she let them have, declaring that each of those precious relics had written the famous phrase: "Madam, your son is my king." The sisters manufactured a chocolate which was sold for the benefit of their work, and Victor Hugo describes a day in the period of his poverty when, going timidly to see Mme. de Chateaubriand, who usually gave him a cool reception, he was amazed to find himself greeted with a smile.

"It was the first time she deigned even to seem aware of my existence. I bowed to the ground. She rejoined 'I am delighted to see you.' I couldn't believe my ears. Then she pointed to a heap on a little table and added: 'I kept this for you. I thought you might like it. You know what it is?' It was a nuns' chocolate, the sale of which she patronised for the benefit of her charities. I took it and paid. The Catholic chocolate and Mme. de Chateaubriand's smile cost me twenty francs, that is to say a week's food. It was the dearest woman's smile ever sold me." But Victor Hugo was unaware that Mme. de Chateaubriand had herself spent more than a fortune on her sick.

In 1838 the Archbishop of Paris, to whom the Chateaubriands had presented the infirmary in 1827, offered to buy the house in the Rue d'Enfer if Mme. de Chateaubriand would give up the direction of the good work. She hesitated for a long time. Her husband begged her to agree. "Hold out against the infirmary; now you'll live a hundred thousand years. Be ready to meet the Archbishop's wishes. Don't grumble or indulge in recriminations." There were three good reasons for which he desired the change—the sale would provide them with a little ready money, his wife's health would benefit by a rest and a move would allow of his living nearer the Abbaye-aux-Bois, whither he went every afternoon.

He did indeed find at 112 Rue du Bac a ground-floor apartment which looked on the gardens of the Foreign Missions. "I am dying with joy at our future arrangements," he wrote to Mme. Récamier, "and at being no more than ten minutes from your door." From that day until his death, there was no further change in the background of his life. After the gilded drawing-rooms, the ministries and the embassies, he had no regret in reverting to the country simplicity of his childhood and, now that he was grown old, and his life was drawing to its close, this Don Juan practised the austerities of a hermit. In his little cell there was no furniture save an iron bed, a table covered with books and papers, another smaller table near the fire, a straw-bottomed chair and a deal box with a broken lock that contained the manuscript of the *Mémoires*. On the wall were a crucifix, a blessed palm and a Madonna, after Mignard, bequeathed him by poor Claire de Duras.

Every morning he rose with the sound of the Angelus, as in the days of Combourg, slipped his feet into down-at-heel slippers, threw on a shabby greatcoat and sat down to work. Later there would appear a secretary to whom he dictated the pages he had just thought out as he walked to and fro in the room. Until 1843 this secretary was the vulgar but devoted Hyacinthe Pilorge, the red-whiskered Breton. In that year Pilorge was dismissed for some mysterious fault and his place taken by the pale-faced Danielo, a failure who, though not without talent, was conceited and lamented leaving his own "vast new studies" in order to act as a literary crutch to the old writer. Chateaubriand's whole morning was divided between meditation and dictation; at its close he lunched and made his toilet.

For long he remained an old beau, tightly buttoned in his "graceful cut-away coat" royal-blue, black or chestnut brown, gloved, gaitered, a flower in his buttonhole, a slim ebony cane in his hand, "his fine eyes still sparkling with fire beneath their thick lashes." At the appointed hour, never changing his route, he set off for the Abbaye-aux-Bois where he arrived shortly after half-past two, went upstairs to Mme. Récamier's apartment and remained alone with her till about four o'clock.

What did they find to say to each other between the portrait of Mme. de Staël and the view of Coppet by moonlight, in the course of those mysterious, entrancing and forbidden moments that were "M. de Chateaubriand's hour"? Hardly anything. "Will you have some tea, M. de Chateaubriand?" For ten years he had answered, "Yes. After you, Madame." "Shall I add a little milk?" "Just a few drops." "May I give you a second cup?" "I cannot allow you to take so much trouble." And so on. Yet it may be that, on this particular day, an eyewitness had frightened away more intimate conversation—besides, what need had they of words? He was content in that harmonious presence; he gazed at the face that had been full of glad grace and was beautiful even yet; he listened to that voice which, said Lamartine, "tinkled against her teeth like the notes of an ivory keyboard softened by her lips," that voice "whose timbre spoke of itself." It was like "a soul diffused through the air, that caressed you with its waves."

With her marvellous sweetness, her wise discretion, Juliette Récamier had become altogether necessary to him. "Never speak of what would become of me without you," he wrote to her. "If you should ask me, I could not tell." If ever she went away he felt lost: "I no longer know what to do; reft of its beauty, Paris is a desert. . . . Come back and be near me; I miss you too intolerably; your absence depresses me so that I cannot even write. I have no strength to do anything and can only await a brief word from you to help me to go on living."

What could the Rue du Bac think of this devotion to the Abbaye-aux-Bois? It was not easy to know, for the Rue du Bac was secret, witty and mocking. There were times when the legal wife complained of the Egeria, and Chateaubriand had to beg Mme. Récamier to pay more friendly visits to Mme. de Chateaubriand. "What do you expect? Since you are bound up with my life, you must needs share it wholly." Old age had changed the child with the pink pelisse into the oddest of old fairies. Titania, at sixty, no longer fed on dew, but a few syrups, herb-teas or soups were enough to keep her alive. In the morning she would work in bed, in a white dressing-grown, surrounded by prayer-books, rosaries and scraps of sewing that she unearthed heaven knew where. "She has," said her husband, "arsenals unknown to us and reading matter of her own." She had always loved writing and was still in the habit of jotting down reflexions in her notebook—some of them very pleasing: "I always hear talk of the insolence of the mob, but I am struck only by its patience. . . . The only flattery for which we care is that which is refused us. . . . After the ladies who do not go in for good works, I know nothing worse than the ladies who do go in for good works."

Her conversation was still brilliant and original. "It was impossible," wrote the secretary Danielo, "it was impossible, when she was in the mood, to hear anything more piquant and attractive. It was gossamer, it was a little carillon, it was a prism." Victor Hugo, as we know, was less kindly in his judgment. "Mme. de Chateaubriand," said he, "had a formal goodness which in no way interfered with her shrewishness at home. She visited the poor, looked after crèches, cared for the sick, yet—at the same time—she bullied her husband, her relations and her servants, and was stiff, prudish, sharp-tongued and bitter. God will weigh all that in heaven."

Hugo and Danielo were probably both right. Wit and shrewishness do not go badly paired. Danielo himself admits that she was not easy to live with, that her husband was afraid of her and that, if she attacked him, he yawned without replying. As do many people who feel themselves neglected, she delighted to rouse his indifference: "You are reputed to be a great man; I make no claim to being a great woman; it isn't fine phrases I want, it's sound reasoning. I reason well myself."

"Indeed you do, my dear," said he, "indeed you do." "He was," adds Danielo, "a pattern of husbands, a hero of conjugal patience and peace at home. I believe he would have given anything, even his renown, to avoid a fuss." He had always been the same, with his sisters, with Fontanes and with Villèle. As for his wife, he loved her in his own way. In fifty years she had become a habit, and he was far from disliking the order and unity she brought into his life. When she cut bread for her little birds in a great leather basin, he looked tenderly at her and called her the "crumb fairy."

Occasionally she was snappish, especially with Mme. Récamier, but she blamed herself afterwards: "Alas! It's a sin I did not carry very far. Do you know how that dear woman avenged herself for my abuse? By sending me a thousand francs to open the subscription I am raising to send Mlle. Lemonnier to the alms house." The unfailing rightness of Mme. Récamier's behaviour could steal away even the most closely guarded hearts.

Mme. de Chateaubriand and Mme. Récamier had, moreover, at

least one interest in common, that of fending off from a gallant and illustrious old age the marauders of renown. "It is the punishment of those who have loved women too dearly to love them always." Often he would set out on mysterious wanderings in Paris and, always with his flower in his buttonhole, would visit ladies eager to be kind. "His day had its times and places as fixed as the signs of the sun." In society he was ever ready to pay graceful and charming compliments to the women he thought attractive. Meeting Rachel at Mme. Récamier's house he said to her: "How sad it is to see anyone such as you come into being just when one is about to die!" "But Monsieur le Vicomte," replied she, "there are men who do not die." And to Delphine de Girardin: "I have never been so tempted in my life. . . . It needs all my forty years of virtue to resist the double attack of your beauty and your wit."

Of the women he had greatly loved, the only one yet living (Natalie de Noailles having died in a nursing home in the Rue du Rocher in 1835) was Mme. de Castellane. But the fiery, delicate Cordélia had turned into a serious and dumpy person whose liaison with Molé had become respectable and respected. Chateaubriand rarely saw her, but now and again he would go walking with Hortense Allart, sit down on a bench at her side and talk of his death for the pleasure of seeing the young woman's eyes fill with tears. His tender friendliness would charm and touch her for, notwithstanding his melancholy, he still had all his old grace and "that distinction, that loftiness of soul, which made him so attractive as a man." To Mme. Hamelin, the fair fashion-plate, he wrote: "I am now old and shrunken. If we should chance to meet, you would not recognise me. Farewell, or goodbye, as you will. Love me always as you did when you used to fetch me from the Ministry for Foreign Affairs. The time has come for me to seek, in some remote corner of the earth, the chief concern of all men." Nevertheless, that concern and even the image of death itself in no way hindered him from taking an interest in passing strangers. "A Louisianian has arrived from the Mississippi. I thought it was the Madonna of Last Loves that I beheld." He was still swift to clothe his withered years with the April poetry of his youth.

In the evening, as he never went into society, he returned home, there to fall into the power of Mme. de Chateaubriand who, now that her turn had come round, made him dine with old royalists, with famous preachers, bishops and archbishops. Until further orders, that is to say till next morning, he became the author of *Le Génie du Christianisme* once more. "The sun rose more brightly; he pricked a flower in his buttonhole, let himself out by the garden gate, and from one o'clock till six in the evening, recaptured joy, liberty, freedom from care, coquetry, a conquering mood and the certainty of victory. Thus did he spend his declining years and as far as in him lay outwit old age."[1]

Relations with the exiled Bourbons remained strained. His ideas found little favour, his books gave scandal and his devotion was felt as wearisome. The Duchesse d'Angoulême thought herself mortally offended by a wholly innocent sentence in the *Congrès de Vérone*. Only young Henry V, now created Comte de Chambord, a young man of sense and sensibility, forgot the grudges of the bygone court. In 1842 he sent to offer Chateaubriand his pension as a peer—an offer gratefully accepted—and, in the following year, when the prince was going to London to receive the French legitimists, he invited Chateaubriand there.

Yet again, and for the last time, the latter was to see the city where he had once lived in poverty and afterwards in pomp. During the crossing, which was long and stormy, this old friend and companion of the winds had the joy of encountering his last tempest. He slept on deck and urged his fellow-passengers to do likewise. "M. le Vicomte," said one, "you would pass for Chactas." "Yes," replied he, "and almost for Atala." Before the coming of the prince, who was then in Scotland, he roamed places which, for him, were steeped in memory and emotion, and dictated fine letters to Mme. Récamier. "I went to walk off my sadness in Kensington, where you too used to roam as the loveliest of Frenchwomen. Once again I saw the trees under which René first appeared to me: this resurrection of my dreams amidst the sad realities of life was a strange experience. Then, when I fell a-dreaming my youth was before me and I could journey towards the unknown goal of my search. Now I cannot take a single stride but I must

[1] Sainte-Beuve.

touch the post. Oh! how glad I should be to sleep, my last dream being for you!"

Again: "Pray tell all my friends that my feelings for them have in no way changed and that when the curtain goes down on the last act of my life, when I make my exit from the play which began for me in this country fifty years ago, everything will still be the same: the setting is more or less like, only the scene-shifters have changed." From his youth up he had regarded the world as a theatre and life as a play staged by a divine manager; the image obsessed him yet.

Henry V had the delicacy to provide a fine setting for the last act. He installed Chateaubriand in his own house in Belgrave Square and, on the day when he received the French legitimists, would not allow the great writer to remain standing in his presence. "M. de Chateaubriand, I beg you be seated so that I may lean on you." The young king seemed even to accept the liberal doctrines with which his family had so long reproached the author of *La Monarchie selon la Charte*. "If ever my thoughts have turned to the throne of my ancestors, it has been only in the hope that it might be granted me to serve my country with those principles and feelings so nobly expressed by M. de Chateaubriand."

Yet once again, in the following year, Henry V desired to see him. It was in Venice. Chateaubriand would have liked to drag Mme. Récamier with him: "That is where we must meet our end, in a city that belongs to us. We shall encounter no opposition to the scheme from the Rue du Bac. Hence you must harvest your strength and your courage." But neither the Rue du Bac nor the Abbaye-aux-Bois had enough energy left to traverse France and Italy. He set off alone, saw his young king once more, decided to return by ship for the pleasure of breathing the tang of the open sea, and was welcomed at Marseilles and afterwards at Avignon by enthusiastic crowds. Glory was more faithful than youth.

4. Work

He had himself divided his life into three parts: the Traveller and the Soldier, the Man of Letters, the Man of Action. No doubt he regarded as negligible a fourth period, which was yet as long as the other three, that of old age and of the "hours for which none had any further use." He was wrong, for in that old age the man of letters brought forth a second flowering and these autumnal roses were perhaps the fairest of all.

In the closing books of the *Mémoires* and in the *Vie de Rancé*, the works of those despised years, he achieves a freedom of style and a daring in the choice of words and the piling-up of images which he was far from attaining in the time of *Le Génie du Christianisme* or of *Les Martyrs*. Attentive to the works of his great contemporaries, Hugo, Lamartine, Sainte-Beuve, incapable of reading them carefully, but skilled in skimming through their books to breathe the new fragrance, he wished not only to imitate, but to surpass them. He succeeded. The style of the *Vie de Rancé* is more modern than that of either *Les Misérables* or *L'Histoire des Girondins*. Chateaubriand's methods of evocation are already those of Proust. His language is more original and richer than ever. In these his last works, he is not only the first of the great romantics, but one of the great French writers of all time.

Granted that in the course of these dreary years his poverty drove him to accept hack work for publishers—he had to live. A translation of Milton, though made with care and "that conscientiousness which he put into everything," was too impersonal an undertaking for a mind of his quality. An *Essai sur la littérature anglaise* seems to have been frankly bad, at least in its general outline. Chateaubriand had thrown into it fragments of memoirs, translations and even a long passage on love letters which he afterwards used in his *Vie de Rancé*. Some of the pages are beautiful, but—put together—they do not make a book. Chateaubriand's opinions on Byron should, however, be read with care, for Byron was steeped in Chateaubriand. As early as the publication of *Atala*, he wrote to the author; all his life he imitated his attitudes, followed in his footsteps as a traveller and borrowed even his imagery. Of all the French writers Byron loved, Chateaubriand was the only one whom he never named either in his journal or in his verse, perhaps because he was fain to banish an untimely ghost. The *Essai* proves that Chateaubriand was by no means unaware of this unconfessed sonship and that he bore no grudge, clearly as he saw the position.

His chief labour during this period was the final revision of the *Mémoires*. Chateaubriand was anxious that future generations should see in them all the splendour of a work of perfect beauty. It was through them he counted to live on after death. Even in 1830 he realised that *Le Génie du Christianisme* and *Les Martyrs* would soon be, not forgotten, but neglected, and quoted rather than really read. His *Histoire de France*, which might have been a great book, had been scamped by force of circumstances and so done harm to the dissertations preceding it. The short novel of *René* alone dominated his work "like a lonely and lofty tower." It was not enough and, after the revolution of 1830, he realised that only through the *Mémoires* would he have a chance of impressing himself on coming generations. It was therefore vital that the *Mémoires* should be unassailable.

It may be remembered that they had been begun in 1809 at the Valley of Wolves and taken up again for Juliette Récamier one day when an ousel, singing in the park of Montboissier, called up memories of Combourg. He had worked on them both in Berlin and London; in 1830 the manuscript formed twelve books, twelve portfolios that contained the story of his youth. There now came to him a vaster project, that of linking the history of his own life with that of his country and of his age, of translating his autobiography to epic. It was a great design and a fine one, but would he have time to carry it out? In July 1831 he wrote to Jean-Jacques Ampère: "At your age, Monsieur, a man must take thought for his life; at mine he must take thought for his death. The future beyond the tomb is the youth of the hoary-headed. I want to make rather better use of that second youth than ever I did of the first."

Hence, from 1830 to 1833, he wrote, corrected and polished. He was determined not to publish his book until after his death. At that time fifty years seemed to him a decent interval. Only, he needed money and what likelihood was there that a publisher would make an advance on so distant a venture? "Many of my friends have urged me to publish part of my history here and now. I have not felt able to yield to their wishes. To begin with, I should—in spite of myself—be less outspoken and trustworthy. Further I have always, in imagination, written from my grave; hence the work has assumed a kind of religious character which I could not efface without spoiling it; it would cost me something to stifle that far-off voice from the tomb which is heard through the whole course of the narrative."

Possibly, however, the delay might be shortened and publishers' curiosity aroused. It was to give a fillip to such curiosity that in 1834 Mme. Récamier, with her usual skill, organised readings in her drawing-room. The guests were few, but in a position—through their ramifications with various worlds—to spread the fame of the work: society people such as Sosthène de La Rochefoucauld and Adrien de Montmorency-Laval; friends of the house such as Ballanche and Jean-Jacques Ampère; writers such as Sainte-Beuve and Edgar Quinet; an ecclesiastic, the Abbé Gerbet; two women. . . . "The reading was a triumph," says Nisard. "Those who had been of the party described it to those of us who had not and we grieved that the salon of Mme. Récamier, a woman renowned for her gracious goodness, was not as large as the plain of Sunium." Every review and every newspaper went to beg of the illustrious writer a few fragments of the *Mémoires*, which appeared on their pages framed in laudatory articles.

These articles were afterwards collected in a book which was not sold, but given away to subscribers to the Collected Works in order to fire them with the desire of possessing the *Mémoires d'Outre-Tombe*.[1] From the time of *Le Génie du Christianisme*, Chateaubriand had proved himself skilled in launching his works. On this occasion such writers as Nisard, Sainte-Beuve and Villemain were allowed to skim through the manuscript of the *Mémoires* as a dark secret. Chateaubriand himself sat at the reader's side. If the latter happened to smile at a jest or shiver at some passage eloquent with feeling, the author—smiling with modest content—asked what had struck him. "You are most kind," said he, "I am very glad you like it," and other little civilities of the kind. Such conversations usually bore fruit in a fine article. Those of Jules Janin and Sainte-Beuve are famous.

"In that narrow drawing-room," wrote Sainte-Beuve, "which was scantily and nobly enough filled to make one proud of being in the circle of the elect, it was impossible, in the intervals and even during the reading—not to lose myself in memories. This huge picture, which takes up all the further wall and lightens it,

[1] *Lectures des Mémoires de M. de Chateaubriand.* (Lefèvre, editeur 1834).

is *Corinne at Cape Miseno*; it is thus that the remembrance of a famous friendship fills and illumines a whole life. . . . Oh! how welcome were such fine confidences in the simple yet ornate frame in which they were tried out! How the delicate composition of this art—whose secret must enter into every ideal enjoyment—intensified the effect of sincerity and completed the harmony of feeling! The great poet did not read himself; he may have feared for the throbbing of his heart and the emotion in his voice when he reached certain passages. But, if one lost a certain note of mystery by not hearing him, he was the better seen; across his strong features the reading was reflected like the wandering shadows of clouds across the tree-tops in a forest."

After such a triumph, it was easy to find subscribers. The publisher Delloye founded a joint stock company to acquire the *Mémoires d'Outre-Tombe*. Both politicians and society people agreed to join. It was decided that there should be a capital of 800,000 francs divided into sixteen hundred shares at 500 francs each. Chateaubriand was to receive an immediate payment of 156,000 francs and for the future, a yearly annuity of 12,000 francs, with reversion to Mme. de Chateaubriand. This was to be increased to 25,000 francs as soon as Chateaubriand delivered the part of the *Mémoires* that dealt with the Spanish war, since it could be published at once. It was a generous arrangement so far as it concerned Chateaubriand and one which ensured a carefree old age; nevertheless, he lamented it. "Since he has paid his debts, he is said to be like a fish out of water; to have his future mapped out and fixed seems to him a burden. In his presence, all the manuscript books of his *Mémoires* have been solemnly put under lock and key in an iron chest and deposited with a solicitor. He says that his thoughts have been imprisoned for debt in his stead."

Regarded as prisoners of a posthumous contract, his thoughts nevertheless remained singularly free. There could be no more daring anticipation than the conclusion of the *Mémoires*. Chateaubriand heralded socialism. "Too great a disproportion in wealth and condition could be endured so long as it was hidden; but the moment this disproportion became generally apparent, the mortal blow was struck." He realised that human societies were threatened by the progress of science: "Imagine hands condemned to idleness by reason of the multiplicity and variety of machines—What will you do with unemployed humanity? What will you do with the passions and the intelligence left without occupation?"

Having thus posed the problem of unemployment and leisure in its most modern form, he ventured yet further into the future. He half realised, as did Lamennais, that socialist equality could assert itself only through despotism and dictatorship, that the remedy would be worse than the ill, and that the abolition of personal property would lead to a slavery to which history "however far one delves into the past can shew nothing comparable." "Weary of private property, do you wish to make the government sole owner, distributing to a beggared community a share proportioned to the deserts of every individual? Who is to judge of those deserts? Who will have the power and authority to execute your decisions? Who is to hold this bank of living chattels and turn it to account? . . . Make no mistake, without individual property none are free. Property is none other than liberty."

Present injustice . . . Future tyranny. What is the solution to such a debate? Chateaubriand could see only one—the Christian solution. As a youth he believed in the *contrat social*; as a grown man he extolled liberal monarchy; in old age he hoped for no salvation save in Christianity. "My religious conviction has swallowed up every other conviction in its growth; here below there is no more believing Christian nor sceptical man than I."

The *Mémoires* were finished at last. But life went on interminably. With no human ore to crush, with no lofty periods to roll off his tongue, what was to be done with a yet vigorous instrument through the long course of a dread old age? The Abbé Seguin, Chateaubriand's director of conscience, was wise enough to set him a task—that of writing the life of the Abbé de Rancé who, in the seventeenth century, founded La Trappe. The work, which Chateaubriand began without enthusiasm, was to give him an opportunity for some of his greatest felicities of style. In this history of a man who left the world to enter into holiness, he found something that moved him. The material for the book was provided by earlier documents and biographies. Such conditions are favourable to a great stylist. On the firm framework imposed upon him he can place, with the scholarly daring of a taste that experience has made all but infallible, the most unexpected of ornament. The *Vie de Rancé* is sown with flashes of beauty: "Even Corneille was caught up by this ultramontane taste, but his mighty genius resisted: bereft of his Italian skull-cap, he had only the bald head that hovers over all. . . . In the shadow of the cloisters there was heard a rustle of papers and of dust: it was Mabillon arising. . . ." And the famous comment on Saint-Simon: "He scribbled for immortality."

The images are thick-coming, condensed and telescoped. "Bossuet rose upon La Trappe like the sun over a wild forest." Philosophy finds expression in dry aphorisms: "There is no more gratitude in history than in man." Constantly he made Rancé the excuse for speaking of Chateaubriand: "Long-vanished societies! How many others have succeeded you! There is dancing above the dust of the dead, and tombs arise beneath the steps of joy. We laugh and sing amidst the spots watered with the blood of our friends. Where are the ills of yesterday today? Where will our present bliss have fled tomorrow? What importance can we attach to the things of this world? Friendship? It disappears with the friend's rise to power. Love? It is betrayed, fleeting, or guilty. Renown? You must share it with mediocrity or crime. Fortune? Can such a trifle be regarded as a good? There remain the days, so-called happy, which flow by unnoted in the obscurity of domestic cares and which leave man neither the wish to lose life nor that of beginning it again."

And the fine passage on love letters in which there go by, silent and unseen, the ghosts of the Swallow and of the Lady of Fervacques: "At first the letters are long, intensely felt and thick-coming; daylight is not long enough: we write at sunset; we trace a few words by moonlight, bidding its chaste and silent haze to veil a myriad desires beneath its seemly cloak. With sunrise came parting; at sunrise we watch for the first gleam of day to write what we believe we left forgotten and unsaid. A thousand oaths cover the paper that flushes with the roses of the dawn; a thousand kisses are imprinted on the words that seem to be born of the sun's first glance; there is not an idea, an image, a dream, an accident, an anxiety, but has its letter.

Towards the Grave

"There comes a morning when, almost unperceived, something falls across the beauty of this passion like the first furrow on the brow of the beloved. The breath and fragrance of love die in the pages of youth's sweet-scented manuscript as a breeze at evening falls to sleep among the flowers; we are aware that something is changed, but will not admit it even to ourselves. Letters grow shorter and more few, they are filled with news, with descriptions, with outward things; some are late in coming, but we are no longer anxious; sure of loving and being loved, we have grown reasonable; we utter no reproaches, we submit to being parted. The oaths come flocking yet; the words are still the same, but they are dead; the soul is out; *I love you* is no longer aught but an accustomed phrase, an essential formality, the *I have the honour to be* of every love letter.

"Gradually the style freezes or grows sharp, post-day is no longer impatiently awaited; it is dreaded; writing becomes a weariness of the flesh. We blush to think of the follies we have confided to paper; gladly would we recover our letters and throw them on the fire. What has befallen? Is it that a new attachment is beginning, or that the old is drawing to its close? No matter: it is love dying before the beloved. We are forced to admit that man's feelings are exposed to the effect of a hidden activity—a seasonal fever that brings weariness, dispels illusion, undermines our passions and changes our hearts as it changes our hair and our years. There is, however, one exception to this infirmity in finite hearts; it sometimes happens that in a strong soul love endures long enough to grow transmuted to passionate friendship, to become a duty and to take on the qualities of virtue; then it loses the weakness of its nature and lives by its immortal spring."

In that last sentence Juliette herself invaded the *Vie de Rancé*. As for Chateaubriand, he was everywhere present. His loves, his repentance and his faith grew fused with the passions and regrets of his hero. With a quaint love of symmetry in the ordering of his life, he had dreamed of giving René, in his old age, "a hoary-headed and failing brother." The novel that he had sketched in a mood of delirious confession, and that he had given up writing for lack of strength and time, was now finely embodied in the form of a biography which, from many aspects, was rather an autobiography.

At last the *Rancé* was finished and published in its turn and—once again—Chateaubriand found his occupation gone, though he was still overwhelmed by his superabundance of life. He therefore prepared the book for a second edition; then—as death tarried—he took up the manuscript of the *Mémoires* once more and went in search of new harmonies. Even with his last breath he was to work. When, in the course of his cheerless days, this silent ghost, this being already numbered by the sleep of the tomb, recaptured a few brief moments of lucidity, he gave them to his manuscript. All had suffered ship wreck with the ship—vigour, understanding, intellect—but, amidst the wreckage of a person, one thing survived, the conscience of a sound literary craftsman. Here and there, with a trembling and paralysed hand, he erased some word that he thought too old-fashioned, tried the effect of a more daring epithet, did away with a repetition, crossed out too highly-coloured a phrase. Not till May 29th, 1847, did he send M. Mantaroux-Vertamy, his literary executor, the final manuscript of the *Mémoires*. On the first page he had written: "Revised. Chateaubriand."

5. The Disparity of Days

There are bodies which keep all the attributes of life to the day of their death; some old ages are Dionysian; Chateaubriand's was all bloom. In 1846 he had his collar-bone broken in a slight carriage accident. Such a mishap, which is a mere episode in the life of a young man, becomes an epilogue in the life of the old. From that moment he began to fail pitiably. A pamphleteer of the time, jesting at the old master's coquetry from beyond the tomb, said that the title page of his Collected Works should bear the inscription: *"Quotidie morior*—I die daily." The irony was superfluous. Crippled with rheumatism, unable—towards the end—to leave his chair, forced—like his old father before him—to steady his paralysed hand with his serviceable arm, Chateaubriand, for many a year, did indeed die daily.

Conscious of his decrepitude, he suffered when—at Mme. Récamier's—he had to be carried to the fireside and the other guests turned considerately away. He no longer went to the French Academy unless it were essential that he should vote for some old friend such as Ballanche; he did not wish, he said, "that they should see him creeping to his bench." Mme. Récamier herself was losing her sight and those who met him at her house thought, as they looked sadly at the two great shades, of those ghosts, described by Chateaubriand, in his *Vie de Rancé*, who—before the sunrise—talk over old, unhappy far-off things amid the tombs.

It was as a ghost that he thought of himself. "It was doubtless by mistake, monsieur," he wrote to a correspondent, "that you were told I inhabited this earth." In 1846 Eugène Manuel, a young student at the École Normale, went to see him with a friend. The visitors gazed in amazement at those "sparse white hairs, that mouth twisted in an enigmatic smile, that thin and shrunken body— that outward man, most human and most mortal, already leaning on the verge of the tomb." It was January 1st and the garden of the Rue du Bac was sprinkled with snow. "You are looking at the snow," said he, "it reminds me of the lonely spaces of the New World. In what countries, beneath what skies, have I not begun and ended the year?" Then, as he did to all alike, he spoke of his death. His sarcastic ill-humour saddened them. They were particularly disappointed to see a comic paper, *Charivari*, open upon their great man's table. "One cheers oneself up as best one can," he said.

More painful still was the visit of a young couple whom he welcomed at first with the exquisite courtesy of an old nobleman, "finding delicate phrases of compliment to the newly-married pair." Then, suddenly forgetting his guests and gazing into space, he began softly to hum this strange refrain—the last one would have expected on his lips: "The little pigs . . . And we eat the little pigs . . ." The visitors were completely taken aback and kept a stricken silence.

Sainte-Beuve, whose feelings for him were compounded of admiration, irritation, jealousy, prudence; perspicacity and pity, thought to pay his last homage by no longer going to seek the sight of such a fall. "M. de Chateaubriand says never a word," he noted in December 1847; "in these days no one can get a sound out of him. Béranger claims that when he goes there he can get him to talk for a quarter of an hour or twenty minutes, but—as

Thiers justly remarks—when Béranger has been talking to someone, he imagines that that someone was talking with him."

Now and again, however, a flame yet flickered from that dead-seeming hearth. When his Westerner, Léontine de Villeneuve, now Mme. de Castelbajac, came to see him with her husband, she found him "warming himself at once by the flame of a little fire and by a gleam of sunshine." He stretched out both hands to her: "It's you." And when the time came for her to say goodbye: "I have loved you well," said he. Raising his eyes, he added hurriedly: "I love you still." He could not keep his tears from flowing. Children, as well as women, sometimes aroused the life in him. He would be seen making painful efforts to kneel and play with one of them. One of his great-nephews, when brought to see him, sang the ballad from *La Dernier Abencérage*, and his tuneless voice made Chateaubriand laugh so much that he dropped the cup of chocolate he was holding.

"A hearth choked by ashes." Behind that flushed face, beneath that crown of silver hair that stood out on both sides in white and impish wisps, there yet brooded sombre and fiery thoughts. Between the man of desire and the man of faith the struggle was not yet at an end. True, he had plumbed the emptiness of the passions. Love? Vainly had he sought among the race of womankind that Eve, sprung from his side, to whom his youth had called. Friendship? It disappears when the beloved falls into misfortune or when the lover rises to power. Fortune? "I have no further concern with the affairs of this base earth. I have seen politics at too close quarters. . . . I no longer believe in anything, I have no more regard for anything, I am content to have been the unrepentant dupe of two or three noble ideas: liberty, fidelity, honour." But can he really be called a dupe when he was it so consciously?

Amid that mounting tide of disillusion, in that twilight of dreams and visions, only a few peaks yet emerged. The highest, the utmost refuge of this drifting soul, the one hope of the despairer, was Christianity. Those who had witnessed his life as a sinner might long have been dubious of the sincerity of his faith. In childhood, it had been ingenuous, in youth—at the time of *Le Génie du Christiansme*—asthetic; during the period when in Mme. de Duras' house and in the presence of Sismondi he defended religion as necessary to the support of the State, it had been political. More than once he admitted his doubts: "I believe in God as firmly as in my own existence. I believe in Christianity— as a great truth, always—as a religion so far as I can. For twenty-four hours I believe in it, then back comes the devil to plunge me into a morass of doubt in which I am still struggling at the coming-on of death."

Towards the end, as he drew further into that mighty shadow which slowly engulfed him, he clung "to the robe of Christ." His own phrase was more true of him than of any other; "Christianity has stirred in human hearts a chord that was mute before; it has created souls made for dreaming, grief, weariness, anxiety, passion—souls that can find no refuge save in eternity." In many guises, he reaffirmed his faith: "Long experience has proved to me that religion is the one true thing on earth." And again: "I cannot be born again into a political faith; I no longer believe in anything save the Christian futurity, that is to say the future of heaven." Was he playing a part, was it the last scene of a sublime comedy and, as Vitrolles maintained, a stylistic effect? "It is not," Chateaubriand would reply, "when one is soon to quit this earth that one would choose to find amusement in lying; if I were so unfortunate as no longer to believe, I should in no way scruple to say so." The simplicity of an old man's faith is often akin to that of a child and we have every reason to believe that it was in peace and trust that Chateaubriand wrote the last sentence of his *Mémoires*: "I have nothing now to do but sit down by the edge of my grave; thereafter I shall go down unafraid, my crucifix in my hand, into eternity."

1847. A system and a generation were entering upon their agony. Chateaubriand rarely left the Rue du Bac. Mme. Récamier, blind though she now was, used to go there every day to see him. But she saw him only "under the fiery gaze of Mme. de Chateaubriand," who had thus "the last word on that sublime and fickle soul." The Rue du Bac had carried the day from the Abbaye-aux-Bois, but Céleste's triumph was brief, for she died the first of the three on February 12th, 1847. Chateaubriand left his room to attend the funeral service. Victor Hugo, in *Choses Vues*, states that he arrived home in fits of laughter. "A proof of softening of the brain," said Pilorge; "a proof that he was in his senses," replied Édouard Bertin.

On learning of his bereavement, Hortense Allart wrote to her old friend. "Next day," she tells us, "I was told that someone who could not come up was waiting for me in his carriage. I flung on a hat and went down. There I found M. de Chateaubriand who asked if I would care to go for a drive with him. I stepped into his carriage. He was all friendly tenderness. As we drove off, he turned round sideways to look at me. He was wrapped in an elegant cloak. He told me he was bored. We talked of Rome. . . . I used often to see him at his house and, when we went for walks, he charmed and touched me. He cannot walk; he is melancholy—but he has all his former charm and that lofty distinction which makes a man so attractive. Age, instead of marring the beauty of his face, has made it yet more striking." The friends about them smiled, amused by this gallant widowhood.

There was another mistress on whom he wished to gaze once more before he died—one far older than Hortense Allart—the Sea, and, in July, he paid a last visit to Dieppe. There he was welcomed with great honour. Women and priests flocked to his hotel. He was treated to a serenade. But the sound of the waves on the pebbles was not so sweet now as it was before, and he was soon back with Mme. Récamier. Now that he was free, he would have liked to win her consent to marrying him. "A wedding? Why? What end could it serve," she asked. "At our age what can the proprieties find to object in my taking care of you? If you are saddened by being alone, I am perfectly ready to come and live in the same house. The world, I am sure, does justice to the purity of our relationship. If we were younger, I should have no hesitation. I should rejoice to accept the right to devote my life to you. That right, years and blindness have already granted me. Let us change nothing in a perfect affection." Victor Hugo has described the visits of his blind old friend to the paralysed poet: "It was sad and moving. The woman who could no longer see groped for the man who could no longer feel. Their hands met. Blessed be God! We are soon to die; we love one another yet."

Towards the Grave

Before long there was another empty place in the group. Ballanche, the trusty Ballanche, a gentle and self-satisfied prophet, died of pleurisy in his room, with his window opening on the apartment of Mme. Récamier. As for Chateaubriand, he lingered on for a few months, "an ancient oak riven by lightning, splendid in its ruin." His silence was now almost unbroken. "His memory was so far gone that he would be heard to ask after a friend who had died twenty years before. He knew that his faculties were failing and he had the proud instincts of a poor man who conceals his poverty." Dreading the things he might say, he strove to be silent. Thus this buttoned-up soul kept its secret to the last.

In these last months Mme. Récamier prevailed on him to pose for the sculptor Étex. The latter made, not a statue, but a painted sketch which is moving and terrible. The hair is still blown back by one last storm, but the head is bowed in despair, the eyes are dark with the sadness of disillusion; the mouth expresses scorn, resignation and indifference. "My God! My God!" he seems to say, "when shall I be at last delivered from this world with all its noise and rumour? When, when, will it all end?"

The revolution of 1848 found him still alive. "Hearing the stir in the street," says Alexis de Tocqueville, "he wanted to know what was happening. They told him that Paris had just overthrown Louis-Philippe's monarchy. 'They did well,' he said." His grievances had outlived his consciousness. Three weeks after the February revolution he was attacked by pneumonia, then by a chill in the bladder which caused him acute pain. This sharp suffering seemed to arouse him somewhat. In June the thunder of the revolt penetrated to his room. "What noise is that?" he asked. They told him there was fighting in Paris and that it was the guns. Vainly struggling to rise he said: "I want to go there," then he fell silent—this time for ever—for he died next day.

By his bed there watched Mme. Récamier, a priest (the Abbé Deguery), his nephew (Count Louis de Chateaubriand), and a Sister of Charity. It was said in the papers that he died in full possession of his faculties and that he had signed a recantation of all the errors which might be found in his books. Sainte-Beuve says that, at the time, Chateaubriand was incapable of sustained thought;

such is not the account of Mme. Lenormand, Mme. Récamier's niece. She says that, during those days in June, Chateaubriand asked eager questions of those who could give him news, and that he was greatly moved by the heroic death of the Archbishop of Paris. She states, too, that he welcomed the last offices of religion not only with full consciousness, but with a deep faith and humility.

From the moment he was given extreme unction, he never spoke again. The fever that flushed his cheeks gave his eyes an extraordinary brilliance. If ever Mme. Récamier left his bedside for an instant, he followed her with anguished eyes, but made no sound, and she—who could not see his look—was heartbroken by his silence. He died on July 4th, 1848. Victor Hugo, who went to see him on his death-bed, found him lying on a little iron bedstead with white curtains. His face wore an expression of nobility. The shutters of the windows that overlooked the garden were closed. "At M. de Chateaubriand's feet were two deal chests, one above the other. The larger contained the complete manuscript of the *Mémoires*. On the mantelpiece was a marble bust of Henry V; facing the bust, a full-length statuette of Chateaubriand. Students of the École Polytechnique, who had arranged that a guard of honour should watch by him, saw a stricken old lady kneeling at a prie-Dieu. It was Mme. Récamier."

On the morrow of a revolt, amidst the funerals of the victims, this death seemed to have failed of its effect. "Poor Chateaubriand," said his old friend and enemy Pasquier, "what a trick to let him die at a time when there is hardly room in the *Débats* for even a few lines about him." The obsequies were held on July 8th, 1848, in the Église des Missions. "Paris," said Victor Hugo, "was still stunned by the days of June; and the noise of fusillades, of the cannon and of the tocsin, which still echoed in its ears, shut out—at M. de Chateaubriand's death—the kind of silence that falls about the disappearance of great men. There was very little crowd and the emotion was lukewarm. Molé was there in his greatcoat, nearly all the Institut, and a company of soldiers under the command of a captain. Taken altogether, there was something pompous about the ceremony which excluded simplicity, and something bourgeois which excluded grandeur. It was both too much and too little. I could have wished for M. de Chateaubriand a royal funeral, Notre Dame, peers' robes, the mantle of the Institut, the sword of the banished nobleman, the collar of the order of the Golden Fleece, the presence of all the authorities, half the garrison to go a-foot, veiled drums, the five-minute gun; or a poor man's bier in a country church." Victor Hugo, another great stage-manager, was to make a greater success of his own death.

During the service, Sainte-Beuve heard the republican Béranger whispering to his neighbour, the legitimist Vitrolles, with marked coquetry: "Oh nothingness! Be Chateaubriand, that is to say Royalist and Catholic, so that at your funeral, all convictions being as outworn as your own, Béranger and M. de Vitrolles may meet, never to part again!"

The real funeral took place at St. Malo. There, in time long past, Chateaubriand had obtained from the town the grant of a few feet of earth for his grave on the island of the Grand Bé. A slab of granite, a cross, no name, he had taken thought for the setting. Thither he was borne, at low tide, between two rows of surpliced priests, following a Requiem Mass in the cathedral where, as a child, he had delighted to kneel among the sailors and listen to the equinoctial gales. The cannon thundered; crags and ramparts were black with spectators singing the refrain from the Abencérage: "*Combien j'ai douce souvenance....*" All Brittany was met to do homage to a great Breton. A storm wind was blowing. Sailors bore the coffin to the tomb. It is there that Chateaubriand sleeps today, lulled by "the unchanging waves" and by the far-off sound of the human waves—blind as those of ocean—that, with the violence of their vain blows, eat into the granite of civilisations.

5. Conclusion

Men who prepare themselves a tomb in strange and lonely places are either consumed with pride or divided souls tortured by a passionate need for rest and silence. From his childhood on, Chateaubriand had never known inward peace. All within him had been contradictions, painful strife, heights and depths, and rending griefs. He had known the love of liberty and the thirst for authority, the hunger for power and the sense of its vanity, reverent awe for marriage and a longing for adventure. He had scorned action, yet desired the triumphs it brings in its train, belittled imagination and found in it his only refuge, united the blackest melancholy with the gaiety of a child, and the utmost violence of feeling with the majesty of utterance.

A man of the eighteenth century and a master of the nineteenth, a disciple of Rousseau and the restorer of Christianity, a libertine and a believer, he had oscillated all his life between faith and doubt. A monarchist, he had chosen for the friends of his old age the enemies of the monarchy. The creator and prototype of René, a distiller of the Romantic poison, he had struck his friends—Joubert, Molé, Fontanes—as the most lucid, the most classical and most realist of intelligences. Finally, like most great minds, he had been an infinitely complex creature who found, in the burning medley of his passions, the elements of contradictory characters all of whom, in succeeding moments of his life, he had sincerely embodied.

He had suffered long from such conflicts. "Life," he wrote, "has no dignity save in its unity and its doctrine." A sincere admirer of that dignity, desperately athirst for that unity, how—from his spiritual disorder—could he bring order? It was a fearsome problem and one that has faced others less great than he. Some have solved it through an emotional unity; love may become the mainspring of a life. Chateaubriand, though capable of affection and of a fitful goodness, had not got it in him to be faithful. He needed, not one especial woman of his choice, but the tender pleasure that all women of a certain type had to give. Even Mme. Récamier, who won him to a strange aesthetic constancy, could never away with the Hortense Allarts, or even more fleeting passions.

Political unity? There was in Chateaubriand at least one unchanging emotion—the love of France, of its past end of its glory; but among the parties which struggled for the government of the country, he could never choose. He strove after a unity of personality and became, if his actions only are taken into account, the most faithful of legitimists and Catholics; but—even if he was often successful in contenting his public in such guises—he never

Towards the Grave

satisfied himself and suffered so greatly from uncertainty of the kind that, since he could not solve the conflict, he more than once came to long for death, that death which, said he, "I have always singularly loved."

Ultimately he found peace, not in real life, but in the picture of his life that, in the *Mémoires*, he drew for posterity. "He writes only for others, and lives only for himself," Joubert had said at the time of the *Génie*. By the time of the *Mémoires* he had come near to writing only for himself. Despairing of understanding his own being, he had recreated himself. From strange dreams and those chaotic deeds that are the stuff of all existence, he wove a fine and consistent narrative. Passionately in love with greatness, he had, in his book, given his childhood for setting a proud and terrible Combourg, for the castellan of the manor a Shakesperian old man, for the companion of his age a Sylph. Having, by the power of his genius, linked his frail existence with the sublime drama of Christianity and with the epic history of the French nation, he had become in his own eyes an epic and dramatic hero. It was the triumph of his art that he had conquered nature within himself. Towards the end, the face beneath the mask became almost like the mask itself. An enemy once accused Chateaubriand of wishing for "a cell on the stage," and for long the reproach was true. The beauty of it was that the actor had been caught in his own toils, and that, in his cell on the stage, he had worked to his dying day with an artistic steadiness no less lofty than Flaubert's.

Spiritual conflict engendered by a difficult childhood, by the ideas of the age and by the ills of his family; an artist fashioned by nature at Combourg and preserved intact by journeying; a romantic hero shaped by youth's disasters; further conflicts between that romantic hero and a classical intelligence; efforts to reconcile those conflicts in action and, following his defeat, their happy reconciliation through style, a vain attempt to make of his life a work of art, then another attempt—this time successful—to make a work of art on his life: such was roughly the history of François-René de Chateaubriand.

THE END

Index

Academy, French, 157, 168, 180-183, 186, 226, 273, 275, 336-337.
Alexander, Emperor of Russia, 194, 249, 251, 253, 263, 264.
Allart Hortense, 284-285, 289, 306-309, 312-317, 336, 344; quoted, 292, 296, 308, 340.
America, C. in, 33-45.
Amiens, Peace of, 108.
Amour et vieillesse, 294n.; quoted, 293-294.
Amours de deux sauvages dans le désert, Les, 98. See also Atala.
Ampère, Jean Jacques, 262, 330, 331.
Anglas, Beissy d', 112; quoted, 26.
Angoulême, Duc d', 255-258, 299, 310-311.
Angoulême, Duchesse d', 229, 262-263, 297, 310-311, 327.
Arenberg, Duchesse d', quoted, 141, 145.
Armand, Colonel. See Rouërie, Marquis de la.
Artois, Comte d', 78, 195, 199, 205, 228, 229, 230, 238, 262, 263, 271; quoted, 265. See also Charles X.
Atala, 44, 78, 79, 85, 96, 97-101, 102, 110, 206, 217, 275, 284, 297, 329.
Augustus, Prince, of Prussia, 217, 218, 317.
Austria, 48, 159, 187, 236.

Baciocchi, Elisa, 89, 107-108, 110, 126, 128.
Bail, *Rêveries de M. Chateaubriand*, 201.
Ballanche, bookseller, 113, 142, 148-149, 213, 217, 219, 262, 298, 308, 331, 337, 340; quoted, 218, 224, 315.
Barante, Prosper de, 217; quoted, 202, 218.
Bastille, fall of, 29.
Beauharnais, Joséphine de, 112. See also Joséphine, Empress.
Beaumont, Pauline de, 94-98, 102-105, 111-113, 115-119, 121-123, 125, 130,

132, 134-135, 149, 167, 173, 209, 223, 243, 267, 274, 278-279, 303, 321.
Bédée, Apolline de, 3. See also Chateaubriand, Apolline de.
Bédée, Uncle, Seigneur de Plancoït, 4, 6, 27, 45, 46, 53, 54, 55, 61, 64, 75, 78.
Béranger, 296, 309-310, 337-338; song to C., quoted, 309; quoted, 343.
Bérenger, Mme. de, 165, 167, 184.
Berlin, C. ambassador to, 233-238.
Bernadette, King of Sweden, 217, 218.
Berry, Duc de, 228-229; quoted, 211-212; C. writes memoir on, 230.
Berry, Marie-Caroline, Duchesse de, 228-229, 311, 317-320.
Bertin, 121, 146, 193, 202, 205, 216, 269; quoted, 340.
Blacas, Duc de, 204, 207, 212, 247; quoted, 197, 198.
Boigne, Mme. de, 115-116, 152, 165, 167, 194, 212, 226, 227, 312; quoted, 143, 163, 276, 315, 317-318.
Donald, 58, 97, 157, 158, 213.
Bonaparte. See Napoleon.
Bonaparte, Lucien, 89-92, 108, 110, 146, 217.
Bordeaux, Henri, Duc de, 230, 237, 299, 301, 302. See also Henry V.
Bourbon, Louis de, 125-126, 127. See also Enghien, Duc d'.
Brest, Chateaubriand in, 11-12.
Broglie, Duc de, 262, 275, 293.
Broglie, Duchesse de, quoted, 224, 276, 306.
Buisson, Céleste, 46-47. See also Chateaubriand, Céleste de.
Bulletin de la Société Chateaubriand, cited, 177 n.

Canning, 242, 243, 253-255, 264, 303.
Carnot, Lazare, 88, 199, 232.
Carrel, Armand, 305, 309, 310.
Castellane, Cordélia de, 259-261, 263, 272, 273, 326.
Cayla, Zsë du, 238, 263, 268.

347

Index

Chamfort, 25, 30, 48, 81.
Charles X, 271-272, 275, 276, 289, 294, 295, 297, 299, 301, 303, 304, 310, 312, 318, 319. See also Artois, Comte d'.
Chateaubourg, Bénigne de. See Chateaubriand, Bénigne de.
Chateaubriand, Apolline de, 3-7, 12-16, 19, 22, 27, 33, 45, 47, 55, 64, 69, 75, 80; quoted, 54.
Chateaubriand, Armand de, 7, 51-52, 176-178.
Chateaubriand, Bénigne de, 4, 11, 13, 24, 134; quoted, 135.
Chateaubriand, Céleste de, 46-47, 48, 49, 50, 54, 64, 90, 104-105, 113, 125, 129-130, 132, 134, 137-138, 140, 142, 145-146, 148-149; quoted, 106, 126, 128, 138, 148.
Chateaubriand, Céleste, 157, 158, 159, 161, 162, 163-165, 167-168, 179, 181, 183, 184, 186; quoted, 157, 164, 165, 178, 190-191.
Chateaubriand, Céleste de, 203, 204, 209, 210, 220, 231, 232; quoted, 198, 206, 220-221, 227.
Chateaubriand, Céleste de, 46-50, 54, 64, 90, 104-105, 113, 125, 129-149 *passim*, 157-168 *passim*, 179-186 *passim*, 203-204, 209-210, 220, 231-237 *passim*, 240, 245, 269-282 *passim*, 292-298 *passim*, 306, 308, 311-312, 316-317, 321-327 *passim*, 332, 339; quoted, 106, 126, 128, 138, 148, 157, 164, 165, 178, 190-191, 198, 206, 220-221, 227, 310, 324, 325.
Chateaubriand, François-René de, ancestors, 1; birth, 4; childhood, 4-7; "Chevalier," 4, 62; religious impressions, 6, 10, see also Religion; at school, 8-12; returns to Combourg, 12-19, 32-33; "Vicomte," 13; pride, 14, 62, 63, 266; subaltern, 20-22, 24; patrimony, 22; at court, 23; Knight of Malta, 27, 35; merchant, 32; Estimates of, 33-34, 55-56, 231-232, 266-268, 303-304, 343-345; beginnings as writer, 38, 56, 58-59, 68; American diary, 41, see also America; marriage, 47; émigré, 50-56, see also London; dread of society, 62; loves, 66-67, see also Beaumont, Custine, Noailles, Récamier, etc.; "insincerity," explained, 67; return to France, 87; early political ambitions, 110; Rome legation, 114, see also Rome; leaves Napoleon's service, 126; buys *Mercure*, 158; buys Valley of Wolves, 160; barred from politics, 174-178; Academy episode, 180-183, 186; appointed ambassador to Sweden, 198, 201; receives Cross of St. Louis, 200, 247; flight from Paris, 203-204; Minister, 204-208, 209-215, 252-266; president of Orléans electoral college, 209-211; political doctrine, 213; Berlin ambassador, 231, 233-238; awarded Legion of Honour, 238, 247; London ambassador, 240-248; at Congress of Verona, 248-252; decorations, 264, 279; causes of his political defeat, 266-268; buys home in Paris, 271, 274; Rome ambassador, 277-295; political allegiances, summary, 303-304; arrest, 311-312; last embassy, 318-321; Paris apartment, 322, 324; pensioned, 327; last visit to sea, 340; death, 341-342; funeral, 342-343; life, summary, 343-345. See also works by title.
Chateaubriand, Jean-Baptiste de, 4, 5, 19, 21-25, 27, 30, 45, 50-51, 53-54, 64.
Chateaubriand, Mme. Jean-Baptiste de, 26, 64.
Chateaubriand, Julie de, 4. See also Farcy, Mme. de.
Chateaubriand, Louis de, 185, 221, 312, 341.
Chateaubriand, Lucile de, 4-6, 13-19, 22, 24-26, 28, 45-50, 54, 64, 69, 90, 104-105, 133-137; quoted, 134-137.
Chateaubriand, Marie-Anne de, 11, 24. See also Marigny, Mme. de.
Chateaubriand, René-Auguste de, 2-5, 8, 10-20, 22, 33.
Châtillon, Duchesse de, 165. See also Bérenger, Mme. de.
Chênedellé, 97, 111, 113, 131, 134-135, 137-138, 140, 141, 160, 301; quoted, 95, 135, 160, 174.
Chénier, Marie-Joseph, 85, 180-182, 186; quoted, 100; C.'s encomium on, quoted, 182.
Cholera epidemic, 311.
Christianity, C. and, 338-339, 344, 345; C. quoted on, 333, 339. See also *Génie du Christianisme, Le*.
Cod-fishing, 2.
Collas, quoted, 2.
Combourg, purchase of, 3; description, 7-8.

Index

Conclave, papal, 1829, 286-288.
Conduct, rules of, for the hapless, C.'s, quoted, 63;
Congrès de Vérone, 327. See also Verona.
Conservateur, Le, 227, 229, 230.
Constant, Benjamin, 218, 270; quoted, 219; *Adolphe*, 222.
Corbière, 230-231, 237-240, 265-266, 268.
Coucher de Soleil sur l'océan, 43.
Coussergues, Clausel de, 126, 146, 164, 167, 187, 197, 203, 270; quoted, 126, 229.
Creed, C.'s quoted, 74.
Custine, Delphine de, 112-113, 115-116, 125, 128, 130-131, 133, 138-139, 144-145, 165, 175-176, 178, 223, 239, 259, 261, 267, 273-274, 279, 291; quoted, 140-141, 144, 147.

Danielo, C.'s secretary, 323; quoted, 324.
Death, C. quoted on his, 185-186, 345.
De Buonaparte et des Bourbons, 188-195, 198, 272; quoted, 188-189, 195; Napoleon quoted on, 192.
Decazes, Élie, 212, 227-230, 269, 303; quoted, 215.
Dernier des Abencérages, Le, 153-154, 167, 168, 171-172, 197, 218, 338; quoted, 168, 172.
Des Beautés poétiques et morales de la religion chrétienne . . ., 82, 105. See also *Génie du Christianisme, Le*.
Dieppe, C.'s last visit to, 340.
Dinan, Collège de, Chateaubriand at, 12.
Dol, Collège de Dol, Chateaubriand at, 8-11.
Druidess, episode from *Les Martyrs*, 168
Duras, Claire de, 165-167, 184-185, 197-199, 201-202, 204-205, 207, 210, 212, 215-216, 218, 220, 227, 231, 234-236, 238, 240, 245, 247, 249, 251-253, 261, 265, 267, 273, 279, 303, 323, 329; quoted, 221-223, 291.
Durry, Marie-Jeanne, cited, 278 n., 279 n., 305 n.

Elisabeth, Empress of Russia, 147; quoted, 194.

Enghien, Duc d', 161, 211, 303. See also Bourbon, Louis d'.
England, C., quoted on discipline of, 65; C.'s debt to, 86; and South America, 264. See also Wellington, Canning, George IV, etc.
Essai sur la littérateure anglaise, 329.
Essai sur les Révolutions, 59, 63, 69-76, 78, 79, 81, 83, 186, 201; commentary on, 274.
Étex, sketch of C., 341.
Études historiques, 163, 169, 297, 306-307; quoted, 309. See also *Histoire de France, Une*.
Eylau, battle of, 156, 157.

Farcy, Mme. de, 11, 21, 24-26, 48, 50, 54, 64, 69, 75, 80, 83, 105; quoted, 21, 80.
Ferdinand VII, King of Spain, 247, 256-258, 264.
Fesch, Canon (Cardinal), 110-111, 116-118, 122, 127, 159, 279; quoted, 124.
Fontanes, Louis de, 25, 70, 76-79, 81, 83-92 *passim*, 97-98, 101-102, 107-111, 113-118, 123-129 *passim*, 138, 146, 157, 167, 175, 178-182, 187, 193-195, 197, 202, 237-238, 267, 325, 344; quoted, 78, 79, 84-85, 90-91, 97, 119, 159-160, 181, 229.
Fouché, 84, 88, 101, 102, 112, 125, 128, 165, 171, 175-178, 195, 205-209, 211, 212, 214, 267; original of Hiéroclès, 170, 175; quoted, 202.
Fougères, C. at, 22, 24, 28.
Friedland, battle of, 156, 159.

Gazette de France, La, 278.
Génie du Christianisme, Le, 81-85, 89, 90-94, 96-97, 102-115 *passim*, 127, 129, 139, 161, 171-172, 174, 178, 180, 186, 193, 195, 201, 205, 277, 283, 309, 327, 329-331, 338, 345.
George IV, King of England, 242, 246.
Gesril, 7, 11, 12, 33, 55.
Ghent, Louis XVIII's ministry at, 204-207.
Girodet, portrait of C., 175.
Government stock, C. and conversion of, 264-265.
Greece, C. in, 149-151.
Guerre des Dieux, La, Parny, 81, 82, 92, 178.
Guingené, 25, 48, 70, 81, 88, 106, 110, 169; quoted, 30.
Guizot, 171.

349

Index

Hamelin, Mme., 258-259, 284, 326.
Henry V, 291, 299, 311, 319, 327, 342; quoted, 328. *See also* Bordeaux, Henri.
Hingant, Councillor to Parliament of Rennes, 55, 59-60, 241.
Histoire de France, Une, 173-174, 273, 291, 306, 330. *See also Études historiques.*
Holy Alliance, 236, 248, 250, 254.
Hugo, Victor, 329, 340; quoted, 310, 318, 322, 324, 340, 342-343.
Hundred Days, 202-209.
Hymne aux vertus maternelles de Marie-Caroline, 318.

Immortality, C. quoted on, 80-81.
Itinéraire de Paris à Jerusalem, 161, 163, 168-169, 172-173, 183, 194. Gassicourt's parody of, 186.
Ives, Charlotte, 65-67, 83, 184, 242-243; original of Celuta, 65; original of Cymodocée, 139.

Jersey, C. in, 54-55.
Jerusalem, C. in, 151.
Joséphine, Empress, 112, 177, 178, 183.
Joubert, Joseph, 79, 85, 92-99, 101-104, 113, 117, 119-122, 132-133, 148, 154, 157, 164-165, 167-168, 172, 267, 278-279, 344; quoted, 93-94, 96, 104, 115, 120, 132, 159, 160, 161, 345.
Journal des Débats, 193, 196, 197, 202, 216, 269, 270, 342; C.'s advice to nation in, quoted, 199.
Journal universel, 205; C. on Waterloo in, quoted, 207.

Kersaint, Claire de, 165, 167. *See also* Duras, Claire de.
Krüchener, Mme. de, 114, 147, 194.

Laborde, Alexandre de, *Voyage pittoresque et historique de l'Espagne,* C.'s review of, 158.
Lafayette, 301.
Lamartine, 273, 329; quoted, 162-163, 290, 324.
Laval, Adrien, Duc de, 154, 184, 222, 247, 288, 295; quoted, 217, 252, 277. *See also* Montmorency, Adrien de.
Law, C. quoted on English reverence for, 65.
Lectures des Mémoires de M. de Chateaubriand, 331 n.

Legion of Honour, 201, 202, 238, 247.
Le Moine, C.'s secretary, 209, 216, 220, 221, 269.
Leo XII, Pope, 279, 285-286; quoted, 286.
Le Roi est mort, vive le roi, 272.
Levaillant, Maurice, cited, 316 n.
Lévis, Duchesse de, 165, 184, 204.
Life, C. quoted on, 344.
Literary fame, C. quoted on, 146.
Literary Fund, helps C., 79, 241.
Literature, C. and Canning quoted on, 242.
London, C. in, 57-61, 67-86; C. ambassador to, 240-248; C.'s last visit to, 327-328.
Louis XVI, 23, 45, 49, 54, 94, 121, 152, 195, 209, 210, 233, 237, 238, 319.
Louis XVIII, 84, 88, 114, 187, 189, 196-203 *passim,* 204-215, 227-232, 250, 252, 262-268 *passim,* 271, 303-304; quoted, 197, 198-199, 212, 229, 238, 252-253, 265.
Louis-Napoleon, quoted, 316.
Louis-Philippe, 301, 305, 307, 312, 318, 341. *See also* Orléans, Duc de.

Madelin, *Le Consulat et l'Empire,* cited, 156 n.
Malesherbes, d', 22, 23, 26-27, 30, 33, 40, 48-49, 50, 53, 55, 66, 152, 162, 165, 216; quoted, 31, 32, 49, 64.
Marcellus, C.'s secretary, 241, 243, 244, 246, 254, 255, 256.
Marengo, victory of, 88, 91.
Marie-Antoinette, 23, 178, 237.
Marie-Louise, Empress, 178, 249.
Marigny, Mme. de, 11, 28, 47, 90, 113, 137, 177, 180, 183, 186.
Marriage, C. quoted on, 185.
Martignac, de, 276, 278, 285, 289, 294.
Martyrs da Dioclétien, Les, 45, 139-140, 142, 147, 160, 163, 167-171, 174, 175-176, 178, 180, 183, 296, 329, 330; quoted, 169, 170.
Maurras, Charles, cited, 303 n.
Mémoires d'Outre-Tombe, 45, 163, 169, 173, 237, 243, 248, 259, 290, 293, 307, 316-317, 320, 323, 329-333, 336, 342, 345; quoted, 109, 196, 216, 220, 332-333, 339.
Men of letters, Napoleon quoted on treatment of, 179.

Index

Mercure de France, 91, 92, 100, 115, 146, 193; C. buys, 158; C. attacks Napoleon in, 158-160, 175.
Metternich, 174, 217-218, 249-252, 321.
Mirabeau, 48.
Moëlien, Thérèse de, 11, 64.
Moïse, 163, 169, 173, 212, 289-290.
Molé, Mathieu, 97, 120, 128, 131, 138, 140, 146, 156, 158, 167, 211, 267, 275, 326, 342, 344; quoted, 143-144, 222, 259.
Monarchie selon la Charte, La, 213-215, 328; quoted, 213, 214.
Moniteur, 108, 215, 239.
Montboissier, Mme. de Colbert-, 216, 221.
Montcalm, Mme. de, 212, 215; quoted, 232.
Montesquieu, Abbé de, 194, 204.
Montmorency, Adrien de, 105, 154, 184, 185, 277, 331; quoted, 217. *See also* Laval, Adrien, Duc de.
Montmorency, "Adrienne" de, 167, 184.
Montmorency, Mathieu, 217, 218, 230-231, 239-240, 245-254 *passim*, 262, 264-265, 267-268, 273; quoted, 224, 226, 250.
Mouchy, Duchesse de, 143, 166-167, 184, 222-223, 259. *See also* Noailles, Natalie de.

Napoleon, 69, 88-89, 92, 95, 107-111, 114, 124-127, 129, 132, 138, 156-157, 159, 174-183, 187, 190-192, 201-209, 215, 238, 303, 304; quoted, 84, 90, 91, 101-102, 114, 118-119, 128, 156, 157, 159, 174-175, 177, 179, 181.
Natchez, 44, 51, 63, 67-70, 73, 78, 79, 83, 142, 147, 274-275.
Neuville, Hyde de, 151-152, 154, 270, 311.
Noailles, Natalie de, 143-147, 151-154, 157-158, 165, 168, 171, 184, 201, 223, 326; quoted, 147, 152-153; original of Blanca, 154; original of Valléda, 170. *See also* Mouchy, Natalie de.
North West Passage, Chateaubriand plans discovery of, 27, 31, 40.
Nuit chez les sauvages de l'Amérique, 43.

Œuvres complètes, 274, 306, 331.
Orléans, C. President of, 209-211.
Orléans, Duc d', 206, 299, 301. *See also* Louis-Philippe.
Otrante, Duc d', 178. *See also* Fouché.
Oxford Movement, émigrés and, 76.

Pailleron, M. L., *La Vicomtesse de Chateaubriand*, cited, 10 n., 246 n.; quoted, 13.
Paris, C.'s early visits to, in, 21, 23-24, 25-27, 29, 48-50.
Parma, Duchess of, 249. *See also* Marie-Louise.
Parny, Chevalier de, 25, 30, 70, 169; *La Guerre des Dieux*, 81, 82, 92, 178.
Pasquier, Étienne, 95, 97, 128, 138, 156, 163, 167, 178, 186-187, 195, 208, 211, 235-237, 267, 275, 312; quoted, 252, 300, 342.
Peltier, Jean-Gabriel, 59, 61, 75, 98, 114; quoted, 102.
Pilorge, Hyacinthe, C.'s private secretary, 233, 235, 266, 298, 300, 319, 323; quoted, 245-246, 340.
Pius VII, Pope, 117, 138, 187.
Pius VIII, Pope, 287.
Polignac, 279, 288, 295, 303.
Poussin, C.'s monument to, 281.
Pozzo di Borgo, 194, 249.
Prague, C.'s embassy to, 318-320.
Press, freedom of, C. upholds, 271-272, 299; C. quoted on, 271.
Privateering, 2.
Progress, C. quoted on, 272.
Prussians, enter Paris, 191.

Raucourt, Mlle., actress, funeral of, 202.
Raynal, Abbé, 16; C. disciple of, 39, 72.
Récamier, Juliette, 101, 145, 197, 217-220, 223-227, 230-232, 235, 238-253 *passim*, 261-262, 267, 273-274, 277-282, 288-290, 296, 298, 306-331 *passim*, 336-337, 341-342, 344; quoted, 217-219, 225-226, 262, 289, 315, 325, 339, 340.
Réflexions politiques, quoted, 200-201.
Religion, Napoleon quoted on, 90, 91.
Religions, C. quoted on, 73, 74. *See also* Christianity.
René, 79, 85, 262, 275, 297, 330.
Rennes, Collège de, Chateaubriand at, 11.
Restauration et la monarchie élective, 307; quoted, 308-309.
Restoration First, 193-203; Charter, 197, 199, 201, 297-298; Second, 207-215, 238-240. *See also* Louis XVIII, Charles X, Louis-Philippe.
Révélations sur le mystère de ma vie, 220. *See also* Mémoires.

Index

Revolution, French, 27-32, 45-46, 48-54, 63-64, 69, 77, 84, 94, 108. *See also* Napoleon; of 1830, 298-303; of 1848, 341.
Richelieu, Duc de, 203, 212, 215, 219, 227, 230, 235, 237-239, 263.
Rochefoucauld, Sosthène de la, 254, 262-263, 267-268, 271, 293, 331.
Rome, Napoleon's negotiations with, 102; C. in, 116-124; C. ambassador to, 277-295.
Rosambo, Mlle. de, 22. *See* also Chateaubriand, Mme. Jean-Baptiste de.
Rosambo, Président de, 22, 25, 26, 30, 50.
Rouërie, Marquis de la, 32, 39, 54-55, 64.
Rousseau, C. a disciple of, 27, 34, 49, 64, 72, 75, 76, 304, 344; Joubert quoted on, 96; quoted, 315.
Russia, 156, 157, 187, 190, 191, 236. *See also* Alexander and Elisabeth.

Sainte-Beuve, 154, 290, 309, 329, 331, 341, 343; quoted, 106, 169, 191, 217-218, 226, 327, 331-332, 337-338.
Saint-Géran ou la nouvelle langue française, parody of *Itinéraire*, 186.
Sauvages, 70, 76.
Ségur, Mme. de, quoted, 165, 166.
Sismondi, 339; quoted, 199.
Slave-trade, 2-3, 251.
Socialism, C. heralds, 332-333.
Souvenirs de Mme. de Ségur, cited, 165 n.
Spain, C. in, 151-154; war with, 253-258, 262, 264, 303. *See also* Verona, Congress of.
Spectateur du Nord, 82.
Staël, Mme. de, 91, 92, 95, 100-101, 105, 111, 142, 217-220, 237, 317; quoted, 102.
Sur la Religion Chrétienne . . . , 82. *See also Génie du Christianisme, Le.*

Sweden, C. appointed ambassador to, 198, 201. *See also* Bernadotte.
Switzerland, C. in, 312-318.

Talleyrand, 85, 88, 102, 114, 116-118, 124-126, 176, 178, 194-195, 198, 204-212 *passim*, 319; quoted, 207.
Tilsit, Peace of, 159.
Tocqueville, Alexis de, 185; quoted, 341.

Unhappy, C.'s advice to the, 63.

Valley of Wolves, C.'s country house, purchase of, 160; for sale, 216, 221; sold, 224.
Verona, Congress of, 247, 248-252. *See also Congrès de Vérone.*
Versailles, Court at, 23.
Vichet, Marquise de, 291, 292; quoted, 282-283.
Vie de Rancé, 329, 333-336, 337; quoted, 259, 334-335.
Vigne, Céleste Buisson de la, 46-47. *See also* Chateaubriand, Céleste de.
Vigny, 290; quoted, 162.
Villèle, de, 227-231, 237-239, 247, 249-254, 256-257, 263-268, 269-272, 275-276, 303, 325; quoted, 264, 266, 269-270.
Villemain, 202, 229, 331.
Villeneuve, Léontine de, 283-284, 291-294, 296, 338.
Vitrolles, Minister of King's Household, 203, 339, 343; quoted, 164.

Wagram, battle of, 178.
Washington, George, 32, 39-40, 85.
Waterloo, battle of, 206-207, 242.
Wellington, Duke of, 194, 195, 205, 208, 218, 219, 242.

Youth, C. quoted on, 34.